Duke McCall
An Oral History

With A. Ronald Tonks

W0006283

BAPTIST HISTORY AND HERITAGE SOCIETY
BRENTWOOD, TENNESSEE
AND
FIELDS PUBLISHING INC.
NASHVILLE, TENNESSEE

Printed in the United States of America

Library of Congress Card Number: 2001095331

ISBN: 1578430119

Published by

Baptist History and Heritage Society
P.O. Box 728 • Brentwood, Tennessee 37024-0728
800-966-2278
e-mail: cdeweese@tnbaptist.org
and

Fields Publishing Inc.
917 Harpeth Valley Place • Nashville, Tennessee 37221
615-662-1344
e-mail: tfields@fieldspublishing.com

Contents

Dedication

To Marguerite Mullinnix McCall, who for forty-seven years of my ministry shared every success and failure. Her partnership doubled the prospects of success and halved the pain of failure. She was involved in every event between 1936 and 1983 as counselor and supporter. To my advantage, she muted her own career as a community and church leader.

—Duke McCall

Preface

In contemplation of my retirement at age sixty-five, which should have occurred August 1, 1980, the trustees of The Southern Baptist Theological Seminary, led by trustee chairman T. T. Crabtree of Springfield, Missouri, made arrangements with the Southern Baptist Historical Commission for an oral history to be conducted with me. Dr. Badgett Dillard, seminary vice president, worked out the legal and financial arrangements. I was happy to cooperate. I thought the process would take two or three days and might be of interest to a few historians. Election to the presidency of the Baptist World Alliance effective in July 1980 and the closing responsibilities at the seminary plus the staff schedule at the Historical Commission delayed the beginning of this project.

The first real break in my schedule came after relinquishing the presidency of the seminary to Dr. Roy Honeycutt February 2, 1982. Marguerite and I had planned to spend the winter of 1982-83 in our condominium in The Summit, 1000 Lowry St., Delray Beach, Florida.

We invited Dr. A. Ronald Tonks, assistant executive director of the Historical Commission, to visit us there the last week of January 1983. He and I set up his tape recorder on the fourth-floor porch, overlooking the Intracoastal Waterway. Marguerite, who had known almost no illness during our forty-seven years of marriage, was not feeling well; so she often rested on the sofa in the adjacent living room.

Recording on that porch was a mistake. The many yachts that passed would blow their horns or whistles three times to ask the bridge tender at the nearby Atlantic Avenue Bridge to open up. While that noise did not bother Dr. Tonks or me, it played havoc with the recording. Miss Clara McCartt, my secretary for most of the past fifty-five years, has transcribed the tape (or at least a re-recording of that tape on cassettes by Dr. Andy Rawls of the Southern Seminary library media service). She experienced great difficulty hearing some of the conversation over the background noise of the Intracoastal Waterway.

Desiring to clarify statements and slips of the tongue, I have edited McCartt's transcript on my own computer. It should be clear to the reader that this record is my off-the-cuff memory. Undoubtedly, I sometimes remember to advantage, and sometimes I mis-remember details. The record, however, is an accurate report of *my memory* of the things we reviewed.

Instead of completing the project in a few days, I am typing this Preface on May 1, 2000. The interviews with Dr. Tonks (all in Delray Beach, Florida) extended over three years and took place during four weeks in January 1983, May 1983, May 1984, and November 1985. These years permitted enough time for me to change my attitude in some cases and also to forget that we had already discussed a subject before. So there is some repetition and sometimes different versions of the same event.

I want to close by saying that I have spoken rather candidly in this interview, sometimes perhaps too candidly about my opinions and my views. They are my opinions and my views, and that's what they are worth. They are not absolute reports of all the facts in these situations. Any historian who uses any of these remarks as a resource is hereby charged to be a good historian and to verify his data and check the accuracy of some of these statements.

New computers and new software furthered our efforts to make an oral history document more readable, but added years to the effort. Our intention was a more homogeneous organization and even less repetition. Finally, we decided that the oral history flavor should remain; so with some revisions and additions we stopped the intermittent tinkering. Here it is.

Duke McCall
May 1, 2000

Publishers' Notes: Throughout this book interview questions and comments by A. Ronald Tonks appear in italics. McCall's responses appear in standard type. Second, the interviews comprising this book were conducted in 1983-85. Therefore, when the interviewer and McCall use the present tense, they are referring to 1985 or earlier, not to years since 1985.

CHAPTER 1

My First Seventeen Years

1914-1931

What is the earliest thing you can remember?

The first thing in sharp focus for me was falling off a fence and breaking my arm in Meridian, Mississippi, where I was born in 1914.

Were you supposed to be on that fence?

No, I was just walking the fence because it was there—like climbing Mount Everest. I was about four years old. I also recall a time when I ran across the street in front of our house to greet Dad as he came home from work. One of the few cars in town was coming down the street, and my father ran out and pushed me out of the way, but the car ran over his leg. I was impressed that he would risk himself for my sake.

PARENTS

What are your first recollections of your parents?

I remember my father in terms of his physical prowess. He had been a football star at the University of Mississippi in 1908, 1909, and 1910. He became the "field captain." That describes both his aggressiveness, and his willingness to commit himself, and also something of his confidence in his own ability.

So your father was a self-confident type of person?

Yes, and he had a deep commitment to right and justice. He would take the side of the underdog any day if he thought that person was being unfairly treated, whether it was my dad's business or not. He was also a southern gentleman, gracious and courtly.

Did you know him well, or was he always busy with responsibilities?

We were not together often because he was busy and worked long and hard as an attorney. But there was good quality to the time we had together. This frequently came in terms of travel together as a family. We often camped out in a tent. This was before the day of tourist courts or motels. If we didn't make the next town, we would put up a tent and spend the night or maybe a couple of days.

How did you travel?

We had a Studebaker. In those days, two hundred miles in one day was a long trip. We made trips as far as the West Coast and New England. By the time I was fourteen years old, I had been in all the states except two—North Dakota and Maine.

Did your father ever take you on business trips?

Most of his business was local as long as we lived in Meridian, Mississippi. We left Meridian when I was about five years old and moved to Memphis, Tennessee.

Why did you decide to move to Memphis?

Dad's father was a lumberman; so he was aware that the long leaf pine was about gone and the virgin forests in Mississippi had been cut over. Lumber was the base of the economy in Meridian and eastern Mississippi; so my father moved his law practice to Memphis, predicting a recession for Mississippi. Along in 1921 and 1922, a recession did hit the country, and the eastern Mississippi economy collapsed and did not recover until after World War II. His prediction was right.

Tell me more about your father.

Dad was a big hunter. I grew up going hunting and fishing with him. He grew up around logging camps, since his father was a lumberman. My father had to earn his way through the University of Mississippi on his own. He told me that he applied to become secretary to the president of the university, and the president laughed at him because he was such a country bumpkin. But Dad lived long enough for the university president to try to borrow some money from him during the 1930 Depression. He reminded the president of that first encounter, and then he lent him the money.

My father and all his brothers graduated from the University of Mississippi. He was the oldest. They all came along and took over the campus store that Dad had started in order to earn his way through college and law school. Dad's nickname was "Scotchie." He was the original "Scotchie" McCall. All of his brothers inherited the campus store and the nickname "Scotchie," and they all played football.

It sounds like your father was something of an entrepreneur.

Yes, an entrepreneur always. He was a lawyer, worked at being a lawyer, worked at being a city judge in Memphis, but he was always involved in a lot of other things, like real estate.

I never had any allowance as a kid growing up, but Dad would always have a job for me to do. One of my early jobs was to paint a rental house. In those days you bought white lead and mixed it with linseed oil and lampblack to make gray paint. I was painting this house gray with green trim. I ran out of lampblack. I didn't want to ride the streetcar to the hardware store to buy more lampblack, so I just painted the sides of the house white and the front gray. I used the bucket of green trim I had left over from trimming the windows and painted the back of the house green because I ran out of linseed oil.

When my father came to inspect my job, he said it was an interesting color combination. Then he pulled out the deed to that house and handed it to me. "Now you own this house," he said, "and what you make is your allowance." There was one other thing: If the rent was more than one week overdue, he could collect it, and if he got it, I would never see it. So I had to collect the rent and then I had to take care of repairs, taxes, and all the other things. That was his way of introducing me to business operations. I was about twelve years old at the time.

I understand you and your family first attended First Baptist Church, Meridian, and then First Baptist Church, Memphis.

Yes. And R. J. Bateman was pastor in Meridian. My father was chairman of the pulpit committee in Memphis after A. U. Boone retired; so R. J. Bateman then came to Memphis. We, therefore, had the same pastor in both Meridian and Memphis for a good bit of my life.

I gather your father had considerable influence in the church?

Oh yes; he was always a deacon, and generally chairman of the deacons. Mother and Father both taught Sunday school. Both were spiritual leaders. Dad's business judgment was very good, and he was quite a diplomat in his own way. I don't know how to describe it except he could take a raw controversy and calm it down quickly. This was due to his presence, his manner. He communicated a sense of authority, and people tended to listen to him.

If things got tangled up in a church business meeting, he was very much the democrat. He would recognize everybody with deference, and then he would say, "We must hear what Joe Blow has to say." And, in effect, he would get the crowd quiet to listen to Joe Blow. This had the effect of quieting and calming the tempers and emotions by his gracious dealing with Joe Blow, with whom he might not agree at all. He did not get reelected repeatedly as chairman of the deacons just by accident; the other deacons wanted him as chairman.

What about your mother?

My mother was the daughter of a judge in the university town of Oxford, Mississippi. After her parents' death, she lived with her half brother, Duke Kimbrough, an attorney. The house was on the edge of the University of Mississippi campus. The William Faulkners, the literary celebrity's family, bought the house from the Kimbroughs. The house, known as Memory House, is a historic shrine now and belongs to the University of Mississippi.

My father and mother's story was a classic: The belle of the town and the football hero finally got together. She represented the culture and wealth of the aristocratic South. His family was climbing by their bootstraps. He did it by strength and courage because handling timber was a dangerous, hard life.

What are your recollections of your mother?

I have tender, warm memories of her. She was a very religious person. She talked very piously, as was characteristic of a very religious person of her generation. She believed strongly in prayer. When I was about ten years old, I fell and lodged a splinter in my knee. The splinter produced blood poisoning. Dr. R. L. Sanders, the surgeon, decided not to cut off my leg because the poison had already moved into my body. I was supposed to die. Mother agonized in prayer for me.

In the wee hours of the morning, she felt that God had answered her prayer. She got in the family car and drove to the hospital to tell my attendants that I was healed. Dr. Sanders confirmed that this was true when he came in to the hospital the next morning. As a young man I was skeptical about prayer, but I could never get away from this event that confirmed the power of Mother's prayers.

Did your parents take you to church whenever the doors were open?

Whenever they were open, and probably from the first Sunday after I was born. I never knew you could eat on Wednesday night anywhere in the world except at church.

Was your mother or your father more influential on you as a young man?

During my high school years and until I went off to college, Mother's influence was probably stronger. But from that point on, my father's kind of religious expression became more of a pattern for me. I have never been able to use the pious language that was characteristic of my mother. I'm not sure what that means, but I simply can't do it.

My father was not expressive emotionally in the way it has become popular for many people to express their emotions today. A strong man in those days was reserved, and he did not show his feelings openly. He showed his emotions by action, not by what he said. That has been both a strength and a weakness for me through the years.

But the early religious training from my mother is still there. I have a very strong pietistic streak in regards to prayer. Real, authentic prayer is very effective and very powerful. I also reflect both of my parents' attitudes toward the Bible. I am not greatly impressed with theology, conservative or liberal, if it is simply rational, with no feeling or emotion.

GRANDPARENTS

What about your grandparents; did you know either of them?

I did not know my mother's parents. Her mother died when she was very young, and her father died when she was in her teens. I did know my father's parents. Both lived until I was in high school. They lived to a very old age. They were in their eighties. Both of them were big people—broad, burly, and strong. My grandfather worked for the Eastman Gardner Lumber Company of Leland, Mississippi. He lived in the small town of Starr, Mississippi, when my father was a boy.

Were they Baptists?

They were Baptists, as were my mother's parents, and both families were very devout. My father's mother, a migrant from England, made her nine children save their shoes for Sunday and church. She also sold her tough kids on education. They all went to college while most of their friends quit school before finishing grade school.

How did your grandparents get to Mississippi?

The McCalls moved to Mississippi from South Carolina. The Kimbroughs moved from Tennessee. Elder Duke Kimbrough was an early Baptist preacher from Jefferson City in East Tennessee, so the Kimbroughs were active Baptists, including some clergymen.

My mother's family was wealthy. Her mother was her father's third wife; his first wives had died. When I am talking about uncles and aunts, they were half brothers and sisters of my mother. Mother had a full sister who died at an early age, but the uncles and aunts on the Kimbrough side were children of the first two wives.

FAMILY TREE

Share some information about your family tree.

My parents: John William McCall, born Summerville (Just south of Jackson), Mississippi, 6/24/1885. Died 4/12/1976. Lizette Kimbrough McCall, born Oxford, Mississippi, 3/22/1889. Died 3/24/1962. Both buried in Kimbrough plot in St. Peter's Cemetery, Oxford, Mississippi.

My mother's family: Judge Bradley Thomas Kimbrough, attorney, bank president, Baptist leader, legislator. Died about age 65. His third wife, Kate Carothers (daughter of William Harvey Carothers, wealthy landowner, founder of Oxford Baptist Church.)

My family: Marguerite Mullinnix McCall 9/1/14–4/3/83. Married 9/1/36. Her parents: Joseph Henry Mullinnix and Lina Stevenson Mullinnix. Our children: Duke Kimbrough Jr.; Dr. Douglas Henry; John Richard; and Dr. Michael William McCall.

Winona Gatton McCandless McCall (married 2/2/84). Her father: R. Harper Gatton, born 2/1/1891, died 10/27/1965. Her mother: Margaret Lackey Gatton, born 12/20/1894, died 12/5/1921.

My brothers and sisters: Katrina (Mrs. James) Flowers; Dr. John W. McCall Jr.; Lizette (Mrs. Ralph) Bethea; Dr. Charles B. McCall.

RACIAL ATTITUDES

What prompted you as a white Tennessean to be sympathetic to integration? That would not have been the usual position of a white Southerner in 1952.

I'm sure I was influenced by my mother. She was a leader in the WMU Goodwill Center movement, at least in Memphis. The center there was ultimately named for her. This was a WMU program in the 1920s. I worked in the daily Vacation Bible School program at the Goodwill Center as well as at my church. Maybe that is where my social conscience was born. The center program focused on the needs of the poor, with an evangelistic purpose. It was "a cup of cold water in Jesus' name"—or a baseball game in Jesus' name.

When Mother died, my father discovered that she had become a one-woman social agency. She started out teaching the Bible to the black women in the Memphis jail—because nobody else was doing anything for them. To Mother, that was just the Christian thing to do—to share the gospel with them. Some of them were converted under her ministry. She believed they were new creations in Christ Jesus. They ought not to be kept in jail for something the old person had done, which was not in accord with their new character.

So she learned how to get them paroled to her. Then she had to find them a job. She became a one-woman employment agency. Then because these people would run into other problems, she was their counselor. The church ended up with a huge program it didn't even know it had. My father didn't know he was supporting such a program until my mother became too ill to keep it up. Then she had to tell somebody so another person could be enlisted to carry it on.

What about your father's attitudes on race?

Some church members came to my father one Sunday as he was finishing teaching his Sunday school class. "Judge, come quick," they told him. "The Negroes are coming." This was during the racial sit-ins in the churches in the late 1950s. Sure enough, there were two or three busloads of blacks that had driven up in front of First Baptist Church, Memphis, arriving about the end of Sunday School, before the worship service. My father went out, and he recognized one of the leaders. He walked over, called the man by name, stuck out his hand and shook hands and asked him, in effect, "Joe, what do you folks want?" Joe said, "Judge, we want to worship with you today."

My father was a Mississippian, and he had all the prejudices of a Mississippian. I'm sure he didn't have the foggiest idea of what he was going to do in that situation. But the man had used the right phrase when he said, "We want to worship with you." "Wonderful," Dad said, "come sit with me." Then he proceeded to usher the whole crowd into the sanctuary of the First Baptist Church. He called on his friends and family to sit in the pews with them to treat them like honored guests.

Actually, First Baptist Church was an integrated church when I was growing up. It didn't become segregated until integration became a national issue. Originally the church was one block from Beale Street, the main street for blacks in Memphis. The church service was broadcast on WGBC radio (World's Greatest Bible Class), a station my father had started and which he owned. When the pastor of First Baptist would recognize the guests, he would talk about "our honored colored friends" who were present and say how glad the church was to have them. That was broadcast on the air. It said to the public, "You're welcome at our church; please come."

And they came. No one in the church thought there was anything wrong with that until the church moved out into the white section of town to the corner of Overton and Parkway in Memphis. Members of the church were basically segregationist in their economic and social dealings, but in church the phrase "the ground is level at the foot of the cross" would have described their feelings. So they would not have stopped to worry about the integration of the church back in the 1920s or the 1930s or even the early 1940s.

How would you describe your pilgrimage on the matter of race?

Of course, I shared the feelings and attitudes of my society in early life. On the other hand, as I grew up my good friends were Carl Stavros, a Greek, and J. V. Mondontico, an Italian. Prejudice was not limited to blacks, but included Greeks, Italians, Jews, and others. There was strong race prejudice in those days, and even national-origin prejudice.

AUNT LOUISE CAROUTHERS, EX-SLAVE

The key factor in my pilgrimage is that a woman who was born a slave of my grandparents, Louise Carouthers, reared my mother. My grandmother's maiden name was Carouthers, so after the pattern of slaves, her name was taken from the family who owned her. Louise Carouthers then reared my mother. Then she had a big hand in rearing me.

When my father married my mother and took her from Oxford to Meridian, Mississippi, he acquired responsibility for not one but two people. "Aunt Louise," as we called her, wasn't going to let her family go off without her. She went to Meridian, too. That was just the way it was. Aunt

Louise was a member of the family. Even more, we were members of her family.

I once offended a Swedish news reporter by telling this story and saying that Aunt Louise never had a salary. I explained, "She got her money the same way my mother did; she simply told my father what she needed, and that settled it." She would say she was going to buy a new dress, and he would reply, "But I just bought you a new dress." I have heard him do exactly the same thing with my mother. But all the time he was reaching into his wallet for the money.

I also heard Aunt Louise say to him once, "Judge McCall, my church is going to build a new building, and I made a pledge. I'm going to need more money every week to pay my pledge." She didn't ask about that; she simply told him how much the pledge was and how much he was going to provide her every Sunday. He took it for granted that this was proper.

Aunt Louise retired and moved to Jackson, Tennessee, to look after her niece. My father figured what he should have paid her in salary from the time he got married until then. She was nearly one hundred years old at that point. Then he charged himself interest on the wages she had not been paid and used that accumulated amount to buy a nice duplex house for her. It was next door to the church that Aunt Louise wanted to join in Jackson. She and her niece lived in one half of the house and rented the other half to generate cash for their needs.

When I traveled from Memphis to Greenville, South Carolina, during my college days, I would always stop in Jackson and visit Aunt Louise. She was a part of our family. We didn't own Aunt Louise; Aunt Louise owned us. In public my mother was "Mrs. McCall," but in private my mother was "Babe" when Aunt Louise was talking to her. When I came along, I was "Babe's Babe." That was her term for me.

Aunt Louise did everything around the house that needed doing, including making chocolate pies for me whenever she wanted to bribe me into doing something for her. She ran the house, and her orders had the same force as parental orders. When I was growing up, you didn't disobey Aunt Louise. Other servants were under her authority.

HOMES IN MEMPHIS
Tell me about the first place where your family lived in Memphis.
Our first home there was a big house with a huge barn out back. The

second floor of the barn had rooms for the servants. That was the pattern in those days. There were always two or three families there, besides Aunt Louise, who were doing something around the house or the garden or the chickens, cows, and horses. This place was still inside the city limits. My father liked his rural background.

The property ran from Vinton Avenue all the way through to Peabody, which, in effect, was two blocks in length. The lot was at least 200 feet wide at the front. It widened to some 400–500 feet for the barn and servants' quarters, and then on back there was an open field all the way to Peabody. This was a good place for baseball and football games. The whole community came there and played ball.

What about other places where you lived in Memphis?

About 1927–28 we moved to upscale 674 West Drive, along the border of Southwestern University (now Rhodes College). We lived there while I was in Central High School. This was a big, prestigious, two-story brick house. Soon after we moved the economic collapse of 1929 swept the country, but somehow Dad didn't get caught in it.

He also bought some property across Wolf River north of Memphis in the old Hyde Park subdivision. This development went bankrupt during the 1929 crash, and my father bought a chunk of it. It wasn't anything except open farmland. He dammed up a stream and made a lake out of it and built a little summer cottage. We would go out there for the summer in my latter high school years.

While I was in college, my parents decided to move out there permanently. They liked living beyond the edge of the city. So they built their house on a hill overlooking the Wolf River and the lights of Memphis to the south. They lived there until their death.

How did your father miss getting caught in the business collapse of 1929?

I can't explain that. He was conservative but smart in his business dealings. He bought farms on all four sides of Memphis where he thought the major highways would eventually go.

He would say, "One of these days they're going to build a new highway, and maybe they'll build it across one of my farms." He hit it right on three out of the four sides of the city. One of his farms turned out to be where I-40 crosses I-240, and just in toward town a little from I-240.

IN THE HANDS OF THE LAW

Why was your father known as "Judge" McCall?

He served as city judge in Memphis at some point. It had to be after I was sixteen years old because I got arrested once for speeding and was taken to his court. His policy was to charge you $2.00 a mile for every mile you were going over the speed limit. I was going 30 miles an hour in a 20-mile zone, so my fine was $20.00. That was more money than I had ever had at one time. It was $20.00 or 20 days in jail.

Dad never gave any indication that he recognized me when I appeared in his courtroom—just another case: "Guilty" or "Not Guilty?" "Guilty" I answered. "Thirty miles an hour in a 20-mile zone?" "Yes sir." "Fined $20.00 or 20 days." All that was just routine. I stood there on one foot and then the other because there wasn't anything for me to do but go to jail. Finally he said, "Come to the bench." Then he gave me $20.00 and said, "Go pay your fine." I have used that as a sermon illustration on the atonement many times.

FATHER'S CAREER ETHICS

Ed Crump was the political boss of Memphis during this time. Did your father know him?

They were good friends and political opponents. In fact, my father ran for mayor as the reform candidate once against the Crump machine. He withdrew from the race because it turned out the people who were supporting him were pulling the same kind of deals he was opposed to the Crump machine for doing. His political allies, from his point of view, were no better than the people he was running against.

I remember meeting Ed Crump one time. He was a courtly, gracious fellow. I heard my father say that he probably gave Memphis the best government of any city in the United States—provided you didn't mind buying it with your freedom.

What did he mean by that?

That Ed Crump ran the whole thing, and if you didn't do what Ed Crump wanted you to do, your taxes went up, or your zoning problems got impossible, and so forth. My father thought Crump and his people were basically honest. They didn't have their hands in the till. That doesn't mean they didn't make a lot of money by having that much power.

21

They happened to know where the roads were going, and those details. They knew where to buy the right property before the state or the city bought it. The Crump Insurance Agency sold insurance on everything in Memphis.

I think they were not a corrupt regime of evil officials. They made their money not by cheating but by the knowledge they had. Yet they used the governmental processes to make it a disability not to be a cooperating supporter of Ed Crump, and that's why the machine worked.

HIGH SCHOOL DAYS

Share a little about the high school you attended in Memphis.

Central High School was then *the* academic high school. I played high school football, and that crowd was always a little aggressive. They had a highly developed sense of camaraderie and fraternity. I also had a little military—because they had ROTC in high school, which was my only military experience.

In 1947 just after World War II, Marguerite and I got stranded late one night in Hamburg, Germany. By mistake the taxi took us to the British military hotel instead of the Red Cross hotel. The hotel staff was going to throw us civilians out on the street. I tried to get permission for Marguerite and me to spend the night in the British military hotel and sleep in the lobby. We didn't have any way to get to another place to stay, and it was midnight in that bombed-out city. I told them I was Lieutenant Duke K. McCall, U.S. Army, ROTC, CHS. You know how the British are about initials. CHS meant Central High School. I signed in, and they accepted me. For one shilling, we got dinner and bed and breakfast and the hospitality accorded to allied personnel.

Everything I told them was absolutely the truth. I doubt the deception would rate high on an ethical chart. But I was not about to spend the night with my wife walking amid that rubble and the roaming, desolate people of Hamburg.

You were involved in forensic debate and that sort of thing all your life?

Yes. Let's put in a word for BYPU. I grew up in BYPU. It was a magnificent training ground for Baptist young people. BYPU was the one place where you could stand on your own two feet and say something to an audience. You had to stand up and read your part from the quarterly. The first time or two, you stammered and stumbled and fell over yourself, but you still did it. Finally you got to the place where you were comfortable doing it, and then you ended up being a group leader. The denomination lost something important when they lost this. A lot of what Southern Baptists have today, they got through the continuing influence of BYPU and the Baptist Training Union that followed it.

I as a Baptist in Central High School in Memphis, Tennessee, was much more comfortable standing up in assembly and speaking to the audience than someone from any other denomination. Young Baptists had done it before in BYPU. Later, I was a member of the debating team at Furman University.

What other activities did you enjoy in high school?

I ran for defending attorney in the high school student government organization. All discipline in that high school was done by the students. The principal had to approve expulsion, but he couldn't expel a student unless he was convicted in the student government court. I wanted to be the defending attorney; I didn't want to be the prosecuting attorney.

We had a system of lower courts. If you went before a judge and were sentenced, you could appeal it. Then you'd get a jury trial. The system had a defending attorney and a prosecuting attorney and a semblance of the entire court procedure—witnesses and everything else. The jury found you guilty or not guilty, and the judge sentenced you. The judge was a student. There were limits to the sentences at different levels. But if that judge sentenced you to expulsion, the principal could override it. But I never in four years knew the principal to override any decision of that process.

One of my great disappointments, both as a student and as a seminary president, was that I could never make student government work at Southern Seminary. Students would do certain projects, like the missions conference. That was their initiative. But I could never make student government work anything like the process I had known at Central High School

ATTENDING THE SBC

Did your family attend the Southern Baptist Convention while you were growing up?

I was involved in a meeting of the Convention in Memphis as a Royal

Ambassador. I spoke to the WMU Convention. I was very young. I asked the WMU Convention if they knew what the letters "RA" stood for. They broke into hilarious laughter, and I didn't know what they were laughing about.

It was presumptuous to assume these women didn't know about RAs?

A little bit. But I knew a lot of women in the First Baptist Church of Memphis who didn't know anything about the Royal Ambassadors. Why should I think all those women knew about the RAs? And if they didn't know about RAs—what it stood for and what it meant—I needed to tell them. I was going to enlist their support for the Royal Ambassador movement.

CHAPTER 2

College and Seminary Days

1931-1940

What prompted you to go to Furman University?

I've always suspected my mother made the decision. W. J. McGlothlin was president of the Southern Baptist Convention and president of Furman. She probably thought Furman was an excellent place to keep me out of trouble. I was adventurous. Authority did not frighten me. Even before I went to college, they sent me off to the first Baptist World Youth Conference in Prague, Czechoslovakia.

THE FIRST BAPTIST WORLD YOUTH CONGRESS

They sent you? Or did you want to go?

Oh, I wanted to go, but they thought it was a great idea. Frank Leavell, the originator of the Baptist Student Union, didn't have quite enough in his party to get a free trip to Prague. He asked my parents if they would send me. He also enlisted Bill Bethea. Both Bill and I were a little young. I was just finishing high school.

You were just sixteen?

Yes. Bill and I technically were too young, not college students. We didn't go because it was a religious meeting; we went to have fun, to see Europe. We joined one of the youth movement groups in Germany, went hiking through the mountains with German young people, and stayed in youth hostels in the Bavarian Mountains. I am sure Frank Leavell regretted the day he invited Duke McCall and Bill Bethea to join his Baptist World Congress youth group!

What expectations did your parents have for you when you returned from the Youth Congress?

My mother thought I ought to be a minister; my father thought I ought to be a lawyer. I intended to be a lawyer. When I came home from Europe, I wanted to go to the University of Virginia because of its law school. I had already pledged a fraternity at the University of Virginia— Sigma Chi, my father's fraternity at Ole Miss. But I found that arrangements had already been made for me to go to Furman. My parents told me, "If you do what we want for one year, then you can go wherever you want to go to college after that."

COLLEGE DAYS AT FURMAN

I went over to Furman and had a great time. I pledged a local fraternity there, because I didn't want to mess up my bid from Sigma Chi at the University of Virginia the next year. The fraternity set up dates for my college roommate, Walton Smith, and me (we roomed together for four years). Five years later, he ended up marrying my date, and I married his date.

After my second year at Furman, I had already shipped my clothes to the University of Virginia at Charlottesville. I went to Furman to pick up some stuff I had left there the end of my freshman year. They were having some big festivities in Greenville—a dance at the Poinsett Hotel. They didn't have dances on the campus at Furman, but the alumni of the fraternity to which I belonged sponsored dances off campus. My parents didn't approve of my going to dances, but I went anyway. I was stubborn enough to hold my own course, and they let it go at that. I think my own sons will tell you that they have had that experience with their mother and me.

I don't like to work with people who can't make up their minds, who won't make a decision, who avoid the hard decisions. Nor do I like people who won't live with a decision after they have made it. I get along a lot better with people who say, "I decided. I was wrong." That doesn't bother me because I do that, too.

You were valedictorian of your class when you graduated from Furman in 1935.

I joke about that because the man who was salutatorian, Charles Townes, got a Nobel Prize in later years for the development of the laser.

I knew he was much smarter than I am, but I took a lot of courses at Furman because I wanted to study the subjects. I took only the courses I liked.

I also spent one summer editing the college annual, *The Bonhomie.* That summer I took third-year Spanish (without the second year). Because of that, I accumulated more quality points than Charles Townes to make me valedictorian. I have always thought that was one of the inequities of life, and it gave me a nice joke. Charles Townes came to Southern Seminary at one point for the Mullins Award. We have stayed friends through the years.

What were your main academic interests?

I ended up with a double major in English and history. I didn't really choose to do that; I just had enough credits, and then finally had to decide. I also ended up liking any of the math courses. After I finally caught up and caught on to physics, I liked that subject very much.

The father of Charles Townes was the physics professor. Somehow I got into a course where everybody else had already had physics. I didn't know what they were talking about for the first few weeks. I couldn't catch on. I wasn't going to pass the course.

A big test was scheduled before Christmas. To that point I did not have a single passing grade in the course. But I started at the beginning of the textbook and worked through it page by page, took the test, and made 100 on the test. Dr. Townes suspected that I had a little extra help, so he called me back in and repeated the test. I made 100 on that test, too, because I really did understand the subject then.

ALIENATED FROM BAPTISTS

Were you active in your college church?

In my freshman year at Furman I taught a Sunday school class. But in my sophomore year, my roommate, Walton Smith, and I were trying to play on the Furman golf team. I was always number five on a four-man team. But it was big stuff for me; it was important to me.

The University of Georgia golf team played the University of North Carolina. After they played in Chapel Hill, North Carolina, on Saturday, the Georgia team came down to Greenville, South Carolina, and spent the night in the fraternity house as my guests. I worked out a deal with them that if they would get up and go to Sunday school and church with me on Sunday morning, Walton and I would play golf with them on Sunday afternoon. This would give them one round on our home course before the match with us the next Saturday.

So I took them to Sunday school and worship services at Earle Street Baptist Church. That Sunday afternoon, in our golf clothes and with our golf clubs, we were standing on the corner near the campus when the pastor of the church passed by. I waved at him, and he acknowledged my hail.

About ten o'clock Monday morning I got the word to come to the college president's office. I went to see Dr. W. J. McGlothlin. "Mr. McCall," he said, "a trustee and local pastor has complained about your playing golf on Sunday. Did you play golf yesterday?" I said, "Yes, sir, and I had a good score." Then he said, "Do you plan to play golf on Sunday in the future?" I said, "Yes, sir; every pretty Sunday that I feel like playing golf." I was angry. Actually I had never played golf on Sunday before nor did I plan ever to play golf on Sunday again.

I've always been grateful to Dr. McGlothlin, who was wise enough to read me correctly. He could have expelled me on the spot. I wouldn't have batted an eye. He just changed the subject, and went on to talk about something else. He joked with me and then dismissed me.

That was the end of it as far as Furman and Dr. McGlothlin were concerned. But I was furious and would not go back to that church. If the pastor had come to me personally with an accusation, I would have acknowledged it, apologized, and explained. If he had not thought my actions were justified, I would not have defended them. But the idea of my pastor, a trustee of Furman, going to the president of the college and not coming to me violated my sense of propriety. I'm still angry, even after all these years.

This may explain why Matthew 18:15–17, about how to deal with an erring brother, has been so important to me all my life. I did not go back to that church. I would go to the Presbyterian church because Marguerite was a Presbyterian, or I would go to the Episcopal church because the father of one of my fraternity brothers was rector of St. Michael's Episcopal Church. But I wouldn't go back to the Baptist church. This is why I graduated from Furman without much religious involvement.

AGENT FOR LYNCHBURG ENGRAVING

I had been editor of the Furman annual, *The Bonhomie,* and I sold engravings for the Lynchburg Engraving Company to other college annual editors. I am not sure whether that was proper or not. A salesman from Lynchburg Engraving came to Furman just before I graduated and paid me the last of my fees, which was about $3,000. That was in 1935 at the bottom of the Depression. That was more than a year's salary for many people in 1935.

I sold the engravings during my junior and senior years at Furman to the editors of college annuals in other schools such as the University of South Carolina. The final contract would be signed by the salesman from Lynchburg Engraving at a lunch or dinner that I would give to introduce the editor to him. I received a percentage of the salesman's commission.

COLLEGE GRADUATE

I graduated from Furman with several awards, including serving as valedictorian and receiving the General Excellence medal. My parents gave me a new Ford car as a graduation present.

That was a good gift in 1935.

Yes. My father was pretty successful at this point. After graduation I went to a house party in Monteagle, Tennessee. Leaving Monteagle, I drove to Nashville, where I stayed at the old Noel Hotel. I just didn't know what to do next. I didn't have anywhere to go and I had $3,000 in my pocket.

While I was in Nashville I finished up my admission to Vanderbilt Law School. After that was done, I had to decide what to do—go home to Memphis or to Greenville, South Carolina, to see Marguerite Mullinnix.

I walked out of the old Noel Hotel on Church Street going nowhere in particular. In the middle of Church Street I met a Furman classmate, Bob Herndon. After quick greetings in the middle of the street, he handed me a Southern Seminary catalog. He was going to Southern, but there was no reason for him to give me his catalog.

RENEWED CHRISTIAN COMMITMENT

I decided to go to Greenville to see Marguerite. The sky matched my dark mood. It was raining as I drove the crooked mountain road toward Knoxville. I was driving too fast because life seemed to be of little value and I did not really care whether I made the next curve or not.

The car radio was blaring with music. Apparently the program changed, but I was so preoccupied skidding around the curves that I did not notice the change. Suddenly the radio broke through with the words of some uneducated mountain preacher. (I would have changed the station if I had realized that a religious program was on.) He asked, "Why not try God?"

I hit the brakes and skidded (literally) to a stop on the edge of the highway. I bowed my head and prayed, "Oh God, I am making a mess of my life. If you want it, you can have it."

When I got to Greenville the fraternity house was empty. It was between terms. Marguerite was at the beach with Wes Singletary. There was nothing to do. The next day was Sunday. Despite my pious commitment on the highway, I did not know where to go to church. I would not go to the Presbyterian church without Marguerite. My fraternity brother, whose father was rector of the Episcopal church, was not home. I was still angry with the pastor of Earle Street Baptist Church, but I felt I ought to do something religious.

Bob Herndon's catalog from Southern Seminary gave me an idea. The best religious scholars are in seminaries. I knew some of the Southern Seminary faculty because they often stayed in my parents' home when they came to Memphis to preach. Why not go to the seminary and give God his best chance through the seminary faculty to let me decide whether this Christianity stuff should be taken seriously? About nine o'clock that Sunday morning, I was on my way to Louisville. The narrow two-lane road wound through mountains much of the way, but it gave me time to think.

ADMISSION TO SOUTHERN SEMINARY

I got to Louisville too late Sunday night to go to Uncle Bradley Kimbrough's house on Chestnut Street. I stayed in a cheap hotel on Seventh Street (in the-red light district of Louisville, I learned later). On Monday morning I walked into President John R. Sampey's office. He recognized my name from staying with my parents in Memphis. I told him I wanted to enter the seminary.

He "harrumphed" a couple of times and said, "We cannot take any more students because we have committed all the student aid we have." With $3,000 in my pocket, I replied that I did not need student aid; I just wanted to study at the seminary. He admitted me on the spot. No forms to fill out, no questions, just a promise of a college transcript. It was easy—too easy, as I later discovered.

Some time along in the fall Dr. Hugh Peterson, the admissions director, got tired of my failure to respond to his repeated notices that I send a copy of my ordination certificate or license to preach to his office. He sent for me to come to see him. I had not responded because I had not been ordained nor did I have a license. Dr. Sampey had said nothing about this when he told me I could enter the seminary.

My plan was to stay at the seminary only through that term, which would end after Christmas, and then go to Vanderbilt Law School. I had paid my entrance fees to Vanderbilt during the earlier stop in Nashville.

When Dr. Peterson found out that I was neither licensed nor ordained, he told me I was not eligible to attend the seminary. I argued that I had paid my fees and was entitled to finish the term. He said he would check with the faculty to see if I could be an exception to the rule. Later I was told that I would have to leave.

When the word got around that I was being "kicked out for not being a preacher," the students were immediately on my side. I complained to Dr. Sampey that I was being terminated as a student because he had made a mistake. He demanded to know what mistake he had made. I reminded him that he had admitted me without asking if I was licensed or ordained. I had complied with every requirement I was told about. He thought about that for a moment. Then he "harrumphed" and said, "I was wrong; I will fix it."

When the students heard I was back in school, they went to work to make me conform to the regulations by persuading me to be a preacher.

THE CALL TO PREACH

One of my Furman classmates, Ed Rouse, worked on me in his room in Mullins Hall. He wanted to know if I had ever prayed about being a preacher. My answer was, "Not much or recently." I argued that no one in Louisville had even asked me to teach a Sunday school class or lead a devotional since I arrived in the city, so apparently nobody thought of me as "preacher material."

He asked if I would agree to pray about becoming a preacher. It is hard to refuse to pray in a seminary. I agreed. He said, "Let's get on our knees." I meant to pray about it at some time in the distant future. He proposed that we pray that God would give me a sign by opening the opportunity for me to preach somewhere. I thought that was a remote possibility, so I did not object. He prayed earnestly along that line and I joined in without much enthusiasm.

When we got off our knees, there was a knock on Ed's dorm door. An upperclassman named Don Myers asked, "Which one of you is Duke McCall?" I responded. He asked, "Do you have a car?" I must have been the only student in the seminary who was not pastor of a church who had a car. He explained that his car was in the shop, and he needed someone to drive him to his little country church in Indiana that Sunday (before Christmas 1935). My pay was that he would permit me to preach on Sunday night.

Immediately Ed Rouse shouted, "That's it. God wants you to be a preacher." I protested that I thought the test was for me to be called to be pastor of a church. That was all I could think of at the moment to counter Ed's conclusion.

We did drive to the church in the snow on Saturday night. We had cherry pie for breakfast—an incredible breakfast dish for a Southerner. I did not know how to write a sermon, so I simply told the Christmas story from the Bible at the sermon time that night. Three men came up to me after the service and announced that they were the pulpit committee from a neighboring church. (I never got the name of the church.) They said they wanted to recommend me as pastor of their church. It scared me so much that I could hardly talk. I explained that I was not a preacher and so could not accept.

I refused to accept the "fleece approach" to finding God's will for my life. But I did begin to pray for God to show me his purpose for my life with the possibility that it was not law. I came to a deep inner conviction that it was God's will for me to enter the ministry. That conviction has never wavered since, even during difficult days like the seminary controversy in 1958.

I notified Vanderbilt that I wasn't going to show up, and I never did get my money back. A generation later my son Duke Jr. decided to be a lawyer and go to Vanderbilt. I told him to tell the school officials that his admission fees had been paid in 1935. But the Vanderbilt officials didn't buy that argument.

Had you at that point been officially licensed to preach?

Not in my own mind. But at some point the First Baptist Church of Memphis had, in fact, approved me as a preacher. What the Memphis church did in 1932 probably meant to me at the time only that I should do whatever God wanted me to do. You have to remember that there was a time when churches would lay their hands on a young man and say, "We believe God wants you to be a minister, and we're going to set you apart for the ministry." It was in that tradition that Dr. R. J. Bateman had led the church to approve me as a minister. I didn't take that seriously, although I expect it was somewhere deep in my psyche.

On March 29, 1986, while preparing a sermon for Broadway Baptist Church in Louisville at the celebration of fifty years in the ministry, I unearthed a document dated September 5, 1932, in which the deacons of the First Baptist Church of Memphis adopted the following: "We heartily commend our young friend for his decision. We also commend him to the Lord and assure him of our prayers for his success in his chosen field of labor." What prompted that action is lost in memory. That was during my sophomore year in college.

While I was president at Southern, I fussed at the students if they did not have a sense of call or vocation. I always told them part of this story to explain that I didn't start out as a seminarian with a sense of call or vocation either, so I was willing to put up with them as seminary students who were looking for themselves for up to one year. But if they didn't find themselves on the seminary campus in a year, then they needed to go somewhere else to look.

The Christian ministry was and is my calling. So until this good day, I have never questioned it. My mother had always expected it to happen and was not surprised at all.

COURTSHIP AND MARRIAGE

How did your marriage to Marguerite come about?

We had a rocky courtship through college—sometimes on and sometimes off. She dated several members of my fraternity all through college. In the long run she ended up having to make up her mind between two guys—Wesley Singletary and me. That didn't occur until after I left Furman and went to seminary. By the time I ended up in Southern Seminary, I got a little more urgent about her and pressed the matter. After I decided to stay at the seminary, I thought that this might terminate relations with a Presbyterian Junior Leaguer. In God's good grace, it happened the other way.

I don't know why she turned away from my rival South Carolina fraternity brother and agreed to marry me. She and I have exactly the same birth date; we were born on the same day. We decided to get married on that day, so I would be able to remember the date of the wedding anniversary. That's what we did on September 1, 1936.

You were married in Greenville?

Yes, in the First Presbyterian Church. Charles Haddon Nabors, a Presbyterian minister, performed the ceremony for us in the First Presbyterian Church. A lot of fraternity brothers, Marguerite's sorority sisters, and all the people of that church in Greenville were present.

The Mullinnix family was important in Greenville. They were active Presbyterians. Marguerite's father was an elder in the church. Mrs. Mullinnix was a quiet, powerful kind of person. She never said much; she simply lived her convictions and values.

I had great admiration and affection for her husband, Joe (Joseph Henry) Mullinnix. He also tended to be very quiet, and yet he was a successful businessman, consistently a Christian in his relations. He often spent time visiting his friends who were in the hospital or sick at home.

FELLOW FOR DR. SAMPEY

What was your relationship to Dr. John R. Sampey at the seminary?

We named our son "John Richard" which will tell you that John Richard Sampey was a personal hero. The "John" is also for my father. Dr. Sampey was an imposing person, quick-witted and quick-tempered, deeply pious and very serious about living like Jesus. He was a member of Broadway Baptist Church, so I knew him as his pastor in later years as well as a student at the seminary. He and his wife were dear friends of ours through many years.

As a graduate student, I was a fellow for Dr. Sampey, and I also worked with Professor Kyle Yates, who was also in the Old Testament department.

YALE DIVINITY SCHOOL OR SOUTHERN SEMINARY
In 1938 you received the Th.M. degree. Then in September of 1938 you were named a fellow in Old Testament. Was that the year you began your doctoral work?

When I graduated with the Th.M. in 1938, I applied for graduate work at Yale Divinity School, and was accepted. Professor Kyle Yates from Southern Seminary was in Memphis for some preaching occasion. He came out to my house to see me.

He offered me the fellowship that he and Dr. Sampey, as the Old Testament department head, had settled on, if I would come back and do my graduate work at Southern. I've always considered that a gracious act of the good Lord. My career would have been entirely different if I had gone to Yale and earned a Yale doctorate instead of staying in the context of Southern Baptist theological education.

I reasoned that the advantages of attending a prestige school in a new environment would be more than offset by having a close relationship with the faculty at Southern Seminary. So I changed my plans and applied for graduate work at Southern.

GRADUATE WORK AT SOUTHERN SEMINARY
Who stands out as your leading professors at Southern?

Dr. Sampey and Hershey Davis in the biblical field. Davis, of course, was a New Testament professor. I always felt the Bible was central to what I was doing. W. O. Carver always intrigued me and delighted me as a student. During those days, the professors used a kind of force-feeding educational process. The professors would give you an assignment and you would have to stand up in class and recite.

Describe how this worked.

The professor would take the class roll and then he would call your name, "Mr. McCall." When he said that, you were supposed to pop out of your seat. You would stand up and grab the desk until your knuckles were white and wait for the lightning to strike you dead. Then the professor would start asking you questions, quizzing you in detail about the assignment for that day. If you couldn't answer the first question, he would embarrass you. He might say, "Thank you, Mr. McCall," and reach over and write a big zero by your name with a flourish. Your total grade was based on how you performed on that day. You might not perform but three or four times in a semester. Or, with the luck of the draw, you might end up reciting three times in one week.

LEARNING TO PREACH

When did you first begin formal preaching?

I started preaching on the street corner in the Haymarket section of Louisville. Nobody asked me to preach in a church, so I would preach on the street to people who were passing by. I had to make them listen, which was marvelous experience.

I later became a Sunday school teacher in Lee's Lane Baptist Church, which was a basement with a tarpaper top. I had an uncle, Dr. B. T. Kimbrough—a half brother of my mother—who taught at Male High School in Louisville. He was a graduate of the seminary, with a doctorate in Latin theology. He wanted to be a pastor, so he started the Lee's Lane church.

I went out there to help him and also because he was the only pastor willing to let me act like a preacher. I taught Sunday school and visited lost people to witness to them. I did not get to preach often, but at least I could try occasionally.

STUDENT PASTOR

Then in the spring of 1937, I was called as pastor of Woodville Baptist Church, about fifty miles north of Memphis and seven miles north of Ripley, Tennessee.

Jimmy (Dr. James L.) Sullivan was pastor at Ripley. At Woodville, we had a "heretical" experience—a revival in the winter. You weren't supposed to have a revival in a country church except in August. Thirty people made professions of faith. But we couldn't baptize them because the pond where we usually did this was frozen over. I made arrangements with Jimmy to baptize these new Christians in a bonafide baptistry in his church at Ripley. I also borrowed his baptismal outfit. We had the service on Sunday afternoon.

I didn't realize there was a hole in the rubber suit until I got in the baptistry. After baptizing thirty people, my boots were full of water, and I couldn't get out of the baptistry. The deacons had to grab me by the arms, drag me out of the baptistry, and empty the water out of the baptismal suit! I've always held that against Jimmy Sullivan. He should have had a new baptismal outfit if he was going to lend it to a green preacher like me.

I used to go down to the church at Woodville on the old Illinois Central Railroad. I rode the "seminary sleeper," which in common parlance was the day coach. I rode it all night and arrived in Ripley early in the morning. I got off the train and walked up to the bus station, where I cleaned up in the rest room. I caught the bus and rode seven miles up Highway 51 North to Curve, Tennessee. Then I walked three miles to Woodville Baptist Church.

Woodville was a half-time church, so I did this every other Sunday. They paid me $10.00 a Sunday—if the collection reached $10.00—and it cost me seven dollars and some cents to ride the train down there and back. So I didn't net much over $2.00 on the best of Sundays. This was in the 1930s during the depression, so $10.00 a week wasn't a bad offering. People rarely put anything more than a dime in the collection plate. It was a great experience; those were great people.

Most of the church families were sharecroppers; only one or two owned the land they worked. Levy Clark owned his farm, and he was the rich member of the church; actually, he was just a small-time, one-mule farmer, but he and his family were the social leaders of the community.

Levy Clark would say to me after each service, "Pastor, that was a good talk this morning." Next time he might say, "Pastor, that was a good—er, ah, uh—sermon this morning." One day I caught him out in the cornfield plowing, and I asked him, "Brother Clark, what's the difference between a sermon and a talk?"

"Preacher," he replied, "a sermon sounds better, but a talk says more."

So I could always tell if Levy Clark thought I had said anything. If I hadn't said anything, he would congratulate me on the sermon, but if he thought I had said something, then he would praise the talk. But he congratulated me either way.

After two years at Woodville, I was called to Centertown Baptist Church, another half-time church, in Ohio County, Kentucky.

Centertown was much closer to Louisville. I could drive down there, and Marguerite could go with me.

After going to Centertown, I used my off Sundays to listen to other ministers preach. I wanted to hear how they preached because I thought that was the best way to get a varied repertoire. My observation was that most people had only one style of preaching. I wanted to have several different preaching styles.

For example, Dr. R. G. Lee of Bellevue Baptist Church in Memphis once preached in Lexington, Kentucky. I drove him from Louisville to Lexington and back to get to talk to him. Then I wrote a sermon for Centertown that imitated Lee's preaching style. It was a case of putting on Saul's armor. I got in the middle of the sermon, and I got tickled at myself trying to use Lee's alliterative description. Then the congregation started laughing. They knew I was in over my head, and we went into hysterics right there in the church! Then I told them what I was doing, and who I was trying to imitate. I closed by saying, "The point of the sermon is so-and-so; now let's stand for the benediction."

Who did you model after most in your preaching? Your old pastor at home?

No, the pastor at Crescent Hill Baptist Church in Louisville— Charles L. Graham. He was a powerful preacher, and I imitated his style more than anybody else's. Another man I imitated was Harry Emerson Fosdick. He was on the radio on Sunday morning, and I'd hear him while driving to my church. While I had a Southern Baptist aversion to his liberal theology, I thought his preaching style was magnificent.

CAREER PLANS

At this point in your life, there was no doubt that you would become a pastor?

I had only one thought in mind—to be pastor of a Baptist church, and maybe some day to be pastor of a Baptist church as strong as the First Baptist Church of Clarksville, Tennessee. That was the hometown of my college roommate, and I have visited that church frequently. I loved Clarksville, and I thought it would be just like heaven to be the pastor of the First Baptist Church in a town of 10,000 people, which was about the size of Clarksville at that time.

COMPLETION OF GRADUATE WORK

You did most of your graduate work under Dr. Sampey?

Yes, he was the head of the Old Testament department, but Kyle Yates was a professor, and they worked hand in glove. Yates was the subordinate professor under the head of the department. Though I as a graduate student was under the head of the department, I worked with both of them.

When did you graduate?

I finished the dissertation ahead of schedule, and it was approved in the summer of 1941. But I actually received my graduate degree in the May 1942 commencement.

So you completed your graduate work in three years. You must have worked hard.

Yes. I'll work as hard as needed to complete a task. If that means twenty hours a day, I will do it. I was probably working an eighteen-hour day at that time in my life.

CHAPTER 3

Pastor of Broadway Baptist Church, Louisville, Kentucky
1940-1943

You went directly from a small rural church to Broadway Baptist Church in downtown Louisville. That was quite a jump for a twenty-five-year-old pastor.

Yes, Broadway had more prestige, history, and heritage than any other Baptist church in Louisville at the time. Broadway was supposed to be the "rich" Baptist church, but they had been in trouble for a while. The city had changed, and the economy had fallen apart in the inner city. The building was a big, imposing, stone structure. It was exactly seventy-five-feet high to the midpoint of the roof, and it had all of the Gothic symbols. It was the only church I had ever been a member of where chauffeurs drove up a sizable segment of the congregation in limousines. Even in 1940, that was still happening at Broadway.

They made me preach in a cutaway. They had gold-plated offering plates, and they wanted gold put in them, not copper. It was quite a church.

What shape was Broadway in financially?

Their membership was deteriorating. Many members had moved out into the suburbs, and they were driving long distances to the church. The church building had been allowed to deteriorate.

Why did they select you as pastor?

H. O. McKinney was treasurer of the seminary and a member of Broadway. I went to him and recommended my friend Guy Turner, who was serving a rural pastorate in Halls, Tennessee, as pastor for

Broadway. Guy had just graduated from Southern. McKinney said, "He'd need to be a great pulpiteer; our church has had great pulpiteers as pastors."

"Mr. McKinney, the trouble is your church is dying of great preaching," I shot back. What you need is a country preacher who will preach the gospel, and Guy Turner is a country preacher who will preach the gospel, but he will do it effectively, and your church will come back to life."

Nothing came of my recommendation, but Broadway apparently got strapped for a preacher one Sunday. McKinney came to me and said, "Have you got a country sermon that you will preach at Broadway?" I said, "Sure." He said, "We need somebody to supply next Sunday."

I had to pay somebody to go down to Centertown for me. I wanted to preach at Broadway. My intention was to get the attention of that congregation. I had visited there because of my interest in great preaching. The pastor, Hansford Johnson, had a reputation as a strong preacher. I had been to hear him and had decided that the church was dead. It was very formal. There was no interaction between the congregation and the pulpit. I was determined to get some response.

I got up at Broadway and started telling one joke after another, but nobody cracked a smile. Finally I told some wild tale. Broadway used to bring the children from the orphanage—the Baptist children's home—which was then on Second Street, near Broadway. They would come to church and sit in a group down at the preacher's right. One of those kids whistled at my wild joke. That caught the congregation. They began to laugh. As soon as they started laughing, I quit the foolishness and went back to a straight evangelical sermon. *Well,* I thought, *at least they responded to one person.*

The next week, John Long, chairman of the deacons, came out to the seminary to talk with me about becoming pastor of the church. I hadn't even thought about that possibility. I was in the middle of the second year of my doctoral program. This was about Christmas.

I finally agreed to be called as pastor of the church with the understanding that I would not become the pastor until the first of May 1940. I would schedule my doctoral exam before I became pastor. I would have my dissertation to write after I became pastor.

You were taking a heavy load if you were planning to do a dissertation as well as serve as pastor.

Yes, but the church agreed to let me do it that way. I would work in the library from six o'clock in the morning until ten o'clock, when I had to be at the church. Then for the rest of the day, I was pastor. Later, because of an injury suffered by Kyle Yates in an automobile accident, I began to teach in his place at the seminary while serving as pastor of the church.

How were you able to do a dissertation, pastor a church, and teach Old Testament at the seminary?

Well, a thing like that is sort of like the fellow who was hunting out on the peninsula with an icy lake around him when a bear came at him. He looked up and saw a limb twenty feet over his head. When he told the story, somebody said, "Now don't tell us you jumped up and caught that limb." "I missed it going up," he replied, "but I caught it coming down; I had no choice." You know, when you have to do something, you do it.

Why did you feel you had to teach that course at the seminary?

I enjoyed it; I liked to do it; I thought I had something to teach. I felt it was a God-given opportunity.

Did you have children at that point?

The twins were born June 27, 1940, after I had been at Broadway a few weeks. When the baby we were expecting turned out to be identical twin boys, I announced their birth at the next Sunday morning service. I was so excited I forgot to take up the offering. The deacons had to remind me to do so at the end of the service.

FINANCIAL DIFFICULTIES AT BROADWAY

Broadway was in financial trouble at that time, and some of this was the result of embezzlement by the church treasurer. The discovery came because I was convinced we were doing better than our books showed. I knew about what the offerings had been, and we hadn't spent that much money.

Deacon chairman John S. Long led in demanding an audit. I worked closely with the laymen. I believe in delegation of responsibility, and I believe in experts. I wasn't a businessman, so I turned this program over to businessmen for them to check it out as they would do in their business. And they did.

I wanted the church sanctuary repainted. It was a downtown city church in a soft-coal town, and the building hadn't been painted in a long time. Some of the deacons came to tell me, "We're having financial troubles, and you're going to bankrupt the church if you get the congregation to vote to repaint the sanctuary at this time." After they had made their pitch, I replied, "Gentlemen, you know this old church is dead, and I know it's dead. I think we ought to clean it up so we will have a decent place for the funeral."

Those high-powered businessmen sat there for a minute, and one of them started chuckling. They didn't say a word; they just got up and walked out. The next Sunday, they and their friends put enough money in the collection plate to pay for the painting of the church. It turned out that the church wasn't dead. The people had just quit giving. Once the church began to be active, people of great wealth in the church began to contribute again.

How much did they pay as salary?
A total of $2,700 a year and no fringe benefits.
Was that a good salary in 1940?
No, but it wasn't bad. It was a lot better than what I was making at Centertown—less than a thousand dollars a year.

PREACHING AT BROADWAY
What preaching style and methods did you use at Broadway?
I would have stood on my head in the pulpit to make you listen to me. But on the other hand, if standing on my head bothered you, and wearing a cutaway coat pleased you and helped you listen to my sermon, I went out and bought a cutaway coat and preached in one every Sunday morning.

That's what I had to do because I had accepted that particular church. I did not argue against conforming to their customs. But I let them know that I would not be as formal in my rhetoric as in my dress.

I deliberately denied in my style of speaking that I was what I looked like. In my mind, I was telling them something like this: "You want me to look like this; that's fine. But now I am going to talk like me, and I want you to hear what I say. I don't want the sermon to be nothing but neatly-arranged pious phrases that say the standard things that slide across your conscience without affecting your life. Let's talk about real issues and real people, not fight the battles that don't matter. In other words, I can't talk about missions to Africa and not talk about witnessing to blacks in the community."

We started having clinics for the people who lived in the rooming houses around the church. We had sewing sessions for the needy. Mrs. George Norton, a woman of social prominence and wealth in the city, worked in the Broadway sewing room every Tuesday. I doubt that she ever sewed at her home. We also had these doctors, prominent physicians, coming and giving clinics for poor people and bankers helping rooming-house residents with their finances.

How did you convince them to do that?

Just as I convinced them to paint the church. There wasn't any use being a dead church; let's get on with the gospel and do something about it. If we believed it, let's implement it. If you are young, you can get away with murder because successful older people look on a brash young person, if he is succeeding, with a sort of patronizing affection. They will follow you.

Now I didn't know all of this at that time, but my instincts were right. I was trading on the fact that these wealthy, prominent people had picked me out to be their boy, and they were going to look out for me and help me. Those doctors would not have gone down to a rescue center and put on a clinic for anybody else, but they did it for their young pastor. If I had been thirty years older, I doubt that I could have talked them into it.

What else did you do to reach the people in the area surrounding the church?

We used motion pictures during the Sunday evening service. We would put fliers advertising these services under the doors in the rooming houses, inviting the residents to come to a free picture show. These poverty-stricken people had no cultural and entertainment outlet, but they could afford a free motion picture. So they would come in droves. We used to average about four hundred people in that Sunday night service.

I remember particularly one of these night services that focused on the story of the prodigal son. I read the Scripture and then I said, "Now we're going to see an interpretation of this parable." The picture came on and they saw an amateurish presentation of this parable. When the picture was over, I preached about twelve minutes. All my illustrations came from the motion picture.

Through all these approaches, the church began to grow. Even if it was growing on Sunday night, the people who came on Sunday morning began to put more money in the offering plate. They developed pride in their church. They talked about it to their friends, so some of their friends came on Sunday morning, and the Sunday morning service started growing.

I didn't intend to be a standard Baptist preacher. I meant to find some way for the Good News of the gospel of God's love and the redemption of Jesus Christ to become an effective and formative part of the life of people. I thought it meant all people. At Broadway, I couldn't work just the suburbs. I had to work the rooming houses because these were the people for whom Christ died. They were on our doorstep, and nobody else would minister to them. I was looking for a way to get the gospel into the lives of people.

MARGUERITE AS A PREACHER'S WIFE
How did your wife fit into being a pastor's wife?

When we were married, Marguerite very quickly became involved as a Baptist preacher's wife. She became president of the WMU on the seminary campus. That causes us to laugh now. She was so recently a Baptist. She just transposed a Presbyterian word for a Baptist word and followed the directions. WMU used to be pretty explicit about what you did if you were president. She just did it. And it worked.

So it was not a particularly difficult transition for her to become Baptist and accept the Baptist way?

No—except that she says she's a "Pres-Baptist." She has never totally renounced her Presbyterian background and convictions. I have gone along with that basic understanding. After we were married we joined Highland Baptist Church in Louisville. The pastor, Dr. Tom Brown, asked me if I would baptize Marguerite. So I baptized her.

BROADWAY DURING WORLD WAR II
What did Broadway do to reach military personnel during World War II?

There was a big military build-up at Fort Knox not far from Louisville. All these men drafted into the Army would come to Louisville on the weekend and walk the streets. They were victims of all the carnality that exists in a sophisticated, hard-nosed city. They couldn't find a place to stay, and they were often robbed in the alleys.

Everybody in all of the churches wanted to help them. We at Broadway had good facilities in our gymnasium, with its bathroom facilities. So we turned the gym into a dormitory for military service men over the weekend. Then on Sunday morning we offered them breakfast provided by the churches.

The deacons or other members of Long Run Association churches would come down and serve the food or just sit with the men and talk to them. The goal was to train these church members to talk to the soldiers about Jesus Christ and their relationship to God. So it was a mix of a social ministry with an evangelistic goal.

Where were you on December 7, the Sunday when Pearl Harbor was bombed?

Dr. John R. Sampey was in the congregation when I preached on that Sunday morning. He jumped up after the sermon and delivered his description of the United States as a "fat turkey gobbler on the low limb of a tree the night before Thanksgiving." It was a troubled time for the nation and our church. Dr. Sampey thought the United States was unprepared. On the other hand, there were people like Bob Herndon and Clarence Jordan, who formed a pacifist movement at the same time.

Was Clarence Jordan a member of the church?

No, but he was a close friend, and he was a sort of mentor for Herndon. Bob was a member of the church. He was an outspoken pacifist like Jordan. Bob offered to leave Broadway lest his pacifism embarrass the church and pastor. I objected, asking, "When are you a pacifist? When the Japanese are at the doors of Manila or of Social Circle (his hometown), Georgia?" Bob later told me, "I gave your name as a reference in my application for the Army chaplaincy." He retired as a decorated colonel after serving through the Korean War.

The church responded to Pearl Harbor, as the nation did, with the sudden casting aside of the ambiguity of the situation in the country before then, and everyone was against Japan, Germany, and Italy.

Some people had been cheering for the anti-communists; they weren't really cheering for the Nazis. They just wanted communism destroyed because of its economic and political threat. Suddenly everything was congealed behind a new patriotism. The church gave the beautiful iron fence around the front of the building to the war effort. It went to the scrap drive. I remember the debate in the church over whether we should do that.

Some church members were indignant at the idea of giving up the fence. I told them I agreed with them, but I didn't think the church could advertise its lack of cooperation by having that ornamental iron fence right out front on Broadway in the middle of downtown Louisville. We had to show our support for the war effort.

Was this especially valuable to the war effort, or was it just a symbolic action?

It was a valuable contribution. Every piece of iron was needed, because we were trying to make enormous quantities of steel for the war effort. They needed scrap iron to work from as well as the iron ore. The scrap people had a tremendous drive for anything metal. It became popular to see how much you could give. An iron fence contained a lot of metal, and this was big, heavy, decorative iron fencing.

What events from the war years stand out most in your memory?

The big thing with the most emotional content that I remember was what was happening to individuals, to the young men going off to war. A son of the Craemers, one of the Broadway families, was killed in action early in the war, and this, of course, shook us all. Guy Turner, probably as close a friend as I had in the seminary in my undergraduate days, was the first Southern Baptist chaplain killed on Aku (an island in Alaska). This was personal. The war hit you with real force when people whom you knew were dying. This went beyond the machinations on a world scale by great leaders.

And then you had all of the economic disruption that accompanies a shift to a war economy.

Give some examples.

The obvious thing was rationing of commodities such as gasoline. I had coupons good for about ten gallons of gas a week.

That would get you fairly far?

Oh yes, I could live on ten gallons a week by careful conservation, but I couldn't have made it on the three gallons that some people were limited to. In fact, people quit coming to church except once a week if they lived a distance from the church. They would be using a good bit of their weekly allotment just to make one trip into town to church.

That must have affected your program.

Very much so. These young professionals whom I was trying to draw into the church for our special outreach programs disappeared. That trend that had built up and seemed to be a wave moving to strengthen the church just dried up.

Our economy shifted suddenly out of the Depression into a controlled situation. You felt it in your membership because people were being moved around in their companies, and their jobs were changing. While they were still working for the same company, there was great stress on the family. Even though a person might stay in Louisville, his role changed, and he would feel the pressure of a new assignment. You had the shift to what was important from a business perspective, what was important in terms of the way you lived, because of the threat of war.

We weren't all that sure that the United States was going to win the war in those early days. As a matter of fact, we lost every engagement in those early days of World War II. The news was all bad, and this had a depressing effect.

Through the church, we were trying to provide a basis for security and confidence. At least, I could live with the fears and uncertainties by focusing on the eternal purposes of God. You couldn't say the economy was going to straighten out next month, and the war would be over, and the boys would be coming home soon. You dared not say to anyone, "Your son will make it." So you lived with the threat, fear, and insecurity. You tried to minister to that urgent need among the congregation.

PASTORAL LEADERSHIP STYLE

Blakemore Wheeler was a wealthy, powerful man who was on the pulpit committee when I was called to Broadway. I told him, "I am young and inexperienced. I know that and you know that. But if you call me to be your pastor, you will do so believing that it is the will of God for the church to have a pastor as young as I am. I will not stand back on my age or do anything because I am young and inexperienced. I will depend on you to give me the benefit of your experience, but I will be the pastor of the church."

Mrs. Blakemore Wheeler broke in and said, "Mr. McCall, what you are saying is that if we call you to be the pastor of the church, you're going to be the boss?"

"That isn't exactly what I said," I replied, "but if it is going to be misunderstood, that's the correct side to misunderstand it on."

These successful businessmen did not have any problem with that approach. Blakemore Wheeler was my friend from that point on. He did many nice things for me. The Wheeler Estate later gave Southern Seminary a quarter of a million dollars when Mrs. Wheeler died.

I don't think you accomplish anything by trying to be patronizing or pandering to people. I think it's better to say, "Isn't this what the Bible teaches? Isn't this the sort of thing Jesus did? If this church is the body of Christ, shouldn't we be doing the sort of things Jesus did? If he healed the sick as a part of his manifestation of the kingdom of God, shouldn't Broadway Baptist Church be doing something about healing the sick?"

Did the church grow under your ministry?

Yes, I think it did; I really don't know the statistics. Although I ended up being an administrator and living by statistics, at that point in my life I really didn't care that much about money or statistics. What I was concerned with was people crowding into that church auditorium and hearing the Scripture and being treated as Christian brothers and sisters. Now that's important, and that's growth. If you mean growth that way, I thought we were succeeding.

Did you speak out on social issues and social problems in the community?

Yes, about poverty, race, and alcoholism. I had a segregationist or two in the membership at Broadway, and the black issue wouldn't necessarily have been expedient to discuss. I did not go at people like some of my contemporaries, who would get out their sledgehammer and smash people over the head with it. I tried to talk in such a way that the people would listen to me and I could persuade them. I did not demand a fight. I expressed concern about this situation, this problem, and then I tried to find biblical rootage for my concern. In my sermons I would ask for response.

Did you get any response?

Oh yes. I tried to get people to see that differences on the issues had nothing to do with personal relations. We sometimes had a debate in a deacons' meeting. But it didn't seem to affect my personal relationships with the people. They seemed to be ready for a new look at the problems. But I always found a way to turn every sermon into an evangelistic sermon. That kept me out of trouble with the anti-social gospel people—and that was and is who I am to this day.

Are there any people whom you ministered to at Broadway that stand out in your mind?

I remember Charles Hager, a sergeant in the army. He was converted by one of the members of the church at a Sunday morning breakfast. He had spent the night in the church dormitory. The layman who had won Charles Hager to Christ brought him to my study, and I talked with him. I told him about the church and the relationship it provided with fellow Christians. As someone reared in an orthodox Jewish home, he wanted to know about baptism. Did the Messiah want him to be baptized, he asked. And I said, "Yes, he does." He wanted to know how to go about this. I tried to explain it to him.

I told him that you come forward at the close of the church service. But I forgot to tell him to wait for the invitation. So when I closed the sermon, Charles Hager got up and walked down the aisle. It shocked the congregation. I said, "Will you tell the congregation what has happened to you today." He didn't know that every convert did not do that. He had never been in a church service before, so it didn't bother him; he just told them. It was a moving testimony to Jesus the Messiah. He had a high view of the Messiah, and the Messiah had come, and he had found the Messiah; the Messiah had died for him. It was a very moving statement.

Was Broadway the most influential Baptist church in Louisville at that time?

Walnut Street was the prominent Baptist church, but Broadway was a more powerful church in terms of leadership. Crescent Hill was coming on strong at that point, but the leaders of Louisville who were Baptist belonged to Broadway.

PRESIDENT SAMPEY AS CHURCH LEADER

Was Dr. Sampey president of the Southern Baptist Convention at about the time you served as his pastor?

This happened a little before my pastorate at Broadway. He was a great church member, by the way. He would sit and listen to my sermons like he had never heard the content before. Once at a revival, I gave an invitation for the members of the church to repent of their indifference and to renew their vows to God and to signify this publicly by coming forward at the invitation. The whole pattern of revival was for evangelism to begin in the hearts of Christians. The first person to come forward was John R. Sampey.

BROADWAY FACES CHANGE OF LOCATION

Broadway moved out to a new location eventually, but was that after World War II?

Yes, their move was made imperative by what happened during the war. The situation around the church changed. The long-time members and leaders of the church began to die out during the war period. The members also got oriented to other situations away from Broadway because of the gas rationing. After World War II, the future of Broadway as a downtown church was in question.

I understand one of the women of the church was anxious for a change in the pulpit furniture?

Yes, the pulpit furniture was classical Gothic, probably made in 1877. The leather had grown old and brittle and was beginning to crack. This was typical; we needed new hymnbooks, new cushions on the pews, and many other things. I wanted the furniture reupholstered. Mrs. Blakemore Wheeler agreed to do it but she said to me, "If you are going to stay as our pastor, I will redo the furniture in leather. But if you are going to leave, I'll have it covered in vinyl."

I gave her my absolute commitment that I wasn't going to leave for any other church. Then a few months later I left for Baptist Bible Institute at New Orleans. As long as she was alive, Mrs. Wheeler always reminded me of this commitment that I did not keep. She had paid for leather upholstery on my commitment that I would stay. I will meet her in heaven some day, and she will probably complain about my not staying at Broadway after she put leather upholstery on the pulpit furniture.

PASTOR AS CHANGE AGENT

What is the most important thing you learned from your pastorate at Broadway?

I learned that we could do what I believed we ought to do. I was not sure a church could change its structure and its organization in order to minister to contemporary needs, or that people would be that responsive. I think it happened as a result of the mix of the times and the situation. The people at Broadway knew that things had to change in the church because it was on a low limb. They were ready to change.

SEMINARY PRESIDENT ELLIS FULLER

Was Dr. Ellis Fuller, president of the seminary, a member of your church?

No, he was a member of Crescent Hill. He broke the traditional pattern and didn't join Broadway as presidents before him had done. The loyal Broadway members never forgave him.

Did that trouble you?

Not really. I tried to get him to join Broadway, but I understood his decision.

What was his response?

He cited the relationship between Crescent Hill and the seminary and its dependence on Crescent Hill. At that time Southern's commencement was held at Crescent Hill. Many seminary events were held in the church. The little seminary chapel couldn't handle the crowds, so the events were moved across the valley to this church.

Fuller's children also wanted to be in the church where their school friends attended. This seemed to be the right decision for him and his family. Of course, I couldn't build a downtown church on that argument. But you win some and lose some.

Were you close to Ellis Fuller?

Yes, we became very close friends.

CHAPTER 4

Baptist Bible Institute
New Orleans, Louisiana
1943-1946

How did you emerge as a candidate for the presidency of Baptist Bible Institute in New Orleans, and what prompted you to go?

Howard Bennett, one of my seminary classmates, was married to the daughter of John Jeter Hurt Sr., president of Union University at Jackson, Tennessee. Hurt was chairman of the search committee looking for a new president of Baptist Bible Institute. Bennett and his wife went home for Christmas to visit with her father and family. In conversation about the difficulty the committee was having, Bennett said to his father-in-law, "I know a young fellow who could do that job. He's young—if you have the courage to hire somebody his age."

Hurt was impressed by what his son-in-law had to say. This did not come about as a political power play by my father, who was chairman of the Baptist Brotherhood. Such a suggestion has been made in the past. It wasn't any big shot who proposed me; it was the pastor of a little church in east Texas.

But west Tennesseans certainly would have known you.

Perhaps so. My father's name would have been known, but I'm not sure mine would have been. John Hurt came up to Louisville to check on me. He liked the aggressiveness and the mold-breaking process that was going on at Broadway. I had picked up some reputation as a pulpiteer, and that got to him. I have a copy of his recommendation of me to the BBI committee. He researched all the prominent people in history who began their careers at about my age and put me in their category. I was twenty-eight years old at the time.

My pride was involved, I'm sure. I was amazed at the idea of being invited to talk to a committee that was looking for the president of a school. It intrigued me, so my wife and I set out for New Orleans. I remember saying to her at one point, "You know, if they ask me if I smoke, I'm going to turn it down." New Orleans had a reputation for being very puritanical. Dr. W. W. Hamilton, president of the school, is reported to have stood outside theaters when the crowd came out after the evening show. According to this story, he expelled on the spot any BBI student who came out of the theater. I had been having picture shows in my Sunday night services at Broadway, remember? I was afraid things at BBI might be too puritanical for me.

When I talked to the committee, I was rather blunt about what kind of school I thought it ought to be. I don't think I so much sold them as I didn't un-sell them. I think John Jeter Hurt had sold them and carried his committee along.

PROBLEMS AT BAPTIST BIBLE INSTITUTE
Did they have any agenda that they wanted you to follow?
No. They had a set of problems; they were in a mess. They had fired the president, W. W. Hamilton, past president of the SBC, because he married his niece. That turned out to be contrary to Napoleonic, or Louisiana, law; therefore, it was an illegal marriage. It wouldn't have been in most of the rest of the United States. Because of the war years, enrollment at BBI was down, and the country's economic situation was bad. The buildings had originally belonged to Sophie Newcomb College, which had moved to a new campus. All the buildings were old and run down.

Things were so bad that the trustees of BBI were willing to take almost anybody as president. That is how I got elected as the "boy president." Roland Leavell had turned them down before I accepted the presidency in 1943. He accepted the presidency immediately after I left BBI in 1946.

VISIT TO MOODY BIBLE INSTITUTE FOR HELP
Did the challenge excite you?
Yes. I didn't know how to go about being the president of a Bible school, so I went to Chicago and spent two weeks at Moody Bible Institute. They were very kind and helpful to me—from the president on down. They took

me through everything they did and explained why they did it this way, and why not to do it another way. This was after I had accepted the New Orleans job but before I had actually made the move.

Where did you live in New Orleans?

The first house was a big house through the block in front of Dodd Hall. It was a barn, but not as good as a Kentucky horse barn. After several months we moved into the old president's home on Chestnut. The war was still on. Only one telephone per residence was allowed, and we had six bedrooms upstairs. Floor heaters flush with the floor were the source of heat.

MAKING DECISIONS

Did you have second thoughts about having gone to BBI after you arrived?

I have never had second thoughts about any place I have gone. Once the die is cast, once I am convinced that, under God, this is my job, I really don't worry about it. I tend to think things over a long time before I make a decision. I'll walk the floor, literally, all night about a decision. When I am trying to think, I can't sit still, and I'll get up and walk.

I spend a lot of effort in thought and then a lot of time on my knees in prayer. I don't like to tell somebody else that I've prayed and this is God's will for you. I figure you have to do your own talking to God. I will firmly tell you that "I believe this is right for me, under God." I used to say to people, "If you don't agree with me, you have every right to try to stop me. But once I've told you what I think God wants, just understand that I'm going to do it. The only way you can keep me from doing it is that you'll have to block me."

Sometimes I reach a conclusion that I don't prefer. I don't pretend to explain it. I believe that God uses the circumstances. He deals with a person as an individual. The person must come to the place where he feels, "This is what I must do, under God."

BIBLE INSTITUTE OR SEMINARY

When I got to New Orleans, I found I was the only person there who thought I was president of a Bible institute. The faculty thought they were faculty members of a theological seminary. The students thought they were students in a seminary. The trustees thought they were trustees of a seminary. The alumni thought they were graduates of a seminary.

So I abandoned the vision that I had developed at Moody. I had to rethink the whole situation. We had this institution called "Baptist Bible Institute," but it was neither a Bible institute nor a seminary. I was willing to be president of a Bible institute for the training of God-called men and women for Christian service without reference to college graduation. I was willing to invest my life in trade school theological education.

A Bible institute is a trade school. That is not a put-down, because a first-class trade school is a fine institution. We need a few more of them in the United States today, in and out of the ministry. So I would have been for the trade-school approach to theological education. But you can't have it both ways. You must follow classical theological education as in a seminary, or you must go the Bible institute route. BBI started as a Bible institute, but very quickly moved away from the characteristics of a Bible institute. They began offering degrees, but they kept a lot of Bible institute characteristics.

Can you illustrate this specifically?

For example, an emphasis upon practical experience is a Bible school characteristic. A student goes out to preach. Nobody will say whether you did it well or poorly. Nobody asks, "What happened? What manifestation of Christian traits developed in those people?" The student just went out and did it. This "learning to do by doing it" is one of the characteristics of Bible schools.

But a seminary emphasizes supervised field education. A student conducts ministry under careful supervision, and he learns to reflect on what happened and what he learned through the experience.

NEW CURRICULUM AND NEW NAME FOR BBI

What changes were needed when you arrived at BBI?

A revision of the curriculum if we were going to be a seminary. We needed to shift some of the faculty. We began to tighten up the curriculum. We began to separate the classes out by academic prerequisites. We urged the faculty to use the college graduate approach to the subjects taught. We added strong new faculty members like Penrose St. Amant and Frank Stagg.

I supported the name New Orleans Baptist Theological Seminary. I wrote the report to the SBC that officially changed the name. But I left BBI just before the name was actually changed by SBC vote.

The decision to change the name and the choice of the name were proposed by a trustee committee. I even arranged for Dr. J. D. Grey of New Orleans to second the motion of Dr. Wash Watts, who was soft spoken. We needed Dr. Gray's booming voice and the support of a person who was not a graduate of BBI. And he did it perfectly.

Just as Watts said, "I move the adoption of these recommendations," J. D. Grey boomed out in the Convention, "I second the motion." It created the feeling that the whole world was in favor of that motion. Governor Pat Neff (Convention President), with the enthusiasm of J. D. Grey, said, "All in favor, say Aye; opposed No; it is so ordered" (in one breath). And it was done. There were people who planned to speak against the change who never made it to a microphone.

CONSERVATIVE BIBLE SCHOOL VS. LIBERAL SEMINARY
Why were they opposed to the change?

Some people remembered the establishment of a Bible institute in New Orleans, and they wanted it to stay that way. They thought a Bible school was more orthodox than a seminary. Of course it appears to be so because, in a Bible school, you don't question orthodox assumptions. You tend to ask questions and provide orthodox answers and therefore the standard answers are always learned by students in a Bible school.

But in a good seminary you are very likely to say, "Here's a problem. Here's what Dr. So-and-So says, and somebody else says, and somebody else says; here are relevant biblical passages; you figure out your answer." A good seminary says to its students, "You've got to become your own biblical scholar. The Bible has to become *your* authority."

DEVELOPING A MANAGEMENT STYLE
Did you go to a seminary to get some training on operating a seminary?

I talked with everybody I could talk to, and I got all the books I could get my hands on. But I did not find these very helpful. I got more out of the American Management Association than I got anywhere else. This provided basic management techniques, without reference to schools. I did my own adaptation of management principles and policies to theological education.

NEW CAMPUS SITE NEEDED

What was your opinion of the site on which BBI was located?

I really despaired of doing the job at the old site of BBI on Washington Avenue. Two trustees—O. J. Farnsworth, a contractor; and Lowrey Eastland, an insurance man and Louisiana politician—and I picked out the site of the present campus of New Orleans Seminary. We were determined to move the campus.

Frankly, I left New Orleans in order to get the money to build the new campus in New Orleans. New Orleans didn't have the alumni, and the local Baptist community could not do it. The only way I could do it was to get funds from Southern Baptists. So the Capital Needs Program, which provided the money to build the new campus in New Orleans, was the best idea.

SYNDICATE TO BUY 480 ACRES

Did you actually buy the property for a new site?

No, I tried to set up a syndicate to buy 480 acres, which was the estate out of which New Orleans Seminary ultimately bought 75 acres. I wanted to buy the entire 480 acres. With a real estate guru like Lowrey Eastland helping me, I wanted to develop a portion of that 480 acres toward the Industrial Canal of New Orleans. I thought this was a sound business proposition where the seminary would make a lot of money and perhaps be able to pay for its 100 acres that we had picked out to be cut off for the campus.

The 75 acres President Roland Leavell eventually bought for the new campus were a part of the 100 acres that I wanted to buy. But doing that kind of "entrepreneuring" in Southern Baptist life was new and different, and denominational leaders were threatened by that kind of operation. I am convinced they thought I didn't have the business ability to pull it off, and the denomination would end up in debt again.

If this business enterprise had failed, BBI would have lost some money—about $100,000, the amount BBI was putting in up front. The collateral was the land we were buying, and the land was going to be worth at least what we were paying for it. The people we owed money to might have foreclosed and taken the collateral away from us, but the denomination would not have been forced to assume the debt.

From my point of view, it was a straight real estate deal in which the seminary would have only $100,000 invested. Because of opposition to this plan, I had to find a different way of getting the money to buy the land and build the buildings.

Did the syndicate go on and buy the property?

No, the syndicate broke up when I left New Orleans because I had put it together. But somebody else bought the land and did exactly what I proposed to do. If New Orleans had bought that 480 acres at that time, it would have been the best-endowed seminary Southern Baptists have right now because that land became very valuable in future years.

Where would the seminary's $100,000 investment have come from?

Out of funds that we were raising to try to build new buildings.

Did you have the cash, or pledges?

We had the cash—actual hard cash that I could put my hand on. The Hibernia National Bank in New Orleans was going to help us with the deal. The bank would have made a little money out of it if it went off as well as we thought.

What happened to that $100,000?

It stayed there, and the seminary used it later to buy the 75 acres for its new campus. It was not designated funds. This was money that I had been raising to use in building new facilities.

DETERIORATING CAMPUS ENVIRONMENT

If the syndicate had bought that 475 acres as you intended, would that have alleviated some of the problems that have come to this area of New Orleans now?

I hope so, but I don't know whether we would have been smart enough to look that far ahead. Every site that you pick will eventually get to be an old site, even if you should choose the Garden District of Louisville. All those surrounding houses will be old houses some day. The only thing a seminary can do is to insulate itself against adverse development and then try to do some things to be a good neighbor and develop its own environment.

Think about the site of the Southern Seminary campus in Louisville. The Crescent Hill area is getting to be an old, dilapidated section. Southern will have some future problems with its location. I predict that the seminary will eventually move. Many of its buildings were constructed in 1925 and are now past seventy-five years old. When those buildings get to be over 100 years old, there will be a question whether the seminary ought to stay at that historic site or abandon it.

DEVELOPING A SEMINARY FACULTY

Did you need to bring in some new faculty members at New Orleans?

Yes, we needed new faculty people and we needed to train some of the faculty we had. We reassigned some members of the faculty to areas where they had more expertise. We had to bring in people in areas where the faculty members had been teaching without adequate training.

We needed a first-rate historian. Penrose St. Amant, a graduate of New Orleans, appeared to be that. He was at Southwest Baptist College in Bolivar, Missouri, but not as professor of church history. He brought the scholarly status of an Edinburgh Ph.D. graduate. We also added Frank Stagg in New Testament.

A seminary must equip its students to answer questions that weren't raised while they were students at the seminary. You've got to give them all of the technical tools and teach them how to use them. That's what I was looking for in a Frank Stagg or a Penrose St. Amant.

Were these two professors kingpins in your rebuilding process?

Yes, although there were other faculty members at BBI who were quite good in their area. Albert Tibbs in religious education, for instance, was already there. BBI was not without some strong people, but it did not have uniform strength across the board.

BBI tended to depend a little too much on retired missionaries as faculty people. When these people taught on the mission field, they dealt with less academically prepared students. They were brought back over to New Orleans, where, in effect, you were mixing the Bible school and the seminary type of students in one classroom.

STATUS FOR BBI IN NEW ORLEANS

What did you do to win friends for BBI in the New Orleans community?

Baptist lay leaders in the community got me an invitation to join the Rotary Club. That provided access to business leaders and civic leaders. I exploited that friendship, legitimately but to the full, in trying to relate BBI to the life of the community. My thought was that the witness of the institution ought to be felt in the life of the community. Further, you need access to the strength of the community for full development of the institution.

I could give all kinds of illustrations. People tend to forget there are such things as zoning laws. Somebody on the zoning board can say yes or no when you want to change the use of a building. In a Baptist institution, you need to know the community. You want the secular press to be sympathetic and accurate in its reporting of Baptist news. I don't think I created any revolution in New Orleans, but it worked. BBI became a community asset when the public noticed it.

THE LOCAL BOARD OF TRUSTEES

What's your opinion of local trustees and the contribution they can make to a Baptist institution?

Local members of the board are important to any institution. They are more important than I think Southern Baptists understand. There have been various efforts to get rid of local boards. That would be one of the most stupid things that Southern Baptists could do. You need the expertise of these local people.

Often local pastors will provide some unique contribution. Their proximity provides a sort of continuous oversight. They hear by the grapevine everything that goes on in an institution, and they have to live with it. The institution has both good news stories and bad news stories. Sometimes they don't deserve the good ones, and sometimes they don't deserve the bad ones. The local people have to absorb the impact of that. Then they have to represent the institution in the local community, saying good words, you hope, about the enterprise of which they are a part.

So you have been opposed to efforts to do away with local boards?

Definitely. Some people think local trustees have too much control over the institution. But I reject that idea. Local boards tend to be very reticent in terms of the activity of the larger board. They feel they are responsible to the larger board, representative of the wider constituency. This seems to be the instinctive reaction, at least with the laymen who are on the local board.

I find myself eager for laymen who are on the local board to be a little more active, to speak up in the annual meetings of the board of trustees more often than they do. At the local level they are very articulate and very quick to give you their judgment. They tend to go into a shell when the rest of the board comes to town because of their feeling that they ought not to try to speak for the whole Southern Baptist Convention. I know there are bound to be exceptions to that in the experience of all agencies, but that has been my experience with local boards.

DECIDING TO LEAVE NEW ORLEANS

Why did you decide to leave Baptist Bible Institute and go to the SBC Executive Committee in Nashville?

Dr. Theron Rankin of the Foreign Mission Board had a lot to do with that. He spoke at BBI for our missionary day emphasis. He and I were on the train headed to Birmingham, where both of us were scheduled to speak. Then both of us were going on to Nashville for the annual December meeting of the SBC Executive Committee.

During this trip we talked about his dream of a big program of Missionary Advance for foreign missions. I told him how much I was committed to helping him, that he could count on me. I told him that if there were some place in the world where my background and experience would fit, I would accept a five-year assignment because of my commitment to missions.

I told him, "Next week, in the Executive Committee meeting, when you need an ally to get the Advance Program for Foreign Missions adopted, just know you can count on me. If you signal me to speak or do anything else, I'll support you."

That turned out to be the reason I went to the Executive Committee as executive secretary—something I didn't really want to do because of my love for theological education. I went for five years because I had told Rankin I would go to the mission field for five years. During that time I thought of myself as an ally of Theron Rankin and the Advance Mission Program. I was in Nashville for the purpose of strengthening the world outreach of the gospel.

CHAPTER 5
The Southern Baptist Convention and Its Executive Committee

1946-1951

Tell me about your dealings with Dr. Austin Crouch, your predecessor as executive secretary of the Executive Committee?

He was a dear friend. While I was in Nashville and he was alive, I saw him fairly often. He suffered from failing eyesight, and this is why he resigned from the Executive Committee. This opened the door for me to come to the Executive Committee.

He was a precise, astute man who lived by statistics. Numbers were meaningful to him, and he could make decisions on things that were measured by numbers. He was a strong denominational man with a deep sense of justice and fair play. He loved the church and was a devout Christian. I had great respect for Austin Crouch.

He is one of those giants among Southern Baptists who probably will never be fully appreciated because he worked behind the scenes. A George Truett would be a highly visible leader in that era of Southern Baptist life, but an Austin Crouch would be back in the committee room ironing out the problems of the Cooperative Program or servicing the debt that was left from the overspending of the Seventy-Five Million Campaign.

Was he ever able even after the debt was paid to get out of the philosophy of the denomination being in debt?

Nobody got out of that. "Debt free in '43," "Owe No More in '44,' or "We'll Skin You Alive in '45." That was J. E. Dillard's set of slogans that capsuled the mind-set of the leadership of the 1940s.

Was it fortuitous that a younger man such as yourself with a different attitude came to the Executive Committee in 1946?

I think so. It was a time when the close of World War II called for dreaming dreams and establishing new programs. When I was with BBI in New Orleans, I wrote a hot letter to all the members of the Executive Committee complaining about their conservative stance. I objected to their effort to make everybody color inside the lines and observe the letter of the law of the Business and Financial Plan.

I think members of the Executive Committee recognized the truth in that letter and said, "We'll elect this guy as executive secretary, and maybe he can implement some of his dreams."

So there was a dramatic change in philosophy and feeling at this time?

Everything had changed. The Depression was over. World War II was over. Expansion was at hand. The boys were coming home from the war. They had new attitudes about the world that they had acquired while serving overseas. They had a new commitment to their faith. A new air of optimism was sweeping the country, and Southern Baptists were a part of that.

The Southern Baptist Convention had come out of World War II in organizational disarray but with a spiritual dynamic that I have no explanation for—but it was there. Something new had arrived on the scene. I think you saw it partially in the religious revivals nationally in the 1950s.

What had happened to Southern Baptists during the war was a pent-up frustration. This impulse was tapped by the Advance Program of Foreign Missions, the world relief offering, and the new Charlie Matthews evangelism developments. The simultaneous revivals were a technique for getting all Southern Baptists together. Before that, we had been more individualistic. The war taught us what we could do if we subordinated our individualism to a cooperative effort.

RELIEF AND REHABILITATION PROGRAM

You were elected at the Convention in Miami in May 1946. How did you begin as executive secretary of the Executive Committee?

The relief and rehabilitation offering at the end of the war—that's one of my traumatic memories, going to Nashville and being told to raise $3.5 million as my first job as executive secretary.

The Convention voted on this in Miami, about the tenth or twelfth of May of 1946. I arrived in Nashville the first of June, and the campaign was scheduled for July, August, and September. How do you organize the denomination while settling into a new home and a new job, and all in four weeks? We spent years raising $6 million to pay the Convention's debts. Now in three months we were supposed to raise $3.5 million. It seemed impossible, but we raised $3.8 million in the three months.

This convinced me that we had a growing, more powerful Southern Baptist Convention that would have the strength to reach further into the world. I thought the Southern Baptist Convention just couldn't ignore those hungry, homeless people whom I met in my travels. Through this denominational program, little Baptist churches overseas received massive relief shipments and became the instruments of aid in the name of Christ to their own countrymen.

GROOMING THE YOUNG EXECUTIVE

What were your dealings with Dr. T. L. Holcomb at the Sunday School Board? Did he view you as an inexperienced young man?

For some reason I didn't seem to threaten anybody. Yet I was so inexperienced and I was so brash. I think they were having fun working with me because I knew how old I was. I knew how inexperienced I was, and I was trying to learn from them. Teachers always take a personal interest in the person being taught.

Holcomb was teaching me, but he wasn't alone. Many people spent a lot of time and energy trying to enlighten me. I had the best school anybody ever had in denominational life. I was only twenty-eight years old when I went to BBI, and just barely in my thirties when I went to the Executive Committee. So you can imagine these denominational elders really took me under their wings. It was a mutual relationship. I was perfectly comfortable with it. It didn't offend me that they were paternalistic.

I thought I was getting more out of this than it was costing me. On the other hand, this is why you will find every once in a while that I would shock the crowd when I would get my back up and refuse to play the game by the established rules. I didn't always win. I sometimes got stubborn and fought—and lost.

Never did the "big people" in Southern Baptist life argue against my position on the basis of my youth and inexperience. People like Louie

Newton and John Buchanan would beat the socks off me, but it was on the issue and not on my age or experience. Dr. Holcomb and I had some clashes, but I felt affection from him and for him.

BAPTIST PROGRAM

In 1947 and 1948 there was an attempt to develop a purpose for the publication known as the Baptist Program. *Was this one of your goals when you came to the Executive Committee?*

When I went to the Executive Committee, the *Baptist Program* was a newspaper style and size quarterly publication. My feeling was that it was issued too infrequently to keep people informed of what was going on in the denomination. People were using it like they did a daily newspaper. They would look at it and then file it in the nearest wastebasket.

What I wanted in the *Baptist Program* was a more frequent publication that would be current in terms of up-to-date emphases in the denomination. It would promote by sharing information, insights, and understanding. We needed to put it in a magazine size and to publish it more frequently. Originally we started with a monthly, but we later dropped out a month or two during the year for economic reasons.

You have to remember the relative independence of the state papers at that time—their emphases, the things they were promoting. There was no unanimity in what was appearing in the state papers. The denomination would adopt a program, but some states would not adopt it. The denominational program never got mentioned in some state papers.

Was this because the states prided themselves on their independence, or had Southern Baptists not yet molded a national identity?

We were very much more "states rights" people in those days. The autonomy of the states was often the subject of debate and discussion. Many leaders at the state level felt the state programs were primary. States cooperated with the SBC only at points of mutual interest and common consent. There was no sense that the Southern Baptist Convention program involved everybody in all the states.

So the *Baptist Program* was part of my effort to mold a sense that we were a national denomination. The two tools I used for this were the *Baptist Program* and Baptist Press.

I thought we could do together in a national organization far more than we could accomplish separately. Organization means that we as free human beings decide to link our arms and do together what we can't do separately. Organization is important to me. I believe in it. I really did visualize the Southern Baptist Convention as a more coherent national structure in which, by due process, decisions would be made and then we would all undertake to reach the goals on which we had agreed.

So that was the perception that I brought to the Executive Committee. Baptist Press was the other arm designed to provide national information to the state papers, which they could use or not use at their discretion. The *Baptist Program* was a way to discuss the program with the pastors and church leaders without depending on any other publication.

BAPTIST PRESS IS BORN

Tell us about the development of Baptist Press.

C. E. Bryant came to the Executive Committee from the *Arkansas Baptist*. One of his assignments was to develop what became Baptist Press. We even had to invent the title "Baptist Press."

Who invented the title?

I haven't any idea. I have a hunch it was Bryant, but I don't really know that for sure. It was an obvious play on United Press and Associated Press, so it would be an easy title to remember. We were trying to say, "This is objective, national Baptist news that is presented to you as AP presents its news to the local newspapers. Use it if you want it, rewrite it if you want, do whatever you want to do with it." So it was not intended to force centralizing of reporting. The idea was that a sense of common identity would grow out of that sharing of information.

So you used the Baptist Program *as a promotional piece and Baptist Press as an information piece?*

Yes, that distinction is valid. There was a strong distinction between the two. *Baptist Program* was always in favor of the official denominational program, even if the executive secretary was not in favor of it personally.

Has Baptist Press done what it was established to do?

I think it's done a magnificent job. It's a great instrument, and I think it's well used. Sometimes it suffers from delusions of professionalism. Sometimes amateurs try to act like professionals and end up acting like amateurs instead.

What do you mean by that?

I mean that they decide to be objective investigative news reporters, fearlessly reporting the news. And when they do that, they nearly always end up in some inept form of reporting. They don't check with all the people involved lest the people influence the news.

So they announce, for example, that Dr. Henlee Barnette of Southern Seminary was demonstrating against the inauguration of President Nixon, when as a matter of fact Henlee wasn't even in Washington, D.C. That's an inept, amateurish kind of news reporting. Yet they published a story that had him in Washington in peace demonstrations at the time of the inauguration of the president of the United States.

All they had to do was to talk with somebody at Southern Seminary. They wouldn't have embarrassed the seminary or the professor, or published a story which they finally corrected after much hard-nosed prodding.

Can you think of any other cases?

No; that's enough because I would begin to sound as though I'm critical of the people at Baptist Press. I really have high regard for them and feel they've done a good job with limited resources.

BULLETIN SERVICE TO SUNDAY SCHOOL BOARD

Tell us about the growth and development of the Baptist Bulletin Service.

The Baptist Bulletin Service was an effort to reach individual Southern Baptists with little vignettes of Southern Baptist life. It's a third cousin to Baptist Press. When I went to Nashville, the bulletin service was a mimeographed publication, and it was losing about a thousand dollars a month.

The idea was to go around the state papers and the Sunday School Board publications, and go straight to the church members. I thought this was a good idea, but I didn't like losing a thousand dollars a month. C. E. Bryant's other big task when he came to the Executive Committee was to be an entrepreneur and make money out of the Bulletin Service. This would be used to fund the publication of the

Baptist Program, which would become a magazine with color and better paper. He was also to provide bulletins once a week instead of once a quarter.

We introduced colored bulletins and began to promote them, and they sold like hotcakes. We began making $40,000 a year net out of the Bulletin Service. Finally the Executive Committee sold it to the Sunday School Board, for $100,000-a-year payment to the Executive Committee, which would be spent on the *Baptist Program.*

C. E. BRYANT'S CONTRIBUTION

I give a lot of credit to C. E. Bryant. He has never gotten as much credit as he deserves among Southern Baptists for his innovation and entrepreneurship. He and I, to this very day, have a great deal of affection for each other. Both of us were brash, inexperienced youngsters who were trying to climb Mount Everest. It was exciting to see our dreams come to pass.

Let me quote from some recent correspondence with C. E. Bryant. He was writing to Bill Sumners of the Southern Baptist Historical Library and Archives:

> Receipt of the 1998 *Annual,* mailed with second-class postage, calls to mind another 'episode' during my two years as Duke McCall's aide in the Executive Committee office. Duke apparently lay awake at night thinking of new worlds to explore. . . . Time was approaching for the mailing of the 1947 *Annuals,* and Duke chafed over the more expensive cost of fourth class (commercial) mail as compared with second class book rate. Duke asked me to check into it, and we argued with the post office that the *Annual* should be consider a book of general public interest entitled to the lower rate. . . . This required visits with the Nashville postmaster and letters to the postmaster general, and possible letters to congressmen, but eventually the reclassification was granted.

In a review of his two-year role in Nashville, C. E. remembered the following things:

I was 30 years old when Duke McCall, executive secretary of the Executive Committee but not much older than I, invited me to fill the publicity vacancy left by Walter Gilmore's death. I had been editor of the *Arkansas Baptist* four years.

Baptist Bulletin Service. Duke encouraged me to enlarge on the base Gilmore and others had started. The Baptist Bulletin Service was producing and distributing a weekly black-and-white cover for churches' order of worship. Our purpose was to deliver SBC program information and promotion on this outside cover, and the churches printed their own information on the two inside pages. We charged a nominal fee for these bulletins, hardly enough to cover expenses. Probably in 1948, with the help of Rachel Colvin, artist for the WMU in Birmingham and later Herman Burns of the Baptist Sunday School Board art department, we introduced color to these bulletins. A bit later Harold Ingraham, business manager of BSSB, argued that the BSSB should be the publishing agency of (all) church materials and offered to assume the publishing and distribution chores, with the Executive Committee still doing the editorial content. The BSSB paid us 15 percent of gross sales, which relieved us of the worrisome distribution work and guaranteed a "profit."

The *Baptist Program.* Duke had said I could use any new income to strengthen the *Baptist Program.* It was at that time an "occasional" tabloid publication for promotion of special projects (mostly Cooperative Program because this predated the Stewardship Commission). The *Baptist Program* may have been born during the Seventy-Five Million Campaign in the late 1920s (by Frank Burkhalter or a bit later by Walter Gilmore). We designed the "new" *Baptist Program* as a 16-page 8 1/2 x 11 monthly for free distribution to all pastors in the SBC, using a mailing list owned by the BSSB. We restricted circulation to pastors to assure them we were furnishing fresh material not available to others in their congregation. I planned to sell advertisements, but Louie Newton, then president of the SBC, thought it would undermine the stature of the publication. (State papers in that era were decorated with Lydia Pinkham and PILES ads.) We agreed to use advertisements only on items sold by Baptist Book Stores, and George Card, the book store man for the BSSB, became both our salesman and bill collector.

Baptist Press. Porter Routh, then director of the information and statistics department of the Sunday School Board, had initiated an SBC news service at the request of state Baptist paper editors. After I came to the Executive Committee in 1947, there was mutual agreement that this news service would be better handled by the Executive Committee. I cannot remember whether we did our mailing on a weekly or monthly basis, but I do vividly recall the morning when Duke and I and his secretary Clara McCartt gathered around Duke's desk to find a name for the news service. Various ideas came up, but we chose to follow the example of Associated Press and United Press and call our fledging "Baptist Press" using the initials "BP."

"We'll have to wait and see," intoned Clara McCartt, "whether it beeps or burps."

The unhyphenated Cooperative Program. The Executive Committee was then charged with promotion of the Co-operative Program. I confess I tired of using two extra finger strokes (we used manual typewriters) to type that hyphen. I proposed that we drop the hyphen, suggested that the dash was divisive in a word that implied solidarity. Clara McCartt accused me of being lazy and pointed out that all "style changes" were the responsibility of the style committee of the BSSB. Bill Fallis was chairman. I took my grief to Bill. He pointed to Webster that the hyphen belonged there. Finally, Bill agreed we could have it both ways. The Co-operative Program, he said, is a proper name for a giving program administered by the Executive Committee. If we wanted to spell our baby's name without the hyphen, we could do so. At the same time the BSSB publications would refer to it like this: "The Cooperative Program (no hyphen) is the plan Southern Baptists use for co-operative (with a hyphen) giving."

Every Baptist a Tither. Louie Newton sat in my office one afternoon seeking an innovative plan for promoting gifts to the Cooperative Program. We were to report to a meeting of the Executive Committee that evening. Nothing seemed to jell. Then Louie used a pencil to write "Every Baptist a Tither" across

the back of a used envelope. We agreed that was it. He presented the slogan to the Executive Committee that night. Next
morning I retrieved the envelope and asked our printer to make
duplicate copies of Newton's long-hand script for distribution to
editors and for poster-size and banner-size enlargements.

SBC press rooms. In my two years at the SBC, I managed the
press room at three conventions. I moved to Nashville in April
1947, only two or three weeks before the Convention met in St.
Louis. We followed precedents set by Walter Gilmore, but far
short of the elaborate setup W. C. Fields later developed. I
remember Harold Fey, editor of *Christian Century,* being there.
When I introduced him to Louie Newton, the president that
year, he commented that ours was the first church convention
he had ever covered where there seemed to be no secrets. He
had gotten answers to all his questions.

The next year, 1948, we met in Memphis. Lydell Sims, colum-
nist for the *Commercial Appeal,* wrote humorously that "Baptists
came to their annual convention with a $20 bill and a clean pair
of socks, and never changed either." The 1949 Convention met in
Oklahoma City. I had already accepted a public relations position
at Baylor, but worked through this meeting.

Flossie and I decided to leave Nashville after only two years
because our children, then five and three, had respiratory ill-
nesses caused by the heavy acrid smoke in Nashville at that time.

(Note: In the 1940's I left my suburban home in both Nashville and
Louisville in bright sunshine, only to have to turn on the lights in order
to see to drive before reaching my downtown office. Both cities were
soft-coal river towns.)

ALBERT MCCLELLAN

*After C. E. Bryant left, Albert McClellan joined your staff. Why did
you choose him? What type of work did you want him to do?*

I had gotten to know Albert as editor of the *Oklahoma Baptist
Messenger,* and I thought he was a self-starting kind of person who
seemed to be an independent thinker. Albert was an extraordinary person with great gifts and abilities. As a former editor of a state paper,

Albert understood the editors and the problems of the state papers and turned Baptist Press into a powerful instrument of denominational unity. He had an analytical mind. He worked hard at analyzing the problem or the challenge. When he came to Nashville, he came well trained in the business of goals, objectives, and program descriptions. He knew how to think in those patterns. His mind actually tracked the patterns that were laid out, and he did it with precision and, above all, he did it with integrity. There was no guile in him. I took seriously anything Albert McClellan proposed.

COOPERATIVE PROGRAM DISTRIBUTION

Tell us about how the Executive Committee allocates funds.

The Executive Committee does not make its allocation of funds on a program budget basis. They make their allocations in terms of their collective perception of political reality. Anybody who can manipulate the political realities of the Southern Baptist Convention can override the power of the Executive Committee Program Committee.

The executive secretary (later president) of the Executive Committee is the most powerful single individual, but his power is modified by a lot of other forces. I have never thought that program budgeting worked because I don't think the Executive Committee has the power to make its decisions solely on the basis of statistical analyses.

What is the best system for determining the Cooperative Program distribution?

In the early to mid-1940s, the agency heads could agree among themselves on how the funds would be distributed. They could do this because it was their responsibility to study their own fiscal situation as well as that of the other agencies. When you argued with the other administrators about your needs, you were debating with people who had a detailed knowledge of your audits and budgets. At that time this approach worked. The distribution was made by a set of percentages. That made the decisions easier.

And there weren't as many agencies then.

Right. My judgment is that the agencies could still do this, but I don't think the ethos, the feel of the times, would permit the agencies to do so. The agency ownership of the Cooperative Program was felt at that time. Now there is a feeling that "somebody else" owns the Cooperative Program and distributes funds.

I have always preferred the percentage form of distribution of Cooperative Program funds as over against the dollar form of distribution. I know the arguments against that because I've been involved in many debates about it. The percentage distribution approach underscores the ownership and involvement of the agencies in promoting the Cooperative Program.

What you have now is a system in which the agency feels it has a certain dollar allocation of funds and that money will be taken care of and come in from the SBC Executive Committee in Nashville. The agency is then free to spend its energy mining any other sources of funds that it wishes.

We see this approach in the Foreign Mission Board, which pours immense promotion into the Lottie Moon Offering—far more than it does into promoting the Cooperative Program. I'm not picking on the Foreign Mission Board, because all the other agencies do the same thing in varying degrees. The Foreign Mission Board promotes the special offering that brings in funds directly, but it assumes that allocated dollars from the Cooperative Program will come in without any special effort on its part.

Preferring the percentage form of allocation of funds, I would make it a little more sophisticated than a simple percentage table. I was involved in the development of the tiered Cooperative Program involving operating funds, capital needs funds, and then advance program tier.

An agency first receives the operating funds. The next tier of funds beyond this are capital needs funds. The third tier, with no ceiling imposed on it, would be the advance program of the mission boards. This does have the effect of a kind of compromise between dollar allocations and pure percentage allocation.

Under a percentage allocation, an agency would not know how much money they would be receiving. Would this not make the budgeting process more complicated?

Sure, but it puts the risk where the risk ought to be—on the agencies. If they go out and promote the Cooperative Program, they get the money. If they set up competing sources of funds that impact on the Cooperative Program, they may get some money from another source, but they may have a shortfall in the Cooperative Program. This seems fair to me.

I think every SBC agency is up against a budgeting problem anyway. Nobody really cries over this. The agencies do their crying when the Cooperative Program allocation is made; then they work up their budgets based on what they were told they were going to get. They are always fairly sure they will get their operating budget funds.

Has your idea for percentage allocation ever been considered or studied?

No. Once the idea of dollar allocations was accepted, it was set in concrete, reinforced by steel. It gives those who are handling the funds a sense of power and control in the decision-making process. I'm not name-calling here; I'm talking about human nature. These are very good people, and I trust them. If I had thought they were operating on improper motives or something of that sort, you could find that in the state papers. So I'm arguing that the very absence of any charge of malfeasance in office is proof that these allocations have been made by good people, who have done a remarkably good job.

This is a difficult and complex responsibility. Is there is a better way to do it than the way it's done now?

Yes, I would refine what the Executive Committee does. For instance, I would not put quite as much weight on the concept of program budgeting as they do because I think it misleads the agencies. The agencies are a bit cynical about the impact of program budgeting on the total number of dollars they are going to receive.

Are you saying that the parade by the agencies before the Executive Committee does not really affect the allocation of funds?

I think it is a public relations type of process that plays an important role in the present system. But I don't think what the agencies say in those ten-minute presentations has any effect on what will be done this year for their budgets.

But Southern Seminary, as an agency within the Seminary Formula agreement, did get the ear of the Executive Committee?

You've got to make a case for theological education because it's the allocation to theological education that will determine what Southern Seminary—or any other seminary—receives. Your problem is to sell on a twelve-month basis theological education and then to present matters that the members of the Executive Committee will consider important enough to receive increased funding.

For example, salaries for seminary faculty members are clearly very low. That is a thing that you will hammer at until it gets into the subconsciousness of the members of the Executive Committee. They will start trying to find additional funds to increase those salaries. A kind of political dynamic determines what the Executive Committee can recommend, and then it is political pressure that determines what they do recommend.

The most difficult problem the Executive Committee always deals with is the Foreign Mission Board allocation. All the Cooperative Program funds could legitimately be used by the Foreign Mission Board. So the question becomes, "How do we take care of the other agencies in the face of the needs of foreign missions?"

STEWARDSHIP COMMISSION PROBLEMS

You attempted in 1973 to have the Stewardship Commission program given back to the Executive Committee. Did you get any support for this viewpoint?

I had a lot of support privately but none publicly. The state secretaries and state editors almost unanimously supported it. The Executive Committee and the Executive Committee staff were almost unanimous in their support privately.

My problem with the Stewardship Commission was rooted in what was, in my judgment, a bit of ineptness on the part of this agency at that time. The leader of the agency was having personal problems, and this eventually resulted in his resignation from the executive's position.

I did not know he was having personal problems at that time. I just knew that the Stewardship Commission was not working. Having said that, I want to go on record to say that it is working today, and that's what changes the perspective. If you'll look back through the leadership of the Stewardship Commission, you'll say, "Well I was for keeping the Stewardship Commission." If you went back and looked at it in terms of the record at the time, I think I proved statistically that Southern Baptists were falling behind in their stewardship response in the early 1970s.

POWER AND ROLE OF THE EXECUTIVE COMMITTEE

Some people say that the most powerful group in Southern Baptist life is the state secretaries, and that the real decisions are made by them and the executive secretary of the Executive Committee meeting together. Do you agree?

I think that's potentially true. But I doubt that it works out this way in practice. You have to ask, How much power does the state secretary have back home? And that varies from state secretary to state secretary and from time to time. How much power does the executive secretary of the Executive Committee have? This also varies from time to time and from situation to situation.

The Executive Committee also controls the distribution of finances. So is it not true that the executive secretary of the Executive Committee has a great deal of power?

I think the executive secretary of the Executive Committee is the most powerful single person in the Southern Baptist Convention. If Southern Baptists ever find out how powerful he is, they'll abolish the office and re-create it under another title.

The myths about the office don't permit us to recognize how powerful the executive secretary really is. But he is not all-powerful, for even the Executive Committee does not have all the power the Convention regulations seem to give it. [Today I would reverse that statement. The SBC Executive Committee has enlarged its power exponentially. –DKM]

What is the exact role of the executive secretary of the Executive Committee in the budget of the agencies?

The agencies really don't want the Executive Committee to meddle much in their internal affairs. If the Executive Committee tried, the agencies would go into revolt. But every once in a while the agencies try to put a guilt trip on the Executive Committee about responsibility for the problems inside the agency. The executive secretary learns after a while not to take those guilt trips.

So the executive secretary has to be a neutral person in dealing with the agencies?

Absolutely. He must not make any decision based on whether he likes, dislikes, agrees with, or disapproves of anything that's going on in the agencies. He must take the position that he exists to serve all the agencies equally. He must serve them within the context of the defined role of the Executive Committee.

To help them is what the agencies are always asking the executive secretary to do; they don't want him to hurt them. If he ever gets out of his role, he will hurt as well as help. He's human; he can't be one kind of person one day and another kind another day.

This is why I've become very sympathetic with the executive secretary. There are times when he's under great pressure to do a good thing, but if he does that, he violates the assignment of the Executive Committee. If he does a good thing, once he's willing to step out of that assignment, he will do what he thinks is right which may, from the agency point of view, be a bad thing. The person who can perform this balancing act perfectly simply doesn't exist.

LONGEVITY AND RISK-TAKING
You stayed with the Executive Committee only a few years. Can a person in a key leadership position such as this stay too long?

About every five years at Southern Seminary, I would start redesigning the way I dealt with the seminary. I did this to make myself uncomfortable, if nothing else. I felt I had to go back to being a little more creative and inventive because otherwise, in five to seven years, I would reach the point where I knew how to make the seminary run. Then I would settle down and get comfortable and say to myself, "No, you can't do that; we've never done that. Let's stick with the proven path." Then the creativity would go out of the agency.

I am saying this because the Executive Committee had the same problem when Porter Routh stayed there for a long period of time. Part of what he did was part of what I did. He changed the assignments of personnel in their relationship to the agency and therefore to himself. He would shift things from time to time. That makes you have a new ball game on your hands.

The time to retire is when you are not willing to start a new ball game for any reason. Whenever you say, "I'm going to ride this out to the end, or I'm going to ride this out until I reach retirement," you have already stayed a month too long. You ought to have resigned a month ago. The pressure to do that is tremendous on every person who would like to get out of the tensions. Risk-taking has to be characteristic of any administrator who is doing anything worth a salary.

AMEND AGENCY CHARTERS
After you left the Executive Committee, a movement developed to

change the charters of all the Convention agencies to conform to the Southern Baptist Convention constitutional requirements. As president of Southern Seminary, you resisted this action.

Yes, because there were legal problems in the Louisville situation with which I was not familiar while I was in Nashville. I finally agreed, and did come up with what, in fact, is substantially what the Executive Committee requested.

But I also quarreled with the idea of the Executive Committee establishing the programming devices and trying to get the charters of the agencies changed to conform to the Executive Committee recommendations. I think the agencies are in serious jeopardy whenever their policies are determined by the Executive Committee.

This is an issue of denominational polity. Once the charter of an agency has been approved by the Convention, then that is the charter of the agency until the agency itself asks for a change. Then the Executive Committee and the Convention can approve or disapprove.

PROGRAM STATEMENT AS A MANAGEMENT TOOL

In the 1950s, program statements were adopted for each of the SBC agencies. Was this something you had considered during your time with the Executive Committee?

No. The programming concept was a new idea that came on the national scene and was adopted as a management tool in many places. It became a management tool from the point of view of the Southern Baptist Convention Executive Committee. I was at Southern Seminary when that happened.

Did it make life easier for agencies within the denomination?

That's very difficult for me to say. It didn't do a thing for the seminaries. As a matter of fact, I've quarreled through the years about this and said the seminaries already had programs because the programs were defined in terms of degrees. In other words, each degree was a program, and we awarded the degree upon the successful completion of that program. But this did not conform to the doctrinaire definition of programs that consultants urged on the Executive Committee, and which the Executive Committee adopted. So we ended up with all sorts of funny programming titles. The programming business never meant anything except "we're trying to keep the Executive Committee happy." The seminary never thought of programs in the Executive Committee's terms except when it was dealing with the Executive Committee.

And you never made an effort to have the program statement amended or changed from what you had originally set out?

No, because it was a dead issue from the beginning. We just didn't want to stir up anything because whatever the program statement said, we weren't going to pay any attention, and whatever we changed it to, we weren't going to pay any attention to that either.

The nature of education means that a Ph.D. degree represents a program of a certain level of education, with certain descriptions and goals—and that's the program. And the seminary, or an educational institution, will think about those programs, work at those programs, budget in terms of those programs, do all the things that programming requires you to do if you pay attention to it. But that did not fit the consultant-recommended program.

What I perceive is that the program statements were designed partially to keep the agencies from bumping into one another, and to assign programs to one agency, and then say to the other agencies, "Don't you do that." That's nice and neat except it doesn't work; people and organisms such as conventions don't work that mechanically. Under the best of circumstances, you will always have some overlap. But the process did improve the relationship of the agencies to one another.

FORMULAS FOR ALL THE AGENCIES

Would it make sense for formulas, such as the seminaries have used, to be developed for other SBC agencies?

The process of developing the formula for the seminaries required years. The earliest formulas were very crude and inadequate, but across the years—through refinement and experience—we gradually developed a reasonably efficient formula.

The six seminaries are as diverse as the mission boards. The commissions are as diverse as the six seminaries. You could develop formulas for agencies with similar structures. But I don't think it will be done. Consider the diversity in the six seminaries and the difference in size alone. How do you distinguish between the largest and the smallest seminary and have a formula that fits both?

In the earliest stage we had a terrible time with that. That's not even a problem any more. We had to learn how to count students to come up with a formula basis. No seminary president has any problem with counting students any more; he knows exactly how to do that. And all of the combinations and permutations of the different kinds of students—graduate students, part-time students, degree students, non-degree students—they got that all worked out.

The formula has forced the seminary presidents to learn to work with one other despite their differences. Without a formula, the other agency administrators—including the mission board presidents—have not learned to work together in the same way.

STUDY OF SBC

Tell us about the Booz, Allen & Hamilton study of the total program of the Southern Baptist Convention.

This is one of those times when I think outside consultants missed the dynamics of Baptists. History has gone on, and new styles of operation have developed. I'm not trying to go back to it, but I think the management concept that the Executive Committee ought not to be involved in stewardship development is wrong. The management group at the top overseeing all the programs would have been the Booz, Allen & Hamilton philosophy for the Executive Committee.

I understand this study identified the Executive Committee as an agency of the Convention?

Yes, it was listed simply as another agency of the Convention. It is the Booz, Allen & Hamilton concept of the management role of the Executive Committee, or the board of directors, which evolved. Then it was later embedded in the bylaws of the Convention by removing the Executive Committee from the list of agencies. So that was an evolutionary concept that is back of the launching of the Stewardship Commission as a program-oriented agency under the management direction of the Executive Committee.

PORTER ROUTH AND THE EXECUTIVE COMMITTEE

Dr. Porter Routh was elected secretary of the Executive Committee, and you were the executive secretary-treasurer. Was he the person who kept the official minutes of the SBC, or was this a position of another kind?

81

Porter was on the board at New Orleans when I was president there. Then he came to the Sunday School Board as secretary of the Department of Survey, Statistics, and Information. At that point, he was elected recording secretary of the Convention, and became a member of the Executive Committee by virtue of that office in the Convention.

It was a natural thing to name Porter the secretary of the Executive Committee because his office was located there. He was available, he had stenographic help, and he was an employee of the Convention. The secretary is preoccupied with doing the secretarial chores and can't involve himself too much in the debate on the Convention floor.

THE BAPTIST BUILDING

What was it like, having the Executive Committee offices in the same building as the Sunday School Board?

These were the days when the Sunday School Board provided office space for the Executive Committee at the Sunday School Board's expense, but we were always begging for more space. I hoped a new office building would be built that would give us adequate space, or that the new Baptist Building would be built on the property provided by the Sunday School Board. From my point of view, it was a blunder to move the Baptist Building to James Robertson Parkway several blocks from the Sunday School Board.

Why do you feel that so strongly?

I think the biggest problem is the competition between the president of the Sunday School Board and the executive secretary (now president) of the Executive Committee as to who is "Mr. Baptist" in the local community. But to me that is a nothing issue. The personal relationships generated by the proximity of these two agencies are much more important than whether the city of Nashville knows that the executive secretary of the Executive Committee is not an employee of the Sunday School Board.

The Sunday School Board dominates Nashville. People of the city tend to think that the Sunday School Board is what is Baptist in Nashville. The Historical Commission, they think, is a subdivision of the Sunday School Board, and so on. It is a waste of time to try to do something about this perception. And it doesn't matter except to the ego anyway.

When other Nashville-based SBC agencies are located close to the Sunday School Board, the personal interlocking relationships will generate a great deal more collaboration than you could get if you have to go from one building to another to sit down and coordinate a program. Just the fact that you can go out and eat lunch together will get more correlated work done than committees. That's my idea about how organizations work.

So I view with favor moving the Baptist Building back over to Ninth Avenue.

GLORIETA ASSEMBLY GROUNDS

One of the things that happened during your administration with the Executive Committee was the securing of property in the western section of the country that came to be known as Glorieta Assembly. How did this come about?

The committee to select a western assembly site chose a place in the Davis Mountains of Texas, as I recall. But on the floor of the Convention, the vote was for Glorieta.

The Executive Committee went out and took title to the Glorieta property. The site was controversial because nobody had ever heard of Glorieta. There weren't many Baptists in New Mexico, and it was a long way from California—a long way from everywhere. The only reason for putting it there was that Glorieta was a stop on the railroad. Nobody goes to Glorieta by railroad any more. So all of the reasons for putting it there have evaporated except that it's a beautiful site in the mountains. But the Lord does lead. This location has worked very well for Southern Baptists.

When I first saw the property, I insisted we had to have the farm that sits where the main entrance to Glorieta is now located. This farm was not a part of the original property. That's the only contribution I made to Glorieta—to insist that we have that farm to give us convenient access to the highway and the railway station.

I understand the Sunday School Board was asked to assume responsibility for both assemblies at about this same time.

Ridgecrest belonged to the Executive Committee at that time, and I signed the deed to sell Ridgecrest to the Sunday School Board for $10.00. The Sunday School Board promised to operate an efficient and effective assembly for the denomination. That is how the Sunday School Board acquired Ridgecrest.

The Sunday School Board was doing the programming for Ridgecrest, and the Executive Committee wasn't. The Sunday School Board had even built some buildings on this property, even though it was actually owned by the Executive Committee. It just made sense for the ownership of the land to be turned over to the people who ran the risks and were responsible for the programming.

RECEPTION OF NEW STATES

During your tenure at the Executive Committee, there was considerable opposition to reception of new states by some of the longtime leaders of the denomination. Kansas and Washington-Oregon were the two main state conventions that came in and moved the SBC across the country.

The opposition grew out of the realization that we were taking in some people who were more likely to be "fighting fundamentalists" than typical Southern Baptists. R. E. Milam was a strong, tough leader who convinced the SBC to take in Washington-Oregon. He won in spite of the strong odds against him. My hat's off to him. I was on the other side from him most of the time, but he was an able, strong fellow.

He and I had a real fine simpatico in the course of time. Originally I thought it was a mistake to move into Kansas, Washington, Oregon, and California. In fact, I apologized to Californians in one of their conventions and told them the most stupid vote I ever cast at a Southern Baptist Convention was in San Antonio against admitting California. That was one of the times when I was badly out of touch with the trends and the future.

SOCIAL SECURITY

In 1950 the denomination changed its position from opposing involvement of ministers in Social Security and recommended that church workers be included. How did this change come about?

At first there was the threat that church workers would be included in Social Security on a mandatory basis. That was viewed as a violation of the separation of church and state. The Baptist Joint Committee on Public Affairs was the coach and the leader in this effort. It called the signals. I ran the plays the way J. M. Dawson and the people in Washington called them.

When the government moved from mandatory inclusion to optional or elective inclusion in Social Security, the Baptist position changed. We didn't think the Relief and Annuity Board retirement plan was going to be adequate for ministers. We told ministers that Social Security looked like something they should consider. A weak recommendation!

Events have proven this was a good deal, in spite of the current concern about Social Security. It has been a lifesaver for many ministers who have retired in the last twenty years or so. At that time ministers' salaries were low, and the percentage of input to the Relief and Annuity Board was also low on these low salaries. The typical Southern Baptist minister did not build up enough equity in his retirement for the inflation that was typical of this country over many years. Inflation would erode his retirement income.

Compromise made it possible for ministers to be included in Social Security. Ministers went into the plan on a self-employed status. Thus, the church was not required to include its pastor in Social Security. This fitted the Baptist position.

LOTTIE MOON OFFERING

Do you remember the discussion with the Woman's Missionary Union over making the Lottie Moon Offering a church-wide emphasis?

The WMU secretary in Virginia, Blanche White, opposed making this a church-wide offering. R. C. Campbell in First Baptist Church, Little Rock, Arkansas, pioneered the church-wide offering for Lottie Moon and got a lot of publicity out of this, and the idea caught fire.

All of us realized that making this a church-wide event would make the Lottie Moon Offering grow. But my position was that this would tend to divert attention away from the Cooperative Program as the channel of mission giving.

So you were opposed to its being made a church-wide offering and in favor of its remaining a WMU offering?

Yes, I sided with the WMU. I thought we would be getting our polity mixed up. Today, the financial effect of turning it into a church-wide emphasis makes the theory seem rather irrelevant, but the fact is the theories were right then, and they still are.

Did you and Kathleen Mallory have much discussion on this?

She didn't care a great deal for the male of the species. If there ever was anything called "female chauvinism," you could have gotten some over in the WMU camp in those days. Things were different then. It wasn't that the Convention was invading the WMU; the WMU didn't want anything to do with the Convention side. They were an independent auxiliary that ran their own show. One of the factors was that when you began to make it a church-wide offering, the WMU couldn't dictate how the money would be spent. In those days, the WMU was telling the Foreign Mission Board where to spend the Lottie Moon money.

It's the old "control of the purse strings" kind of thing. Part of the argument issued in an agreement that the money would go without designation. Originally the Lottie Moon Offering went to capital projects, and these were specific capital projects chosen by the women. Maybe the Foreign Mission Board influenced the decision, but in the final analysis it agreed with the WMU.

The WMU would decide where they wanted the Lottie Moon money spent. But once buildings were built with these funds, the Cooperative Program had to maintain them. That was why I thought the Cooperative Program had something to say about that whole process.

The problem was a little more complex than my first description; it had to do with that problem of designation of Lottie Moon offerings (and Annie Armstrong offerings). In addition, I theorized that when these offerings became church-wide, the churches would think, "Now that's our foreign mission support effort, and the Cooperative Program—who knows what it's for?"

COOPERATIVE PROGRAM

How have we failed—or succeeded—in educating people about the Cooperative Program?

I don't know that we will ever succeed. We can't get the attention of Southern Baptists long enough to educate them. It's not that urgent in their minds; they feel no need to understand it. This is one of the incredible things about the Cooperative Program: the people give to their churches and the Cooperative Program on the assumption that this is a biblical injunction, and how it is used is not their problem. This is both the strength and the weakness of our Southern Baptist funding method. It's rooted in a biblical theology that satisfies our members. When you ask them, "Where does your money go?" they reply, "Wherever the Lord wants it to go." They hope that whoever made those decisions was led of the Lord, and they're satisfied.

Besides, it sounds so complicated; who really wants to sit still long enough to understand it? I doubt, frankly, if very many members of the SBC Executive Committee really understand the Cooperative Program. They understand their decision-making process, but they don't sit still long enough to learn about the different effects on the agencies. I'll get shot for saying that, but I think it's true.

For a number of years I've been part of a group trying to explain to a subcommittee (the Program Committee) on theological education what the Cooperative Program does with reference to the six seminaries. About as fast as we get the committee educated to where they understand it, there is a turnover in the committee membership. Then you have to go back to square one and start all over again. New members don't come on the Executive Committee with any understanding of the Cooperative Program except in the most general terms.

THE SOUTHERN BAPTIST FOUNDATION

While serving as executive secretary of the Executive Committee, you were instrumental in establishing the Southern Baptist Foundation. Tell us about this agency and how it fits into the fund-raising efforts of all SBC agencies.

About 1947 I proposed that the Speight Fund of about $250,000 serve as the basis of a new SBC agency: The Southern Baptist Foundation. The Speight Fund was left to the SBC Executive Committee for use in providing education to mountain youth. The Executive Committee personnel were not equipped to handle the investment of the money or its distribution. On the other hand, the Southern Baptist Convention needed a foundation.

The foundation was a way of anticipating that we had to have another kind of fund-raising other than the collection-plate dollar. The Southern Baptist Foundation was supposed to be the agency that would develop the expertise and the personnel to do the capital and endowment fund-raising for all SBC agencies.

This got lost because the state foundations were hard-nosed about not wanting the Southern Baptist Foundation to come into their states. Where it was supposed to go if it didn't go into any of the states, I don't know. But the state foundations insisted they would serve the SBC agencies. That is sheer nonsense. The state foundations do not conduct fund-raising for SBC agencies.

I have strong feeling about this. I could document the fact that state foundations have diverted donors from SBC agencies to state agencies. The reason is very simple: the state foundations' staffs are paid by the states. Their jobs and records are judged by what they do for the state agencies. I have no quarrel with that.

I am hard-nosed about it because I think that *some* of the state foundations misrepresent things to gain an advantage. They don't all do it, but some of them do not serve the SBC agencies, or at least they have not in the past. The point is that by claiming they would, they said the Southern Baptist Foundation ought to be just an investing agency. It ought not to be a fund-raising agency.

That, in my judgment, was a major policy mistake, a strategic blunder on the part of the SBC. It ought to have in its foundation the expertise for capital and deferred giving. The Southern Baptist Foundation ought to be out in the field raising the money for things like the Baptist Building in Nashville. The present Southern Baptist Foundation does not have the expertise or the staff to do that.

The Southern Baptist Convention would be far better off if it had let one agency do capital funding and deferred giving. This agency could be monitored and controlled if it got out of bounds.

It was only after the decision was made in the SBC Executive Committee to restrict the Southern Baptist Foundation from soliciting funds that I, in turn, created the Southern Seminary Foundation. I had to do for our agency what I thought should have been done for all the SBC agencies.

Did the Southern Baptist Foundation become the custodian of the endowments held by all the SBC agencies?

No. There was a time when that might have happened. There was a movement at one time to discount the endowment of any individual agency. This would have made up to other agencies for the endowment possessed by any individual agency. There have also been movements to force the agencies to put their endowment in Nashville in the SBC Foundation.

None of these efforts have gone very far. But all you have to do is wave a flag in either of those directions, and you make the agency people very nervous. Frankly, before I would have agreed to do that, I would have dumped the Southern Seminary endowment into the Southern Seminary Foundation and turned it loose, with the restriction that the income would come only to Southern Seminary. Now there are a lot of reasons for that. Most of them are rooted in fears or cynicism about human nature and the power-and-centralization syndrome.

There was one other risk that I saw, and that risk was quite different. It was the risk that you were going to undermine the local boards of the agencies. A board with members scattered over the Southern Baptist Convention cannot invest money. They (full trustee boards) just can't meet often enough.

How often do they need to meet?

In one year—it was a critical year—there are minutes for seventy-two meetings of the local financial board of the trustees of Southern Seminary. At that level, these local boards are giving close supervision to the financial interests of the agency. To get yourself locked in to the point where you have to wait three months before you can do anything about an investment can absolutely ruin an endowment. The agencies that have endowment funds either must have a local financial board or they must put these funds in the Southern Baptist Foundation, an agency with investment expertise.

I have no real objection in principle to endowment funds being placed in the Southern Baptist Foundation. But this would mean you would have to develop the investment expertise and appropriate safeguards. I might as well say that Mecca is viewed with suspicion by everyone who doesn't live in Mecca. Mecca, among Southern Baptists, is Nashville.

These suspicions are not justified, but they are normal and inevitable. You won't get rid of them unless you take precautions to guarantee certain things to the agencies. The people in Nashville tend to think, "We're nice people; we're honest people; we're people of high motives." What they don't understand is that the people across the

Convention think, "Yes, that's true, but what will your successors be like?"

Does this suspicion extend into the matter of how the Southern Baptist Foundation invests these funds?

Sure. The foundation was showing high returns on investments for a while by investing in mortgages. This was while the interest rates were high, but what was the total return on their investment? Since they were so heavily invested in mortgages, they obviously weren't doing much with capital gains.

From my point of view, I would have argued, "A mortgage is fine, but let's get some funds invested in some capital growth stocks. We need capital growth as well as high dividends. I won't be impressed by your report unless you talk about 'total return.'"

1949 CONVENTION

Dr. James Sullivan described the 1949 Convention in Oklahoma City as the Convention that did several things against the wishes of the leadership, particularly with reference to the location of a new assembly in New Mexico as opposed to Hot Springs. And the decision was made to receive new areas into the Southern Baptist Convention as well. What made this Convention so disquieting and controversial?

Geography always affects the character of every annual meeting of the Southern Baptist Convention, whether it is in Atlanta, Miami, Houston, or San Francisco. That's why it has to be moved around if the mind-set of all Southern Baptists is to be expressed.

The Conventions are often erratic in their character; that is, they are one type of convention one year and a quite different type the next year. They will vote for a thing one year and vote against it the next year, so it is proper that the bylaws require two consecutive votes on certain types of action.

This was one of the major questions of the 1949 Oklahoma Convention: Is the Southern Baptist Convention going to include the entire United States? Will it break the "comity" agreement with the American Baptist Convention—or at that time the Northern Baptist Convention? Are we going to move out of the Southeast? Will we change from the leadership of the traditional South in the Southern Baptist Convention? It was a very tense meeting. I guess I was more uptight about the Oklahoma Convention than any annual meeting in my experience until 1979.

But I must admit that the Oklahoma Convention was a good expression of the democratic process of Southern Baptists. Today, who would move Glorieta back to Hot Springs, Arkansas? That was the direction of the flow of Southern Baptist life at that time. That flow was also expressed in our reaching out to new state conventions. It was one of those turning points in the direction of Southern Baptist life.

SOUTHERN BAPTIST CHANGES

What was the biggest change in the SBC during your term with the Executive Committee in Nashville?

It was the growth of the Southern Baptist Convention into a national body. Southern Baptists also moved from a rural constituency to an urban-rural group, not so much in membership as in leadership. The leadership began to be urban rather than rural, which involved a higher level of administrative sophistication. Then with all of this, the homogeneity of the Southern Baptist Convention broke down. It became a very diverse group ethnically, culturally, economically, and educationally.

The representative style of operation also became more popular in the SBC. For example, we began to do things through a committee process rather than subjecting every decision to debate on the Convention floor. A committee would deal with an issue or problem and report its recommendation to the full Convention. Once in a blue moon there would be a debate at the Convention over the committee's report. Once in seven blue moons, a committee report would be rejected and alternatives would be adopted. There was a modification of the egalitarian democracy that had characterized decision-making in earlier periods of our history.

THE NORTHERN BAPTIST CONVENTION

You were the executive secretary of the Executive Committee when major changes were made in SBC territories. How did you and others feel about this?

We were ambivalent about it. On the one hand, we felt that Southern

Baptists had a strength and a know-how and a will to reach out in the name of Christ. On the other hand, we weren't entirely comfortable with how territorial expansion would affect our relationship with another Baptist body, the Northern Baptist Convention, in those days.

Were you closer to Northern Baptists and Northern Baptist leadership in those days than is the case today?

Yes, because there wasn't a sense of competition. You just took for granted that Northern Baptists had an assigned area of responsibility, and you hoped and prayed they were doing a good job at it. There was much moving back and forth from one group to another. People came out of the North to Southern Seminary and became pastors in the South. They came out of the South as students and went to Northern Baptist churches. One student from the South, Dr. Ed Willingham, even ended up being the secretary of the Northern Baptist Foreign Mission Society.

CHAPTER 6

A Time for Personal Decision

1950-1951

I understand you were considered for the presidency of the new seminary in the Southeast.

Let me mention first that I was one of the people that the Baptist constituency of North Carolina tried to run for president of Wake Forest College. But I immediately declined to be considered for this position. This must have been about 1949. Harold Tribble eventually went to the Wake Forest presidency. The reason why I mention this is that this whole process got my name prominently before the North Carolina leadership.

SOUTHEASTERN SEMINARY PRESIDENCY OFFERED

So you were at the Executive Committee when your name was mentioned as a possibility for the Southeastern presidency?

Yes. The Baptist World Congress was held in Cleveland, Ohio, in 1950. Perry Crouch, pastor of First Baptist Church, Asheville, North Carolina, was the chairman of the presidential search committee for the new seminary at Wake Forest—Southeastern Seminary. Perry called me in Cleveland and got me to agree to stop off and talk to him on my way back from the BWA Congress.

So on a Saturday night enroute from Cleveland to Marguerite's parents in Greenville, South Carolina, I stopped off in Asheville. Perry Crouch told me he and his committee had agreed to propose me as the president of Southeastern. I was about ready to leave the Executive

Committee because I went there on a personal promise to myself. I was determined that I would stay in Nashville no longer than five years, and the time was about up.

I told Dr. Crouch, "Your timing couldn't possibly be worse. I can't make a decision now. I leave tomorrow afternoon for Miami enroute to the Nigerian Baptist Convention. I'll talk to you when I get back if your committee wants to wait for me."

He agreed they would wait. So I dropped my wife and children with her parents in Greenville. Then I continued on by myself to Nigeria. This was in August of 1950.

In Cleveland I had been with the pastor of the Baptist church in Tokyo, Pastor Yuyu, and he and I had made plans for me to preach in his church. Meanwhile, the Korean War had caused the cancellation by the U.S. government of all civilian flights across the Pacific. That caused the Foreign Mission Board to cancel a preaching mission scheduled for that fall in Japan.

When the preaching mission was canceled, Pastor Yuyu cabled Theron Rankin in Richmond asking permission for me to come on to Japan, traveling east. That would mean I would not get involved in the government's prohibition against crossing the Pacific, traveling west to Japan.

That cable got forwarded from Richmond to Nigeria, where Rankin was involved in the same centennial celebrations in Nigeria that I was participating in. Rankin asked me, "Would you consider going on to Japan? Besides, we are having trouble placing missionaries who have been run out of China by the Mao Tse-tung takeover in 1949. We are having trouble getting visas to relocate them."

He asked me, as executive secretary of the Executive Committee, to go to some of the countries where Southern Baptist missionaries had been turned away. "You will be a different voice," he said. "Because other people don't understand Baptists, they'll think you are the top CEO of the Southern Baptist Convention. You go back and put the pressure on and see if you can get their attention and get some visas we've not been able to secure."

So a round-the-world trip born in Lagos, Nigeria. W. A. Criswell was there also, and he volunteered to accompany me. Marie Mathis put up the money from the Texas WMU for the two of us—because the Foreign

Mission Board didn't have that kind of money in those days. Besides, they couldn't afford to spend money for such a trip on two non-missionaries for fear there would be criticism for wasting money.

Marguerite was a heroine if ever there was one. I called her up and said, "Honey, you know I am supposed to be home in two weeks." She said, "Yes, and we are eager for you to get home." I said, "Well, make that four months. I'm getting ready to go on around the world on this trip." She got that over the telephone from Rome.

"I'm for you doing that," she replied. "Mother and I will work out the problems with the boys, and we'll take care of the home front; just keep in touch."

W. A. Criswell and I went from Rome on up to Zurich for the installation of George Sadler as the first permanent president of the Ruschlikon Seminary. I had proposed in 1947 to George Saddler in Rome that Southern Baptists set up a European Baptist Seminary somewhere in Switzerland. When it was set up in Zurich and Sadler was elected president, you can see why I wanted to be there for his installation.

SOUTHEASTERN SEMINARY PRESIDENCY DECLINED

In Zurich I sat down and wrote a letter to Perry Crouch about the Southeastern Seminary presidency. I said, in effect, "You have asked me to be president of Southeastern Seminary. But time is one part of God's providence, and you've asked me at a time when it is impossible for me to say yes. I take that, therefore, as God's leading that I must say no. Therefore, proceed to look for a president and take my name out of the picture."

So that trip around the world was costly from my point of view. I wanted to be president of Southeastern; that's the first time I've ever said that in a record anywhere. It was a new seminary. I wanted back in theological education, and here was a chance to be in on the founding of a new seminary and be a part of the structuring of the whole thing from the beginning. You can't offer a person a more exciting opportunity than that.

Could you not have asked the seminary to wait?

I don't like for people to delay their decisions. If you're going to say yes, say yes; if you're going to say no, say no. I hate people who string committees along and finally say no. If you string them along, you've got to say yes. I wasn't prepared to say yes. You've got to understand my method of decision-making and my relationship to Marguerite and her involvement in that kind of decision. I couldn't follow my standard operating procedure. She and I could not sit down and talk about it and pray about it together, and therefore I could not make a decision under those circumstances.

All my life I've taken the position that if I got where I am under God's leadership, I must stay there until there is a clear sense of direction to move. The prejudice is in favor of staying, not moving. Whether you're comfortable or uncomfortable is irrelevant. Somehow the conviction must form that God would have me do this new thing. So I said no to them.

But the Southeastern search committee met and decided to wait. They wrote me a letter telling me they were going to wait for me to get home. They sent it to me in India. The mails were too slow, and it got there after I left. It was forwarded from India to Singapore, to Bangkok, to Jakarta, Indonesia, to Manila, to Tokyo. It dropped further behind me every time it was forwarded. I finally got the letter about two weeks after I arrived back in Nashville. That was the first time I knew that they were waiting for me. I thought my letter to them from Zurich had closed the discussion.

DEATH OF ELLIS FULLER

I was supposed to be on that preaching mission, rooming with Ellis Fuller. But I got a cable on my last day in Tokyo that Ellis Fuller had died in Los Angeles from a heart attack.

Was he a close friend and confidante?

Yes, close enough to sit on the deck of the *Queen Elizabeth* and weep about his problems at Southern Seminary. This occurred enroute to the BWA meeting in London in 1948. He told me about his problems with the faculty at Southern Seminary and his desire to be their pastor and to love them and to look after them. Their reaction, he thought, was hard, harsh, and hostile. He sat there and wept about his experience with them. I sympathized with him, and my attitude toward some of those faculty members was generated at that point. I believed Ellis Fuller. I never have had any reason to believe he didn't tell the truth.

Soon after this overseas mission, I did agree to meet with Perry Crouch and the Southeastern search committee in North Carolina. By then I had received the letter they had sent me while I was overseas. I called him up and said, "I apologize. Believe it or not, I've just today gotten the letter that tells me you are waiting for me and to let you know I'm home and ready to talk to you. I'm home, but I'm not ready to talk to you."

I don't know how to explain this. I really wanted the Southeastern job. But that decision I had made in Zurich was like turning the dial on a safe. The decision was made, and it was locked; and I could never unlock it. If I had gone to Southeastern, I would have gone because I wanted to go and not because I thought, under God, I ought to go. Somehow I thought that God's hand was in that timing—that I couldn't go, even though I wanted to.

If I'd had a week between the BWA in Cleveland and leaving for Africa, I would have gone to be president of Southeastern Seminary. There isn't any question in my mind about that. I took the job in Nashville when I didn't want it, and I turned down the job at Southeastern that I did want. Unbelievably, in the face of my eagerness to go, I ended up not going. The only way I know to explain it is to declare that it was God's leadership.

TRUSTEE MEETING TO REPLACE FULLER
There was a meeting of the board of trustees of Southern Seminary at the funeral for Ellis Fuller. They had to elect an acting president and name a search committee for a new president. Do you know what happened at this meeting?

Either in the board or in the search committee, an effort was made to nominate me and elect me president of Southern at that meeting. But you won't find this in the official records. This initiative was beaten down. J. B. Weatherspoon led a section of the faculty in pushing Theron Rankin for the presidency of Southern. Weatherspoon was opposed to my being president because he wanted Rankin in the job. So by the time I got the word that the Southeastern Seminary board was waiting to meet with me, I had been turned down for the presidency of Southern by the search committee in at least an informal discussion. There are no records, I repeat. But people who were there told me about the situation.

97

MCCALL REJECTED BY SOUTHERN FACULTY

Did the faculty support or oppose your election?

There is no question about that because J. B. Weatherspoon met me in the First Baptist Church of Knoxville at the Tennessee Baptist Convention in November 1950 and said, "Duke, I want you to know the faculty doesn't want you to be president of Southern Seminary."

That was just after you got back from Japan?

Just back from Japan. I remember saying, "Well, Dr. Weatherspoon, I am trying not to use your tone, but I don't want to be president of the *faculty* at Southern Seminary." I said this because of my background with Fuller and his report of the faculty's relation to him. I was saying, "I want you to know I don't want to be president of that faculty." I was making the point that I didn't want the job.

Up to the time of Ellis Fuller, the president of Southern Seminary was chairman of the faculty?

Yes. And part of Ellis Fuller's problem was that the trustees changed his job description and left him to tell the faculty about it. I think the faculty always believed that he engineered the new job description himself. But I can tell you absolutely that he had nothing to do with it. John R. Sampey had far more to do with the change in the job description in the presidency of Southern than Ellis Fuller did. And Sampey did it by accident.

President Sampey had asked for the dismissal of Frank Powell, professor of church history, after Powell had been professor for twenty years. The trustees asked Sampey, "Why have you waited so long to recommend this?" Sampey replied, "Because I didn't have the authority to do it; I am just chairman of the faculty, and that was not my responsibility to pass judgment on a fellow faculty member."

That created a major controversy in the last days of Sampey's presidency. It set the trustees up to determine that Sampey's successor would know that he not only had the right but the responsibility for making such recommendations.

Sampey was about to retire anyway, and he was cleaning up the situation before he left. By the way, this is the work of a good administrator. He doesn't leave the problems behind him. His instinct is to clean up the problems before he leaves so his successor will have as clear a deck as possible. I applaud that.

Fuller perceived his job to be different from that of Sampey. Dr. Sampey wasn't an administrator; he was a professor. He was elected to be president as a professor. His colleagues supported him as a professor. He perceived himself as "primus inter pares," whatever in the world that means, and he functioned that way. But Fuller was an aggressive administrator. He tried to change things. In effect, he put the car into third gear, but it kept kicking back into first.

FACULTY OPPOSITION TO HOBBS

So you knew what a president faced at Southern Seminary before you agreed to go to Louisville?

Yes. This was about the time the *Baptist Standard* began to push Herschel Hobbs for president of Southern. Herschel came to Nashville and said to me, "Should I let them run me for president of Southern, or should I try to stop my friends?" I said to him, "Herschel, only a fool would jump into that meat grinder."

After I accepted the Southern presidency, Herschel wrote me a letter: "Dear Fool, I want to congratulate you upon your position in the meat grinder." When things at Southern blew up in 1958, I sent him a telegram that read, "Dr. Herschel H. Hobbs, Pastor, First Baptist Church, Oklahoma City, Oklahoma. I was right. The Fool." He knew who sent it.

TRUSTEES BEGIN PRESIDENTIAL SEARCH

The records show that the members of the presidential search committee at Southern were H. I. Hester, as chairman, Wallace Bassett, Wade Bryant, Millard J. Berquist, Harwell G. Davis, W. R. Pettigrew, and Norman Shands. When did you begin talking to them?

Hester asked me to meet with the committee in San Francisco, where the annual meeting was held in 1951. Something came up in my duties as executive secretary with the Convention to require my attendance and create a conflict with the time of their meeting. We went on a tour of the West in a vacation after the Convention. So a couple of weeks later I ended up in Kansas City on our way to Nashville.

I called Dr. Hester to apologize to him for not showing up at the meeting and to say that I was not being rude. I really was caught by my other primary responsibilities. I didn't think I was a serious contender for the position. I think I told him at that time, "I am a supporter of Theron Rankin. I hope you will decide to choose him as president. There are a lot of reasons why I am just not your man, and you don't really want me."

I think it's clear that I wasn't hankering to be president with such zeal that I would brush aside all obstacles to meet with the committee. I really was quite busy because of my duties as executive secretary of the Executive Committee in San Francisco.

PRESIDENTIAL SEARCH COMMITTEE—KNOXVILLE

Dr. Hester wanted me to meet with the committee in Knoxville, Tennessee. I agreed to the date and place because I was on my way from Nashville to Ridgecrest to speak. I met with the committee enroute and said to them, "Well, I have two conditions for being president, and you can't meet either one of them. I know you can't meet one of them. My first one is that the trustees would have to be unanimous, and the second is that the faculty must be unanimous in wanting me."

I made the search committee angry by my insistence on the faculty agreement because I was not aware then of the tension between the faculty and trustees over the power in the selection of a president. I do not know to this day why they didn't choose Theron Rankin. That seemed like such a good idea, and it had faculty support. I don't see why they didn't do it—unless he was the faculty candidate and the trustees were determined not to have the faculty's candidate win.

Did you and Rankin ever talk about that?

No. You know, he turned out to have leukemia and died within two years. So I would say however it happened, God knew what was in the future in a way that no trustee or faculty member did. It would have been a tragedy if Rankin had gone, but only because of the health factor. I really was for him. I had great admiration, respect, and affection for Dr. Rankin.

You and he were close friends?

Yes. We were close friends. One thing that really bothers me is when someone thinks of me as being less than a total supporter of the foreign mission enterprise. I've always perceived myself as being totally committed to the foreign mission enterprise. Therefore, I would be for what Rankin was doing; I thought he was good at it; I thought he was moving Southern Baptists into a new era of foreign missions after World War II. I thought he was God's man for the job.

You had known him many years before he went to the presidency of the Foreign Mission Board.

Yes. He was a missionary to China, and I knew him only intermittently before that. Our friendship really evolved after he became the executive secretary of the Foreign Mission Board. So that's why I really wanted Rankin. I thought he would be the best thing for the seminary. I was prejudiced enough that I didn't plan to be the president of that group of people who had so injured my friend Ellis Fuller. It's probably no deeper than that. I resented anything that had happened to a friend.

TRUSTEE MEETING TO ELECT PRESIDENT

The trustees of Southern had a meeting about August 3, 1951, to report and recommend me as the new president. I went from Nashville to Louisville, again enroute to Ridgecrest. I told Marguerite that I wouldn't make any decision until I got home. I think one thing she never forgave me for was that a reporter told her I had been elected president of the seminary before I could get word to her about it.

I met with the trustees, and they were unanimous in their support. Old Dr. Taylor, a life trustee from Mississippi—an elderly man—really pushed it over the top because he got up and said, "I've been listening to what you've been saying. I don't know the young man, but what I hear is that everything is good except that he is a young man." He said, "Gentlemen, I want to tell you this is a fault that will be less a fault every day he lives." With that the vote was unanimous.

After my meeting with the trustees, I insisted on meeting with the faculty of the seminary. The trustees insisted that the search committee meet with me and the faculty. I thought that would intimidate the faculty, so I said, "No; I'll be glad for Dr. Hester or Dr. Turner (the chairman of the board) to go over and introduce me to the faculty, and I'll be glad for you to tell the faculty what you've done. But then I would like for whoever goes to leave and let me be alone with the faculty."

MEETING WITH THE FACULTY

All the faculty members were not at this meeting. E. A. McDowell, for example, was not there, and that later presented a problem. But everybody who was in Louisville came to the meeting in the basement of Faculty Center.

I said to them, "Gentlemen, I don't think you want me to be your president. Dr. Weatherspoon has told me specifically as much. Now, I am going around the room, and I want each one of you to tell me whether you want me to be president of this institution or not. I will gladly hear what you have to say. When this meeting is over, I'm going to get on a plane and go to Ridgecrest. You will relieve me greatly if I can say no to the trustees."

So you at this point had not specifically told the trustees you would accept the presidency?

No, I had not. I didn't think I was going to accept the job. I thought my answer was going to be no. The surprise to me was that we went around the circle of the faculty members and each one of them said why he wanted me as president. They were very positive, very supportive, and they were honest enough to be convincing. That is, they were willing to say, "You were not my first choice, but for the following reasons I want you to say yes and accept." This absolutely surprised me.

Was Dr. Weatherspoon at this meeting?

Yes. His line was, "I had another choice, but he cannot be elected, and you are now my choice." His answer was convincing. If he had said, "I've always wanted you," I would have known he was not straight with me.

ACCEPTANCE OF THE PRESIDENCY

After this meeting with the faculty, another trustee meeting was set up. I was to meet with the financial board of the seminary because there had been no decision about the house, salary, or anything else. At this meeting we were to negotiate the terms of the offer. I still had not said whether I would accept the presidency at that point.

That night I had dinner with the financial board of the trustees at the Pendennis Club. V. V. Cooke was always the horse trader, and he started out trying to find out what they had to offer me. I guess I've got a little horse trader in me—or at least I recognize a horse trade when it is going on.

We sparred around for a while over dinner. Then I said, "Gentlemen, I'm not going to trade with you. You've got to make me an offer. But before you make it, I might as well tell you that I'm going to accept it. I believe the hand of God has been in this situation. Otherwise, I don't see how the faculty could have talked to me as they did this afternoon."

There was no question about whether I wanted to be president of a seminary. The job I really wanted was to go back to New Orleans, by the way. I would have been glad to take Southeastern, and I would go to Southern—but I really wanted to go back to New Orleans. At the time, that job was not available.

CONDITIONS FOR ACCEPTANCE

During the discussion with the financial board, I accepted the presidency of Southern. Then I told them, "I have only two conditions: (1) I will not accept a salary greater than my salary has been as executive secretary of the Executive Committee. (I didn't want anybody to say that I had taken the Southern job because it paid more.) (2) I will not live in the Norton Estate." As it turned out, I didn't get either one of these two conditions.

My salary was set at $8,000—as opposed to the $7,500 I had been earning in Nashville—and I ended up living in the Norton house for ten years. The only way I got out of the Norton Estate as the president's home was to sell it to the Presbyterian Seminary.

I am telling this because I was surprised by my acceptance. I did not mean to say yes or no to the financial board, but I didn't want to negotiate with them or horse trade about it. I wanted a flat offer, and I had already reached the conclusion that somehow, under God, this was the job I should accept. I knew I was going to say yes, but I was also committed to talk to Marguerite about it. The Southern presidency is the only job I ever took without first talking to her. But the truth is she had suspected all along that this is where I would go.

After the acceptance was formalized, I called Marguerite as soon as I could. Meanwhile, the press had learned about it and had called her in Nashville to get her comments. So I was a little late in getting word to her, but she was a good sport about it.

All of this happened in August. I accepted the presidency of the seminary effective September 15, 1951. The week before September 15 was the regular Executive Committee meeting, at which I could resign and my resignation could be accepted.

PORTER ROUTH ELECTED EXECUTIVE SECRETARY

Dr. Porter Routh was elected executive secretary of the Executive Committee in September 1951 after your departure. Did you have any part in the discussion about his election?

I had conversations which are more or less traditional in which friends say, "Do you know any reason why he wouldn't be a good choice." I was supportive in my comments about Dr. Routh. I take it as a matter of pride that I try to stay out of any initiative with reference to the selection of my successor.

To the surprise of everybody, they elected Porter Routh immediately upon accepting my resignation. Louie Newton's nomination speech for Porter resonated with the judgment of all present. There was no "search committee" or any public discussion. Porter was an excellent choice. I liked it because he had been a part of all I was attempting and would carry it on with his own flavor. Besides, I would have a friend in the office of the executive secretary of the SBC Executive Committee.

CHAPTER 7

First Year As Southern
Seminary President

1951

Were you pleased that the faculty at Southern turned a picnic into a formal banquet to welcome you?

No. All of that affirmation that I was the faculty choice to be president of the seminary lasted from the time of the trustee meeting in August until the first day I was in Louisville. The big banquet was really to honor Dr. Gaines Dobbins as the acting president. Then it dawned on them that they needed to do something about the incoming president, so they included Marguerite and me. It was to be an informal affair, sort of a picnic, that we were invited to.

We were in the process of moving to Louisville. Our clothes were in transit. The furniture was being placed in the president's home, and we rushed over to Faculty Center from moving to get dressed for the occasion. We discovered that the dinner had been changed from an informal picnic to a formal dress affair with long dresses and tuxedos—and nobody had bothered to tell us.

My wife was embarrassed because a blue corduroy suit was all she had to wear. All the other women at the banquet had on long dresses. I wore a business suit, and all the other men had on tuxedos. She sat by Mrs. W. O. Carver, who said to her, "You know, I'm so nervous whenever I have to make a speech in front of Dr. Carver."

Marguerite said, "That would make me nervous, too, if I had to make a speech in front of Duke."

Mrs. Carver said, "My dear, you have to make a speech tonight in front of Duke; you've got to respond to my speech." That was the first time Marguerite had heard that she was making a speech to the assembled faculty and wives of the Southern Baptist Theological Seminary.

I discovered that I was supposed to make a speech to them in response to an address of welcome from "Pistol Pete" Estill Jones, the newest and youngest member of the New Testament faculty. The speech of welcome was a careful set of instructions on how the new president would act if he wanted to get along with the faculty.

It was probably one of the half dozen times in my life when I was furious. I was embarrassed for Marguerite because I knew she was embarrassed. I was embarrassed, and I felt that a welcome to the seminary might at least have said something like, "We're glad you're here," rather than, "These are the terms under which we will cooperate with you."

When I get to heaven, I'm going to check to see if one of the stars in my crown isn't for what I did not say that night. I really was within a hair's breath of saying, "Well, if the young professor has spoken for all of you, you are still looking for a president. Marguerite and I will withdraw at this moment." This is the first time I've told anybody out loud what is a sharp memory with me. I was indignant. I thought the whole thing was thoughtless; it was gauche; it was gross; it was careless; it was inappropriate.

Do you think this was deliberate?

No. I think they were honoring Dr. Dobbins. I think they decided to upgrade a picnic into a formal dinner. They forgot they were also welcoming the new president. Instead of having a senior member of the faculty welcome the new president, as an afterthought they decided to let the junior member of the faculty welcome him. Thus the welcome was by a man who had not been a member of the faculty and therefore had not been in the faculty meeting in August. I think he reflected in his speech the mind-set that he had picked up from his faculty colleagues earlier.

How did you respond?

I responded in words like these, "I thought Dr. Jones was a New Testament professor, but he must be an Old Testament professor because he sounds more like Amos at Samaria than Jesus of Nazareth." Beyond that I refused to acknowledge that I had heard his speech. Then I spoke about something entirely different. I discussed whatever I had in the back of my head that I thought would be appropriate for me to say on an ad-lib basis to the faculty. I tried to keep my indignation out of my response.

PRESIDENTIAL INAUGURAL

At your inaugural, W. O. Carver is reported to have said that until Dr. Fuller became president of Southern, "the captain had always been a player." Was he referring to the president also being a professor or teacher?

Yes, it was truer than I knew at the time because I tried repeatedly to teach at the seminary. Every once in a while I would be listed to teach a class. I never could meet the class often enough to be happy about the results. My administrative duties would always interfere with the class meetings. I would end up with other people substituting for me too much. Still it was probably about ten years before I finally gave up trying to be a professor in addition to serving as president.

In your inaugural address you quoted your predecessor, Dr. Ellis Fuller, as follows: "A demagogue may mislead some session of the Southern Baptist Convention, but Southern Baptist Theological Seminary will serve as a gyroscope to bring it back to the middle of the channel." What did you mean by that?

This came out of a discussion I had with Fuller. He was stating how he perceived the seminary theologically and as an entity within the Convention. In my inaugural address I made the point that the relationship of the seminary to the Convention is a little different than that of most of the other denominational agencies. Fuller thought the seminary had to be so sound biblically and theologically, in terms of the heritage of Baptists, that it would tend to pull Southern Baptists back from the edges toward which demagogues have repeatedly sought to push the Convention.

Then you went on to make reference to some of the other Southern Seminary presidents and their contributions.

I had been studying the history of the seminary. I had read all the trustee minutes from the beginning. This was my impression of the impact of the various presidents on the life of the seminary. I was trying to find my position in that succession. I insisted that the problem is not so much biblical authority and trustworthiness as the barnacles that accumulate on the minds of people. It is the purpose of the seminary to chip the barnacles off the minds of people—in order to get away from the culture-conditioned, time-conditioned attitudes that interpret the eternal revelation of God in such a way as to make it fit into the cultural context of a particular era.

You also mentioned the growth of religion departments in Baptist colleges.

I was trying to make the point that the seminary was going to have to move up the academic ladder in its emphasis because it couldn't stay at the level that was now being preempted by the religion departments in the colleges. We would have to be able to take the students after they graduated from those colleges with perhaps a major in Bible and carry them further in their biblical studies. I've also been concerned more than once about the tendency of the colleges to provide a terminal form of education for religious workers. I've always opposed that.

You also mentioned your concern about the student-faculty ratio of the seminary in your inaugural address. What was the basis of your concern?

I thought the student body should be limited to an appropriate set of faculty members who could give first-class theological education. I still think that it is short-sighted simply to keep adding students to classes just because they say they want to be in your seminary. There are other seminaries with smaller student-faculty ratios.

Didn't you at that time advocate reducing the student body to 750 by making the courses harder?

Yes. One way to reduce enrollment is to raise your standards. I thought that was an appropriate response to the improved quality of religious teaching at the undergraduate level in the Baptist colleges. At the same time, it provided a way of maintaining an acceptable student-faculty ratio at Southern Seminary. Enrollment was burgeoning, and the faculty was not growing fast enough to keep up. We didn't have the money to enlarge the faculty. On various occasions I tested the waters to try to get a lid on enrollment at Southern Seminary. The trustees always voted me down.

FACULTY CONTROL

How did you perceive the issue of faculty control at Southern when you first arrived on the scene as president.

Before my time as president, there were minutes recounting the faculty deciding to buy a professor a desk. When I was president somebody said,

"What in the world are those boxes out in the hall? So, I asked, "What are those boxes?" Bob Allen, the seminary building and grounds manager, said, "I had a good price on a dozen faculty desks, and I bought them. We don't need that many now, but we'll need them shortly."

Here is the president of the seminary not even in on the buying of a dozen desks, as over against a time when a faculty meeting would devote its minutes to a decision to buy one desk. My predecessor, Ellis Fuller, was primarily a pastor-administrator, not an academic administrator. As a pastor, he administered a great church, and he tried to apply these skills within the seminary. The faculty wanted no administrator, pastoral or any other kind. They simply wanted someone to preside over their faculty meetings, a person who kept quiet because he was presiding and therefore didn't have the privilege of the floor like the rest of the faculty. So Fuller struggled with that while the seminary was growing and the faculty was growing.

Ellis Fuller had the vision to dream a music school for the seminary and to start such a school with the minister of music from the First Baptist Church of Atlanta, where he had been pastor. Mr. and Mrs. Donald Winters, with Westminster Choir School background, came to Louisville to start the music school at Southern Seminary.

Fuller had to agree with the faculty that no money available for the theology school would ever be spent on the music school. That was the kind of impasse he struggled with. To achieve his dream, he had to raise the money through other sources in order to found the music school. And he did it very successfully.

On the other hand, let me add that a man like T. R. Allen and some of the seminary staff and a few of the faculty came to love Ellis Fuller. They had great personal affection for him. I've heard Allen talk about walking out to the president's home—at the old Norton place, just before Fuller's death—and finding Fuller out in the yard behind a tree, down on his knees, tears running down his face, as he prayed for God to help him win over the faculty. He prayed that what was needed could be done in a Christian atmosphere and spirit.

After World War II, Ellis Fuller had to deal with the influx of war veterans into the seminary. This meant adding a bunch of new faculty members about the same age—recent seminary graduates. That set up another problem that I inherited—now you had the old guard who were, by seniority, the heads of the departments. The new, younger faculty members were low people on the totem pole within the faculty's relationships. That meant they taught at eight in the morning, and they taught what the senior professors did not want to teach.

This was actually the first controversy I ran into. It had nothing to do with president and faculty. Fuller, in his eight years as president, really struggled with this problem. He wanted to handle it by being the loving, caring, hard-working pastor who would meet the needs of his flock.

The faculty didn't want a pastor, and they resented Dr. Fuller in the pastor-administrator role. Some of the hard-nosed professors would reacted vehemently to his efforts that were the best intentioned in the world. There is a real sense in which the word *heartbroken* in describing Ellis Fuller is a figure of speech. But there is also a sense in which *heartbroken* describes the tension, pressure, and frustration that caused his death.

Did he feel he could do nothing about it?

Very little—nothing that would hold. He could force it, but it would come unstuck as soon as he got it done. His real success was in building and fund-raising. He could do these things with no faculty opposition, and he did a good job at these tasks.

ADMINISTRATION FORMALIZED

One gets the impression that the seminary was a very casually run institution before the coming of Dr. Fuller?

Yes. You see that in the fact that as a student I could just walk into the president's office and get admitted to the seminary. I didn't fill out any forms; I didn't see the registrar or the director of admissions. The president said I could come, so that settled it. During my administration, I implemented specific procedures that had to be followed. If a student came to me wanting to be admitted to the seminary, I told him, "Wonderful, I'm glad you have come. Go down to the admissions office and make application. If you have any problems, come see me." I would have expected everything to be taken care of in the admissions office.

Sampey was the kind of administrator the seminary faculty wanted. The trustees were happy with the working relationship he had with the faculty, and that made everything work just fine. To illustrate,

Sampey had a part-time secretary who was housed in an office down the hall from the president's office. Professor Gaines Dobbins was the treasurer of the seminary. Professor Hershey Davis was the librarian. Leo Crismon was the assistant librarian, but a faculty member had to be the head librarian. The faculty ran every facet of the seminary.

That was the background for the desire of the trustees for a new administrative style when Ellis Fuller came on board. Beginning with Fuller, the president was to be the chief executive officer of the seminary. Fuller never succeeded in making this transition. I thought I did, but it blew up because the traditions were very deep. I miscalculated the depth of this pattern in the psyche of the faculty.

OPPOSITION TO A DEAN

One of the things the seminary trustees had agreed to, apparently even before you came on board, was that the president would have responsibilities and powers of an executive administrator, assisted by a dean of the faculty. How was this supposed to work?

I told the trustees at one point that if they were going to elect a dean, I would take that job and they could get a new president because the deanship was the job I wanted. If they were going to have a dean between the faculty and me, I didn't want the president's job. Being president meant pure administration, and I could administer by staying with the SBC Executive Committee in Nashville. It was dealing with the faculty and the students that made the job at Southern attractive to me. So they took that provision out somewhere along the way, and I didn't have a dean of the faculty when I first went to Southern. Then about seven years later, I found out I had to have one.

Later, the School of Church Music and the School of Religious Education were established. These two schools had trustee-elected deans, and I served as dean of the School of Theology and president of the seminary.

Does that mean you presided at faculty meetings?

Yes, and I was involved in curriculum decisions of all sorts—the academic decisions. That's why I didn't want the job of president without the job of dean because that would divorce me from the curriculum and other academic matters.

111

LIVING IN THE NORTON ESTATE

What was it like living in the president's home formerly known as the Norton Estate?

The problem was it was just too big. I had lived in big old houses in the Garden District of New Orleans. I knew what they were like. When we went to New Orleans, we had furniture that we had bought for the normal-sized house on 119 Gibson Road in Louisville when I was pastor of Broadway. When we got to New Orleans in 1943, we discovered that all our furniture was out of scale—too small to be used.

We went out and bought all this big antique furniture to fit the house in New Orleans where we thought we were going to live forever. Then we ended up moving to Nashville, to a modern house, and our furniture didn't fit that place. At that point we had to buy furniture again. I didn't want to do this a third time when we moved to Louisville.

But in Louisville, here we were again in one of those big old houses, four floors high. To this day I don't know how many rooms that house had. I never counted them because it made a better story to say, "I don't know how many rooms it has." It was so big that we didn't live in the whole house. Our living quarters were in the east end downstairs and in the west end upstairs.

The master bedroom was on the west end, overlooking Cherokee Park and the beautiful sunsets. It was a marvelous room! It had a bell so when you got up and it was cold in the bedroom, you pulled the bell cord, and the butler came and built a fire in your fireplace to warm the room. This was wonderful, except we didn't have a butler. Every time I pulled that bell, I had to get up and build a fire because we didn't have central heating in the bedrooms.

The best story is to describe the garage. There was a little three-bedroom, two-and-one-half-bath cottage on one end of the garage. On the other end of the garage there were rooms for about six servants to live. The garage itself would take either eight or ten cars. I never did have enough cars to test the exact number it would hold. It had a private phone line from the garage to the house, so you could call the chauffeur and say, "Bring up the blue Cadillac; I'm wearing my blue tie."

Since we didn't have a chauffeur, we just let our car sit in the driveway for ten years. It was a city block from the garage to the house, and too far to walk, especially in the dark on the unlighted, winding driveway. That really explains what living in that house was like.

It was very impressive; it was very adequate—but it was very impossible to live in. When you have a young wife and four relatively young children, including one two years old, that's a pretty dirty trick to play on your wife—to put her in that kind of house to manage.

Did you entertain officially on behalf of the seminary there or at another place?

At this house most of the time. We used to have graduation receptions for seven hundred people—little affairs like that, plus state dinners and so forth. We could handle that many people with no difficulty at all—except we had a little problem the first time. We discovered our twin sons were charging twenty-five cents per car admission at the big iron gates at the Alta Vista Road entrance. That's how they learned to drive—by parking cars for people at the graduation reception. That's less than most parking lots charge. I guess people got their money's worth!

We got some bad publicity when we arrived in Louisville because of where we lived. It was Labor Day, and the picnickers in Cherokee Park got up on our property and left their trash. The park officials wouldn't clean it up because it wasn't on park property. So my boys had to clean it up.

They made a sign that said, "Trespassers will be shot on sight." But they made the same mistake the picnickers had made. They didn't know where the property line was, so they put the sign in the park. *The Louisville Times* got hold of that and printed the sign on the front page of the second section of the newspaper.

Then the newspaper found who put the sign there and interviewed my children with their air rifles. The boys were smart enough to say, "We wouldn't have shot anybody; we were just kidding." But the truth is they weren't kidding. They really meant, "Keep your trash in the park because if you bring it up on our property, we have to clean it up." That happened during our first week in Louisville, so that was our introduction to the public by the *Louisville Times*.

Really, it was a fun place, and the kids loved it. But their mother and father thought it was a little much. You know, twenty-two acres is just a little too much yard. We had amateur gardeners—that is, seminary students—to look after it. One smart Georgia farmer-student was out there looking after the grounds. He came in and said, "Mrs. McCall, I checked out those peach trees along the driveway. You're not going to have any peaches on those trees, so I cut them down." They had been planted so the driveway would be lined with alternating white and pink blossoms. He had cut down the decorative trees.

We finally put Dean Allen Graves's family with their six children in the caretaker's cottage attached to the garage. There was plenty of room for the Graveses and their six children in the cottage and the rooms for single servants.

Then the McCall children and the Graves children got into the cat-raising business—not intentionally. One of the funniest sights in the world must have been when Mrs. Graveses and Marguerite tried to take all their excess cats—about twenty-seven—down to the Humane Society. The cats got out of the box in the car, and they had cats crawling everywhere while they were driving down Broadway. I wish I had a picture of that!

The tales go on and on, and they are related to the inappropriateness of people like us trying to live in a house like that. It was too massive, too imposing. We could never maintain it in the manner to which it was accustomed.

Yet you wouldn't have noticed it if you visited us. Marguerite would have kept you in the center and the west end downstairs, which were public rooms. We never went there except when we had entertaining to do. She managed to make it quite livable, along with Mary Jo Gheens and Mary Jo's decorator, Mrs. Mendel, a marvelous Jewish woman and friend of Marguerite. Mrs. Mendel helped Marguerite solve the impossible decorating problems of these crazy quarters.

Why did you not encourage the trustees to put you somewhere else?

I brought it up repeatedly in trustee meetings and reminded them they had promised we would not have to live there. They were always willing to put us somewhere else, but what do you say when they ask, "What do you recommend we do with the Norton Estate?" It was cheaper to keep us there—as long as the seminary owned it and couldn't do anything else with it—than it was to put us in an efficiency apartment.

INFLUENCE ON SONS

Your children have remained close to your convictions, and they are leaders in their own churches and communities. To what do you attribute your success in having raised your children so well?

Picking the right wife. All the jobs I have held required a great deal of travel. I was an absentee father much of the time. Marguerite was a great mother and frequently filled the father's role as well.

I have tried to support my children and express confidence in them. I stood up for them once on the dancing issue. They made the headlines of the Louisville newspapers. Douglas, one of the twins, was courting the daughter of Wilson Wyatt, the lieutenant governor of Kentucky, who was a neighbor. Somehow Duke Jr. also got involved. To shorten a long story, he ended up being the date of the hostess of this Saturday afternoon tea dance. Her escort was in an automobile accident on the way to the party.

Well, if you are going to make pictures, here are identical twins with the daughter of the lieutenant governor of Kentucky and the hostess. They made the front page of the second section of the afternoon paper.

Louisville Baptists split right down the middle, east and west, on this issue. Some of the prominent pastors in the West End of Louisville really read me out of the kingdom of God over this. The East End Baptists thought I had struck a blow for freedom.

Our boys were worried about it. They were aware that this was a job attack—get rid of this seminary president who has dancing children. This became an issue with them. I asked, "Did you do anything wrong? I don't want to know what other people said; I want to know what you think. Do you think you have done something wrong." They said, "No, sir." I responded, "All right; why are you running; why are you apologizing? Just say, 'Yes, we went to the dance. No, we were not forbidden to go.'"

I talked to Dr. E. F. Estes, one of the West End pastors. He had jumped on me about this, and he told me I had ruined his ministry. I responded, "Dr. Estes, I have greater confidence in the lasting quality of your ministry. I am sorry that I can't tell you I feel real apologetic about what the boys did. But what I feel apologetic about is that I was busy traveling around the Southern Baptist Convention trying to serve you Southern Baptists. I wasn't in town and didn't even know my children were going to that affair. If I had been there and known about it, I might have asked them not to go just to avoid this kind of encounter."

What kind of advice would you give to parents in terms of what you and Mrs. McCall did for the boys?

I think you have to teach your children what you believe is basically right and get that separated from the popular culture and customs of the times. Then you have to insist that the things that are fundamentally right must be observed.

We used to have one such rule on which there was no compromise. When the boys first began to drive, I told them: "I have only one rule. If you ever take a drink when you are driving, when you get home, and your mother and I are asleep, you wake me up, and you must tell me about it. If I am not in town, you must tell your mother. If I ever hear that you did drink while driving and you did not tell me about it, that will be the last time you will ever drive any car I own."

But parents need to be flexible on matters of secondary importance. Then you have to trust your children, have confidence in them, and believe in them. They must know you believe in them. You are not going to teach them you believe in them unless there is a chance for them to do something that you would be very upset about.

On the things that really matter, I don't bluff much. This has gotten me in trouble sometimes, but it has kept me out of a lot. I don't really bluff with you. If I tell you I will do something, I may hope I won't have to, but if you call my bluff, I'll do it. That is almost a basic principle—in denominational life, in the seminary, and anywhere else.

DECISION-MAKING AND ADMINISTRATIVE STYLE

Very early in your administration, you dealt with the issue of a salary scale for the professors. Was this a priority concern of yours?

I thought that what was going on at Southern was so idiosyncratic. I couldn't make heads or tails out of it. It put the faculty members too much at the mercy of the presidency—if I didn't like a faculty member, he didn't get a raise. I was trying to move to what I perceived to be a better administrative technique.

I proposed that we employ Booz, Allen & Hamilton as an outside consultant to improve the administrative techniques at Southern Seminary. The institution was a very informal, family-style operation in which, theoretically, the president had no power of decision, but de facto he had all the power of decision because nobody else had it. This was a strange situation in which, literally, the color of the paint in the men's dormitory couldn't be changed without my approval. That was because nobody else had the power to make that decision.

I was trying to put in place a participatory decision-making process, but I was trying to get it in a very structured format so everyone would know exactly who was responsible for making these decisions and how they were to be made. That's my due process emphasis—including how decisions are to be reported and how they are to be implemented. I had no problem with sharing the decision-making process.

I would prevent the trustees from intervening in a faculty decision. There actually are instances of that happening, where I wouldn't let the trustees make a decision because that had been delegated to the faculty by the trustees. And once a decision was delegated to the president, I wouldn't let anybody else make that decision either.

The trustees are the policy-making body for the seminary, and all policy is in their hands. No seminary-wide policy could be adopted except by the trustees. Then the academic decisions are made by the faculty within those policies. Then the administration of those policies belongs to the administration of the seminary. Once you agree to these principles, I would not agree to let any of these groups invade the territory of the others.

I have been known to say to the trustees, "That's an administrative matter, as part of your policy. Now you can vote to change your policy, but until you do, you can't do that." I've said that when the trustees were trying to do something administratively. On the other hand, I've also said to the trustees, "In your policy you have established that this is a faculty matter. You can change your policy, of course, but until you do, you can't usurp what you have delegated to the faculty."

The faculty salary scale was an early and very crude attempt to come up with something other than the individual opinion of the president as to what the salary of Professor Joe Blow ought to be.

FACULTY RETIREMENT PLANS

Were there other matters involving faculty benefits that you tackled early on?

I was very concerned about adequate retirement for the faculty. The seminary had a retirement plan that I thought was totally inadequate—which was that a faculty member would retire on $100 per month. I thought that was unrealistic and unfair. I knew that most faculty members were not economically oriented in their priorities, and they weren't likely to make adequate plans for retirement on their own.

Through the years I worked hard to develop an adequate retirement plan for faculty and staff. If you read all the official minutes of the seminary, you will see that we kept upgrading the retirement plan and working to get to the place where at least 20 percent of salary would go into the retirement plan. That was what I wanted.

That backfired on me in an interesting way. Some seminary faculty members started out so young that by the time they got to be sixty years old, they could hardly afford to keep working. They could retire on more money than they were making in salary. I never really thought it would work that way, but it's hard to argue with a statistician. The fact of the business is that recent inflation has forced salaries so high, relative to the past, that the 20 percent really was a very modest retirement provision. [A faculty member who retired in the mid 1990s told me that by following my plan to the letter, his retirement fund was worth over a million dollars!—DKM]

PRESIDENT'S SALARY

What about your salary when you went to Southern Seminary in 1951?

It was more money than I ever thought a Baptist preacher ought to make. My salary as pastor of Broadway Baptist Church several years earlier was $2,700 per year, and there were no fringe benefits. They didn't provide an automobile, a house, or anything of that sort. What I'm really trying to say is that I felt that maybe the seminary salary was rather high. It was not high comparable to similar salaries, either within the Southern Baptist Convention or within religious circles generally.

Or as the president of a major educational institution?

No. It was not a high salary. About what I would have received as pastor of First Baptist Church, Dallas—$8,000 per year.

EXECUTIVE SECRETARY VS. PRESIDENT DIFFERENCES

How did serving as president of Southern Seminary differ from being executive secretary of the Executive Committee of the Southern Baptist Convention? What were the difficulties or challenges you faced in this new job?

I really expected the seminary to be a more difficult job than the Executive Committee, and I knew where the problem would be. It had to do with the proximity of constituencies. Most of the constituencies of the Executive Committee were at arm's length or at some geographical distance.

At the seminary, you had these same distant constituencies—the Southern Baptist Convention, the Christian world, etc. But in addition, you had faculty and staff members and students right on your doorstep. And my decisions were known immediately. If a decision was made by a small committee with a high level of confidentiality, I could go over to the dormitory that night and find out what the decision was.

How that happened, I never have fathomed. I chuckle at the president of the United States who tries to stop the leaks in the White House and say, "If you ever do it in your context, you are a superman genius. I could never do it at Southern Seminary, a much more tightly knit context with less personal animosities and hostilities than you're up against." That's the big problem—the constituencies are at your elbow.

Every time you make a decision with that larger constituency, if it is good for 98 percent of the people, it will be a bad decision for somebody. Some percentage of the constituency involved in the decision is going to get hurt. If you raise all salaries the same number of dollars, the high-salaried people feel they don't get adequate recognition. If you raise all salaries the same percentage, the high-salaried people get huge increases, and the low-salaried people get a paltry increase.

In the seesaw of the process, even if everybody is better off, somebody is less better off than somebody else. To be less better off is to feel that an injustice has been done. And the people affected by the decision are right on your doorstep. They will be in your office within a few minutes. They will come by your house tonight. They will call you after you've gone to sleep, and you will feel in your spirit the hurt and the disappointment of people you didn't want to hurt or disappoint. You cannot get away from them, no matter how hard you try. You carry these aches with you, even when you go on vacation. You really want to be omnipotent and omniscient, but you can't pull it off. That's the big difference.

CHAPTER 8

Southern Seminary President

1951-1957

In March of 1952, the trustees of the seminary passed a motion to increase the endowment of the Broadus Chair as well as some other endowments. Was this a goal of yours when you came as president?

Yes. We were naming certain professorships or chairs for professors that we wanted to endow. Some of these chairs had a little money in endowment but not enough to employ a professor. We were spelling out a fund-raising goal in terms of endowment.

In June 1952, the seminary studied the auditing procedures and the handling of funds. Was this a move to develop a more systematic method for the handling of funds?

Yes. I thought the procedures being used at the time were a little too loose and informal, considering the amounts of money involved. I have wanted very tight controls over the fiscal affairs of any institution I have been associated with.

What was the general rule of thumb on which you operated regarding gifts of real estate to the seminary?

We would accept anything anybody would give us that had potential cash value, but not if we had to make cash commitments to receive the gift. We would run no risk. While I was president, we actually sold off bits and pieces of real property we owned, maybe unwisely. By Kentucky law any real property owned by an educational institution is tax-exempt. The seminary owned several bits and pieces of property that were tax-exempt.

My attitude was that we either ought to use them or sell them and put them back on the tax rolls. I do not support tax exemption for property owned by educational or religious enterprises if these properties are not used directly for the enterprise itself. Now let me say that some property is tax-exempt pending its disposition, and it may take some time for an educational institution to dispose of it properly.

The most recent real estate transaction I was involved in was the disposition of Barnard Hall, across from the president's home on Alta Vista. Dr. Ellis Fuller, my predecessor as president, got the gift of the original piece of property, and I bought all the additional acreage around Barnard until it consisted of about twelve acres of land. Then I found out that it was not feasible to build apartments on that property that faculty and staff could rent. Nor was it feasible to build any other kind of educational enterprise there because of zoning regulations. Since I didn't think the seminary would ever use that property, I recommended that we sell it as soon as we got a good offer.

HIGH MORALE IN 1955–56

In March 1956, there was a statement from the students in the record of the meeting of the trustees. This statement approved the effort and work you were doing as president. How did you feel about this?

From 1955 to 1956, I thought we had found utopia. Both the faculty and the students thought the millennium had come. We had succeeded in making a major revision of the curriculum. The faculty felt good about academic freedom. The RSV translation had just been released, and the faculty had gotten out on a limb in defending the right to have new translations such as that. Faculty members were integrationists, and the 1954 Supreme Court decision had come down. While there was criticism about this decision by the court, there was no anger at the seminary. There seemed to be a feeling that a theological seminary ought to be an integrated school. The fact that it had done it early was good, not bad. All of these things contributed to a high morale on campus.

STAFF SELECTION

What was your philosophy of staff selection? Did you provide training for the staff whom you selected?

I think there ought to be a back-up for every important staff member. In the early days of my administration, I was looking for young staff members who could potentially fill in for other staffers who carried heavy responsibility. The salary scales of the seminaries, particularly in the early 1950s, were very low. We were so far under almost any other scale that the mature person, already established with family responsibilities, simply could not accept a job at Southern Seminary.

So I looked for bright, talented, personable young people who were interested in working at the seminary. I put them in roles where responsibility would at least test their ability. I started them out by getting them involved in an elaborate training program. Even when I worked at the SBC Executive Committee, I had a policy that any staff member could take any course anywhere related to his or her work, with the tuition or fees being paid by the employing organization.

That wasn't something invented at Southern. But Southern as an academic institution tended to make it more appropriate to say, "Education is the name of our game; if you want education to equip you to do your job better, we will provide it for you." The seminary paid for staff people to attend evening school, or short seminars, or other training events.

Sometimes a job required additional training. There were numerous instances in which personnel left Louisville to get valuable training. Usually that was at seminary expense. My policy was, "You must be equipped to be a professional in your area of responsibility."

Out of this grew a kind of ownership of the job and a sense by staff people that "the seminary has invested in me, and now I'm giving them a return on its investment." That is part of the explanation of the longevity of members of the seminary staff, at least at the upper administrative level.

STAFF DEVELOPMENT
What else did you do to develop the staff?

I moved staff around from job to job at the seminary. There was almost no one during my administration who worked at only one job. They worked in various facets of the seminary before finally settling into a specific responsibility.

Badgett Dillard is the prime example of this principle because he did almost everything at Southern Seminary except be president and teach New Testament. He held almost every administrative job in the institution at some point. He was a marvelous vice president for business affairs because he had such a broad perception of the enterprise.

As a seminary student, Badgett was secretary to the acting president, Dr. Gaines Dobbins, when I came as president. He graduated and became minister of education at the First Baptist Church of Gainesville, Georgia. I brought him back from there to the seminary because we lost Erwin McDonald, who moved to Furman as director of public relations. My secretary Clara McCartt and I were editing *The Tie* and doing all the public relations work. So I got Badgett Dillard to come back to the seminary and pick that up.

He went up to Bloomington, Indiana, for a half sabbatical leave as an administrative staff member. The faculty at Indiana University invited him to stay on and do doctoral work, but that would have involved more time. I told him, "There's no way I'll agree to that. That would mean for me to work hard to get rid of a good staff member. When you get your doctorate, somebody else will offer you a job at a higher salary, and you'll leave." He replied, "No; I wouldn't." And I said, "O.K., I'll be the business manager for the year-plus that is required for you to complete the degree."

So Badgett earned his doctorate in business administration at the University of Indiana. For his thesis he used the Association of Theological Schools' computer and provided a definitive work on the financing of theological education.

By the time he came back, he and I had a mutual investment in each other. Through the years he turned down several job offers and stayed with the seminary. Some of that was personal, but a lot of it was a sense of God's call on his part.

Another member of the staff who comes to mind in regards to this principle of multiple responsibility is Pat Pattillo. He stayed in a more defined area of the seminary, public relations. But he did move from one type of role in public relations to another. For instance, he was a first-rate fund-raiser. I can still remember the weeks of argument I had with him trying to get him to move into fund-raising. He said what everybody says, "I don't know anything about it; I don't like it; I can't do it. My personality is not suited to it."

But he did finally move into fund-raising, he developed skills at it, and he discovered he could do the job. Success is a pleasant feeling in any arena.

CURRICULUM REVISION

A change in the academic requirements of the seminary was approved and implemented at the beginning of the school year in September 1956. How did this come about?

I started talking with the faculty about curriculum revision in 1955. We had worked on revisions all the way through the academic year ending in 1955 and had reached the point of concurrence. At this point I suggested we let the decisions soak for a while.

These changes related to the School of Theology and requirements for the B.D. degree. The faculty actually took the lead in these revisions, since this was an academic matter. They went through very tricky waters trying to work out these changes. When I was a student at Southern, the curriculum of the seminary was painted on a plaque in the corridor of Norton Hall; it just never changed.

But in 1955 the faculty accomplished the first total overhaul of the curriculum. They had fine-tuned some requirements over the years. But now they were saying, "This is post-World War II. This is a new era. We are in this explosive era of Southern Baptist church life and the growth of churches. We need to take a new look at how to educate ministers." And they did a massive study.

My memory is that Professor Henry Turlington was the chairman of the faculty committee in charge of the revision. I can visualize him bringing in the final report for my inspection. He was a little disappointed that I indicated I wanted to postpone asking for a vote on the changes.

I was totally supportive of the recommendations. But because there were so many people and so many factors involved, I felt we needed to let it soak for a while. My recollection is that I told him we would look at the proposed changes again in about a year to make certain this was what we wanted to do.

A major curriculum revision affects the careers of individual faculty members. You are wiping out, in some cases, their reason for coming to Southern Seminary to teach because their favorite course may no longer be a required course. Or a four-hour requirement is cut to two hours. Perhaps new courses are introduced, and faculty members must prepare to teach courses that have never been in the curriculum before.

The faculty had done a magnificent job with these suggested revisions, even though there were tears and anguish in the cutting-and-adding processes. Everybody was ready to vote unanimously for it. This was one evidence of the high morale in the seminary at that time.

PROBLEMS IN REVISING THE CURRICULUM

It has been suggested by some people that the new curriculum grew out of the dissatisfaction of many professors with the academic character of some of the practical studies that had been introduced into the School of Theology. Is that correct?

There was always objection among some of the faculty to the introduction of psychology of religion and counseling in the curriculum of the School of Theology. The faculty wanted to introduce some other things into the curriculum such as enlarged Old Testament and New Testament requirements. They moved certain things like preaching a little toward the edge. We later had to turn around and fight to get it back.

If you include speech, preaching, psychology of religion, and so on, there undoubtedly were those who were trying to capture more time for the body of divinity from those areas. But the flip side of the coin was that there were efforts to strengthen some areas that would have been called the practical field.

The faculty recommendations included the requirement of Greek and Hebrew about this time that moved the student toward a heavier biblical orientation. The survey courses in Old and New Testament, as I recall, were almost doubled in requirement, so the biblical content was heavily increased. I happened to agree with that. I am not saying in my enthusiastic support for the faculty recommendations that I agreed with every detail of the change, but I agreed with the thrust of the change. I felt it had been accomplished by due process. I was delighted that the faculty was happy with it.

And there was also a feeling that more attention should be given in the curriculum to pastoral care, psychology of religion, preaching, and other practical courses?

Yes. I was trying to get supervised field training, as it came to be called later, included in Southern's academic program. That was rooted partly in my New Orleans Seminary experience. The field work program in New Orleans for the entire student body had impressed me. I believed in it, and I was trying to bring some of that to Southern.

Field work had always been a part of Southern's program. Originally it was every student for himself. He just reported on whatever ministry he was performing. Nobody helped him get placed in a ministry role or gave him much help in what he did. Once he got the job, it was sink or swim for him. I was trying to introduce something of the New Orleans pattern of aid in placement and supervision.

THE BOOZ, ALLEN & HAMILTON STUDY

Tell us about the report to the seminary of the Booz, Allen & Hamilton consultation.

After completing the restructure of the seminary's curriculum, I thought we needed a thorough study of the total organization of the institution. We turned to an outside firm, Booz, Allen & Hamilton, a national consultant firm of highest reputation. We asked them to study how to organize an educational institution like Southern Seminary. As far as I know, that had never been done for a theological seminary before by such a consultant firm. They were basically oriented to the business community, but they had a division that served educational institutions.

Booz, Allen & Hamilton had no particular expertise with Baptists, but I didn't think that would be a problem. I never thought a theological seminary was a Baptist church. Some people think church polity ought to determine the administrative processes in an educational institution. That is a basic attitude that I never shared.

The Booz, Allen & Hamilton investigation was a very thorough study of every aspect of the seminary's life, and it involved everybody in the seminary. The report is a huge volume that is still available to anybody who wishes to read it. It covers almost every aspect of the administration of the seminary, including, for example, even the work of the executive committee of the board of trustees.

This report recommended that the president of the seminary not function as chairman of the trustee executive committee. This was a situation that had existed since the administration of Dr. Ellis Fuller.

The powers of the president were not uniformly increased through recommendations made by this study. Here was a specific case where his powers were actually decreased.

But the Booz, Allen & Hamilton report insisted there ought to be a dean of the School of Theology, that the president should not try to function in this role. So when the report was adopted, the president lost one of his favorite roles in the seminary. I'm trying to make a point that I didn't like all of the recommendations of this consultant group, although I supported the package. I doubt if anyone connected with the seminary liked all of the changes.

Salary scales were set up, and all members of the faculty and staff were pleased with this. But this was a problem for some trustees because the scale contained automatic escalating increases. This report was not uniformly pro-administration, pro-trustees, or pro-faculty. It was a first-rate academic consulting firm recommending to the seminary, "After careful study, this is what we think you ought to do in your institution." That report, with some modifications, was finally adopted.

The final report was actually not adopted until 1957. But Henlee Barnette was named acting dean of the School of Theology in 1956.

That's right. We began incremental implementation of recommendations as they were adopted. We were in an evolving situation. I didn't think we should wait until we had a final document and then suddenly be faced with a thousand decisions to make all at once.

Did you foresee having Barnette as the permanent dean?

No. In fact, I chose him for recommendation as acting dean precisely because I did not think he would be a candidate for permanent dean. He was acceptable generally to the theology faculty, but they would not coalesce around him as their permanent dean and thereby create future problems. He was a good choice; he did a good job as acting dean.

What were the major recommendations of the final Booz, Allen & Hamilton report?

They recommended that the School of Theology faculty be divided into four divisions: (1) biblical, (2) historical, (3) theological, and (4) practical. They also recommended a new procedure for hiring new professors, which provided the president with veto power over faculty suggestions, so that the procedure was tied into the presidency. There was also a recommendation for presidential authority to make interim appointments to the faculty between trustee meetings.

Another recommendation was to increase the number of deans at the seminary from three to five, and to establish a Deans Council. They recommended that the seminary create the position of business manager. Additionally, they recommended that the seminary discontinue some of the basic degrees, which were Bachelor of Religious Education and Bachelor of Church Music, as a means of cutting enrollment. Finally, they recommended a new salary scale for the faculty and a process by which this would be implemented.

This final report wasn't just a general policy statement that the president would be the chief executive officer of the institution. His duties were now set within a specific structure, with certain responsibilities assigned to the faculty and trustees as well. Some of the recommendations dealt with the procedures for the faculty to use in making academic decisions that impinged on the policy-making operation of the seminary. The primary decision-maker at each point of the seminary's life—administration, faculty, and trustees—was now spelled out precisely and formally.

Did you feel that this report and its adoption would be a bridge between the administration of the seminary and the faculty?

No. I thought there was some understanding of the need for this holistic approach to the administration of the seminary. All the way through that March trustee meeting in 1957, there had never been anything without faculty involvement. I'm trying to avoid saying there had never been any disagreement. But there had never been any faculty versus administration, or faculty objection to the Booz, Allen & Hamilton report, or faculty objection to the direction of the report. It was simply a normative kind of participatory decision-making, with the lead being taken by the outside consulting firm.

Some have suggested that the prestige of the faculty was diminished by this report and its adoption. Up until this time, they had nominated for election, directly to the trustees, all new faculty members. Now the president was making the nominations, based on their recommendations, to the board of trustees.

Now the faculty decision was on the front end where the real decision gets made. I know the difference in perception. The president's perception was that he was surrendering the initiative in faculty search to the faculty. Now he would have to influence the process by either approval or veto of the faculty's selection.

MCCLANAHAN ADDED TO FACULTY

In 1956 you added a second full-time instructor, Dr. John H. McClanahan, to the department of psychology of religion. He stayed only one year, and then there was a replacement. This has often been suggested as the precipitation issue that led to controversy and conflict in the later period at Southern Seminary. Is that true?

If so, I didn't feel it at the time. Dr. Wayne Oates would have used his clout and leadership to get that approved. Adding a faculty member was not an administrative decision without faculty concurrence, so the faculty concurred in the addition. I don't remember the exact process at that time, but there was never a point where the administration said, "We're going to add a professor to a department"—and did it without consultation with the faculty.

Some faculty members probably did not want a faculty addition in psychology of religion. But this would have been true if we had added someone in New Testament, Old Testament, or any other discipline. Whatever the background noise for the decision was, it was routine noise as far as the administrator was concerned. I don't remember it as a particular problem at all.

You would not agree with the statement by some that McClanahan's addition was an administrative decision?

No. Due process was followed in the McClanahan addition, or there would have been a faculty explosion that you could read about in the records. But perhaps I should add that Wayne Oates was perceived by some faculty members as an empire builder. At some point Dr. T. C. Smith in a faculty conference complained about the qualifications and competence of Dr. Oates.

I defended Dr. Oates rather vigorously. Maybe I was perceived after this by some members of the faculty as being "on Dr. Oates's side." Maybe some faculty members thought I would do anything Dr. Oates wanted—even give him an extra faculty colleague for his department. My personal focus on "due process" could have blinded me to any notion of favoritism at that time.

SOUTHARD ADDED TO FACULTY

After McClanahan left, Dr. Samuel Southard was added to the faculty as his replacement. Some professors claimed that his appointment occurred in spite of some opposition by the faculty. What is your response to this charge?

The charge actually was that the president added Southard without consultation with the faculty. Henlee Barnette was the acting dean of the School of Theology at this time.

Henry Turlington of the faculty of the School of Theology had reported to the acting dean that the faculty had approved Southard. Henlee Barnette had me meet Southard in the Louisville airport. I was leaving town as Southard was coming in. We met and ate lunch together. I later told Barnette that Southard was acceptable from the president's point of view. Barnette reported to me that he had faculty support for this addition, and that he had faculty support specifically for Dr. Southard.

In testimony before the trustees in their hearing in 1958, Barnette said, "If anything was done wrong about the Southard appointment, the president didn't do it, because Southard was my recommendation. And I didn't do anything wrong because I acted on faculty approval."

Barnett subsequently forced Henry Turlington to concede that he had somehow gotten ahead of the hounds and reported to Barnette that the faculty approved something that he expected the faculty to approve. But the faculty apparently had not approved Southard at the time of Turlington's report to the acting dean.

SEMINARY FORMULA

You had a role in developing what eventually came to be known as the "Seminary Formula." What exactly is this formula?

The Seminary Formula is a procedure for evaluating certain elements that go into the budget of the six SBC seminaries. It gets amended from time to time when the entire budgeting process begins to shift, for various reasons, among the seminaries. There are a lot of reasons why the formula is flexible. It is a way by which the six seminaries do part of the work of the Executive Committee. If the six seminaries agree on a funding arrangement that is mutually beneficial to all, then the Executive Committee can deal with six independent agencies as if they were one single entity.

The seminary presidents, across the years, have evolved a sophisticated way of working together, and it involves very fine cooperation. They work hard at the business; they worry about the funding of foreign missions, or home missions, or other agencies. They also worry about the effect of their operation on all the agencies. If they worry for you, they also can worry on the other side about being sure that they don't get maneuvered out of their end of the Cooperative Program trough.

The Seminary Formula is simply a way for the seminaries, as a group, to put their request for funding on the agenda for consideration by the Executive Committee.

I understand that the Executive Committee of the SBC and the seminary presidents hired an outside consultant to help develop this formula?

Yes. One of the smartest things the seminary presidents ever did was to persuade the Executive Committee that it ought to have a vested interest in that report—that the consultant ought to be the Executive Committee's consultant since this was an Executive Committee decision that was being made.

Orin Cornett was the person primarily who served as the consultant, was he not?

Yes, over a longer period of time than anybody else. Dr. Doak Campbell, president of Florida State University, was a very effective member of the consultant group for a period of time. There were others. Orin Cornett was the most effective consultant precisely because he understood the political dynamics of the seminary presidents as academic administrators and the political dynamics of the Southern Baptist Convention.

The Seminary Formula is a compromise situation. It always favors one seminary more than the other five. Yet they unanimously agree to its being that way. When the chips are down, the seminaries want quality education for all students, wherever they are. They will worry about Southwestern coming out with enough money—even though it gets more money than any other seminary.

After the 1958 controversy, Southern Seminary had a sudden drop in enrollment. The presidents of the other seminaries became concerned about this situation. The precipitous drop in enrollment affected Southern's income because of the Seminary Formula. They knew that no institution could adjust its budget downward that fast. So the seminary presidents introduced a three-year rolling average at that point. This meant that a seminary would not feel a drastic drop in income all at once. The income through the Seminary Formula would drop over three years, during which time a smart administrator ought to be able to adapt to the drop in enrollment.

The three-year rolling average can also work the other way. If one seminary has a sudden surge in enrollment, it doesn't get the immediate benefit of this increase. Southern Seminary had a 42 percent jump in its entering class one year in the early 1970s. But under the formula arrangement, we only received a one-third-of-42-percent increase in our funding for that year. We had to pick up the other two-thirds increase in the next two years. The three-year rolling average stabilizes the allocation of funds to the seminaries in the face of drastic fluctuations in enrollment. It's a good principle.

It almost seems that the Seminary Formula is a very flexible thing and more an "arrangement" than a "formula."

This is a very complicated subject with a lot of legitimate differences of opinion. I have never thought we were able to isolate the ingredients of the formula with such absolute accuracy that when you put all of the ingredients together you had an absolute formula.

Let me illustrate. One student enrolls in the seminary and takes only one two-hour course. It doesn't cost the seminary as much to teach that student two hours as it would cost to teach another student who's taking eighteen hours. So what is a student? Defining a student is a very complicated thing into which value judgments go. Consequently, when the seminaries ended up by defining a full-time student as one who carried a twelve-hour load, they were describing very few of their actual students.

My point is that the basic data used to construct a formula is debatable. It is value judgment. It is an estimate. The Seminary Formula is one package of statistical analyses over against other possible statistical analyses.

How is this formula funding arrangement for the seminaries established on a year-by-year basis?

It has happened in several different ways across the years, but let me describe what is the almost normative way. First of all, the SBC Executive Committee would agree to employ a consultant to recommend a funding arrangement for the year. This task would be assigned to some Executive Committee staff member. This staff member would negotiate with the seminary presidents about who would be acceptable to them as a consultant, because both sides had to agree.

Generally, this Executive Committee staff member was Albert McClellan. This was one of the great stabilizing forces in handling this whole formula thing and all of the attendant problems. We had the same person who became highly knowledgeable. He developed sophisticated knowledge about theological education and the personalities of the presidents and the political dynamics between the seminaries.

And Dr. McClellan prided himself always on being a neutral person?

I never heard any seminary president imply that McClellan was not neutral. If he had so much as batted his eye at the wrong time, it would have been noted in the minutes—or at least in the private record of the president who saw him do it. It would have been recalled at some other time. It's a fantastic achievement of McClellan that the seminary presidents would fight with him sometimes, didn't always agree with him, but they never questioned his integrity or his neutrality.

Let's say that McClellan, as the associate secretary of the Executive Committee in charge of the institutional work group, would call the chairman of the presidents and say, "Will you agree on Orin Cornett as the consultant?" Albert would wait until the chairman of the presidents called him back and said, "Yes, Orin Cornett would be acceptable to the presidents."

Once that was agreed upon, then McClellan would go to Cornett and employ him for so many days as a consultant. Orin would probably come down to Nashville and talk to McClellan. He would ask him, "What are the issues? What are the problems? What is it I'm trying to solve?"

Then Orin would go off and work on the assignment for a while. He would then have a meeting with the six seminary presidents in terms of what he had worked out as his tentative proposal. All the ground rules could get changed at that point. By the end of the two- or three-day meeting, almost everything in Orin's proposal could be out the window. He could be off on a brand new track because now he had gotten the presidents' perception of what the problems were.

I've known situations in which the final recommendations were almost diametrically opposite from what Orin brought in to the first meeting. He would go off and, without the presidents around, would work with his statistical analyses of theological education, including the six seminaries. At that point Orin probably had asked the six seminaries to provide him with massive batches of data.

They would provide him with anything he asked for, and he would get it in infinite detail. He was an excellent mathematician and, as a statistician, he really did a magnificent job. He might rework the whole proposal.

Then he would probably talk to Albert McClellan before he talked to the six seminary presidents to see if the change in direction was acceptable to Albert. If it was, then he would have another conference with the presidents. But McClellan might say to him, "No, the Executive Committee can't let it go in that direction." Then, without telling the presidents, Cornett would probably go back from that conference and rework it in light of the conference with McClellan. Then he would come back to McClellan to be sure McClellan thought this was a viable direction to move. It took constant negotiation like this to get the Seminary Formula to work on a year-to-year basis.

SEMINARY PRESIDENTS' WORKSHOP

Tell us something about the Seminary Presidents Council, where the negotiations among the seminary presidents themselves occurred.

The Presidents Workshop is their public relations title for it, and this title was suggested by Olin Binkley. He was absolutely right. The presidents make a mistake when they forget to call it a workshop.

But is it really a workshop?

Sure, it's a workshop. It's a hard workshop. Getting the seminary presidents to agree that today is Tuesday is hard work. Some of them will say "not everywhere in the world," and they'll be right.

Were the presidents responsible for forming this workshop? Or was it imposed from above?

It was imposed by the SBC Executive Committee. They got tired of us competing with one another on their turf. And there were some casualties of that competition back in the earlier days. So the Executive Committee finally ordered the seminary presidents to agree on their appeal for funds. Why did they do that to the seminaries and not the mission boards? They are as much alike as the six seminaries. The six seminaries are not that much alike.

What happened in these meetings of the seminary presidents?

All sorts of correlating problems, decisions, and even counsel to one another. General problems were on the agenda. The meetings normally lasted from Monday night until Friday noon. All decisions had to be made unanimously. If a president agreed to a decision, his integrity demanded that he go home and implement that decision in the life of his institution. But remember that presidents are not omnipotent in their institutions. They might have to go home and get the faculty to agree to something that all six seminary presidents had agreed to. Or they might have to get their trustees on board with a decision.

Did these week-long meetings involve a great deal of negotiation among the presidents?

The presidents were always deadly serious advocates of the welfare of their own institutions, of theological education, of the Southern Baptist Convention, and of the cause of Christ. All of these factors were always behind the discussions.

You were never sure which one of these factors was controlling a specific president at a given moment. You could know what a specific decision would mean to his institution. But you couldn't know whether he was willing to sacrifice the advantage to his institution for what he believed was an important contribution to the cause of Christ in the world.

The atmosphere in the meeting ran all the way from friendly game-playing and jesting to intense discussion and hard-nose negotiations. Each president put items on the agenda. The agenda was a compilation of items sent in advance to the chairman of the group, plus the items that were agreed to at the opening of the meeting. The agenda would usually be expanded in the brainstorming about the agenda in the first session.

You met twice a year officially?

The official workshop was held once a year—the week after Thanksgiving. We might meet twice or ten times during a given year. But these were usually ad hoc meetings with a limited agenda. They were called by the chairman for the corner of a corridor or his hotel room. They might be arranged in connection with a meeting of the SBC Executive Committee in Nashville or the Inter-Agency Council, or the Southern Baptist Convention, or the inauguration of a new president at one of the seminaries.

In these extra meetings, the president/chairman usually had two or three things that somebody had asked him to handle. We might meet and eat lunch together, and the chairman would run through six items and say, "I think we ought to do this." "O.K." "I think we ought to do that." Five heads would nod.

This varied, and there was no single pattern, but there was a pattern to that annual meeting of the Presidents Workshop in early December. We learned, first of all, to bring our wives.

All twelve husbands and wives would meet for dinner on Monday night of that week. It would be a happy reunion, everybody would love everybody, and all would be friends. Information would be exchanged about children and grandchildren—just a bunch of friends having a wonderful time together.

Then when dinner was over, the wives would go off and do whatever they wanted to do. They usually ran their own version of the workshop somewhere along the way. Not as formally, of course; they would get together and talk about the problems of being a seminary president's wife. The wives of seminary presidents have never been given enough credit for their part in the achievements of their husbands.

The first order of business for the presidents would be to set up the agenda for the meeting. It might take an hour or so to hammer out a consensus agenda for the week. Then we would dip into the first items of business. We would try to begin with the items that we could tick off quickly and unemotionally. Sometimes we made mistakes and grabbed a hot potato at the beginning sessions.

We would generally get through Monday night with little flack. Everybody would go to their hotel room and get a good night's sleep. Then the presidents would start again early Tuesday morning. By

Tuesday noon some of the seminary presidents wouldn't be speaking to one another. So they would have lunch with their wives. Each one would explain to his wife what a bunch of rascals the other five were, how stupid and stubborn they were. The loving wife would listen sympathetically and absorb all the venom that had built up.

By the time we got through lunch with our wives, we could go out to Key Biscayne, which was one of the most frequented meeting places, and play pitch-and-putt golf. All of us didn't get together like this, but maybe two couples here and two couples there would get together, or they would go swimming in the ocean. We never worked in the afternoon.

We needed recreation in the afternoon to bleed off all the hostility that had been built up in that morning's session. Then all twelve of us would have a big dinner on Tuesday night—going back to the Monday night pattern. Again, by the time dinner was over, everybody loved everybody again.

Then it was back to work again after the dinner on Tuesday night. The chairman would cut off the meeting about eleven o'clock. By then the odds were that not a single one of the presidents could go to sleep.

That's why each president's wife had to be at the workshop. She knew her husband. She might ask, "Is there any place around here where we can get some ice cream?" She knew her husband needed to release some of the tension that had been generated in the meeting if he was ever going to get to sleep.

By the time the meeting ended on Friday, the agenda items consisted of Mickey Mouse stuff—settling the expense accounts and so on. The expense was split six equal ways. No matter where the meeting was held, the most distant seminary paid transportation at the same rate as the nearest seminary. If you didn't bring your wife, you would still pay one-sixth of the cost of the meeting.

On one occasion we had a sharp disagreement over the Seminary Formula, and I was the bad boy on that one. I said to the other president who was asking for special treatment, "Where are your statistical supports for your claim? Your quotes from your faculty and your trustees and your students and your own opinions are very interesting. But they must be supported with statistical evidence out of your financial reports. Where's your evidence?"

The president went back to arguing, and I finally ended up by saying, "Forget it. My vote is no, and it will continue to be no until you come up with some data to prove that you have a special problem." About that time the meeting broke up. In my room I had the audits and the most recent financial reports of all six seminaries. I sat up for about two or three hours doing a statistical analysis of that seminary's financial situation.

The next morning I ate breakfast with Goldie and Bob Naylor. I said, "Bob, after I got to my room last night, I did a statistical analysis of the presentation this president had made. He is right. He really is in trouble. The institution has a first-class problem on its hands. The emotional overload has blocked his ability to make a coherent presentation. So I've changed my position. Now I'm on his side. We have to pitch in to help him solve the problem."

I took the paper placemat and turned it over and said, "This is how I think we ought to go about solving the problem for him." Bob said, "O.K., I agree to that." Then I asked, "Bob, will you present it to the group? If I do it, he will have trouble believing I have reversed my position overnight?"

When the meeting started, Bob said, "During the night, I've looked at these figures, and I want to make a proposal." So he read the analysis off the placemat—what the problem was, the level of the problem, and what ought to be done to solve it.

This other president said, "I'll move that." Bob Naylor said, "I'll second the motion." Everybody sat around and waited for me to make a speech. I said, "I'll vote for it." So the solution to this seminary's problem was voted unanimously within a matter of five or ten minutes of the presentation.

Did the seminary presidents bring staff members to the Presidents Workshop, or was it always just a head-knocking between seminary presidents?

There was an absolute rule that nobody else would be present in a workshop unless there was unanimous agreement to this among the presidents. In the workshop in which the transition from Naylor to Dilday took place, it took unanimous agreement of the presidents to let Dilday sit in a workshop before he actually took over as president; he was president-elect. He was on the payroll at Southwestern. That will tell you how rigidly the rule was observed. There were occasions on which, for a specific reason, somebody except the presidents might be allowed to sit in. Not even a member of the SBC Executive Committee staff was allowed in one of the meetings of the workshop without the same kind of vote.

SOURCE OF GOOD STUDENTS

During your presidency at Southern Seminary, was there some feeling that Southwestern graduates were more conservative than Southern Seminary students? Were the churches concerned about that type of thing?

I am not denying that this concern did evolve, but it was not in the bloodstream at that time. Something else that hasn't been discussed about seminaries was happening. If you get the reputation as a strong, academic institution, a great many "ordinary" Baptist ministerial students don't want to be subjected to that kind of discipline.

Now don't hear this as a put-down because I want to underscore the next statement: In that group will be some of the smartest students that any seminary can get. They don't aspire to be scholars. They aspire to be effective pastors, so they will avoid getting on the scholarly track. In the academic situation, they will turn out to be among the best scholars.

Some Southern Baptists used to say that Southern was the academic seminary and Southwestern was the evangelistic seminary. That made both Southern and Southwestern mad because neither one of us would admit that we were exclusively either academic or evangelistic.

But that perception has something to do with the selection of a seminary by students. Selection by students is really going to work to the advantage of the seminary that is perceived as evangelistic. It won't like the characterization at the time, but it will end up getting some of the best scholars among Southern Baptists.

I might throw this in—and this is the kind of thing that can get me in trouble. But if you really want the best seminary students, you'll probably get them out of Arkansas precisely because of the culture patterns of Baptist churches in Arkansas. In Virginia the churches tend to say to the bright young men, "You are so smart, you'd make a good doctor. You'd be a fine lawyer." In Arkansas, they say to their brightest Baptists in the church, "You ought to be a preacher." That does something in terms of the quality of students that go into the ministry.

This would be true in terms of Boyce Bible School. You would have seen this as a ministry to some other people who would not normally have chosen Southern Seminary?

Or even any seminary, but they were going to be SBC pastors. We've had students come into Boyce who had never been to college, who didn't think they could do college work. But they were so good when they got into Boyce Bible School that the faculty tried to convince them to go back to college.

Some of these students did go back to college and graduated high in their class. They came back and ended up doing doctoral work at Southern Seminary. So Boyce Bible School was a recruiting tool for a small number of exceedingly competent students. That's a little superficial to say "recruiting tool" as if that's the end. The end is to graduate this kind of highly-trained, highly-motivated minister.

Is it fair to say, then, that the concept of Boyce Bible School came out of your basic thinking and initiation?

I think that is correct with modifications. There was opposition to Boyce within the faculty of Southern Seminary because this cut across the grain of the true academician's approach to ministry education.

AFRICAN-AMERICAN STUDENTS

On March 12, 1952, you reported to the trustees on five black students who had enrolled at the seminary. I understand this was a delicate situation because of the laws of the state of Kentucky at that time.

Yes, because of the old Day Law, which forbade the teaching of blacks and whites in the same classroom. My memory is that we decided to ignore the law. We thought we had the moral ground—and probably the legal ground as well—to ignore it. We didn't think the authorities were going to challenge the seminary over the admission of black students. We thought if anybody did, and it got into a federal court, it probably would get thrown out. The faculty of the seminary had voted to admit blacks during the preceding year.

The first decision I made as president was on this issue. Dr. Hugh

Peterson, dean and director of admissions, came into my office. He asked, "What do we do about Negro students?" I replied, "We don't do anything about Negro students." He pressed the question, and I responded, "We don't have any policy about brown-eyed students, or blue-eyed students, and we're not going to have any policy about white-skinned students and black-skinned students."

He then ran me through the whole rigmarole of dormitory and dining hall and swimming pool and apartment buildings. I insisted that the seminary had to be color-blind in terms of its student body. That was the first decision I made as president of Southern Seminary.

I understand some black students had received training at the seminary before this?

Yes, but in the professor's office, not in the classroom, and not as enrolled, matriculated full students with full rights as students. Garland Offut was such a *sub rosa* African-American student in the seminary in my time.

Garland and I have been friends through the years. Not too long ago we were talking about blacks in the seminary, and he was surprised at the open policies. I was surprised that as a Louisville pastor he did not know of the change. (He took his classes in the professor's office until the professor got tired of covering the same material twice and invited him to sit in the back of the room during the regular class.)

Can you relate any other incidents regarding these students becoming a part of the seminary community?

Our policy was that they would be admitted to all the classes. Then the question arose, What about admission to the dormitory: do they get special privilege, are they put at the bottom of the list, or are they put at the top of the list for vacant space in the dormitory? The answer was, Wherever their application comes. They got neither an advantage nor a disadvantage because they were black.

I discovered that the past discrimination and refusal to admit blacks meant we had to recruit blacks specifically in order to get them. I hired Bob Herndon, a former military chaplain and Southern alumnus. For two years his job was to visit campuses where there were collections of black students. He would try to find black ministerial students who were Baptists to convince them to come to Southern Seminary.

It never worked well, because by then they were convinced they wouldn't get good treatment in a southern institution. The title "Southern Baptist" didn't reassure them at all. Besides that, by then the ministry was not the key profession of blacks. Bob would sometimes find nobody who knew whether there was a black ministerial student on a big black university campus.

Bob's technique was to sit and eat an apple on a bench on the campus until somebody sat down by him. Then he would start a conversation and find out if that person knew whether there were any black ministerial students on campus. He did recruit some black students. But we never could get much beyond twenty or twenty-five black students on campus at any one time.

INVESTMENT PROCEDURES
I understand Southern Seminary developed a fine investment program during your administration. Tell us about it.

The seminary had a very fine investment-counseling firm. When we were not happy with the results, we fired an investment firm and got a new one, making it clear that their track record and nothing else would help them keep the job. We have kept the current firm for twenty-plus years because they have done well with the seminary's investments.

The account executive we had when I was president is now head of the national firm, so I guess we got a pretty good man, and we stayed with him. Southern Seminary is one of the few accounts he handles personally. He likes handling it—and this will say some things, too.

Because the financial board of the trustees of Southern Seminary has a lot of investment expertise, this account executive liked to come and sit with them and bring his counsel and take home some counsel with him. He would learn from them. I'll use the name of Homer Parker, who retired as president of Capital Holding, a company that owns a handful of insurance companies. If you want to know about insurance investment stocks, get Homer Parker to tell you about them. You will end up knowing more than you will ever discover by reading the investment advisory services.

For that reason Southern's investment program was a two-way street, and it meant that the investment counselor could not give superficial counsel. If he didn't know what he was talking about, he was going to be queried by some people who didn't know the answers, but they would find out in a hurry whether he knew the answers. They were ruthless in their handling of their experts. A phenomenal bond of friendship and respect developed. I have great admiration for these laymen who made up this financial board of Southern Seminary.

They got regular reports and compared the performance of the seminary endowment with all sorts of averages, like the Standard & Poor's average, or other investment portfolios. They would ask, "How is our track record as compared to theirs?" As long as their investment portfolio was doing as well or about as well as the best, they were reasonably happy.

There could be a bad year, and the investments might not do as well?

Quite so. They didn't get out of the stock market even if it took a nose-dive; nor did they put all of their cash into volatile stocks just before a surge. They were too conservative to do that. They got caught every now and then. If one of their stocks turned out to be a dog, they didn't keep it. As soon as it barked once, they sold it. They were absolutely ruthless about that.

They must have had certain policies and procedures about what they would and would not do. Can you recollect what the parameters were?

For instance, they would never invest in liquor or tobacco stocks. If the seminary was given stocks of that type, they would dispose of them immediately. By the same token, if they wanted to lease property, they would put something in the lease to protect the seminary. The person leasing the property could not use the premises for the sale of alcoholic beverages.

Did you engage in active discussion with this group?

I always sat with them, partially because they taught me a lot, and partially because by being there I symbolized that this was a very important function in the life of the institution. I was asking them for a big gift. Here was a lawyer who would be in a two-hour meeting. That was two hours where he would have no client billings. Or here was the president of a corporation. The fee for being a member of the board of directors of a corporation would be very high, but he was serving without compensation on the Southern Seminary board of trustees and its financial board.

When did the financial board begin to feel comfortable enough to invest in stocks as well as bonds?

This was one of my big problems—to get them to be willing to buy as much as 40 percent of their portfolio in stocks. It took a long time to get to 40 percent, but they finally got there. I think it now could run as high as 73 percent in the course of the years, but it would be well down from that level now.

What was the standard fee the seminary expected to pay for this kind of service?

I can't really answer that, and I ought not to guess at it, because that is a very precise figure. We usually ended up with a contract that specified a dollar amount. The attitude was that we were buying a financial consultant's time.

The financial board never asked for donations at that point. They paid for the service, and then they would want the service delivered. When they wanted the consultant to come down from Chicago for some special reason, they didn't mean to get a lot of explanation about why he couldn't come this month. They meant to know which day this week he would be there.

GREEN TREE MANOR/SEMINARY VILLAGE

How did the seminary come to buy Green Tree Manor, an apartment complex that was later renamed Seminary Village?

When Green Tree Manor was built, I was a student in the seminary. My wife and I tried to move out there, and they wouldn't rent to us because we were students and therefore transitory tenants. When I came back to Louisville as president, I found seminary students paying rent as high as $125 a month for a cold-water, over-the-garage apartment. I was outraged by what I considered to be gouging by apartment owners in the community. I was determined to break that. I set out to build 200 to 250 apartments along Grinstead Drive, but I couldn't find any way to fund it. Then I came up with the idea of buying the Green Tree Manor complex.

I found out that a man by the name of Lloyd Goode from Charlotte, North Carolina, owned Green Tree Manor. I chased around all over the country and finally found him in Sarasota, Florida, where I tried to negotiate with him. He wasn't interested in selling because the apartment complex was somehow mixed up in his corporate structure—locked into other projects that he owned.

After I got back to Louisville, I asked Faris Sampson, who had been sort of a business manager for the Norton interests and who was on the seminary board, to go to Charlotte and see if he could negotiate the purchase of Green Tree Manor with Lloyd Goode. He talked with Goode and got exactly the same answer he had given me.

As he got ready to leave Goode's office, Faris Sampson said, "I want to go to the First Baptist Church to see Pastor Casper Warren (who had been a seminary trustee)." Lloyd Goode said, "Well I am leaving my office; I'll take you by the church." They went to the church and entered the wrong door and went into the sanctuary of the church instead of the office section.

When Faris Sampson got back and was reporting on his trip, he told me, "I couldn't get any opening to buy Green Tree Manor, but I had a funny experience. Going through the sanctuary of the church, Lloyd Goode said, 'They've moved the baptistry.' Faris Sampson asked him, 'How do you know?' Goode replied, 'I ought to know; I was baptized here.'"

I had investigated Lloyd Goode every way I could, and there was absolutely no reference to religion anywhere in any report about him. I wanted to know who he was and how to get to him. I told Sampson, "That's what I've been looking for."

So I picked up the phone and called Mr. Goode. "I've been making a mistake," I told him. "I didn't know you had been a Baptist. I've been trying to buy Green Tree Manor from you, and I ought to have been trying to sell you Southern Seminary. I want you to come over here and give me equal time. I chased you all the way down to Sarasota, Florida, and sent Faris Sampson over to Charlotte. Now you ought to come over here and let me try to sell you on Southern Seminary.

"I want to tell you quite flatly what the deal is: First, I want Green Tree Manor Corporation. The second thing I want is a friend of Southern Seminary. Now I want two things for you: I want you to make a *little*—underscore *little*—money on the deal. But the second thing I want for you is that you will get a new grip on your religious faith and find your religious commitment again."

As foolish as that was, Goode said, in effect, "You're crazy, but I'll do it." So he flew over to Louisville one morning. I took him to the worship service in the seminary chapel—the good Lord does provide. The service was absolutely wonderful, the music was magnificent, the speaker was impassioned and intelligent and had a spiritual message of great power.

Then I took Lloyd Goode down to the meeting of the financial board of the trustees at the Pendennis Club for lunch. He got in with these other businessmen. They batted ideas back and forth, tested each other every way there was. He tried to pull some smart stuff on them, and they tried some on him. They both decided they were first-rate professionals. With that he just sat back and laughed, and said, "All right; I'll sell you Green Tree Manor Corporation for your price."

His idea was that he was not going to sell us the real estate; he was going to sell us the stock that represented the corporation that owned the Green Tree Manor property. Joe Stopher said, "Not on your life; we'd have to audit the corporation; we'd have to check the title of the real estate, and everything else. We couldn't settle that today."

Lloyd Goode looked down the table at me, and my face must have fallen two feet. I had worked so hard to get to that point, and then my lawyer friend was saying "nothing doing." With that Lloyd Goode took the stock certificate for 100 percent of the stock of the Green Tree Manor Corporation, turned it over, and wrote his name across the back of the stock to indicate he had sold it. He flipped the certificate down the length of the table where I was sitting, and said, "All right, Duke, you own it. You all figure out how much you owe me."

Then Goode went out and caught the plane. As I put him on the plane, he said, "My secretary's going to shoot me. I don't even have a receipt for the sale. If something happens to this plane, you'll never have to pay a dime for the Green Tree Manor Corporation."

That isn't the end of the story. When we did an audit of the corporation, we found out there was $40,000 in the corporation—money that we didn't know about—which we had bought. So I called him and said, "Lloyd, we found you sold us $40,000 cash that we don't think you meant to sell us." "Oh," he said, "you're right; I did forget that." And I said, "Well, how do you want it payable—to what corporation?" He replied, "Oh, no; that was an honest mistake I made. You just got a $40,000 better deal than you thought you did."

To finish my story, we got the Green Tree Manor Corporation, but we also got a friend. I never went to Charlotte after that without seeing him. I never saw him without getting a nice gift for the seminary. And he went back to the St. John's Baptist Church and became an active member for the rest of his life.

As it turned out, we paid $1.7 million for Green Tree Manor—less $40,000. The local daily newspaper, the *Courier-Journal,* had a fit about our buying it because they thought it was a speculative investment. Some of their staff lived out there, and they didn't like being told to move. Nobody believed that the seminary wanted 265 apartments to rent to students. But we did rent it to students, and we reduced the rent from what the Green Tree Manor Corporation was charging.

BUSINESS MANAGER

During one of the meetings of the executive committee of the trustee board, you asked for a business manager.

I don't think I got the request affirmed. I once offered the job of business manager to Bruce Heilman, and he may have been the prospect at that time. I believe he was at Peabody College. He was a very able fellow who has ended up as president of Meredith and finally the University of Richmond—a very astute academic administrator.

I thought the seminary needed a business manager. The business operation was growing bigger and bigger, and it involved all sorts of things—data processing, a department where stenographic work was done for a growing number of faculty members, and all sorts of strange and wondrous devices. Later on, it was computers and data processing machines, as well as maintenance of buildings and grounds and the handling of funds. The treasurer would keep the financial records, but I needed someone to do more than this—serve as purchasing agent, for instance.

The treasurer, P. H. Bufkin, had a big responsibility and served in that position for a number of years.

Yes, P. H. Bufkin did a fine job. He succeeded a member of the First Baptist Church of Atlanta—a Mr. Anderson—whom Fuller brought up to be the business manager of the seminary. He was apparently a high-powered businessman who came to Louisville with a sense of calling and dedication to serve the business interests of the seminary. So the idea of a business manager was not new to the institution.

In early 1956, Leslie Wright was considered as business manager. Is this the Leslie Wright who became president of Samford University?

Yes, that was another abortive effort to get a business manager. He was not interested in coming to work with us at that point. I thought he was available or I would not have brought his name before the trustees. We never could get our offer straightened out as a clean offer or get a clean response from prospects. It was a clumsily handled job, which may mean that I never knew exactly what I was talking about. Besides, Joe Stopher of the local trustees would not support Wright, with whom he had grown up.

FACULTY ATTENDANCE AT SBC

In January 1955 at the meeting of the executive committee of the trustees, it was agreed to pay expenses for professors to attend the Southern Baptist Convention in Miami. What was this about?

I wanted the whole crowd to go to Miami. I thought it would be fun, good for the morale, and good public relations for the Convention if we all showed up. I asked my public relations associate, Cort Flint, to go down and look up a place called "Key Biscayne Hotel and Villas" and see if he could get enough rooms for the seminary faculty and staff.

When he came back, I asked him, "Did you get enough rooms?" He replied, "It was such a good deal, I just rented the whole resort." This included about seventy-five villas and the entire four-story hotel.

Then he proceeded to sell rooms to various groups, like the state editors, as being a delightful place to stay. He filled up the whole thing and got the rooms free for the seminary faculty and staff. So it was a pretty good deal. It also meant the faculty could take their family if they wanted and then they could keep the children in one of the villas, which were right on the ocean. The Convention meeting place was in the southern part of Miami, so it really was quite convenient. This was one of the most delightful episodes in my thirty years at Southern Seminary.

Not long after this we set up a fee system for each professor, which provided for him to attend the Southern Baptist Convention and a professional society meeting. Because the amount of money involved was not enough to pay all of his expense every year, he was allowed, at his initiative, to accumulate the money for two years.

He could either go every year or he could save up and have twice as much money to go every other year. Most of the faculty saved up their money and went every other year, both to the Southern Baptist Convention and to their learned society meeting.

SOCIAL SECURITY AND RETIREMENT

In 1955 the trustees increased payments for Social Security for faculty and staff. What was behind this action?

The seminary agreed to pay half of the Social Security for ordained self-employed personnel, just as we were required to pay half for those non-ordained persons who were employed by the seminary. It may have been an effort to equalize what the seminary did for the ordained employees as well as for the non-ordained—the ordained being "self-employed" as defined by the Social Security Act.

At the same time the statement that the seminary was no longer responsible for widows of professors was approved. What prompted that action?

My guess is that this was related to the development of a retirement program. The seminary was pulling out of the original agreement that they would pay $100 a month to the professor and/or his widow. So the trustees were probably getting rid of that provision in favor of an adequate retirement program.

I'm sure we weren't reducing what we were doing for the widows of professors, because the effort was to enlarge what the seminary was paying rather than reduce it.

FACULTY RETIREMENT

About the same time (1955), it was indicated that there was no policy on retirement of the faculty and no policy on use of the faculty after retirement. Why was this?

Because the assumption originally was that when you started teaching at Southern Seminary, you would die in the classroom some day. If you could teach until ninety-eight, you would always be teaching on the faculty. That's why the seminary didn't need much in the way of a retirement program. Professors were expected to be on full salary until they died. But the seminary and the trustees were beginning to learn that this approach didn't work anymore. The student requirement of professors, for one thing, meant that a time would come when you couldn't get the students to accept a professor if he couldn't remember what he came to the classroom to talk about.

In addition to that, the retirement age was being moved downward in American society. Sixty-five was becoming the standard retirement age. So the seminary did the same thing, proposing to make retirement standard at sixty-five, with the possibility of extension up to age seventy. That meant we had to fund a retirement plan adequately so professors could take a fully-funded retirement at that age.

You are now retired. It has been almost thirty years since these discussions about faculty retirement took place. What's your philosophy of retirement now?

I told you at one point that I thought every school needed a new administrator about every five to seven years. When you get to the place where you can't project for the next five to seven years—how you're going to function and what you're going to do—you ought to retire. When you get to the place where there's a lot of day left at the end of energy, an administrator probably ought to consider retirement. When you get to the place where the pressure is getting to you and your zest for bouncing out of bed and rushing off to the fray is dissipating, the time for retirement is at hand.

Then a person needs to ask himself, What do I want to do in retirement? I'm going through the throes of agonizing reappraisal myself right now because my wife and I had some things in mind that we wanted to do in retirement. Her sudden death just a little over a month ago has thrown all of those dreams and plans out of focus. I'm now having to decide what I will do with myself in retirement. All of us need to realize that "the best laid plans of mice and men" with reference to retirement may not develop. But retirement depends so much on the individual person that I don't know if there is a single answer to that question on a philosophy of retirement.

Some people are such workaholics that they have only one set of interests. They will be absolutely lost when retirement comes. I've been a workaholic, I think. But I also have a variety of interests and many things I would like to do. Fortunately, my election as president of the Baptist World Alliance added a five-year extension to my working life, and I have more work to do than I will ever get done in those five years.

Would you favor, in looking back, a mandatory retirement at a younger age than sixty-five?

No, I think age sixty-five is about right, and I base this on observation of a great many people in professional education over the years. Very few professional educators have difficulty making it to sixty-five. A few begin to lose their effectiveness as early as sixty, with a rapid deterioration setting in toward sixty-five. By the time they get to sixty-five, everybody's glad for them to retire. If they hadn't retired, they might have been dismissed. I'm not being cruel about this. I'm just talking descriptively about what is a natural human process for many people.

Not many people go beyond sixty-five without beginning to show changes in personality, drive, and their commitment to goals. I think the retirement policy that Southern Seminary had is almost ideal: normal retirement at sixty-five, with one-year extensions going up to seventy, and then mandatory termination at age seventy. The normal person ought to retire, in my judgment, at about sixty-five, and it's wonderful if there is some expansion of that for two or three years that lets him coast to a stop.

Even after retirement, those who still have the energy and capacity for work ought to continue to do so. I think the denomination has some older ministers, for instance, who are exceedingly valuable. I think of Herschel Hobbs and J. D. Grey and some of that crowd. They are doing some fine things even during their retirement years. They are passing on the heritage of the denomination and its churches to newer generations of people and church leaders.

It would be marvelous if everybody could be reasonably comfortable economically in retirement so they could either work or not work, depending on their wishes and desires. I think the denomination makes a mistake in not using its older, mature people. We have been using such people at Southern Seminary for a long time—and with great profit to the seminary.

SABBATICALS INAUGURATED

Some people have charged that Baptists tend to inbreed—that we train our professors in our own institutions and then put them on the seminary staff to teach other people. Did you see that as a problem?

This was a very obvious problem in the early 1950s. It was an insoluble problem in that the seminary had to have a professor who was Baptist, and it had to have a Baptist who was at least sympathetic with the Southern Baptist Convention. Given those criteria, the best scholars you could find were Southern Seminary alumni. Now that did not continue to be true, and it is not true today. But in the early 1950s Southern Seminary, academically, was far beyond that of any other Southern Baptist seminary. Where did they get their faculty members? They elected Southern alumni.

The only solution I could find to the "inbreeding" problem was the sabbatical program, which we installed at Southern. It was designed not just to *give* sabbaticals, but to *require* sabbaticals. We tried to make it clear that the faculty member earned the right to a sabbatical but that the seminary's interest was best served if the professor actually took the sabbatical. Therefore, the seminary had some controls over where a professor should take his sabbatical.

There were numerous cases at Southern where faculty members did not want to take sabbaticals but were forced to take them. There were instances in which I called in a faculty member and said, "You are not due a sabbatical, but you're going to get a paid leave of absence. We can call it a sabbatical or a leave of absence. You're going to get it next year, and you're going to a certain place and stay there until you complete your doctorate because we need someone with a doctorate teaching in your area."

An illustration: Hugh McElrath didn't want to do that. But after he did, his wife thanked me for putting the pressure on him to complete his doctorate, which he did at Eastman. He has been a very effective member of the music faculty down through the years.

At Southern while I was president, we specifically required people to take sabbaticals who didn't want them. Further, we sometimes vetoed the purpose of a sabbatical or the place where a faculty member wanted to take a sabbatical. All this had to be reviewed and approved. The departments and the deans usually made the judgment call.

Clyde Francisco never forgave me for not letting him teach in the school in Beirut, Lebanon. But that would have had him teaching at a lower academic level than the seminary. I wanted him to do some work in very technical areas of Old Testament studies.

Subsequently his colleague, J. J. Owens, got to teach in Beirut by a fluke. J. J. was studying and teaching in Zurich and living in the home of a professor at Ruschlikon seminary. Something happened, and the plans of that professor were changed. He came back and ousted Owens from his living quarters and out of his teaching responsibilities at Ruschlikon. The only thing on the spur of the moment that Owens could do to finish his sabbatical year was to teach in Beirut.

I agreed to this. To his death Clyde Francisco never let me forget that I did something for Owens that I wouldn't do for him. He never knew that his colleagues recommended the restrictions on his sabbatical.

Was there resistance to this program on the part of the trustees?

Not real resistance, but trustees by the nature of things are never enthusiastic about sabbatical programs. As businessmen—or as pastors—they don't enjoy sabbatical programs, so you have to sell it. It's a continuous selling job. With the turnover in trustees, you will wake up one day and find that the trustees have discovered you are more valuable on campus teaching than you are off studying somewhere. This could cause them to pull the plug on the sabbatical program.

This is also why Southern had a strict rule that a professor couldn't take a sabbatical in Louisville. The reason for this is that the professor was too visible. Here was somebody who could come and go as he pleased. Now he could come and go as he pleased in Zurich, but he was not visible. So I always felt it was not wise for professors on sabbatical to be too visible, lest even their colleagues begin to complain about the way the sabbatical was being used.

What about mini-sabbaticals for the administrator? You took one for six months at one point.

I took two: one for six months and one for six weeks; one at Columbia and one at Harvard Business School. I really believe in education, even for presidents. And if I really believe in education, why not believe that a dean of students or a vice president for business affairs could learn something that would make him or her more efficient on the job? So we instituted a more limited program of sabbaticals for administrative personnel. In my judgment, it explains the strength of the administration at Southern Seminary.

I'm very proud of my colleagues in administration at Southern. They are a remarkable group of people with levels of skill and a repertoire of skills that is very impressive. I think the sabbatical program had a lot to do with this.

FACULTY STATUS FOR THE LIBRARIAN

At the March 1956 trustee meeting, the librarian of the seminary was accorded faculty status. Why did it take almost twenty-one years for the librarian to get that status?

Because of the system. He wasn't a teacher in the classic theological discipline. He was sort of an administrator, and you don't give administrators faculty status. Most of the time in the history of Southern, some faculty member like Hersey Davis was the librarian, and the actual librarian was the assistant librarian by title. The faculty would not let the person who actually operated the library be a faculty member.

I did insist that Dr. Leo Crismon get his master of library science degree before I would recommend faculty status for him. His doctorate was from Southern Seminary, but that was not the degree for a professional librarian—even if it helped him do his work. I thought the librarian had to be part of the teaching team of the seminary. Regardless of what other functions he had, he deserved to be a faculty member.

You use the terms "faculty status" and "administrator." What is the distinction in your mind?

To the faculty, someone who does classroom teaching is a faculty member. In my mind, there are various people involved in the academic operation of the institution who are bonafide faculty people. They deal with the teaching responsibility, the learning processes, just as much as the professors. To me, even field supervisors might be considered members of the faculty. But that wouldn't go over too well with some professors.

OPEN TRUSTEE MEETINGS

Were the meetings of the trustees at Southern always considered "open meetings" during your administration?

Yes. No meeting of the board of trustees of Southern Seminary was ever a closed meeting unless the body voted to go into executive session. They did that from time to time. But normally, any Southern Baptist could walk into the meeting. The full board meeting was always open to the press, the general public, the student body, and the faculty. From time to time, students would get irate about some issue and demand to be allowed to come to the trustee meeting. We always told them, "Any time you want to come, you're welcome."

So they would come and sit through about three or four meetings and find that it was hard work. I've never known the students to sit in board meetings more than about three years in a row, and then they would drop out. Certain faculty members will nearly always sit in on part of trustee meetings. But most faculty members never sit in on any of these meetings because they find them boring, routine, and just plain hard work. They are not really exciting meetings because they are work sessions.

ADMISSION OF WOMEN TO SCHOOL OF THEOLOGY

At the March 1956 meeting of the trustees, they adopted a policy on the admission of women into the School of Theology. Do you remember this?

I remember the struggles that went on. The School of Religious Education was against this, because they had traditionally trained women for the educational ministry in the church. By agreement between the School of Theology and the School of Religious Education, a man preparing for the pastorate couldn't enroll in the R. E. School. So now the R. E. School said, "If we can't train pastors, then you can't train women for religious education."

There was an evolution on the role of women going on in our society. Women were aspiring to roles that were not traditionally open to women, and they were preparing in the colleges for such roles. Then they began to come to the seminary and say, "We want to be prepared to do these ministries." For instance, one of the early specializations in the School of Theology was counseling, and then that evolved into chaplains

156

in the hospitals, and then that became ordained chaplains in the hospitals. No one ever challenged this development seriously because it was a part of the changes happening in society. Southern Seminary wasn't particularly leading the way in these changes. In fact, it was just one of the boats in the bay that were being raised with the tide.

At a certain point the consciousness of the faculty and the administration of Southern Seminary was raised. We came to discuss some serious biblical and theological issues. At that point the seminary began to ask, "What about that wall of partition that got broken down? What are the distinctions that are left in the religious community?" Very quickly the seminary moved to declare that we could not determine or stand in the way of what God was calling women to do.

LOCAL CHURCHES CERTIFY SEMINARY STUDENTS

Every student at the seminary must be approved and recommended for admission by a local church. Is this a responsibility that churches take seriously?

I've agonized over this situation many times. There was a time when the churches took this recommendation very seriously. The seminary could depend on it as being an authentic judgment of a local congregation who knew the student and who concurred in the student's sense of call to some aspect of ministry.

I do not think Baptist churches these days take very seriously even the ordination of ministers, much less the recommendation to a seminary. I could tell many stories about ridiculous things that churches have done, proving that local church recommendation is worth far less than it ought to be to the seminary. But the seminary, in terms of Baptist polity, has no way to substitute some other criteria for the church's endorsement.

If you assume, as I do, that the local congregation controls the matter of ordination of its ministry, it also controls selection, credentialing, and approval of its ministers. There is no way that the seminary can start deciding whether people are called to the ministry. It has to turn back to the church and say, "What do you want us to do about this person?"

Originally the seminary would not accept any person for admission as a student unless he or she was licensed or ordained. There was so much objection to the licensing or ordaining of musicians or religious educators that the seminary dropped this requirement. We only required a recommendation of the individual. This has been a major disaster because until that time, the churches would never license or ordain anyone unless that individual was a person of character, of proven Christian commitment, and had at least minimal gifts for functioning as a minister. Now none of those factors are necessarily implicit in a church recommendation for a student to be a candidate for the ministry.

I could tell horror stories about churches that recommended emotionally disturbed students, knowing they were emotionally disturbed but hoping the seminary might help them. That is exactly what won't happen. The pressures of the seminary are the wrong things to subject an emotionally disturbed person to. The seminary is a professional, graduate school, and the pressures on its student are rather high. If a student should break down, the seminary has done a great disservice to that student—but it did it on the recommendation of a local church.

Was this a continuing problem for the seminary during your administration?

Yes. It was there when I arrived as president in 1951. This problem did not exist at New Orleans between 1943 and 1946. It apparently developed during World War II. Churches began to say, "We must not fight against the Holy Spirit. If this person says he's called of God, who are we to say he is not a proper instrument of God?"

This is a denial of the assumption that the church is the body of Christ, and that the church as the body of Christ is capable of knowing the mind of Christ. If you drop that basic concept out, then the church cannot know the mind of Christ in an important matter, such as the choice of the ministers of Christ. This is a major flaw in current Southern Baptist church life.

SECRETARIES

Tell us about those who have served you as secretaries across the years.

Fortunately, both in Clara McCartt, who was then succeeded as my secretary by Bonnie Stowers, I had magnificent help. Other people recognized this. If Clara McCartt or Bonnie Stowers called somebody on the campus to say, "I've talked with the president about the question you asked, and his answer was such and such," that settled it. It got to the place where many people would call my secretary and ask for the decision and never even talk with me.

My dependence on excellent secretarial assistants goes all the way back to New Orleans Seminary. I've never mentioned in this context Theresa Anderson because she would be known as a missionary to China and to the Philippine Islands—a very competent foreign missionary. But Theresa, the daughter of one of the professors at New Orleans, was my secretary there. I have great friendship and affection for her.

When I went to Nashville, Miss Edwina Wenz was Dr. Austin Crouch's secretary. Unfortunately, we didn't know at the time that she was suffering from cancer. Illness forced her retirement and rather early death.

I hired Clara McCartt, who had worked for the Sunday School Board but was at that time secretary to Paul Caudill, pastor of the First Baptist Church, Memphis, Tennessee. My father recommended her to me. Clara McCartt came back to Nashville and went to work for me. She served five years in Nashville and then for another twenty-five years in Louisville. Then she found Bonnie Stowers, who was the executive secretary for the head of the Baptist Hospitals in Kentucky. Bonnie (Mrs. Earl) Stowers spent a year working with Clara McCartt, so the transition was smooth. Bonnie is now assistant to the president of Southern Seminary, a job she held long before she held the title.

Before I anticipated the death of my wife, Clara McCartt had come back the week of Marguerite's death to be secretary to me as chancellor of Southern Seminary. On Easter Sunday when she heard in Crescent Hill Baptist Church of Marguerite's death that morning, she walked out of the worship service and came over and went to work as my secretary. She took over matters in my home, as she would have in an earlier time.

My children know her as "Aunt Clara." They were the ones who insisted that she sit with the family at the funeral. She is now functioning as my secretary as president of the BWA. Clara and I have worked together for over fifty years. It continues until today as she helps edit this oral history for publication.

These marvelous secretaries, or assistants, or executive assistants—whatever you want to call them—have been colleagues in the enterprise. They've never worked a forty-hour week; they've worked until the job was done. They haven't worked for the salary. They've worked because they felt they were called of God to serve. I have profited greatly from their expertise and commitment. Their efficiency and intelligence always made me look good.

CHAPTER 9

Southern Seminary Controversy

1958

In 1957 there was a new order at Southern Seminary. Some of the faculty members were sympathetic to the changes that were taking place, and some were diametrically opposed to them. Is that true?

Yes, we had completely revised the curriculum. There were still some open wounds from that revision. Some people weren't delighted with what had happened to them in that revision. Then we started revising the structure and procedures of the seminary, spelling out some things that had been implicit.

To illustrate how these changes were affecting people, it took the faculty a long time to learn to go to the dean, or—before that—to the acting dean. They wanted to come to the president directly to get the decision. I kept saying to them, "I'm interested in the problem you pose, but you know that is a matter that has been put in the hands of the dean. You need to talk with him." Faculty members would always take this as a put-down, no matter how I tried to soften the rhetoric.

There was a point at which I went to each of the dissident faculty members and visited him privately, and said, "Now let's forget all of this high-toned rhetoric. The question really is, What is it you have to do that you don't like having to do? What is it you are prevented from doing that you want to do? What is it the president does that you dis-like? What is it the president doesn't do that you want him to do? Your answer will never be used by me outside of this room. All this stuff about academic freedom and the rights of the faculty are general terms, but where does the water hit the wheel (to use Louie Newton's phrase)?"

Out of that discussion I received only one complaint. One faculty member said, "Mr. president, the problem is you ask the faculty's advice, and you don't take it, and you never tell us why."

My reply was, "That is a legitimate complaint, and I will try to correct it. I should have told you why I didn't take your advice. I do insist that all I ever asked for was advice, not instructions, so the fact that I didn't take it was legitimate. But I am in error, and I apologize, and I'll correct my failure."

RESPONSIBILITIES OF THE PRESIDENT

After the acceptance of the Booz, Allen & Hamilton report in 1957, you became, strictly speaking, the chief executive officer of the seminary and had responsibilities in several different areas. For example, responsibility to the faculties of the three schools, the trustees, the Convention, and the American Association of Theological Schools, as it was called then. So you had a real balancing act to perform.

Yes, but I had all of those responsibilities before. During the earlier years as president, I had to deal directly with thirty-plus faculty members as dean of the School of Theology plus all the students in the School of Theology who wanted to talk to the dean.

The Encyclopedia of Southern Baptists *makes this comment about you: "As one trained in theology himself, he sympathized with the then sizable portion of his theology faculty who stressed thorough academic training in theology." Then it goes on to say: "He possessed a keener sensitivity than many faculty members to the gap that separates the seminary from the churches," and then further on, "so the president also shared the view of those who advocated a practical training for the churches in their current state." Is that substantially true?*

To a large degree. I had to look at the denomination as a whole. But the faculty didn't buy this, and it doesn't even today. I have talked to individual faculty members saying this kind of thing: "You tell me that you've been out among the churches. But the problem is you've been out to the churches that shared your views and invited you to come to speak to them. I have to deal with associational missionaries and state secretaries and editors and members of the SBC Executive Committee."

I wasn't alone in this experience. There were other faculty members who sensed exactly what I did. They argued along with me for responsiveness by the seminary to the average Southern Baptist.

There were also members of the faculty who, for philosophical reasons, opposed any movement toward practical training. They thought that the body of divinity was all that the Bachelor of Divinity degree ought to signify, and that staff members of churches ought to get all of their practical training after they graduated from the seminary. That was a minority view, but it had its articulate supporters.

You also produced a book on Baptist ecclesiology, or edited a collection of essays, published by Broadman, entitled What Is The Church? *Evidently you made some effort to urge faculty members to participate more actively in academic debate and discussion of this kind.*

Not only that, I did several things to try to get them to write more and to participate more in denominational affairs. For instance, if they taught in the area of Christian ethics, I urged them to participate in what later became the Christian Life Commission's work and programs—to attend the meetings if they could. I offered to fund travel to certain types of meetings. This, by the way, was done not out of the seminary's budget but out of a discretionary fund underwritten mostly by Maxey Jarman, a Baptist businessman from Nashville, Tennessee.

I could use the Jarman Fund for anything except the president's interest. I could use it to say to a faculty member, "If you want to go to this meeting in London, or in Nashville, I'll find the money to pay your expenses." That would come out of this discretionary fund. The use of these funds did not require trustee approval, although it was always audited and reported.

Apparently your efforts and the changes you were making produced some serious misunderstandings within the faculty. They had a series of informal faculty meetings between 1957 and 1958. Did you know about any of these at the time?

No, I did not. Henry Turlington was very prominent in faculty leadership at that time. Maybe he was chairman of the biblical division, or something of that sort. He had a way of making accusations that the president was taking over the duties of the faculty. At some point I said to him in a faculty meeting, "Let's discuss these matters, but move away from your accusations because I'm having trouble controlling my temper when you do that. I don't want us to get into an angry confrontation."

But then he did exactly the same thing in another faculty meeting, after I had asked him not to do it without specific charges that he could support. When the meeting was over, I called him into the president's office, and I let my temper fly. I raked him over the coals, up one side and down the other. I probably threw every charge I could think of against him. I indicated that as far as I was concerned, his usefulness at Southern Seminary would approach an end if he couldn't stop making these unsupported accusations.

After this confrontation was over and I reflected on it, I was furious with myself. I went back to Turlington and apologized. My recollection is that he accepted my apology without accepting any responsibility for provoking the situation.

One other thing that happened about this time needs to be told. At some point Professor Guy Ranson came on the faculty. I thought he was supported by and advocated by Theron Price, who later indicated that this was not true. My respect for Price's judgment had tilted my support for Ranson. We did not have a set procedure for faculty additions at that time, and I was trying to demonstrate my confidence in the faculty's judgment.

When Price withdrew his support from Ranson, I went to my true position, which was a sense of discomfort about him. That brought out the fact that Ranson had already resigned as professor at William Jewel and had no job if we didn't hire him at Southern Seminary.

In an effort to cooperate with faculty members, I did not veto Ranson's appointment. I should have. As a faculty member, he never cared much for the president. He expressed his displeasure by referring to the president with the initials SOB. [At that time television and movies had not made this term little more than slang. SOB was the ultimate slur. The involvement of one's mother made this the occasion for fisticuffs between strangers in those days.—DKM]

I was told about this and promptly called him into my office, along with Dean Hugh Peterson. I was following Matthew 18 by confronting Ranson in the presence of a witness.

I told Dr. Ranson that if he used these words about me one more time, he would be dismissed from the seminary. This was a major blunder on my part. I should have fired him or found some other method of handling the problem. What I did was to drive him underground. He never appeared to take any opposition to the president after that—at least, in a public sense. But I think he was the source of the infection in faculty morale and relations as far as the president was concerned.

Ranson's addition to the faculty was a blunder, a major blunder. I regretted that long before the 1957–58 controversy, but I came to regret it more before the controversy was over. This blunder made me feel that I was left out on the limb because of placing too much confidence in the process of faculty recommendations or faculty additions.

Perhaps this illustrates that the president as well as the faculty was having some difficulty working into the new procedures—which were in flux for some time before the Booz, Allen & Hamilton report recommended that they be restructured.

FACULTY COMPLAINTS

According to the Encyclopedia of Southern Baptists, *some things the faculty objected to were the delay in promoting some faculty members compared to the rapid promotion of others, the apparent arbitrariness of adding new faculty, the representation the president was making of the seminary to the denomination, and the failure to appoint a permanent dean. Were these charges true?*

All those charges have some element of truth in them, although they are not of equal value. These charges came from a group or bloc of faculty members, not the whole faculty. A group of professors was beginning to form a coalition that was becoming very aggressive in airing their complaints and discussing the problems relating to the seminary.

The trustees had indicated they sensed this problem developing. In my report to the trustees in their annual meeting in 1958, my report gave quite a list of charges I would make against myself. It has always intrigued me that the faculty members never did use that list. In other words, I had pled guilty to some charges that were, in my judgment, more serious than some of the charges they were bringing—for example, the Turlington issue of impatience and bad temper.

In my report to the trustees, I spelled this out; I also spelled out the element of fatigue and difficulty in responding quickly to the legitimate complaints of the faculty. I felt that one of the problems with the faculty was that they were uncomfortable in their economic situation. That was partially reflected, for example, in the absence of promotion and raises for the faculty.

FACULTY INVOLVEMENT IN PROMOTION

The faculty—specifically the senior professors—was a part of the evaluative process that determined who got promoted and who got the salary increases. That's one of those details that the faculty ignored. Since the president would make the recommendation to the board of trustees, the president did it all. They didn't like to remember that maybe the president had not even been in favor of that action in the meeting of the full professors. That was a part of the process. The full professors would meet and go over the matter of merit ratings and promotions with the president.

In at least one instance, the president struggled to get promotion to full professorship status for a certain man and was voted down by the written ballot by which the full professors make their decision known—an anonymous yes/no written ballot. The president advocated the promotion of this man, but the full professors voted him down. Later they told this professor that the president had kept him from being promoted. So they got it a little garbled about exactly who was not supporting whom for promotion.

I think I need to call names or this will sound like remembering to advantage. I was for promoting J. J. Owens, but the full professors voted against his promotion. Then J. J. Owens was enlisted as a part of their group on the basis that the president had objected to his promotion. Well, it was clear the president hadn't recommended his promotion to the trustees because Dr. Owens didn't get promoted. The president could refuse to promote with a majority vote of the full professors, but he couldn't promote with a majority vote against a professor.

Was this the procedure followed after the Booz, Allen & Hamilton study, or the pattern before that time?

This was a pattern evolved before that time, and it involved a very formal procedure. The full professors met on a certain day, usually in the president's home on Saturday morning, and we started with breakfast. We fed them lunch, and even ended up once having to feed them supper because the meeting lasted so long. This wasn't a perfunctory meeting, and the whole business of promotion of younger colleagues was aired. This process went through many versions and variations because the full professors disliked being involved in it.

Then, as you've read, they turned around and complained that the president was arbitrarily making decisions about faculty promotions. The president would say, "There isn't anybody else but the president and you making these decisions; and unless you're going to help make the decisions, I stand alone. Then they wanted it arranged so their action would be anonymous. In this way, they would never be held responsible by their colleagues for what happened. This left the president as the only person in the spotlight.

If the entire system involving faculty promotions is considered, the complaints from the professors begin to appear ridiculous because there was a conscious effort by me as president to involve the faculty in the decision-making process. I got the feeling that the faculty members were as angry about being partly responsible for the decision as they would have been if they had been left out of the decision. If a full professor participated in a tough decision, he didn't want to be identified with it among his colleagues.

I kept trying to involve the faculty in the decision-making process in a way that they could be comfortable with. I never succeeded. We (the full professors and I) formalized it; we made it as mechanical as we could. We set up the criteria for judging a professor, by secret ballot, on a scale from 1 to 5, so that, in effect, they could say, "Yes I recommend his promotion, but in terms of my evaluation of the important characteristics, I evaluate him as 1," which would mean well below promotion. That way they could have it both ways: They could say, Yes I recommend promotion on that line of the form, but then they could rate him so low on the other items that promotion was impossible.

A rating of 3 was the minimum rating for recommending promotion. Theoretically, a professor had to average 3 for the president to think that promotion had been recommended by the full professors.

In the end, after the full professor had filled out the eight items on a 1-to-5 rating, there was this question "Do you recommend promotion?" This required a yes or no answer.

The faculty member could actually give the professor a low 1 on all eight items and then say, "Yes, I recommend promotion." Then he was on record so, if he were queried, he could reply, "Yes, I recommended promotion." But he knew full well that the president, reading that evaluation, would read it as a negative evaluation.

Some senior professor in the meeting would have to advocate each professor's promotion and would make, in effect, a little speech. By the way, the full professors would have in their hands the vita that the faculty member himself had completed about what he had done, was doing, and had achieved. He was the one who provided the information about himself, in writing, to each of the full professors. He always had an advocate who spoke in his favor, and then he might have some people who would raise questions about facets of the vitae. Then all the full professors had to rate him.

The other problem I could never solve was that these full professors would not keep what went on in that meeting confidential. At least one of them would feel obligated to tell the candidate what somebody else in the meeting had done or said about him because the rating would be made after discussion.

We never cut down the leakage. I understand the problem the president of the United States has in stopping leaks from within his own staff. I actually threatened to recommend the firing of any professor identified as leaking information from that meeting. I never identified anybody, although I suspected a few.

The leakage didn't usually hurt the president. The leakage generally hurt another faculty member. It wasn't the president trying to stop the leakage to protect his position. There was a sense in which the president would have been better off if the whole meeting had been available to the general public. Then it would have been apparent that his influence and power were highly modified by the counsel he received from the full professors.

This faculty group also raised questions about the fact that some professors weren't being promoted very quickly, and others were promoted rapidly. Do you know what they had in mind in this suggestion?

A majority of the full professors had voted no on promoting those who weren't promoted, and a majority of the full professors had given 4 and 5 ratings to those people who got fast promotions. Again, that rating sheet was unsigned. All the full professors had to do was to write figures rating each candidate for promotion and then to check yes or no for promotion. There was no way for the president to know how any full professor had rated professor John Doe.

SEARCH FOR A THEOLOGY DEAN

How do you respond to the charge from some faculty members that you had failed to appoint a permanent dean for the School of Theology?

To answer this, I have to go back to early 1958. Henlee Barnette was acting dean; and we were looking for a permanent dean. One of my closest friends on the faculty was Dr. William Morton. He and his wife Thelma were also close friends of my wife Marguerite.

Let me illustrate how close we were with this anecdote: The only woman other than my own wife whom I ever carried flowers to for no particular reason was Thelma Morton. She was feeling badly about something, and I bought a bouquet of flowers and went by her house to try to cheer her up. My closest confidant was Bill Morton.

At an early point in the search for a permanent dean for the School of Theology, I had asked Bill to come into my office. I told him, "Bill, the faculty is trying to find a permanent dean. They are looking for the one they want to recommend. Eventually they're going to think of you, and they're going to recommend you. I want to look you square in the eye as a friend and tell you that I do not want you to be dean. I'm prepared to tell you why, if you want to hear it."

He immediately responded, "You don't have to tell me why; that's the act of a friend. I must not be dean; I shouldn't be dean; I don't want to be dean."

"O.K." I said, "with that out of the way, I'll tell you another reason why I called you in. I would like to have as dean your younger colleague, Morris Ashcraft, who has been on the faculty too short a time to have proven himself to the faculty. But he's proven himself to me, and I believe in him, and I would like for him to be dean. I'm going to need your help in either delaying this decision until we can get him ready and move him into position from which the faculty will be willing to accept him. Or, I'm going to need your help in advocating him as the dean. He's my choice for the permanent dean of the School of Theology."

My tendency was to name young persons to administrative jobs, with the idea of on-the-job training. I felt that Ashcraft was very talented, very gifted, and very able. He had military experience and organizational know-how that would equip him to understand what he was dealing with. I thought he would not threaten the faculty because he was so young that they wouldn't feel he might lord it over them.

After this conversation with Bill Morton, someone in a faculty meeting did propose Morton as dean. Obviously, I expected Morton to remove himself from any possible consideration because I thought it was clear to him what my position was. I had been quite explicit about that. I assumed that by the time we got into other meetings dealing with this issue, he either would already have eliminated himself or he would eliminate himself in the meeting.

Why do you think he didn't?

It's one thing to say, "I don't want to be president of the United States," and it's another thing to tell the Democratic Party, "I won't accept the nomination that you have tendered me." When the job was actually available and offered, Morton gave a perfectly human reaction: "I hear a mandate from my colleagues and therefore I'm going to reverse what I said to the president." I won't quarrel with him for doing that. But I do criticize him harshly for not coming back to me and telling me he had reversed his position. I assumed the commitment we had made to each other was still in force. I had restated my position in his presence at the faculty meeting on March 19.

At the next faculty meeting, on March 27, the faculty presented Morton as their recommendation for dean. There were four dissenting voices from the faculty—from four professors who had talked to me about being opposed to Morton for various reasons. These were differing reasons of their own, not my reasons.

My reasons for not wanting Morton were fairly clear, and one of them was basically health. I did not think he could manage the job in the face of his asthma attacks. As dean you can't be present for meetings only when it suits you. You have to be there on certain occasions, whether you are healthy or not, because the decisions have to be made. Further, I thought Morton was capable of becoming one of the world's best biblical archaeologists. I wanted a famous biblical archaeologist on the faculty. Those were my only two reasons for objecting to Bill Morton as dean.

The faculty then voted on Morton. There was no dissenting vote, I believe, in the March 27 meeting to support him as dean. I publicly rejected the recommendation and substituted the name of Cornell Goerner as the president's recommendation for dean—because Morton had now blocked my choice of his younger colleague, Morris Ashcraft, by being willing to accept the job himself. (Ashcraft later became dean of Southeastern Baptist Theological Seminary). I recommended Goerner to the faculty for their support or rejection.

GOERNER OFFERED THEOLOGY DEANSHIP

We had an agreement among the SBC agencies that we didn't approach one another's personnel without notifying the executive of that agency. In one of those peculiar twists that doesn't make any sense to anybody, the Foreign Mission Board had approached Cornell Goerner to be secretary for Europe, Africa, and the Near East and had failed to notify me. And Cornell Goerner had told the Foreign Mission Board he would accept the job.

I not only crawled out on a limb; I crawled out on a limb that had already been sawed off when I got there. I knew nothing about Goerner and his acceptance of the Foreign Mission Board job; as Goerner himself will verify. This was just one of those times when the routine procedure of notifying the head of an agency of an employment offer to somebody in that agency broke down. The Foreign Mission Board hadn't notified me. They couldn't know the harsh consequences of that oversight.

I had let the faculty of the seminary recommend as dean a professor whom I wouldn't accept. After vetoing their choice, I recommended a person who had already taken a job with another agency! It was just one of those days when the cookie crumbles wrong, whatever you do. Then Bill Morton showed up as chairman of the group of thirteen dissident professors to present the supplemental report to the trustee committee in June 1958.

The warm relationship with him and his family disappeared, I assume?

Yes, though it has been reactivated to a small degree. I have just this morning read for the second time a Christmas card with a very warm, cordial communication to my wife from Thelma Morton. There's no active hostility between Bill Morton and me, but we've never attempted to reestablish the close ties of friendship that once existed between us.

Was that a bitter disappointment to you?

Very much so, because I had confided in Bill what was in my mind and heart. I had been open with him about all my problems, dreams, and plans. For him to reverse his position on the deanship without communicating with me and then to end up as the secret leader of the opposition were two of the most bitter personal elements in the entire 1958 controversy. It's one of the few things that really kept on hurting long after the controversy was ancient history. I still feel betrayed by a friend.

He should have been the first person to tell me not only about my problems but also about my mistakes, my failures, and my faults. That would have been the act of a true friend.

Incidentally, I've reestablished a fairly cordial friendship with most of the thirteen professors. But this does not include Bill Morton, Theron Price, or Guy Ranson.

1958 FACULTY REPORT TO THE TRUSTEES

The first open expression of resentment came at the trustee meeting of March 11–12, 1958. With only two dissenting votes, the School of Theology faculty adopted and sent to the trustees a report that expressed concern over the Booz, Allen & Hamilton report and cited "low morale existing in the faculty." They raised questions about the power of the president to appoint non-permanent faculty for three years. When did you learn of this report?

I learned about it when the report was made to the trustees. And there was no reason why I should have known about it sooner. It was the regular faculty report to the trustees. I was surprised at some of it because the three-year temporary appointment for faculty members was something the faculty had to be involved with. The only way you could hire a faculty member was to elect him at an annual meeting of the board of trustees.

With the faculty involvement in the selection process, the president could appoint a professor for a maximum of three years. This was long enough to entice him to take the job, but it also gave the faculty and president enough time for him to be evaluated. By the end of the three years the faculty and administration and the trustees would agree either to keep him or to give him a gentle farewell.

So this matter of three-year appointments for faculty was actually a way of meeting another faculty demand—namely, give us more help. It was an attempt to try to give more help to the faculty by adding teaching personnel for a short period of time. It bought us time to make the decision for permanent appointment at some other time in the year besides the mid-March annual trustee meeting.

It interests me that you did not know the details of this faculty report before that March meeting of the trustees.

If I had been a member of the faculty committee, I doubt that I would have wanted to take that report to the president's office. As a matter of principle and policy, I did not seek to find out what the faculty had done, whether it was to commend or condemn, or what issues they would raise with the trustees.

Would you say a little more about the specific disagreements with the faculty, based on this faculty report to the trustees?

This was the first time the faculty as a whole had said, in effect, "We're unhappy, we're dissatisfied, things are not going well, the Booz, Allen & Hamilton report is taking our rights away from us." They really thought that. By now, they had discussed the matter until they had concluded that the function of the Booz, Allen & Hamilton report was to centralize all power at the seminary in the hands of the president. But I did not see any place where I thought the faculty members were reduced in their decision-making power with reference to the academic functions of the seminary.

I need to share a yarn here that may illustrate what I'm talking about. At one point, Dr. E. A. McDowell of the seminary faculty had come in to my office to complain that the seminary was putting up a maintenance building, and the faculty hadn't approved it. I said, "Dr. McDowell, I can tell you how many square feet the building will have. It will be over behind the heating plant, and it will be constructed of concrete blocks with Flemish bond brick on the outside."

I had insisted that it be Flemish bond so it would match the other buildings on the campus instead of looking like a different type of building. That was my total contribution to the plan. And I said, "When you get to asking me about the plans, I don't know how many square feet are in the paint shop, or the carpenter shop, or anything else. That's something I've left to the architect and T. R. Allen. I know how much that building will cost per square foot, but you and any other faculty member are welcome to go by Mr. Allen's office at any time to take a look at the plans."

He was complaining that the faculty didn't know some details about a new structure that the president didn't even know about. This shows that faculty members were still thinking they ought to be in on deciding whether to build a maintenance building, where to build it, how big to build it, and what its layout should be. But the faculty had already lost decisions about buildings. They lost that back when Ellis Fuller was elected president, and they certainly lost it when I was elected because I never even considered that to be an issue.

Decisions about buildings and grounds were staff and trustee decisions. Remember, however, that faculty additions, faculty promotions, and all curriculum matters required decisions by the faculty.

A great deal of emphasis was made at the time the faculty issued this report to the trustees and throughout the controversy that only principle was involved and not personalities. Is that true?

No. Personalities were very much involved in this controversy. It is not at all unusual—with this many different people—that there should be conflicts and personal clashes between individuals. It's normal. The 1958 controversy moved very quickly away from principle to personality.

It was March 11–12, 1958, when the trustees met at their regular annual meeting. In early April, Dean Allen Graves of the School of Religious Education and Dean Forrest Heeren of the School of Church Music either were on the campus of Mississippi Baptist College, or had gone to Clinton, Mississippi, and had told Howard Spell, the chairman of the trustees, that tension had erupted at Southern Seminary. Did you know anything about that meeting?

No. I knew they had been there, but I had nothing to do with their going. I did not send them. They may have gone on their own out of concern. And this would have been within a pattern that I've described to you—that they would have the authority to do what they perceived to be in the best interest of their respective schools. As deans, they would have been justified in saying that what was happening would be disruptive, although it was happening in the School of Theology.

What was your relationship generally with Howard Spell?

I had a warm relationship with all of the trustees. I would have been very comfortable with him, and I think he would have been very relaxed with me. Since he was the chairman of the trustees, I would have looked to him to speak with candor and freedom. There was never any real difficulty between us. The problem was that I needed help.

COALITION OF THIRTEEN FACULTY MEMBERS FORMED

On April 28, 1958, a committee of the trustees met in Louisville to assess the situation that, as they said, involved the dissatisfaction of the faculty with the seminary administration. Four days before this meeting, William L. Lumpkin of the faculty wrote to the trustees that they did not get a full report of the recent trustee meeting. He asked for an occasion to meet with the trustees. At about the same time, apparently, a coalition of thirteen professors who were defending the dissident position was formed. Had many of the other professors been pacified or satisfied? What did you think had happened?

Thirteen professors could get a majority vote for the faculty report. This means that the entire faculty would vote to tell the trustees that a problem existed that demanded their attention. But not every member of the faculty felt they had said, "I have these problems." The faculty instinct is to support its committee. It's understandable that they assigned a committee the responsibility of drawing up the report.

When that report was presented to the faculty before it went to the trustees, they tended only to add some things to it, never to take anything out of it. Psychologically, their position was that if anybody was having these problems, they ought to tell the trustees.

What I finally concluded was that the hard-nosed, organized group of thirteen professors had drawn up the report and gotten the full faculty to support the report to the trustees. I never did think that the entire faculty was on that side. A full faculty vote did not necessarily mean that every faculty member agreed with what was in the report. It meant they agreed that what was said ought to be shared with the trustees.

The chronology seems to be that thirteen faculty members who felt deeply on this issue were organized in the latter part of April just before this special meeting of the trustee committee.

Of the thirteen, five had been appointed before you became president; the others had been added by you. Let me list the names: John J.

Owens, professor of Old Testament, joined the faculty in 1948. William H. Morton, professor of archaeology, joined the faculty in 1948. Theron D. Price, professor of church history, joined in 1948. Henry E. Turlington, associate professor of New Testament, joined in 1949. Taylor Clarence Smith, associate professor of New Testament, joined in 1950. J. Estill Jones, associate professor of New Testament, joined in 1951. Guy H. Ranson, associate professor of ethics, joined in 1952. William L. Lumpkin, associate professor of church history, joined in 1954. J. Morris Ashcraft, associate professor of archaeology, joined in 1955. Heber F. Peacock, associate professor of New Testament, joined in 1956. John M. Lewis, associate professor of theology, joined in 1956. Tom L. Hall Jr., associate professor of Old Testament, joined in 1956. G. Hugh Wamble, associate professor of church history, also joined in 1956.

So there were at least six of the thirteen—almost half—who had joined the faculty a short time before this meeting. All of them were alumni of the seminary, and five of these had received promotion at the trustee meeting in March. This is interesting—that they were promoted just before they raised such strong opposition.

It probably reflects some of their frustration and anxiety before the 1958 meeting of the trustees because they weren't supposed to know they were going to be promoted. The anxiety factor sometimes doesn't go away with the realization of a goal. They probably felt they should have been promoted two or three years earlier.

SUPPLEMENTARY REPORT OF THE THIRTEEN

These thirteen professors next proposed a supplementary report and presented this report to the committee of trustees when it arrived?

That's my recollection. The supplemental report was very interesting in a lot of ways. First of all, it was at the point of this report that the thirteen almost lost their case. They had asked for the privilege of making a report to the trustees. This was not out of line or unusual. I met with the trustees about noon when they came on campus. Then I absented myself from the meeting while the faculty members came to make their report.

It was dinnertime by the time the trustees called me back in to the meeting. That night at dinner I was the only happy person there. I wondered what the gloom was all about, and I was trying to joke and exchange pleasantries with the trustees.

Finally one of the trustees said, "You don't know about the supplemental report?" I responded, "I don't know what you're talking about." They said, "You mean you've never seen a copy of the charges in the supplemental report?" I said, "I've never heard of the supplemental report or any charges."

PRESIDENT'S CONFERENCE WITH THE THIRTEEN

On May 12, 1958, there was a long meeting between you and this coalition of thirteen professors. Were you told by the trustees to try to resolve your problems?

I understood that I was under such a mandate. But I don't want to take responsibility for calling the group together, although I would have wanted such a meeting. I can't remember whether I called it or somebody else did. The meeting started with my insistence that our proceedings be kept out of the press. Dr. Hugh Wamble insisted that there would be no such limitation on the meeting. I responded, "In that case, I might as well withdraw because I won't talk with you. There's no way we're going to make any progress unless we can talk candidly to one another without what I construe as your misrepresentation to the press of what I say."

We spent the first thirty or forty minutes arguing about that. I left the meeting so they could iron out their differences. They did call me back; and then they argued among themselves for a period of time until they got consensus. They operated, basically, on this premise: All thirteen of us must agree on everything, and then all of us are bound by everything we agree to.

What happened at this meeting? Did you just argue back and forth and get nowhere?

Essentially so, because they were operating as a bloc. I became aware that this was a major problem. I felt I could reach agreement with individuals, but coming to terms with a group was another matter. They were determined that no one of them would reach an agreement with me separately from the others. I've always thought that if they had functioned as independent persons, I could have negotiated a settlement with at least eight or nine of them without any problem.

BROADMAN COMMENTS

One part of the faculty's charges against you related to alleged plagiarism in Broadman Comments *for 1958.*

We need a little background to understand that charge. Southern Seminary had never espoused the Landmark view of the church. I had quarreled with the Sunday School Board people from time to time because only the Landmark view of the church appeared in Sunday School Board literature.

The first quarter of Sunday school lessons in 1958, I believe, was on the doctrine of the church. So the Sunday School Board asked me to provide the *Broadman Comments* materials for that study. I indicated there was absolutely no way I could write the material because of my other commitments.

They responded, "You're always complaining that we don't present the alternative to the Landmark view; now you have an opportunity to do it, and you're not willing to take the assignment."

I said, "Why don't you let Southern Seminary professors write the material?" I tried to get the Sunday School Board to let me edit what the faculty would write.

"No," they replied, "because this is very controversial. You will have to take responsibility for the material because that is one of the ways we will defend ourselves from the Landmark element. They will dislike what you say as much as you dislike what they believe. If the fall-out is dispersed among all the Southern Seminary faculty, the Sunday School Board will still take all the heat."

I agreed to this approach. Then I called a group of faculty members together and said, "I'm not very enthusiastic about this approach. But I've worked so long to get an alternative view of the church in the Sunday School Board literature that I don't want to pass it up. What do you fellows think about it?"

It didn't take long to generate plenty of volunteers to write the material that I would edit. We agreed that the material would be published under my name. I did take the precaution of writing a contract with each professor. It was clear that I had not imposed this on anybody. The idea of plagiarism had not occurred to any of us at this point. We agreed to collaborate to get a different point of view on the church into *Broadman Comments.*

Did the names of the others who participated in this project appear anywhere in the literature?

No, they did not. There is another twist to this that must be added. I still have the original faculty contributions. To my horror, some of them were poorly done. So I ended up writing about half of the material myself. I did use all of the faculty material that I found useful. I didn't use any given percentage of their material. If I could have used 100 percent of what they wrote and none of my own, that's what I would have done.

Later on, in the midst of controversy, some of those professors who wrote the material began to use the word *plagiarism*. They said they didn't expect me to use the material they turned in, whereupon I always asked, "How much of your material did you sell me?"

I purchased their material by diverting to the faculty members every penny that was paid by the Sunday School Board for this material. I received not one red penny from any of this. It was a way to let the faculty make a little money and to get their views published. I still have the checks I wrote to them with their endorsement to indicate that they accepted the pay. I divided the compensation equally among the faculty members who agreed to do the writing. They weren't under any illusions about what they were getting that money for.

Did you get criticism from people who read the material?

Of course. I got none of the money, all of the criticism, and then the charges of plagiarism after the seminary controversy erupted. It was a bad deal all the way around. I hate to think I was ever that stupid!

PRESIDENT'S LETTER OF RESIGNATION

After the subcommittee of the board of trustees met during the week of April 28, they notified the thirteen professors on May 9 that they would support the president at the full trustee meeting, which was scheduled during the Southern Baptist Convention in Houston. This trustee committee made this statement: "On the basis of the charges made and the testimony heard, we have full confidence in the integrity and character of the president, recognize that in the administration of duties errors of judgment were made which contributed to the president's difficulty. Despite these errors, we have confidence in him as an able administrator." I heard somewhere that you had prepared a letter of resignation that you were prepared to give to the board of trustees.

I wrote out an undated letter of resignation, presented it to the chairman of the board of trustees, Dr. Lamar Jackson, and he carried it around in his wallet for two years.

When did you write that letter?

I'm not sure, but it would have been after the actual dismissal of the dissident professors. I would have done it then because I also said to Dr. Jackson, "The trustees may think they've ended this, but they really haven't. With the dismissal of this many faculty members, I suspect that it won't take long for the rest of the faculty to decide they want a new president. You hold this letter in your pocket. When you feel that the trustees really would like to have a new president, you pull it out and read it."

I also told Dr. Jackson, "I'm not going to resign immediately, and here's why. First, I have made some pretty bad mistakes, but I don't think there are ethical issues involved. Second, I think it is important for me to try to stabilize the seminary before you get a new president. If he comes in right now, he will come in on one side or the other of a controversy."

THIRD BAPTIST CHURCH OF ST. LOUIS

Did you ever seriously consider leaving the seminary on your own to bail out of the controversy?

Yes, and I almost accepted the pastorate of the Third Baptist Church of St. Louis in the midst of the turmoil. This was a great inner-city church, and I had been pastor of another inner-city church—Broadway Baptist Church of Louisville—so I had something to offer. I would have been going back to something that I would have felt comfortable doing.

It was a real option for me, and I was tempted to go. I finally decided that pessimism about the future at Southern was why I would accept this pastorate. I would be running away from something rather than going to something. This would not be fair to the church or to me and my family. I decided to stay at Southern and tough it out.

ULTIMATUM TO TRUSTEES

I understand that on May 15, 1958, this coalition of professors sent a copy of their supplemental report to all the trustees. A covering let-

ter indicated, "If we receive no specific proposal from the Board of Trustees, you may expect to receive our resignations." Is that correct?

Yes. I didn't think they had the guts to resign. Excuse me, that's raw—but that's exactly what I thought. I didn't think most of them would resign.

The trustees then met as scheduled during the Southern Baptist Convention in Houston on May 23. But the issue never went to the floor of the Convention in any way.

The thirteen professors didn't believe the Convention would help them. From my point of view, I was trying to contain the arena of the struggle and keep it as small as possible. I thought it was probable that it would come up during the Convention.

ALUMNI TRY TO MEDIATE

I understand some of the alumni of Southern Seminary tried to get you and these professors to reach an agreement at a meeting during the Houston Convention?

Yes, there is an unrecorded meeting that Claude Broach, then the president of the Southern Seminary Alumni Association, set up trying to reconcile the situation. He correctly identified the chief protagonist of the different points of view, and really identified Theron Price as being the opponent of the president. He got us in a room and tried to work out some understanding between us.

Finally, the alumni proposed an agreement, and I agreed to it. Theron Price did not agree to it. The alumni became upset because he wouldn't agree to it. Basically, it was a "you'll agree to treat one another as Christian brothers and forget what's been said and done" agreement. It was read to me, and I said, "Sure, I'll sign that or anything else you want."

But it involved something that had to do with Dr. Price's sense of the integrity of the position he held. He wasn't about to agree that there was any lack of integrity in his position. This was not what Broach meant for it to say. But Price would use words so precisely that I could understand why he wouldn't agree to it. The proposal broke down because of all the emotions involved in the situation by this time. This caused the alumni leaders to throw up their hands in despair at the unreasonable nature of both sides.

TRUSTEES SUPPORT ADMINISTRATION

During the formal meeting of the trustees on May 23 in Houston, by a vote of 42 to 7, they approved your administration, but the professors were not dismissed as some people had expected.

No. The trustees didn't intend to dismiss anybody. They told me that I was to work toward reconciliation with the thirteen and that they would meet again in Louisville on June 12 to hear my recommendation and to give the professors a full hearing.

What happened between the May 23 meeting and June 12, when the meeting in Louisville took place?

I visited each faculty member and tried to ask, "What is your complaint? What is it really—let's get away from the big general terms that sound good, like academic freedom. What is it you have to do that you don't like to do? What is it you'd like to do that you're not permitted to do? Let's get specific about that, and move away from the charges and find out what's behind them."

Did you meet them as a group or individually?

As a group and individually because I was trying to pry them loose from the group. I was trying to get beyond their coalition so I could deal with them individually.

I believe you had the last of your meetings with this group on June 10. Your conditions for reconciliation were the repudiation of their supplemental report to the trustees and the disintegration of the coalition. It's my understanding that they viewed this as totally unacceptable.

That's correct. I wanted them to drop the package of charges they could not prove, and to disband the coalition and become individual members of the faculty who would vote their own opinions. I didn't get any information from these thirteen professors that was really useful to me, nor did I find any inclination on their part to engage in reconciliation dialogue. Finally, I prepared a recommendation to the board of trustees for the June 12 meeting.

During the trustee meeting, each of the thirteen professors was heard separately, and then the group was heard together. There was no evidence to suggest that the thirteen were willing to retract the charges they made, but they were looking for some kind of relief from the board in the future. How did this meeting go?

The trustees planned for the faculty members to be dispersed in a sort of camaraderie fashion, with trustees and faculty members all sitting together. The group insisted on bringing thirteen chairs up to the front of the room and sitting together. In this way, they symbolized their stance as a group. This was a major psychological blunder on their part because it set them over against the trustees.

The other thing that happened was that Newton Rayzor, a trustee, asked the professors, "Why did you release a statement to the press before our committee dealing with this problem could report to us?" Dr. Ranson replied, "Because we didn't trust the committee to tell the truth." There were ten trustees on that committee, so this wasn't a very diplomatic statement. In fact, it infuriated the entire board of trustees.

PRESIDENT DEFENDS THE THIRTEEN

I made the mistake of saying to the trustees, "Don't take what Ranson said the wrong way." He is simply saying that the trustee committee is not able to interpret their position accurately." This was like throwing gasoline on the fire. For me to defend the thirteen professors made them angrier than almost anything that could have been done. I'm sure they saw it as patronizing.

The hearing went down hill from there. At one point in the meeting, V. V. Cooke said, "I want you to adjourn for a few minutes; I'm going to settle this matter." He called for Theron Price and me to go with him. We went upstairs to the parlor of Faculty Center. Mr. Cooke said, "You two men are the key to this problem. If you two will resign, we can resolve this whole situation."

I said, "I will resign if Theron Price and Guy Ranson will resign. But I will not step down unless they do." I thought Ranson was the infection that had spread this antagonism among the group of dissident professors. Theron Price said, "I will not resign." So we went back downstairs, and Mr. Cooke admitted that his effort had been futile.

Theron Price had been part of this group that had said either they would get what they wanted or they would resign?

Yes. But he changed his mind in this confrontation with V. V. Cooke. I think Ranson poisoned Theron Price's attitude. My wife used to get furious with me all through the controversy because I defended Price as a man of intelligence and integrity. I took up for him because I thought he was the victim of the propaganda that Ranson was feeding him. I never believed that Theron Price would lie or misrepresent the truth about anything.

Later in the meeting you apparently leveled charges against these thirteen professors. The charges were threefold: "(1) They did breach the fellowship of the faculty to effect changes in the life of the seminary. (2) They did thereby create a grave and disastrous division within the faculty. (3) They brought reproach upon the Southern Baptist Theological Seminary throughout the Southern Baptist Convention and discredited the name of Baptists and the cause of Christ." Then you recommended the resignation of the thirteen be accepted and that they be dismissed from their position as members of the faculty, effective June 12, 1958. Then you recommended that they receive severance pay through July 31.

Was that my recommendation, or was that the action of the trustees?

My understanding from the information I have is that those were the charges you leveled against the thirteen.

I don't really remember that, but it sounds like what I would have said.

The trustees voted 32 to 9 to dismiss the thirteen professors effective June 12, and they continued their salary until July 31, or until such time as the financial board of the trustees deemed it wise. They authorized a committee of the board to reinstate any of the thirteen, if the committee was fully confident the professor would cooperate with the administration and serve in good conscience.

I want to go back because you've raised a good question. I haven't seen the record you quote. It doesn't jibe with my memory.

Now about the charges I brought against these professors. I was to make a recommendation to the trustees, and I would always put a "whereas/therefore" in a recommendation like this. So the charges sound like the "whereas" of my recommendation. My memory is that I asked for continued support of the trustees for the administration and to advise the faculty members that unless they found it possible to work with this administration they should resign, as they had indicated they would.

So you did not make the specific proposal that they be dismissed?

That's right. And this is the reason why I'm so sure about that: After the hearing, somebody moved to adopt the president's recommendation. After the discussion a substitute motion was made to replace "accept the resignation" with "dismiss."

Now that is my memory. I wish I had the documents to go back and verify this because it's very important to me to be accurate at this point. I know that the dismissal was on the basis of an amended motion to dismiss, rather than to stand ready to accept their resignations. I think my phrasing was that the trustees would act now "to accept the resignation as of the date it was proffered," so in effect there would be no way for them to resign and expect a hearing at some later date. I was asking for resignation rather than dismissal. I know there was a motion that amended my recommendation.

You did not want to "fire" thirteen faculty members?

Right. And I was trying to find some way the trustees could slap the wrists of the faculty members and get them to sit down and negotiate an arrangement for the future. Subsequent events will show I was willing to negotiate their future connection with the seminary.

Let me go back. I'm sorry if I'm confused at this point. I'm quoting here, "that their resignation be accepted and that they be dismissed from their respective positions as members of the faculty."

That was the final form of the trustee action, as amended by Joe Stopher

It would be fair to say that some of the records of this issue have been sealed. At the time of our conversation in 1983, they are still sealed, and you are drawing upon memory. I'm drawing upon miscellaneous materials that are available to the public.

These professors had said clearly to the trustees, "If you don't do something, we will resign." This was the basis for advising the thirteen professors that their resignations were hereby accepted, effective upon the date proffered.

I still was hoping that if all hope of winning as a group was lost, they would then be willing to deal on an individual basis. I believed that if I could crack the group, eight or nine of the faculty members could be kept at Southern Seminary and the situation could be worked out. I was not optimistic about more than eight or nine staying. I was not willing for two or three certain ones to remain.

That isn't the end of the story, but that's what I thought I was recommending to the trustees in their June meeting. I knew what the AATS would do if these professors were summarily dismissed.

The thirteen professors later charged that they were never given a full hearing that had been promised them by the trustees on May 23 in Houston, even though ten of the thirteen met with the trustees, individually and as a group, on June 12. Their greatest complaint was that they were informed of your plan to recommend dismissal only a few hours before the meeting convened.

I wouldn't have told them that, because I did not plan to recommend their dismissal. I did plan to put it squarely on them that they had said they would resign unless they got their way; and they didn't get their way. The trustees came out of those hearings the angriest group of men I've seen in any board meeting in my lifetime. They didn't want to leave it open for any of the thirteen to stay at Southern except on the basis that the trustee committee approved their reinstatement.

I know I didn't recommend that last part: reinstatement. The trustees put that in as a sort of sop to my insistence that you just can't fire thirteen faculty members at one time. I know I didn't recommend that. What you are reading was not what I recommended. I think what you read is substantially the amendment of my recommendation.

My secretary Clara McCartt always served as assistant to the secretary of the board of trustees. She has written that she thought she made a bad mistake by recording only the motion adopted as amended by Joe Stopher. She did not write into the minutes the exact wording of my recommendation.

Along with these thirteen professors leaving, two other professors had also resigned to accept other posts—Cornell Goerner and Clyde Francisco, who subsequently rescinded his resignation. This meant the School of Theology was losing about half of its faculty. Did you ever reflect on whether you would be able to find competent people to teach during the upcoming fall semester?

Dr. Goerner left for the Foreign Mission Board job before the controversy. Dr. Francisco resigned to go to Southwestern Seminary, but withdrew his resignation when it became clear that the thirteen were leaving. The need to have a full complement of faculty in the fall of 1958 was a priority issue in my mind. But the trustees had indicated that the seminary couldn't go through another year with this civil war going on. On the other hand, if none of these people were going to stay, we needed their resignations so we could get on with finding their replacements.

After this happened in early June, there was an attempt to find some sort of grounds for reinstatement of these thirteen professors. There was a four-member reinstatement committee of the board of trustees.

There was no way this attempt was going to work with many of these professors because of their bloc action. They had pledged to one another that all of them would stay at the seminary, or none of them would.

The only person who actually met with this reinstatement committee was J. J. Owens. He has been both a friend and a professor whom I have respected through the years. I had advocated his promotion with some of the thirteen, specifically Theron Price, opposing his promotion. Therefore, there was more psychological ground for rapprochement with Owens than with others because he had no business being a part of that group to begin with, in my judgment. I never felt that he was a fully committed member of their bloc.

I understood why Dr. Owens felt that these professors were his friends and supporters and I was the cause of his not getting promoted. Once this thing got hot enough—I don't know this, but I would guess offhand—some of the other faculty members who were present in the full professor meetings finally broke the rule and told Owens that I had supported him for promotion. I think they also told him that some of the people he had thrown his lot in with were actually opposed to his promotion.

A report in the Louisville Courier-Journal *in December 1958 charged that the dismissal reinstatement process was a device to secure the firing of Theron Price and Guy Ranson and the reinstatement of the other eleven professors. You indicated earlier that you felt the resignation of Guy Ranson would have provided some help in the situation, but you did not include Theron Price.*

No, I didn't include Price, but I could have told you there was no way that Price was going to come back. It didn't matter whether I would have accepted him; he was not going to come back to teach at Southern.

You said you thought you could get eight professors to come back; this report implied eleven.

At least one of the eleven was trying to leave the seminary before the controversy developed. I was trying to help him in his job search because he was not happy as a professor at Southern. He wanted to go back into the pastorate.

187

Who was this, and did he subsequently go to the pastorate?

It was Bill Lumpkin, and he did go into the pastorate. I don't want any of this to be interpreted in a bad light as far as Lumpkin was concerned, because he was one of the professors whom I wanted back. He told me when I approached him that he would continue as a professor, but the next day, after conference with the others, he advised me that he could not do it.

BREAK IN THE IMPASSE

Did you have any other contact with these professors immediately after the meeting of the trustees at which they were released?

I need to tell you about something that's not in the official records because it throws light on some other things. Along in late July 1958—and I ought to date it exactly—on a Monday morning, Morris Ashcraft showed up in my office.

He said, "I have spent this weekend with a fishing line in the water, but I have not been fishing. I have been sitting there meditating and praying and thinking, and I've come to the conclusion that the historian will not deal kindly with either you or us. We have both been badly wrong. We have not dealt with you as Christians should. I have come to beg your forgiveness and ask you to forgive me as a Christian brother."

I replied, "Dr. Ashcraft, that is what I've been trying to say all along. My phrase about this whole thing has been, 'There are no angels and no devils in this controversy.' There are a lot of good Christians who have been caught in a demonic situation in which we are not dealing fairly or rightly with one another as Christians should. I wish to apologize to you and ask your forgiveness."

In the somewhat emotional scene, both of us apologized, asked forgiveness, gave forgiveness, and reestablished our relationship as Christian brothers.

Then I said, "Morris, is there any way I can get you to come back to Southern Seminary as a member of the faculty?" And he said, "Yes, I will come." Then he said, "Is there anybody else among the thirteen that you would say the same thing to that you've said to me?"

I replied, "Morris, there's nothing I've said to you that I would not say to any or all of the thirteen."

He asked, "Can I bring some of the fellows over to your house tonight?"

I replied, "Yes, you may; I'll be glad to see them."

They came over to the old Norton Estate; and we sat in the living room. I even remember that they were on the sofa on the north end of the room, and I was in a chair facing them. I'm giving details because it shows how deeply this is etched in my memory. We talked as Morris Ashcraft and I had talked, and in a little while all of them were saying, "We want to do the same thing."

Then we had a great confessing of sins and admission of errors and begging of forgiveness and reaffirmation of Christian relationship and brotherhood. They asked, "Would you take all of us back?" I replied, "I'll take you all back but Guy Ranson."

Was he there?

No, he was not present. They said, "Duke, it's all or none of us. Please take us all back. But we understand why you are saying that. If you will take Guy Ranson back, we will handle him for you, and you won't ever have any problem with him again."

I finally said, "All right. I don't want him; I don't trust him. But I trust you. On your promise, I will agree and recommend that all thirteen of you be reinstated."

They asked, "Will you write out the agreement that we have reached here?"

I replied, "No, I won't write anything out because every time I have written anything, one of you has misunderstood some phrase in it, something I said, or something I didn't say. You write the agreement, and I'll sign it." So they agreed to this on that Monday night. They wrote up the agreement.

How many of the thirteen professors were at this meeting? Morton was in Palestine; Ranson was not there; and J. J. Owens had already been reinstated. That left ten.

I don't think all ten of the others were there. I think it was eight or nine.

What about Price?

I don't think Price was there. I think he was out of the city. I was not sure whether they could speak for those who were absent, but I knew they meant to speak for them. I knew if they couldn't, they would tell me.

I trusted these men; I believed in them with all my heart. I still think they are men of integrity and competence. Now they were acting like the people I knew they were. I also knew the problem of trying to rebuild the seminary. They wrote the agreement and I signed it. There was to be a meeting of the executive committee of the seminary trustees about August 1 or 2. The problem was that they made one technical mistake in their proposal. They asked the executive committee of the trustees to rescind the action of the full seminary board on June 12. The executive committee, technically, cannot rescind the action of the full board.

I signed the document the way they wrote it because I thought I could correct that technical problem very simply. I went into that executive committee meeting on cloud nine. The professors who were at the meeting did get in touch with Morton as well as the other members who were missing from the meeting. They assured me that all thirteen professors had agreed to the statement that they had drawn up. I didn't want to amend it in any way. Therefore, I took the original statement just as it had been written to the trustee meeting.

I thought the trustees would hear that report, love my recommendation, sing the *Doxology*, pat me on the back, and tell me I was the greatest seminary president since creation. Newton Rayzor, a member of the executive board, had written articles in the Virginia Baptist paper defending these professors and criticizing me. He picked up immediately on this technical flaw in the document. I told him they could recommend to the full board that these men be reinstated. That is really what I wanted them to do—call a meeting of the board and recommend their reinstatement.

Rayzor responded that the board had set up a procedure for the men to come back individually as provided and to confess their sins, in effect, and to beg for reinstatement. I knew they would never do that. The thing then got into a debate. Finally, V. V. Cooke turned on me and said, "Duke, you are filibustering to keep us from voting on the motion to reject this document."

I responded, "Mr. Cooke, I am filibustering; I'm filibustering and praying that the Holy Spirit will lead you to see the light. You are about to do irreparable damage to Southern Seminary. You have within your hands the healing of this whole situation; you have the opportunity to salvage the careers of some fine faculty members. You needn't worry about the fact that some of these people cannot be reintegrated into the life of the seminary. If you will take this action, they will leave as quickly as they have a place to go. But in the meantime I will guarantee there will be no trouble between the administrator and these faculty members. That is what this agreement means. If they don't mean what they've agreed to individually, their colleagues will enforce it. I'm safer as president in promising you no trouble out of these men now than I've ever been."

I pled, I begged, I argued; but Newton Rayzor's motion to reject the document prevailed unanimously. I was devastated. That was the absolute low point of the whole 1958 controversy for me. Up until then, I really believed that, by the miraculous intervention of God, we were going to resolve the problem. But I had overlooked one vital fact—one major thing that every administrator ought to know.

I thought the trustees were on my side. I did not understand that the trustees had their own side, their own agenda, that they were not just supporting the president. They were also voting on the integrity and authority of the trustees. I was, in effect, compromising the role of the trustees by trying to handle the controversy. They were saying, "We, the trustees, have spoken, and neither you, nor the faculty, nor anybody else can change what we've done."

But the thing gets worse. Newton Rayzor told these professors that I did not present their proposal to the trustees. This absolutely closed all communication between me and every one of them except J. J. Owens. Rayzor, as the defender, advocate, and friend—presumably—of the thirteen faculty members, moved that their compromise not be accepted and then told them the compromise was not presented. I do not understand it. It doesn't match up with anything I know about Newton Rayzor, common sense, integrity, or human experience. It just is demonic; that is all I can say about it.

Did you have any further contact with this group of professors, now twelve in number?

I called Morris Ashcraft that night when I got home. I told him, "Morris, I know what you've been told. Some day you will discover that it's a lie. I know you won't negotiate or talk with me further. But I affirm that I kept faith with you. I did present the proposal. I begged for your reinstatement as provided by your document. If you ever want to talk, I'm available." He indicated that he did not believe me and that there could be no further conversations between us.

The miracle that I believe God had worked through Morris Ashcraft, and for which I had been praying, was aborted by the powers of darkness! Ever since that event, I have taken the devil more seriously as a force within the life of the church.

Do you have any reason to believe that this group of twelve former professors now believes what you have just related?

I think most of them do. Tom Hall came across the Austin Crouch Room in the Baptist Building on James Robertson Parkway in Nashville at a meeting one day. I said, "Tom, there are some things I want to say to you." He interrupted me and said words to this effect: "I have learned that what you said about your presentation of our agreement was true, and I want reconciliation with you as a Christian brother." Other things that have happened since then show that he didn't just say it; he meant it.

ASSOCIATION OF THEOLOGICAL SCHOOLS

There was a meeting on July 9 with Charles Taylor, executive director of the American Association of Theological Schools, and he requested financial provision for these professors beyond July 31. Do you remember anything about that?

I'm nervous about the timing. Charlie Taylor was in Louisville. The trustees asked him, "How much severance pay should we provide to these professors?" And he replied, "You ought to provide six months." On his recommendation, the trustees changed the provision for these professors to six months.

Later the AATS clobbered the seminary and the trustees for not giving these professors a year of severance pay. Charlie Taylor forgot to tell his body that the six months was not the action of the seminary independently but was his recommendation to the trustees.

AATS through its executive had recommended the six months severance pay. Furthermore, prior to the actual meeting at which the AATS clobbered the seminary for this, the trustees had met and extended the severance pay to one year. My respect for Charlie Taylor is somewhere less than zero because he was not a man of character or integrity in his dealing with me or the seminary at this point.

That includes his dealing with me in terms of my not attending the meeting of the Accrediting Commission of which I was the chairman and my resignation as vice president of the AATS. On principle, I would have voted to fire him for incompetence and lying. Maybe he was just as incompetent in the midst of a controversy as I was.

I proposed not to attend the meeting of the Accrediting Commission which would deal with the Southern Seminary problem, provided he would agree that the action of the commission would be communicated to the Southern Seminary trustees through their chairman before any news report was released. Despite that agreement, the trustees received word of the commission action from the press at least twenty-four hours before Dr. Taylor communicated with them. I was very much embarrassed because I had assured the trustees of the procedure Dr. Taylor had committed himself to follow.

CRITICISM OF CHARLES TAYLOR

I detect there was some discomfort on your part with the way in which Charles Taylor of the AATS handled certain parts of this investigation. What was the problem?

Part of the dilemma is to get this timing straight in my memory. One of the conversations, for instance, with Charlie Taylor about the meeting that I was talking about not attending—that has to be the December executive committee meeting in 1958 at which the Weigle committee would report their findings on the seminary. One of the items involved was a firm commitment from Charlie Taylor—which I still have recorded on an old Dictaphone belt—that whatever action was taken by the AATS would be reported first to the trustees of Southern Seminary. Under no circumstances would the AATS recommendations or actions be released to the press until the trustees of the seminary were notified.

How could he give you that kind of commitment when an independent committee was investigating the seminary?

Because there was always a press release from these AATS meetings that dealt with accreditation matters. What I was asking was that the normal procedure be followed by the AATS. The problem was that I assured the trustees they would have the press release before it was released to the public. But that was not done. Taylor gave a press release in New York, so even I learned of the report from the morning newspaper rather than through an official communication from AATS. This was a violation of standard AATS policy.

Obviously, a reporter would go to the AATS and verify the findings, and then AATS would deal candidly with the press about the matter, but the news release would come initially from the institution. But that didn't happen in this case. The news release went straight from the executive secretary of AATS to the press, and the institution (Southern Seminary) had to read about the action in the newspaper and then wait to get an official copy of their action and recommendations.

That is precisely the sort of messy mistake that we at Southern Seminary had made in our controversy, and AATS did the same kind of thing while criticizing us.

REQUEST THAT AATS VICE PRESIDENT RESIGN

This was the report released after the AATS meeting on December 8? And this happened after the committee had been to Louisville and returned and made their report to the AATS?

Yes, and in that same release they requested that I resign as vice president of AATS. More than a year later they contacted me and told me they hadn't received my resignation. My response was, "You'll never get it until you ask for it. You haven't asked for it yet. I read about what you did in the newspaper, but you've never notified me or dealt directly with me. I consider you to be in an ethically untenable position because you're the people who insisted that I allow myself to be elected to the office, even though I told you clearly what was going on at Southern Seminary. You have tried to score Brownie points through the press at my expense, and you haven't had the courage to give me an official report of your meeting."

The AATS had roughed up a person—namely, me—in the same careless fashion that they accused Southern of doing to these thirteen professors. What we did at Southern may not have been right, but other smart people probably could not have improved on it in such a tense time. Of course, the AATS did not damage a professor; that makes it different. For administrators, such treatment is simply an occupational hazard.

When did this conversation with Taylor take place?

More than a year after the AATS report on Southern Seminary was issued. The AATS was planning another meeting. I was still vice president and chairman of its Accrediting Commission. Taylor was trying to get it cleared so they could nominate and elect a new chairman of the Accrediting Commission. I was saying to him, "You'll never get my resignation until you formally notify me of what the executive committee of AATS did in terms of asking for my resignation, as well as what the Accrediting Commission did in terms of Southern Seminary. I'm angry about the use of the press as the method of communication with Southern Seminary and with me."

My due process instincts were coming into play. I think I could prove that Charlie Taylor had made several firm commitments to me that he violated. They were legitimate commitments; they were not anything that meant that Southern Seminary was going to get some special treatment. It was just the sort of thing that "we will notify you formally of what has happened, and then you notify the trustees of our decision." That kind of commitment was made, which the AATS did not follow.

The trustees did agree to continue the salaries of these professors to January 1, 1959, or until such time as the men secured employment?

Yes, that was the six months; and they subsequently extended that to one year.

Some have suggested that Dr. Taylor's appearance in Louisville before the trustees was a subtle warning about a forthcoming investigation of Southern. Is that true?

Sure it was, but it was something that ought to be expected. I, for one, expected it. I knew it had to happen. After all, I was chairing the body that dealt with accreditation of schools that got into this kind of trouble. I knew exactly the policies of AATS in situations like this. These policies were that they would hold hearings on the matter and determine whether the institution had acted properly.

What I didn't anticipate was that they suddenly adopted the procedures of the American Association of University Professors and tried the seminary on the basis of the AAUP document. This was not an official document of AATS. AAUP was at that time an organization to which Southern Seminary could not have belonged, even if it had wanted to. Therefore, the AATS used a set of standards that should not have applied in this situation.

CHRISTIAN CENTURY CRITICISM IN 1958

On September 2, 1958, the Christian Century *published an article by Paul Ramsey of Princeton University criticizing the seminary adminis-tration for its action and calling for a full investigation of the faculty dis-missals. Then a short time later, there also appeared a critical letter in the* Christian Century *from Alan Gragg, who was a past president of the student body at Southern. Some have suggested that these two articles were what really brought the American Association of Theological Schools into the fray. Is that true?*

Absolutely not true. It was inevitable that the American Association of Theological Schools would be involved. If it had been any other institu-tion, as chairman of the Accrediting Commission of the AATS, I would have insisted that the Accrediting Commission review the matter. That was absolutely inevitable.

Ramsey was most unscholarly in experting on something that he had no direct information on and had not investigated. Alan Gragg's letter was a perfectly appropriate thing for him to do. The point of view he expressed was one that I would be very disappointed if a student body president had not held. If the student government doesn't feel they have the finest fac-ulty anywhere around, you have real problems in your school.

The investigation into the Southern problem was on the agenda at AATS. In fact, the negotiations were going on between Charles Taylor, the executive secretary of the AATS, and me about how this was to be done. That very summer just a few weeks before the controversy came to a head, I was nominated as vice president of AATS.

I told Robert Handy of Union Seminary, chairman of the AATS nomi-nating committee, that I didn't think I should be nominated as vice pres-ident. I told him clearly that I was in the middle of a controversy that AATS might have to handle.

Handy replied, "The committee has met, and they're going to nomi-nate you unless you refuse to accept it." That was one of the mistakes I made. I should have refused. When the chairman of the committee insist-ed on the nomination, I let it go on through, protesting that AATS had to deal with the Southern Seminary matter but hoping it would straighten out before the AATS had to get involved.

They were saying, in effect, "You will know how to deal with that if it happens." They wouldn't deal with the Southern Seminary problem until they got to their regular meeting, which as I recall was in December. That would be the normal time for the Accrediting Commission to put this matter on its agenda. By then the situation had solidified in disastrous configuration. But in the summer before the whole thing blew up, it was hard to make anybody believe that this could happen. The people in AATS thought I would succeed in straightening out the problem.

You and the executive secretary of the AATS (Taylor) had a conversation in July in which there was some suggestion of paying additional funds to the professors. Are there other things you could relate about that particular meeting?

The big thing I remember about that July meeting was that Charlie Taylor came as a kind of consultant to help the seminary resolve its problems and give counsel to the president and the trustees. We talked about the situation, and we talked about what AATS could do to come in as a mediator. There wasn't unanimity on the seminary's side about how much they wanted the AATS to be involved in the situation. But I would have been happy to have them as the arbiter of the case at that point.

Later on I was very disillusioned and upset with the AATS, but at that point I trusted them implicitly. I had great confidence in these people. I voted for Charlie Taylor when he was elected executive secretary.

Some of the businessmen among the trustees didn't want any arbitration. They had their reasons for thinking that arbitration was not the way to solve problems. It was a good meeting. Charlie Taylor told the trustees that their action in June on salaries was inadequate, that they ought to extend that action to a flat salary for six months regardless of when these professors might be employed elsewhere. Six months severance pay was what was proposed—and the trustees bought that proposal.

We didn't know the rules of the game. We had been through a process in which thirteen faculty members had been dismissed, and one had been restored, and there were no guidelines. We didn't have them in our own documents, and AATS didn't have them in their documents. We didn't know what we were supposed to do in such a situation. We were flying by the seat of our pants and ad-libbing our decisions. We were looking to AATS to say in the larger academic community: How do you perceive this? What's right? We want to do what is right, and if you'll tell us what is right, we'll do it.

Maybe we should have found out what was right in advance, but then we always thought we knew what was right: let's get reconciliation of this problem. So Charlie Taylor's coming was on his initiative, I suspect, but quite welcome.

Do you remember having any other contact with Charles Taylor before the AATS investigating committee came to campus?

Yes, there were a lot of conversations. One of them, at some point, was over whether I should come to the December meeting of the AATS Accrediting Commission. That would have to be before the December 1958 meeting of AATS. My position was, in effect, "This is an awkward situation; I'm chairman of the commission that will have to deal with Southern Seminary. Obviously I can't chair the commission while it deals with my own seminary."

REPORT OF AATS COMMITTEE TO EXAMINE SOUTHERN

What procedure did the AATS follow in investigating the situation at Southern?

Dean Luther Weigle, chairman; Oren H. Baker; Gray M. Blandy; and Frank B. Lewis came to Louisville from the Commission on Accreditation October 24–28, 1958. I want to put in the record that I said the following to the chairman of this committee in the Brown Hotel: "Dr. Weigle, we're prepared to respond to any initiative your committee takes in terms of what you ask us to do, who you ask to interview or investigate, or any documents you want. They are all available to you. But the question is whether we should present a case to defend the action of the institution. So let me ask you, 'Is there any way, in your judgment, that an institution could justify the dismissal of thirteen faculty members?'"

His answer was: "If a professor raped the wife of the president of Harvard at high noon on Harvard Square before 1,200 witnesses, you might have a case."

I said, "Thank you, Dr. Weigle. I understand exactly what you've said. You have explained the environment and the circumstances in which our presentation is to be made. So we will not attempt in any way to justify what we have done. We will simply be available to explain to you the answers to any questions you have."

Did that work out to be a positive thing from your point of view?

I felt he was stating an attitude that was so endemic in the academic community that he was just reminding me of the law of gravity. I didn't really see it as anything very unusual. I knew that was the attitude we would have to contend with.

Obviously any professor in any school anywhere in the world will feel exactly that way. There is no ground for dismissing a faculty member except moral turpitude. That is why Luther Weigle chose this illustration. Even on grounds of moral turpitude, he was telling me, any educational institution and its accrediting agency would have a very difficult problem with the dismissal of thirteen professors.

The other ground would have to be incompetence, and we weren't charging these men with being incompetent. It's impossible to prove incompetence of a professor because there's at least one student and one colleague who will testify he's competent. So you really can't prove that a professor is incompetent in any way that I know other than that he would be psychologically incapable of meeting his classes.

The committee stayed in Louisville for two days. Do you remember those meetings?

They were not meetings; they were hearings. They heard individual members of the faculty. They heard the faculty collectively. They heard individual trustees; they heard trustees collectively. They queried administrators of the seminary. They also heard from most of the professors who were being dismissed. This was standard procedure—to ask everybody, to view the documents, to try to figure out what the mitigating circumstances were.

In its report, this committee noted "positive steps to repair the damage done to the seminary by the events leading up to the dismissal of the thirteen faculty members." But they remained unconvinced "that the seminary has taken adequate steps to repair the damage to the dismissed professors," citing a generally accepted principle in instances of dismissal on grounds other than that of moral turpitude "which would require extension of salaries for a year." This committee also expressed doubt as to whether "adequate measures have been inaugurated to insure the proper exercise of administrative authority in academic matters and to protect the rights of the faculty."

Did you have any problems with the way this committee conducted its investigations?

I did have one strong criticism. Luther Weigle, the chairman of this committee, represented Yale Divinity School. Yale Divinity School was a member of the American Association of University Professors. This professors' organization has standards that are applicable to its member institutions. Luther Weigle imported the Association of University Professors documents and standards and used them to apply to the Southern Seminary action.

There was no such thing as a set of standards in the American Association of Theological Schools for judging a situation such as this. So, in effect, the AATS went outside its domain and established the standards by which Southern Seminary was judged.

As a result of the report of this committee, the Accrediting Commission did not withdraw accreditation from Southern Seminary, but cited: "The Seminary's unfavorable faculty-student ratio, the inadequacy of its faculty and library for the ambitious program of the school, and especially the shortcomings of its facilities for the advanced study leading to the Master's and Doctor's degrees in Theology."

The Accrediting Commission proceeded to recommend: "A temporary discontinuance of admissions to the Th.M. and the Th.D. programs, and specific measures to strengthen the faculty in respect to salaries, opportunities for sabbatical leave and research, and the appointment of scholars trained in other graduate schools of theology, including schools in a university setting" (AATS Accreditation Commission Report).

Southern Seminary was given one year by the AATS to get its house in order, so to speak, in order to preserve its accreditation. Southern was also called upon "to take steps to repair the damage" that had been done to the school and to the seminary professors. How did you interpret that?

I interpreted that as the best thing they could have done because they didn't withdraw accreditation. They were saying, "We will give you one year to see if you can meet our standards." When the AATS reviewed us the next time, they not only reaffirmed our accreditation; they took off notations the seminary had had since the earliest days of accreditation. "Notation" was a note of some defect in the institution.

And the seminary, by retaining its accreditation at this point, had gained a much stronger lease on life.

Oh yes; it was being granted the time it needed to put its house back in order. Obviously, we opened in the fall of 1958 with barely enough faculty to meet all the classes. I thought that was a pretty heroic accomplishment—to have all the classes manned by at least credential-qualified personnel. But we needed more time than that. We had to get the dean of the School of Theology installed. And you don't recruit that many faculty members in three or four months.

ELECTION OF ST. AMANT AS DEAN

One of the issues that emerged in 1958–60 was the selection and election of a dean for the School of Theology. Dr. Penrose St. Amant assumed that position. What was your relationship with him in those early years, 1961 and 1962, when he first came to the seminary?

You may remember that I employed Penrose St. Amant as a professor at the Baptist Bible Institute, now New Orleans Seminary, when I was president of that school. But during the late 1950s at Southern, we were having a hard time finding the right dean. I had reassumed the role of dean of the School of Theology, replacing Henlee Barnette as acting dean after the controversy.

One day in a faculty meeting, Dale Moody did a typical Dale Moody thing. He announced suddenly, with vision from Olympus, that he knew who we ought to choose as dean—Penrose St. Amant. This would have been about 1959 or 1960. I didn't do anything about this suggestion at first.

The members of the faculty were meeting about a week later. Dale and his friends jumped on me because I hadn't done anything about getting Penrose St. Amant as dean. And I said, "Well, you've got to be formal about it. Do you really want to recommend Penrose St. Amant as your dean?" The faculty responded that they wanted to recommend that he be invited up for a consultation so they could decide what they would recommend.

I said, "Fine. But I need to tell you that you've just recommended a very close personal friend of mine. I wanted you to be absolutely sure he was your man before you found out how much he would be my man. That's why I haven't moved; I was afraid you might change your mind."

So we agreed and approached Penrose. It was an involved thing—it was on again, off again, on again. Penrose finally turned me down. I then turned and discussed Wayne Oates as a possible dean—not my first choice but perhaps the only choice under the circumstances. The problem with Dr. Oates was that I didn't think he could unify the faculty. He was often controversial himself.

The Sunday morning after I had discussed the deanship with Wayne, St. Amant called me up and said, "I can't live with my decision; I'll accept it if you'll elect me." So on Monday in the faculty meeting, I announced that St. Amant had accepted and that Wayne was not the candidate. That created some problems that stayed with us later in dealing with Wayne, particularly when Bill Hull replaced St. Amant.

I really believe in the delegation principle. So when St. Amant came in, he was the dean, and it was up to him to do the things the dean was supposed to do. He moved in, did his job with crispness and clarity and decisiveness, and provided a strong, healing force in the academic arena of the seminary. We had the problem of rebuilding the faculty, and he moved very well in that arena. He made a few mistakes, but then so did I. I'm trying to say I don't give him a thousand in his batting average, but I would say he performed with great skill.

I don't have any better friends than Penrose and Jessie St. Amant. So when I talk about them like that, I'm trying to say that he is a rugged individualist, he has his own lifestyle, he operates his own way, he has his own value system. He is primarily a church historian, and he thinks like one twenty-four hours a day. His emotions are geared to that role. He knows how a faculty member feels, and he respects that as legitimate. So he was a good choice as dean.

The appointment of a dean for the School of Theology was one of the recommendations of the Booz, Allen & Hamilton consultant group. What did you think of this particular recommendation?

I didn't like it. I wanted to be dean of the School of Theology. In fact, I later said to St. Amant—not entirely in jest—"I'll trade jobs with you; you be president, and let me be dean." That was an impractical thing, so in that sense it was a joke. But emotionally he understood I was saying I liked his job better than mine.

Did that make the job of the dean somewhat difficult?

I guess it could have, but I never heard of a dean complaining about it or objecting at all. As president I was *interested* in everything, but this doesn't mean I insisted on *doing* everything. I've been known to argue with a dean about a recommendation he had made, and end up by saying, "I still don't agree with you. That is not what I would support myself, but I believe you believe in it, and you've got the responsibility for making it work. So I'm going to go with you, and I will carry your recommendation to the trustees and make it mine."

How much input did St. Amant have in formulating what this job was going to be like?

The job description was handed to him when he arrived. But then, being St. Amant, he didn't revise it formally; he just lived with it the way he wanted it. He just functioned as dean the way he wanted to function as dean. Repeatedly he wrote to trustees or faculty members—or made a speech—saying how he viewed the deanship. I doubt if he ever meant to revise the Booz, Allen & Hamilton report or even implement it as such. But he fitted easily within the guidelines they had written.

Would the relationship between the president and the dean in those years be described as times of creative tension?

No—cooperative tension.

You knew that's how St. Amant operated?

I knew exactly how he operated. I didn't have to like what he did, but there wasn't any other way to have a dean. I wasn't going to like anybody else as dean any better than St. Amant. In fact, I knew I would like St. Amant better than anybody I knew. I never presided over the School of Theology faculty meetings after St. Amant became dean.

How would you characterize Dr. St. Amant's style of operation as dean?

He was very forthright. He had an interesting style of handling potential controversy. He would come in and say, "This is what I came to see you about." And he would tell you. It was all out at once—very clean and crisp with no emotion.

St. Amant didn't like precipitating a disagreement of any sort, or even making demands. But if he thought it ought to be done, there wasn't any question about whether he would do it. I understood his style, and really admired him, and admired the precision and candor of his mind. There never was a dean with whom I couldn't disagree on something, or sometimes even just be the devil's advocate. In other words, sometimes I would challenge the dean to be sure that he had covered all the problems and was absolutely convinced this ought to be done.

My theory is that once a job is delegated to someone, he must have power and authority equal to the responsibility. My idea may be a better way to do it if I were operating it, but he'll be in Saul's armor if he has to implement my ideas all the time. The seminary will be a lot better off to give him the freedom to be himself and use his style of operation rather than mine.

There is no adequate recognition of the role of Dean Penrose St. Amant in the 1959 report of AATS. He did a heroic job. He implemented much of the Booz, Allen & Hamilton report in his own unique, personal style. The faculty applauded him for doing exactly what precipitated the controversy. I can only boast that I supported him to the fullest in his dealing with the faculty.

A DEMONIC TIME

Looking back on this controversy after all these years, how do you assess it and its effect on you, other people, and Southern Seminary?

There were a lot of individual tragedies. I tend to think of it as a catastrophe and a very great tragedy from a personal point of view. Then you have to add all the faculty members who were involved and what it did to their psyche as well as their careers across the years.

But you haven't begun to measure the tragedy when you get through with that. You have to talk about all kinds of people, including lay people whose ideals about the ministry were destroyed. So a major controversy of that sort really ought to be beyond thought, much less occurrence.

I want to use a phrase about this controversy that I've used before: I thought at the time, and I still think, that there were demonic elements involved. I'm using the word in the biblical sense, declaring that there were demonic elements in this controversy so that good people on both sides did not act as well as they ought to have acted.

Does that include you?

Yes, definitely me. It's unbelievable some of the things that people did during this controversy that were out of character. If there had been that much change for the good in some of us who were involved in this controversy, everybody would have marveled at the miraculous grace of God. To have that much change in character and personality for the bad—I have no explanation except the term *demonic*. I'm using it as the reverse of the miraculous intervention of the grace of God.

I have never been able to explain the entire situation from a rational perspective. I've never been able to explain, even satisfactorily to myself, some of my own actions. This was not a quarrel between demons and angels, with one side representing the angelic and the other the demonic. It was a group of demon-possessed human beings who were doing utterly unbelievable things to one another, to the cause of Christ, to Southern Seminary, to students, and to other faculty members.

EFFECT OF CONTROVERSY ON STUDENTS

The other constituency involved in the controversy was certainly the students at Southern.

Oh yes. That trauma still exists in Southern Baptist life. President Roy Honeycutt is trying to wipe it out. For example, he has named Dr. Estill Jones seminary chaplain. Several years ago I approved a New Testament job offer for Jones, and I never learned why the faculty or dean did not go through with it—or maybe why he did not accept it. This was after his departure as one of the thirteen dismissed professors.

Some of the graduate students felt especially shattered, I suppose.

Yes, because they had vested interest; many of them lost their major professors. They had an immense investment in a situation that couldn't be recouped for them. Some of them never finished their doctor's degree because of the dismissal of these professors.

I have a dear friend who didn't get into Southern Seminary's graduate program because of the fall-out over this controversy. He has always ridden me pretty hard about this. He was an alumnus of Southeastern, but he was scheduled to do graduate work at Southern, and the door was closed to him. He ended up getting his doctorate much later from a Methodist institution, Emory University.

I run into people every now and then who will talk about the bitterness and the hurt of what happened. The bitterness and hurt often are verbalized in terms of the inability of Christians to resolve their differences. That is one of the things that absolutely shattered the students. Their idealism about the way Christians ought to deal with one another was shattered because their mentor, their professor, was involved in this situation. Usually they felt badly treated. But their loyalty remained with the professors.

TRUSTEES ASK SBC HELP

The trustees met in mid-December of 1958 and voted to request the SBC Executive Committee to form an advisory committee for Southern Seminary. This committee was composed of the current SBC president and five former presidents. Where did that idea come from?

It grew out of the fact that I thought I had been double-crossed by Charles Taylor of the Association of Theological Schools. I was very angry about what I thought—and still think—was utterly immoral action on his part. He agreed on a procedure that would be followed by the AATS and then double-crossed me by following a different procedure.

What the American Association of Theological Schools had done was to condemn the seminary. I discovered later that what they did was to make a lot of noise but put no substance in their condemnation. It took a little while for me to get beyond the sound of what they did to examine the substance. They may have been a little more thoughtful and kind than I thought they were at the time, but their violation of the procedure we had agreed on is clear to me.

The Association of Theological Schools had examined the situation and made pronouncements that condemned the trustees and the administration of the seminary and exonerated the faculty members. It seemed to me that the only defense mechanism was to have somebody from the denomination conduct an investigation. A prestigious, objective group to do this would be the current president and several former presidents of the Convention.

Who was named to this committee?

The six men were J. D. Grey of New Orleans, Brooks Hays of Washington, D.C., and Little Rock, Arkansas, Louie D. Newton of Atlanta, R. G. Lee of Memphis, Casper C. Warren of Charlotte, North Carolina, and J. W. Storer, who at that time was with the Southern Baptist Foundation in Nashville. He was a former pastor in Oklahoma.

Do you remember any particular involvement of any of these individuals?

I felt that J. D. Grey was the most effective member of this Presidents Committee because he was the only one who stayed through all the meetings and listened to all the hearings, and stayed alert enough to ask the right questions of everybody, including the administrators.

Since the meetings ran until three or four o'clock in the morning, that was quite a feat. He took his responsibility seriously. He was not a spectator at any point. He was a participant. He was emotionally and intellectually involved all the way through. He was caught up in the work of the committee. He was responsible for something of significance in the life of Southern Baptists and the cause of Christ, and he intended to do his job. He didn't care who liked what he did or said or the questions he asked. He was just being old J. D. Grey, and he was after the truth, and he was going to get it, no matter who got hurt. I'm more grateful to J. D. Grey for what he did in that committee than anybody else.

His papers on that era have been turned over to the Historical Commission, SBC, archives [now in the Southern Baptist Historical Library and Archives]. *He has kept careful records of his involvement.*

I would judge that those records will be very important. Without having seen them or knowing what's in them, I would say that anyone who wanted to know about that particular episode would get the best report from J. D. Grey. I can't say the same for some of the other presidents—at least one of whom was not present for the meeting but who after the meeting was the most vociferous in his writing about what went on. He was, in my judgment at that time, considerably wide of the mark regarding his own role and the actual events. But his report was readable.

Would this have been the pastor of Druid Hills Baptist Church—Dr. Louie D. Newton?

It would. J. D. Grey's record would be more complete and more accurate than that of any of the other former presidents.

Louie Newton was elected chairman of this committee. Was that just the nature of things?

At that time he was of that stature in Southern Baptist life, and he was not a seminary alumnus; therefore, he was considered neutral. Perhaps another reason why Louie was chosen as chairman is that he generally ran almost any meeting he was in, whether he was chairman or not. He would run it from the floor or from the chair; either way didn't seem to make much difference to him. His skill and political astuteness, his quickness on his feet, and his ability to choose the phrase that would summarize a position—all of those things were characteristic of him in any setting.

But I recall that Louie didn't stay through the whole meetings—I believe he had a funeral. Louie always came late or left meetings because of funerals. That was a wise crack, not meant to be taken too seriously. He left before this meeting was over and relinquished the chair.

Had this idea of a committee of SBC presidents been used before? What prompted you to get this group together? Why the presidents?

It may have been used before, but I'm not aware of it. But it is an obvious idea. If you are looking for a prestigious group, chosen by the body itself, in whom the Convention membership has confidence, where else would you look but to the presidents?

The diversity of the presidents makes them a rather objective cross-section of the Convention itself. I thought what they would say would have some effect on Southern Baptists and also, frankly, that the hearing would buy some time. There would be some people who would wait to arrive at a conclusion until they heard from the Southern Baptist presidents. I felt strongly that whatever these people said would probably be accepted by the Convention as an objective evaluation of the actions of the trustees and the administration.

We were hoping their report would counter what AATS had said. I'm a little less emotional about this today than I was back then about the AATS statement, but at that time we were pretty vehement about what we construed as misrepresentation of the facts in the AATS report.

Were you happy personally with the Presidents Committee?

Yes, I thought it was an excellent committee because I had no hand in determining who had been elected president of the Convention. These were responsible people. They ranged from R. G. Lee and Jim Storer, who had not been to any seminary; to Casper Warren, who was a doctoral graduate of Southern Seminary; to J. D. Grey, a doctoral graduate of Southwestern; to Louie Newton, not a seminary alumnus but an opinionated and outspoken person. That was one whale of a fine committee. I think R. G. Lee, regrettably, didn't participate in any of the meetings.

There were actually several meetings of this group.

But the investigative meeting—the digging-for-the-facts meeting—took place on January 8, 1959.

After several additional meetings, this committee suggested that all possible efforts to reconcile the differences had been dealt with and that they felt there could be no real reconciliation between the seminary and these professors. Do you remember those events?

No. You resurrect some emotions from the time, but I don't have any new information to offer.

THE FRIENDS OF A PRESIDENT

I detect from all your reflections that there was a type of loneliness connected with being president of Southern Seminary.

Yes, very much so. I thought one of the wonderful things about going back to Southern was that I would have so many close friends. But one of the toughest problems I faced was that I couldn't play golf with the faculty. I never could communicate to the faculty member that, on the third tee, he shouldn't ask me for permission to do something that I wouldn't have given him permission to do in my office. They would do this instinctively; it was not a planned kind of thing.

These encounters had the effect of placing me "back in the office." I was just playing golf with a friend, but then I had to put my presidential hat back on. Faculty and staff, with rare exceptions, could never let the situation remain solely friendly for long.

So you developed a community of friends beyond the faculty group?

Yes, I had to find intimate friends beyond the seminary community. That always frustrated me because I couldn't be with the friends beyond the community except for a limited amount of time. I never could be close to the people I most wanted to be close to.

There's one story from 1958 that illustrates my point. This happened before the controversy had erupted. I realized a certain amount of tension had developed, so I invited about a dozen faculty members to be my guests for lunch at the Pendennis Club in Louisville. I wanted us to sit down as colleagues and talk about the situation at the seminary. The purpose was to dig out what they wanted, what was happening that wasn't good from their point of view. We had a long session.

In the course of that session, somebody prompted me to wisecrack, "The reason I like being president of the seminary is that the trustees meet once a year, and the deacons meet once a month." This was an exaggeration, and it was meant as a joke. The faculty response at the time was laughter.

In the special faculty report of the thirteen professors in this controversy, this wisecrack was quoted to prove that I liked being president of the seminary because I was not subject to supervision by anyone. At the Pendennis Club, they knew this comment was made in jest. Then it got played back to me later as a pronouncement. That has happened to me more than once; a friendly wisecrack on a golf course would get turned into a presidential decree.

That always bugged me. I never learned how to anticipate when I could relax and say whatever popped into my head. As you have seen in these interviews, I like to wisecrack, and I like to try to say something that puts common expressions in a crazy-quilt pattern.

There was a definite loneliness associated with the job of serving as president of Southern Seminary. I told you about the support of the wives of the seminary presidents in connection with the Presidents Workshop. The wives of seminary presidents are always having to serve as confidants to their husbands because the presidents don't have anybody else to confide in.

This lack of real friends is one of my problems, and I guess it is an idiosyncratic personal problem of mine. What happened to me with Bill Morton was disastrous because I could never really bring myself after the controversy to have that kind of openness with any other faculty member. I had been so confident of the ties of affection and friendship and mutual trust and mutual support between the two of us. In the back of my head—though I tried to get it out—I would always think, "Be careful about this now; you're talking about sensitive things. If he doesn't understand all that's involved, he may decide one of these days to let you have it with both barrels."

No seminary president thinks he's right all the time. No president thinks he is at his best all the time. He is acutely aware of his finitude and humanity. He knows he isn't omniscient, but he still has to make a decision. He's got to go ahead and settle the issue. He realizes that he needs another month to study the problem, but the deadline for decision is today.

I suspect what I'm describing is true for everybody. But the difference is that a seminary administrator has responsibility for the welfare of so many other children of God. And that includes the janitor as well as the head of the New Testament Department. All of these people are linked into what you do. If you're wrong and the situation turns out badly, everybody will pay for it.

In 1958 it did turn out badly—and all of us paid dearly.

CHAPTER 10

The Good Times

1960-1970

As I worked through the seminary records of the early 1960s, I sensed a certain peace and harmony. Was this the calm after the storm?

We had been through a trauma, and we were trying hard to learn how to work together in a better way. Everybody was trying—including the president.

There were also major changes in the graduate program during this era; there were attempts to introduce new degrees and a new emphasis in religious education. Did you have a lot to do with that?

No, I worked in the background on these things. By this time, I was administering some of this by veto. If a dean proposed it and I agreed, it flew. But I didn't go through the early stages of hammering it out in the faculty processes. That was up to the dean of the appropriate school.

And what about the director of graduate studies?

We had a hard time putting that on a chart, but *de facto* the director of graduate studies was under the dean of the School of Theology.

Some of the personalities in these responsibilities were not "unopinionated individuals," such as Ray Summers.

It was a real coup to get Ray to leave Southwestern and come to Southern. He brought maturity, stability, scholarly commitment, denominational savvy, and commitment to the campus. He was a very fine addition to the faculty. He was the first director of graduate studies at Southern. I regret we couldn't keep him. He eventually went to Baylor.

FACULTY SELECTION

In early 1960, the trustees approved a basis for election to the faculty and a method of election. Tell us about this.

There never had been any real problem with the faculty being involved in faculty selection. In principle, I would have insisted that to select faculty members without consultation with the present faculty just wouldn't work. You would be mixing conflicting elements. If you have any confidence in the faculty, you have to believe they know more about people in their field than anyone else in the institution.

The process is still going on today, although it gets amended and refined and adjusted periodically. The blunt truth is there is no ideal way to select new faculty. The current agreement is always a kind of compromise reached by the personalities involved at the moment. You try to get a balance between all the factors involved. A balance is needed between the powers of the faculty, the powers of the dean, the powers of the president, and the powers of the trustees. All these are involved in faculty selection. If you get these powers balanced properly, there is some hope of consensus.

I've known a department not to want a senior professor because all the faculty in the department were junior professors, and a senior professor would outrank the incumbents. On the other hand, I've seen it work the other way where a department made up of senior professors wanted only senior professors added.

From an administrator's point of view, the time of retirement, or the time of the maturation of the scholarship of different members of the department, is important and must be balanced so that you don't end up with all four-star generals in one department at one time. On the other hand, you don't want all your scholars in a department to retire in the same twenty-four-month period. So there are many factors to be considered.

The way it works at Southern is by veto. It starts out usually with the department and the dean, and then it goes from there into the larger faculty, to the president, and then to the trustees.

Any faculty member can propose a candidate and put in a proposal in the initial process. But the proposal that gets lifted to the working process is determined by the department and the dean. From there on it becomes a veto procedure. The faculty can veto the proposal. The president can't name somebody else, but he can veto the present proposal. The trustees can't elect somebody else besides the person being proposed, but they can veto the recommended person.

Did you like the idea of getting different points of view among the faculty members in a department?

Yes. The departments themselves prefer unanimity or uniformity among their professors. But I prefer diversity in terms of academic background, general personal background, the faculty members' areas of interest, and even personality differences, as well as theological differences. I preferred a department that forced dialogue among the students between the theological perspectives of different faculty members.

Some people can tolerate more difference and more disagreement than others can. So we never achieved any uniformity in the degree of diversity. That varied from department to department. Some departments would opt for a more "open" attitude, and some would opt for a very conservative doctrinaire theological line within the department. I think variety is necessary for a good educational environment.

SCHOOL COMMITTEE ROLE IN FACULTY SELECTION

In June 1965 the trustee minutes noted that certain faculty members "had been approved by a Committee on the School of Church Music." What did that phrase mean?

The organization of the trustees provided for a trustee committee on the School of Church Music, a committee on the School of Religious Education, and a committee on the School of Theology. The deans of the appropriate schools carried recommendations for trustee action to the appropriate school committee of the trustees, and the school committees then brought these as recommendations to the full trustee board. I thought we had begun to follow this procedure earlier than this. Maybe this is simply one of those times when the record raises to the surface something that had been going on for a while.

So the pattern was for the dean of the appropriate school, in consultation with the president, to be in contact with a prospective faculty member. If the process moved down the line with the approval of the president and the dean, it would then be taken to the appropriate school committee of the trustees?

Actually, it was a very formal procedure involving formal documents in which we filled in the name of the prospective faculty member and his rank and his grade in rank. This had to have the dean's signature, recommending it, and then the president had to sign off on it. Then that document went to the school committee of the trustees, and the school committee chairman affixed his signature. Finally, the secretary of the trustee board signed the document, and a copy went to the faculty member, indicating he had been approved by all of these trustee processes and administrative processes. This process, in turn, was rooted back in faculty support because the dean could not make the recommendation to the president without faculty support.

Would you delineate how this worked in practice with a prospective faculty member?

Generally, the rule was that there was no vacancy on the faculty until the president declared a vacancy. For example, nobody could look for an Old Testament professor until the president formally said there was a vacancy in the Old Testament Department. And he might add, "a senior vacancy," or he might add, "a junior vacancy," which is to say, "look for a young men in the early stages of his teaching career," or "look for a mature man, a senior professor."

Once the president had declared a vacancy, the next step was for a search committee of faculty members to be formed. The most recent development would make the dean the chairman of that search committee. In the earlier stages—and this is one of those things that varied—sometimes a faculty member would be chairman of the search committee. But we found that it worked better if the dean was the chairman of the search committee. If the dean was chairman, he had secretarial help and access to budgeted funds that were necessary in conducting this type of search.

When you say that a vacancy was declared, would that be a budgetary decision?

Yes, that would be essentially a budgetary decision. That's why this declaration had to come out of the president's office. If the budget was tight, the president might choose to leave that vacancy unfilled. And the opposite was also true. If funds were available, he might declare the need for an additional professorship within a department that could be filled.

This declaration by the president would relate to teaching loads, student enrollment, budget, and so on. The president would not make this decision all by himself; the deans were always making recommendations to him on behalf of the faculty that additional professors were needed here or there, or reminding him that Professor John Doe had resigned or retired and he needed to be replaced.

When the deans and the respective committees had worked the process to the point where they had two or three good prospects for a faculty vacancy, the dean would approach the president. He would come in and say, "We have these three prospects for the vacancy; do you have any objection to any one of these three?" The president at that point might say, "Yes, I have an objection to Number 3," in which case the dean would drop this person. He knew at this point early in the process that there was no use asking for a presidential veto.

But the dean was also in a position to argue with the president that Number 3 really ought to be kept on the list. I have known the deans to win those arguments—not often, but sometimes. Then the committee would move ahead and interview these three people. Let's assume that they agreed on candidate Number 2. Then there would be a conference between Number 2 and the entire faculty. The dean and the president would meet with this candidate. After that the faculty of the school involved would formally vote to support or not support the prospective professor.

Presumably the dean by this time was willing to recommend this candidate to the president, and presumably the president was willing to support the nomination—unless the president, in the conference with the prospect, happened to reverse his position. This has happened.

I recall one or two occasions in which everybody cleared a prospective professor, but the president refused to endorse this person and take his name as a recommendation to the trustees. That was very rare, and it was always an agonizing presidential decision, but there was always a reason for it. Usually it had to do with the candidate's compatibility with Southern Baptist goals and lifestyle.

Once the president's approval was secured, he signed the appropriate documents. The president's signature on these document threw the ball back into the dean's court because the dean was the staff member of the school trustee committee. The president rarely attended those committee meetings. He was available, if needed, but he generally showed up only if the dean or the committee called for him.

The dean was the chief administrator as far as the school committee of the trustees was concerned. Once everything was done, the school committee took the recommendation to the floor of the trustee board, and it was now a trustee matter. The president's recommendation had been processed, and now it was in the hands of the trustees to settle the matter. The president might be called on to speak for the recommendation, or opposition by trustees other than the members of the school committee might come up. But that didn't happen very often.

EFFECTS OF A ROTATING TRUSTEE BOARD

You are on record as opposing the rotating trustee board for SBC agencies. Why your objection?

The rotating trustee board for SBC agencies came in during my era at the Executive Committee, although I was opposed to it. The rotating approach puts the emphasis on letting somebody else have an opportunity to serve on the board rather than asking the more important question, "Is this person knowledgeable, competent, capable, interested, and willing to work at being a good member of the board."

With rotating boards, you end up choosing someone to serve because he's a young man, and there ought to be a young man on the board. There's nothing against having a young man as a trustee. But what knowledge, experience, or dedication does he bring to the task?

I knew of one situation where a man was named to the board of an agency—and he was in the process of suing the agency! Then there was the trustee who used to come and answer the roll call, collect his expense check, and that was the last time you ever saw him at the board meeting. He was out visiting his family who lived about fifty miles from the site of the agency.

Admittedly, these are the extreme horror stories. But what you had under the old stable board system was just the opposite. These trustees were present for the meeting, they knew the history of the agency, they understood how it worked. Their leadership grew out of their dedication to the affairs of the agency. Of course, there were also the old settlers who thought they owned the board and who knew enough to make it hard for any newcomer to break into the leadership of the board. That is the sort of thing that caused the shift from a stable board to a rotating board.

LOCAL BOARD OF THE TRUSTEES

What's your philosophy of the local trustee board and how it should work?

The local board also rotates, but the selection process means that the members of the local board—especially the very useful members—tend to come back on. They will be off the local board for a year or two, and then they will get reelected. This tends to keep people with good experience and valuable skills on the local board.

But this creates another problem. The members of the local board, unless they are briefed and carefully trained, will tend to dominate the full board meetings. They know so much more than the people who come in to direct the agency intermittently and who have been on the board for only a short time.

The local board at Southern Seminary briefed themselves about this problem. They agreed among themselves that they would not discuss some matters in the annual board meeting that they were very knowledgeable about. They would sit back and let the other people handle them simply because they thought they might be accused of trying to control the agency.

Let me illustrate. Here's a lawyer, Joe Stopher, who has been on the local board for Southern Seminary off and on for thirty-five years. He stays on the board for ten years and goes off for a year. As soon as there's a vacancy on the Southern trustee board, he is put back on. He has a powerful reputation as an able Baptist in the local community and in the state, so it doesn't take any administrative maneuvering to get him named again as a trustee of the seminary. The SBC Committee on Board members will go right back to him as a strong man. They think of him as a Southern Baptist who is committed to evangelism and to the ministry and who works hard for the agency.

But out in the whole Southern Baptist Convention, the choices for board members are too great. Once a person away from the site of the agency has been on the board, it's very rare that he gets reelected—unless somebody is pulling strings to make it happen.

LOCAL TRUSTEES—TERM OF SERVICE

The trustees of Southern Seminary in the early 1960s determined that the local trustees could serve indefinitely. Were you a part of initiating that?

I was in favor of that, and I guess I joined in initiating it. But it didn't do any good. This proposal was voted down by the Southern Baptist Convention. Perhaps as vigorously as any agency, Southern Seminary has opposed the rotation system of trustees. I think the rotation system is using a meat ax to do a fine operation. Trustees who don't function ought to be severed from the board of the institution. I think that is the job of the SBC Committee on Boards, if it had the courage of its convictions.

How do you counter the argument that this does not give much opportunity for all people to serve as trustees?

Out of thirteen million Southern Baptists, I don't think any one person is going to have much opportunity to be on a board—even if you rotated them every six months. Only an infinitesimal fraction of Southern Baptists will ever have an opportunity to be on the board of any agency. So the opportunity of getting on the board is almost non-existent.

Besides that, what's your goal? Are you having trustees in order to let people be on boards, or are you selecting the most competent people to run that portion of the Lord's work? And the latter is what I would insist on.

I think the trustees of every SBC agency ought to be reviewed by some external body to ascertain whether they are active participants in operating the agency. I don't care whether they've been on the board one year or not; they ought to be dropped if they are not functioning members.

EDUCATIONAL LOAN FUND FOR FACULTY

One program that was adopted at Southern Seminary during the 1960s was to have an educational loan fund for the children of the faculty. What was the philosophy behind this?

The problem was that the seminary couldn't pay the faculty enough. I considered the faculty at Southern to be terribly underpaid. I thought the faculty members with family responsibilities were suffering more than anyone else.

But I couldn't raise salaries on the basis of how many children a professor had. So the only way to help them was to provide an educational loan for their children. One-tenth of this loan would be canceled for each year of service rendered to the seminary by the professor after the loan was made. If a professor stayed at Southern for ten years after he received the educational loan for a child, he wouldn't have to pay the money back.

There was a pragmatic twist to this loan system. It was one way to stabilize the faculty and keep the good faculty members. We made it clear that if they left before those ten years were up, they would have to pay off that educational loan. By the way, that was always collected. As long as I was president, those who left made those payments. But we did have some harsh feelings with a few people who wanted to be relieved of repaying the loan.

LIVING ENDOWMENT FUND

Another idea developed in the 1960s was a fund known as the Living Endowment Fund. What was that about?

I think that began before I arrived. It was an Ellis Fuller idea. The Living Endowment is rooted in the fact that seminary alumni generally don't become very rich people. Yet every institution turns to its alumni for funding. You couldn't expect Southern Seminary alumni to leave a million dollars to the seminary, or to give a building.

So Ellis Fuller had the idea that if every alumnus would make an annual gift, that would be the equivalent of income on so much endowment. That's the Living Endowment idea. He originally figured the gift on the basis of a return of 4 percent. He translated a $100 annual gift from an alumnus as 4 percent of $2,500. Then he would say to an alumnus, "If you'll make an annual gift of $100 you're worth $2,500 endowment to Southern Seminary."

So it was intended simply as another endowment fund that would build?

It had the effect of raising money, and it also had the effect of tying the alumni to the institution. It's an interesting thing that Southern Seminary has had a great deal of difficulty eliciting loyalty out of its alumni for the ongoing welfare of the institution. Perhaps this is because the alumni reason in circular fashion like this: "I'm pastor of a church; my church gives to the Cooperative Program; the Cooperative Program supports the seminary; I give to my church; therefore I'm giving to Southern Seminary."

I've noted over the years that alumni of the seminary tend to be more loyal to their collegiate alma maters than to the seminary. It's been a struggle to elicit loyalty from the alumni for the seminary as such. I can talk about that now because the alumni seem to be doing better. Now there is a very commendable level of participation and loyalty between the alumni and the ongoing life of the institution.

What do you think has changed that?

Inman Johnson and Pat Pattillo. What they did as alumni secretaries made the difference. Grady Nutt was popular but not so effective. Patillo has worked very creatively and very effectively across the years. He has done a magnificent job of involving the alumni in the ongoing life of the institution. He did it through man-of-the-year awards and that sort of thing. He did it through continuing education, which he is gung-ho about.

SALARY SCALE ADOPTED IN 1960

In 1960 a salary scale for the seminary was adopted by the trustees. How was this formulated?

This was part of the Booz, Allen & Hamilton study. It was so comprehensive that it took probably ten years for all of its proposals to be worked into the life of the institution. The concept of a salary scale was a revolutionary idea at Southern Seminary. I wanted some specific policy about salaries rather than a system in which the president negotiated a salary with each person.

My personal idea of a salary scale was relatively primitive. Before the formal study by consultants, Trustee Homer Parker, president of Commonwealth Life Insurance, lent the seminary his "salary scale expert." Finally, Booz, Allen & Hamilton refined a program tailored for Southern. I grabbed it with enthusiasm.

It was a better way to administer the institution. The salary system featured a formal rating process, under which each position was put somewhere on the scale without reference to the holder of the position. The job or position itself was rated as being of a certain level. Whoever was put into the position was rated and placed somewhere within the scale applicable to that position.

When you install anything like this, there are some people who are already so far out of the scale—either on the low or the high side—that it takes what they call "red-lining." These situations are marked as exceptions to the scale. We had to "grandfather" in any person whose salary was over the scale, even though his or her salary might be 150 percent of the maximum for the job. People in this situation were just lucky. But time eventually solved this problem.

This entire salary scale system was established basically through a committee process. It took a long time for a committee to identify what the various positions at the seminary were. After the positions were identified and people were associated with these positions, then came the moment of truth. Where could we find the money to pay these salaries, and how much of what the seminary ought to pay could it afford?

A school is labor intensive. Most of the money goes into paying salaries. Some agencies of the Convention put 60 percent of their funds into their programs—which is wonderful. That's what the agency is— the program it carries on. Then it can raise salaries and put maybe 50 percent into its programs. A seminary doesn't have that cushion. Something in the 90 percent range of all money the seminary spends is on people and salaries. So the only way you can save money is to get rid of people.

In Southern Seminary's new salary scale, the base of a full professor's salary was taken as 100 percent. We had to have some base line from which to work. So if you say the bottom salary of a full professor is 100 percent, you can work down from that or up from that. After that you move the base of the full professor up in light of the cost of living. Whenever you move the salary of the full professor up 7 percent, it doesn't have an exact 7 percent effect on all other salaries. But it will affect all other salaries in a coherent way. All salaries will maintain their relationship to one another.

Was there any reason that a full professor's salary was set at 100 percent as opposed, say, to the president's salary?

It is better to tell a professor that his salary is 100 percent than to tell him it's 92 percent. Besides, that's what education is all about—it's not presidents. Presidents are a necessary nuisance in educational institutions. Professors are essential. And I'm not trying to be clever about this. It really is true. You could operate a school without a president, but there's no way to operate a school without a professor. You can operate without business managers and deans of students, admissions officers, but you can't operate without a professor. So philosophically, even, a full professor is the proper base line for a salary scale for an educational institution.

FINANCING OF SABBATICAL LEAVES
The trustees had already adopted a sabbatical plan for the faculty. Was there any tying together of this 1960 salary scale and the sabbatical plan?

Yes. The sabbatical is a delightful fringe benefit for the faculty. All of them think it's a wonderful thing. The sabbatical program was a way to enrich the salary scale without putting much more money into it. If a professor took his sabbatical overseas, the seminary paid travel expenses for him and his wife.

A lot of professors from Southern Seminary received help from the AATS sabbatical support program. Did you have any part in that?

The funding for this came from the Sealantic Fund, a part of the Rockefeller Brothers operation. AATS asked for and got them to be involved in providing sabbaticals. I was simply one of many in the AATS at that time arguing that a good sabbatical program is one of the best ways to enrich theological education. I had already bought that in my own institution, so I obviously argued for it in AATS.

Nothing you could do would mean as much to theological education as to pull small seminaries out of isolation geographically, denominationally, and so on, and expose their faculty to the wide world of academics and theological discussion.

MARTIN LUTHER KING JR.
Martin Luther King Jr. spoke at Southern Seminary in 1961. Do you remember the events leading up to this?

Dr. King was invited routinely to be a lecturer at the seminary. I didn't invite him as such. My only role in his coming was that I appointed the guest lecturers committee that invited all guest lecturers. But I never admitted during the ensuing controversy that I didn't invite him personally; this would have sounded like I was trying to say something was wrong in the invitation being issued to him. I think Southern Seminary was the only Southern Baptist agency to which he ever spoke. I thought it was appropriate for the seminarians to hear such a prominent person who rooted his position in the Bible.

I must add that we also invited the head of the White Citizens Council to lecture at the seminary, but nobody had a problem with that in those days. The truth is that the guest lecturers committee was trying to get people to state their position on major issues in detail during that particular era in American life.

Did you receive some flack over Dr. King's appearance on campus?

Yes, all my speaking engagements in my native Mississippi were canceled. A fellow Baptist in Dothan, Alabama, assured me that he had $40,000 that he was going to use to get me fired. I told him if he'd give me $25,000, I'd quit, and he'd save money.

Was he serious?

He was serious. He said frankly, "You're not the worst of the integrationists in the Southern Baptist Convention, but we're going to make an example of you, so that nobody else will do that kind of thing." He sent messages and letters to the chairmen of the deacons of all the Baptist churches—some things like that. It wasn't a very intelligent campaign, and it never had much effect.

Did the attacks on you spread to others in the seminary community?

Some faculty members defended having Dr. King speak on campus, so they became targets. The White Citizens crowd were mean. I especially resented their attacks upon my family. They would call my wife and children and tell them all sorts of nasty stuff.

DALE MOODY AND THE OKLAHOMA CONTROVERSY

Let's talk about the Dale Moody controversy in the 1960–61 era in relationship to Oklahoma Baptists.

What happened with Moody and his discussion under the tree at the Oklahoma Assembly, and his argument about the security of the believer, is general knowledge. The question, then, was what the seminary would do with this. Moody was on sabbatical at the time, but he was given an extra year's leave of absence. Newton Rayzor of the board of trustees of Southern Seminary put up the money at my request to pay his salary for the extra year. Mrs. Rayzor admired Dale Moody, so they supported Dale for that year.

In my view, the problem with Dale was always to get him to keep quiet long enough to let somebody else solve his problems for him. Dale would get a "bulldog" attitude toward controversy in which he would worry the issue to death, and he could never let it die. Keeping him out of the country for a year gave the controversy time to run its course and die out.

You must have felt considerable pressure from the people in Oklahoma.

Oh yes. Seminary presidents try to pretend they don't feel any pressure from anybody, but it keeps them awake at night. The question at Southern Seminary for any professor has always been, "Are you operating within the Abstract of Principles, or not?" There has never been any occasion in which a professor who was operating outside the Abstract of Principles was allowed to stay at Southern. My position has always been this: If you are outside the Abstract, you have already resigned.

The problem is that human language is slippery and imprecise. Sometimes it's hard to tell exactly what someone is saying. "The faith that fizzles had a fatal flaw from the first" is Dale Moody's old position on the question of the security of the believer. That position obviously fits within the Abstract of Principles. But was he saying that in different language, or was he saying something entirely different, which, subsequently under Honeycutt's administration, he affirmed he was saying.

This was before the Baptist Faith and Message, which is specific on this point. It's much more narrow than the Abstract of Principles.

Only the Abstract of Principles has ever been authoritative with Southern Seminary. Later, in the 1980s, Dale said his position was not in accord with the Abstract of Principles. But in the 1960s, he was saying it was.

ACADEMIC FREEDOM AND TENURE STATEMENT

Just after the March 1961 meeting of the seminary trustees, Southern Seminary developed a full statement on academic freedom and tenure. What brought this about?

This development went back to the 1957–58 controversy at the seminary because neither the Association of Theological Schools nor Southern Seminary had any relevant documents that addressed academic freedom issues. A third organization not related to Southern Seminary, the American Association of University Professors, did have a document.

By 1961, Southern Seminary was ready to adopt its own document on academic freedom and tenure. These two things go together because tenure means a professor is beyond being dismissed except for just cause. Tenure was tied to the academic freedom document, which defined what freedom a tenured professor had. Our thinking was that any future challenge of the seminary's dismissal of a professor would be measured by that document. The document has been slightly revised from time to time, but the basic elements in it are unchanged since 1961.

Apparently this document on academic freedom and tenure preceded the events related to Dale Moody by a few months. In a July 27 meeting there is a record indicating that you protested to the editor of Baptist Press about a premature news release on certain action taken by the Oklahoma City Baptist Pastors Conference. Do you remember that?

It had to do with the fact that Baptist Press carried a story that was incomplete. This news article did not, according to my authorities in Oklahoma City, reflect accurately all that happened in the pastors conference. It did not give the full story.

The controversy that Dale got involved in began after one of the sessions in which he was lecturing at Falls Creek assembly. He was standing out under a tree talking to several people. He had his old battered Greek Testament, and somebody challenged something he had said in his lecture. He challenged them to show him in the inspired Word of God where he was wrong.

Of course, they didn't. But when he does something like that, he is rather combative. He tends to beat his opponents over the head. It was a case of "a man convinced against his will is of the same opinion still." So he won the debate, but he lost the war. Then some of these people accused him of not teaching in accordance with the Abstract of Principles on the security of the believer. At that time he was pretty clear about where he stood, and he had no hesitancy in affirming that he was operating within the Abstract of Principles.

What was your general method or strategy in dealing with these theological controversies stirred by seminary professors?

I would always call a professor in and discuss it with him. I always asked, "Are you within the Abstract of Principles?" I wanted him to be clear that he had to make the case that he was inside the Abstract of Principles. If he once stepped outside of the Abstract of Principles, he was out, and neither he nor I could do anything about that. That was the first thing I did.

The second thing was to plead with him not to argue his own case, but to let me argue his case for him. I would be glad to defend him if he was inside the Abstract. If he would be quiet and let somebody else defend him, we had a chance of defusing the situation. It was the old lawyer thing: "The lawyer who defends himself has a fool for a client."

A theologian is the worst illustration of this principle. He generally tries to defend himself in the terms a technical theologian uses and not in the popular terms in which his critics attack him. His response is highly technical, very precise, and very abstract. What he says may be quite good and convincing to another theologian. But he usually loses the argument because the public doesn't hear the careful distinctions he tries to make.

Initially, this type of dialogue and confrontation about controversial statements threatened faculty members. But they gradually came to understand this as a routine response to any criticism of them that I had received or heard about. Once that was cleared and they were proven innocent, I would become their defender. Most of them preferred for me to deal with their critics rather than their doing it themselves. I confess that was not the most pleasant role I had as president, but I thought it was a part of my job.

CARVER SCHOOL AND SOUTHERN SEMINARY

Southern Seminary has had a long relationship with Woman's Missionary Union Training School, later the Carver School of Missions and Social Work. When did this relationship begin?

Originally, this agency was the WMU Training School, and it became the Carver School of Missions and Social Work in later years. The WMU Training School began with W. O. Carver and other seminary faculty teaching women who came to Louisville to study to become missionaries. That was in the early 1900s.

This school met in the area of Louisville near the seminary? And it had its own campus?

Yes. The WMU women raised the money, bought the property, and started a new school for women downtown. They owned a house downtown for the WMU Training School. Later, "House Beautiful" at Preston and Broadway was built for the WMU Training School, and it was operated by the Southwide WMU. The seminary was located on down Broadway from the Training School at Fifth and Broadway. The seminary moved in 1927 to a new campus on Lexington Road. The Training School stayed downtown.

Then about 1943, the WMU Training School moved from Preston and Broadway out to the Lexington Road campus. They built their own facilities across the valley from Southern Seminary. The teaching for its students was still done mostly by Southern Seminary faculty members. It was the women's division of Southern Seminary, but it was under the control of the Southwide WMU. All women were enrolled in Southern Seminary through the WMU Training School. (There were administrators and faculty members of WMU Training School who were not on the Southern Seminary faculty.)

This was in part because women were not admitted to the seminary program in those days?

Admission to the seminary program required licensing or ordination, and women were not licensed or ordained, so they couldn't enroll as degree candidates at Southern Seminary.

This arrangement with the Training School continued. But with the development of the School of Religious Education and the women's involvement at Southwestern and New Orleans, pressures were on Southern Seminary to open its program directly to women students. The changing role of women in society and in the church added greatly to the pressure. But tradition ruled.

Then, with the retirement of Miss Carrie U. Littlejohn, and the election of Miss Emily Lansdell, the name of the Training School was changed to Carver School of Missions and Social Work. This change was designed to create a new type of school that was not in competition with Southwestern or with New Orleans. What the WMU didn't realize was that once they weren't in competition with those two schools, that left Southern without a program for women in the standard mode of Southwestern and New Orleans.

Carver School people would not agree that they had dropped all religious education courses from their curriculum. But if you talked with them about this, they would say, "We're doing this new form of religious education." They weren't training people to fit into the Sunday school organization and the young people's structures of Baptist churches. The social work motif was more dominant in their thinking. They thought that emphasis also equipped people better for mission activity, whether at home or abroad.

But that left Southern Seminary, then, with no religious education program for women. We were also setting up the School of Religious Education for another set of reasons. So we began to admit women to the R. E. School. That had the effect of appearing to go into competition with the Carver School of Missions and Social Work.

The Carver School people felt it was competition. We felt that we weren't competing with them any more than they were competing with Southwestern or New Orleans. We were offering the standard religious education-type program. We already had the Music School, and women were enrolled there. There was no women's music program in the Carver School, so they didn't object to the Music School; they did object to Southern Seminary's School of Religious Education.

The president of WMU, Mrs. George Martin, from Norfolk, Virginia, decided I had set out to wreck the Carver School of Missions and Social Work. I kept saying to her, "If I did, the trustees of Southern Seminary ought to fire me, not because you object to what I have done, but because it would be a stupid move on the part of Southern Seminary. The longer you represent the WMU next door, the longer we have an inside track here in terms of the women. I want Carver School to stay alive. I'll do anything to help you, but I'm not going to cut Southern Seminary out of religious education for women simply because you've abandoned that program."

The Carver School administrators also stopped using Southern Seminary professors as their essential faculty and hired their own teachers. Therefore, they had become a separate school. They essentially put all their eggs in one basket—and that was to become an accredited school of social work. I don't know why they did this because the accrediting agency for social work schools, by their rules, could not possibly accredit Carver School. It didn't matter how good they were at social work. It was the category of institutions Carver belonged to that eliminated them from accreditation. They were not associated with a university. To be accredited, they had to be a school that was part of a university.

There was no way, technically, for Carver School to be accredited as a social work institution. I never interpreted the denial of accreditation for their program as a put-down of the quality of their work. But alas, that was the interpretation generally, and that had the effect of forcing the closing of the Carver School of Missions and Social Work.

When did you see the handwriting on the wall? What were the dates?

The handwriting was on the wall as soon as they committed themselves to accreditation by the Council on Social Work Education. I can't give you the dates when accreditation was denied. But by the time this happened, they were operating at arm's length from Southern Seminary—by their choice, not by ours. Miss Lansdell had left, and Dr. Nathan Brooks had come as the principal.

Did that change things substantially?

Not really. Nathan had been a trustee of Carver School during Miss Lansdell's tenure. He was elected because he knew her policies and was committed to and wanted to carry on the same policies. He was a very good man, and he did a fine job.

CARVER SCHOOL AND SOUTHERN MERGE

There was some discussion by 1963 regarding the Carver School endowment. Was there much to fight over?

About a million dollars, which was a lot of money in those days. Nathan Brooks, as principal, and John Sandridge, as chairman of the Carver School board of trustees, came to my home one evening. They said, "We want to discuss whether we should merge Carver School of Missions and Social Work with Southern Seminary."

I knew this kind of talk was going around, but this was the first official notification I had received from any of the Carver School personnel. My answer to them was, "Gentlemen, that's a good subject, but I'd rather not discuss it with you until you've discussed all your other alternatives. If you know that there is no other good option, I will discuss it with you. I don't want to be accused of having plotted whatever it is you decide to do about Carver School."

In my memory, I can hear John Sandidge now. He was an attorney in Louisville and the chairman of their board. He laughed and said, "You drive a hard bargain. We've already explored all the other options. We're here because this is the only option we have." I said, "All right, we'll discuss it." I relate that because I had no part in any early discussions about the future of Carver School. I did nothing to precipitate their dilemma.

Exactly when did they make you aware that they were considering a merger with the seminary?

My guess is that it was about February 1963—just a few months before the final action in regard to Carver School's future was taken.

The record seems to imply that this occurred rather quickly, but I'm sure deliberations must have been going on for some time.

It did happen quickly from Southern Seminary's perspective because of the arm's-length relationship with Carver School. The seminary didn't know what the school was doing. We could guess, and we heard the rumors, just like everybody else. But we wanted to get as far away from that situation as we could. It was going to be an explosion, particularly if anybody could tag the seminary with having done something to cause the closing of Carver School.

My position in relation to Carver School was that we were not in a position to do anything more than preserve the history and heritage of the institution, which began as a part of Southern Seminary. We promised we would reincorporate it into Southern Seminary. And the seminary kept its promise. We changed our colors to scarlet and gold to incorporate the Carver School colors (purple and gold). Some other things were done to pick up the heritage, but we were not willing to accept any of their program.

We did agree to institute a church social work program and to use Carver School's endowment. The agreement was, "If you give us the endowment, we will use it to set up a church social work program. But we can't take on your personnel. We will try to work it out with your students so that their credits will become our credits, your alumni will become our alumni, and their degrees will become our degrees. They won't be graduates of a defunct institution; they will be graduates of Southern Seminary."

So most of the personnel did leave Carver School, and the school closed when it merged with Southern?

The programs were discontinued, except for a couple of things: We set up a program of church social work and hired Dr. Walter Delamarter to develop it. We also tried to get the Foreign Mission Board to tell us what kind of special courses they would like for the seminary to offer. It was their policy in those days to say, "That's none of our business." They had a doctrinaire notion of the separation of institutions.

We kept saying, "O.K., we understand what you're saying, but you are the major employer of our foreign mission graduates. We'd like to equip these people the way you want them equipped. Do you want us to teach linguistics, for example?"

Were there other aspects to this negotiation you could tell us about?

I had no desire to merge the two schools, because their buildings were white elephants at the time we acquired them. The merger gave us an addition to the campus that we couldn't use. It took us a decade to figure out what to do with the Carver School facilities.

Finally, we moved the business offices of the seminary over there. We put the Boyce School in the building. We used some of the dormitory space. We converted their old Rankin Hall, the Carver School's administrative office building, into a child care center. It's a good child care center. It's just in the wrong location on the seminary campus. But that's where we had an available building. So, in effect, we had buildings that didn't meet our needs. And we had building needs we couldn't get met because we had empty space as a result of the merger.

We were in the post-1958 period still. We were still in the process of recovering from the controversy. So we had space. We had faculty members. In some areas we had more faculty members than we needed for the student body. In other areas we didn't have enough faculty members. We were scrambling to try to balance the faculty out and get good people. We had a full agenda without having the Carver School merger added to our plate.

But had you not accepted the Carver School property, there is a good possibility that the land and the buildings would have just gone to creditors?

They would have sold the property and given the money to some cause. And I suppose every school wants all of the land contiguous with what it owns. The Carver School property was contiguous to the seminary campus, and it tended to fill out the block. Now the seminary campus runs on Lexington Road from one street to the next.

The kitchen of the Carver School sat vacant for years. It now houses the computer activity of Southern Seminary. It was wonderful because it had all the electric power we needed. It's halfway underground. This doesn't bother the computer; it works well down there. It's protected, and the temperature is controlled. The old walk-in refrigerator is a marvelous storage area for our computer records, a nice fireproof safe. So we are using most of the old Carver School facilities now.

And the Boyce Bible School has used the auditorium, the classrooms, and the offices. And, by the way, the chancellor (me) now has an office over there away from the new president. In spite of my pessimism about the merger at the time, we would have made a major blunder if we hadn't agreed to the acquisition!

Did the WMU continue to put any money into the former Carver School?

Not a dime. It stopped with the merger. We've never been able to raise any money, by the way, through WMU. Efforts have been made to do so, but we've never succeeded. We have WMU Drive and WMU Chapel, and all sorts of references to WMU in those facilities. The building became Carver Building, following the Carver School idea. So we've tried to preserve their heritage.

It was important to the alumni of the Training School and Carver School that they became alumni of Southern Seminary, so that they were not academic orphans. That was the most substantively important thing, of no value except to individuals. But certain individuals found that their degrees turned out to be more rather than less because Southern Seminary was accredited by both the Association of Theological Schools and the Southern Association of Colleges and Secondary Schools. That ascribed an accreditation to their degrees that they had not had in the past.

There's a funny twist to this story. Carver School tried to effect an affiliation with the Kent School of Social Work in the University of Louisville and could not do it. But within a year after they joined the seminary, we had that affiliation because of a change of personnel at Kent.

Could you summarize the liabilities and assets the seminary gained in the Carver School merger?

The building was not in the best of shape, but it wasn't in horrendous shape. We tried moving the Music School into the building. But that didn't work. It wasn't sound proofed; in fact, it was anything but sound proofed. It turned out that the building just had a dropped ceiling. The light fixtures would transmit the sound into the open space above and travel all over that floor. Nothing was right for the Music School, so we went back and built Cooke Hall over by the chapel. Then we were back with an empty building again.

The renovation of the Rankin Building to create a child care center cost us about as much as it would have cost to build a brand new one. The difference was that by spending that amount, we could use what we had and not have to pay for an empty building as well as a new child care center. We would have preferred to put the child care center in another location instead of on the front edge of the campus.

This merger added about eight acres to the seminary property, a million dollars worth of buildings, and over a million dollars worth of "funds functioning as endowment," which is in the hands of the Southern Baptist Foundation. We continue to report to WMU about our use of the endowment.

LIMITS ON FACULTY ABSENCES

In January 1963 the trustees expressed appreciation for the "self-imposed limits of the faculty being away from the classroom." What did this mean?

We had been through a period with a shortage of faculty in certain areas. The faculty members buckled down and committed themselves to being on campus and to carrying whatever load was required to see that the students got the education they were entitled to.

This recognition from the trustees was a well-deserved accolade to the faculty. They had voluntarily imposed limitations on their absence from the campus. This was very different than the situation that existed back in 1958. In those days every faculty member was viewed as a law unto himself. The professors tended to come and go as they pleased. It was a situation where every department was a school within the seminary, so every professor was president of his own school.

The professors were entitled to one week per semester out of the classroom by this new statement.

Yes, one week for their interests. In addition, they could have one week out for the seminary's interest. So they might attend a state convention but not charge it against a week they would use on a revival or something like that.

STUDENT AID

How did the student aid system at Southern work during this era?

Normally the Louisville community supplied sufficient employment for students. The problem was not that students went hungry. The real problem was that they didn't have time to breathe because they would end up with two or three jobs. Some students would be making too much money, in the sense that they worked too much. Beyond that, the seminary had enough money to sort of tide the students over a brief crisis. What the seminary couldn't do was provide living expense for a student over the next six months. But we could help him with student aid funds for a month or two.

Did you work to expand those funds?

Yes. We worked very hard to expand student aid funds. That's the easiest money at the seminary to raise. When people won't give you money for anything else, they will give you student aid money. And they will especially give you money if it is paid to the student for something he or she does. The seminary employs a great many students, and that employment is related to their classroom responsibilities.

I used to be able to say that no student ever left Southern Seminary for lack of money. I don't think that's true now. I think the last few years have created crises, particularly for the student with two or three children, which the seminary couldn't handle either through its resources or through its friends or through employment in the city. A student couldn't get a job that would pay him enough to support a family of five.

One area, perhaps, where student aid comes in is through churches?

Yes, you get a lot of money from the home churches of students. A church will send money to help John Doe.

And also the churches in the Louisville area that employ student pastors?

Yes, student pastors. Members of the churches meet a student, find he's in need, and pitch in to help out. I'll see somebody, and they'll say in an off-hand way, "I've been helping this student."

It's remarkable, really, when you think about the degree to which the church members in Louisville accept the seminary as a part of their parish. They look after the students, worry about them, and get angry at the seminary if a student doesn't live and act like they think a seminary student should. They won't handle that problem; they'll see the president about that one. And unfortunately, with 3,000 students, almost everything that happens to people in the course of time will happen to seminary students.

SEMINARY VILLAGE
On January 14, 1964, an offer was reported by trustee V. V. Cooke for $1 million for the Seminary Village property. Were some of the trustees anxious to sell the property?

Until the decline in enrollment at Southern following the 1958 controversy, the students were standing in line begging to get into Seminary Village. While the rents were considerably below the market for rents in the area, we were actually paying for Seminary Village out of rental income.

I think we put $400,000 of the seminary's money into buying the property for $1.7 million-plus. So $1.3 million of the property's cost was paid by rental income. In fact, other housing was subsidized by Seminary Village, we found out, when we did a more careful check. By "other housing," I'm referring to Mullins, Rice, Fuller, and so on. Our rents were too low on those facilities. But the total housing bill was coming out zero because of Seminary Village.

That raises an issue that came up later when the seminary attempted to raise the rent on on-campus housing and the students were unhappy about it.

That occurred when we finally figured out what was happening with the total housing picture. The reports didn't accurately reflect the personnel costs, where the maintenance people were doing their work. Seminary Village was carrying the overhead. The other student housing wasn't carrying its part of the load.

So Seminary Village was an asset; it paid for itself; the students loved it. But then with the downturn in enrollment, we had to rent to non-students in order to fill it up. That made certain trustees less than happy. A few trustees, including Mr. Cooke, didn't want to buy Seminary Village in the first place. They remembered it as the first government housing project built in Louisville.

Was it inexpensive housing when it was first built?

No, it wasn't inexpensive, but it was a government-funded housing development by a private developer. This offended the pure free-enterprise people.

RENOVATION OF SEMINARY VILLAGE

Did Seminary Village reach the point where it was expensive to maintain?

Yes. The complex was getting older. The bills for maintenance were beginning to come in. The plumbing was not as new as it used to be. The wiring was bad. The heating plants were old. We did eventually renovate Seminary Village from stem to stern, adding additional bedrooms to certain apartments. We spent about $3 million renovating a building complex that we had bought for $1.7 million. That will tell you something about the situation with this property.

Was $1 million a good offer for the property in 1964?

It was ridiculous, nowhere near what the property was worth. The local trustees would have sold Seminary Village almost any time, and I would agree to sell it, provided we were in a position to build apartments along Grinstead Drive along the north side of the campus. This would have brought the seminary community into one campus. I wasn't totally opposed to selling it. But then by the time we got around to selling, the pressure for housing was so great there wasn't any way we could provide 265 apartment units to replace Seminary Village.

FELLOWS AND PROFESSORS' ASSISTANTS

In January 1964 a new pattern regarding fellows and professors' assistants was adopted. Tell us about this.

A fellow was a graduate student who assisted a professor. Each professor had one fellow. Each fellow got to be very close to his graduate professor. I served as a fellow when I was a graduate student at Southern. We students would have taken the job for free if necessary. But the seminary paid us $30 a month whether we deserved it or not. That was the old pattern.

By 1964 the enrollment at Southern was building back. The faculty still wasn't adequate for the size of the enrollment; classes were getting to be the size of congregations again. Faculty members had grown accustomed to having small classes, even if it was just a temporary situation. Now they wanted two or three fellows because of their big classes. They also wanted fellows related to their instructional task rather than simply an honorific relationship of a graduate student. This required fellows who would grade for the professor as well as teach for him when he was absent from class.

But there were not enough graduate students to go around, or the graduate students didn't want the jobs because they had more lucrative jobs as pastors of churches. Grading and teaching for a professor was hard work and took a lot of time. The old fellow system just collapsed of its own weight because of all these changing circumstances.

So I tried to do a different thing. What I had in my mind was to give the professor a stipend to employ assistants. Now I didn't care how he spent it; he could hire somebody to cut his grass if he preferred to grade papers. I thought that was a good investment in the professor. It was a marvelous idea, but there was just one problem: it didn't work because faculty members didn't want it to work. This new approach meant they had to do more decision-making and make more judgments than they wanted to make. They liked the old system where fellows were attached to them, and they would do whatever they could make them do.

There was some funding given by a Mr. Garrett for the institution of the Garrett Fellows?

He was a friend of my father in Memphis, Tennessee, who left an estate to the seminary. We designated the income from his estate to create the Garrett Fellows.

Each department had one Garrett Fellow, as I understand it, and then there were other fellows and professors' assistants.

That was a way to raise the salary of graduate fellows in the old-fashioned fellow pattern, to give status, and to memorialize the Garrett name, which we were supposed to do. So we carried out the terms of Mr. Garrett's will and did something that was useful to the seminary at the same time.

SEMINARY CHARTER STUDIED

The minutes of the trustee meeting in March 1964 note the beginning of a study of the charter of the seminary. What was the background for the study of the charter?

We were still trying to resolve the matter of the election of trustees. The seminary's Fundamental Laws, which were a part of the charter, required that the Convention nominate three trustees for each position, and the trustees of the seminary would select one from those three nominees.

I had been the author of the SBC Executive Committee recommendation that the Convention require all of the agencies to amend their charters to provide that charters could not be changed without Convention approval. I really didn't change my judgment, but I just ran into a legal thicket when I got over on the other side as chief executive of an agency.

About 1964, I think, we discovered that the seminary was all fouled up in ways that nobody had ever dreamed. The Fundamental Laws of the seminary had never been registered in Kentucky. These Fundamental Laws were incorporated in the charter of the seminary in Kentucky by reference only and, as such, had never been put into the Kentucky documents.

We hired a very efficient law firm to sort it out. We amended the charter and cleaned up the whole legal mess. The charter for the seminary that's registered now in Kentucky is correct. It includes the Fundamental Laws provision for the Convention to "nominate one or more" trustees for each vacancy on the board of trustees.

The Convention decides whether it will nominate one or two or three or ten trustees for Southern Seminary, and then the seminary's board of trustees elects from that slate somebody to fill the vacancy.

DEAN OF WOMEN

In July 1964 a job description was approved for a dean of women at the seminary. What brought this about?

At this point we had a lot of women on campus, but there was nobody on the staff whose specific job was to look after the interest of women. Dr. Louise Foreman Blount had done this earlier for about ten years. Contrary to the tenets of the women's liberation movement, there is a difference between men and women; their needs are different. The situation works differently for them, especially in a theological seminary. We needed to have an advocate of the interests of women in the administrative structure of the seminary.

In my thinking, this person would relate to the seminary's dean of students. It would be a number two slot under the dean of students. Later, we ended up with the dean of students being a woman. This development meant that a woman was a part of the Deans Council, but that was not the same person we began with as dean of women.

So, basically, the dean of women position was gradually moved out of the dean of students' office?

Well, it didn't fly too well, to be honest about it. Allen Graves was then dean of students, and Pitts Hughes became the dean of women, on his recommendation. Later on Graves was moved out of the dean of students job, and later she moved out of the dean of women position. Then I believe Elaine Dickson came in as dean of students. Then Arthur Walker came in as vice president for student affairs, a somewhat different job from dean of students, but including dean of students. Then we went back to a dean of students, and the present woman dean of students was elected.

There is no longer, then, a dean of women at Southern Seminary?

No. If we had a male dean of students, we would probably end up with a woman somewhere in the organization as director of admissions, or director of student aid, or something else, to keep a woman's perspective at a high level. A male-dominated institution, like Southern Seminary, needs to hear the points of view of women. We made an effort to try to equalize the opportunity for men and women students.

GRADUATE PROGRAM

What effect did the 1958 controversy at Southern have on the graduate program at the seminary?

The bark of the accrediting agency was so loud that the general public thought accreditation had been withdrawn. We were so shaken by the entire controversy that we thought we had weakened our graduate program considerably. So we closed the graduate school admissions for awhile. This temporary closure to new students was necessary because we didn't have the personnel to supervise as many graduate students as we had, much less any new students. The faculty members who remained had to take over the graduate students of faculty members who had left. The faculty was overloaded, so we just shut down new admissions to the graduate program temporarily.

This move, by the way, was what convinced the accrediting agency of our good faith. This showed them that we were a responsible graduate school that would go beyond what was required because of its high standards. When the accrediting agency returned, they not only did not withdraw accreditation; they withdrew all the notations they had issued against us to point up our areas of weakness. They indicated we had shown the character of a first-rate academic institution through this trying situation. We have the faculty and Penrose St. Amant to thank for that.

Was this substantially his idea?

No, I think it came out of the faculty committee. The professors were the ones who felt the pinch. They were the ones who complained and said, "We're going to use all the resources we have to keep faith with the students who are already in the program."

You also added to the faculty at that time—graduate students who were in the process of graduating, had just graduated, or who graduated a little later. Two of these were Bill Hull and Glenn Hinson.

They were in the pipeline or were added to the faculty before the other professors left. I know Hull was, and I think Hinson, too. So they were not replacements. They were young fellows just coming into the system. They just happened to come on stream at the right time. And they were two of the people whom we overloaded because we rushed them into doing some graduate supervision. Under normal circumstances, we would not have let them supervise graduate students so soon after joining the faculty.

BILLY GRAHAM CHAIR OF EVANGELISM

In January 1965 the Billy Graham Association promised support for a chair of evangelism at Southern. I believe their commitment was for $10,000 per year for three years. Tell us about this development.

Billy Graham and I have been friends since back before he became a famous personality. I met him about a year or so before his crusade in Los Angeles that projected him onto the national scene.

He came to hear me preach at Ridgecrest. I tell people that I've known Dr. Graham so long that when we met, he came to hear me preach. Which is true. But the reality is that both of us, during World War II, had been Youth for Christ speakers in various parts of the country. We read each other's publicity as we saw the Youth for Christ materials. He saw in the paper that I was speaking near his home at Ridgecrest, so he came over to hear me.

Afterward we went to his house; he gave me one of his loud, youth evangelist ties that were in vogue in those days, on the condition that I would wear it at Ridgecrest when I preached that night, which I did. I don't know who threw that tie away—probably my wife—in a fit of good taste.

That's when we met, and our friendship continues today. It is a rather peculiar order in that it's possible Billy Graham might call me tonight and talk for an hour because he has some problem. Or because he has no problem and has time on his hands, and just happened to think of it. On the other hand, we may go a year and never speak to each other. Our friendship does not require tending. It just is always there.

I'm talking like that because ours is a very warm relationship. I have great admiration and affection for him and Ruth. I've not really been with Dr. Graham since his crusade in Tampa back in the spring. I spent some time with him then. He came to Louisville in December 1972 to launch an evangelistic conference that I had dreamed of for Southern Baptist evangelists. He spent a week in Louisville with much of his team to launch that conference.

One day I was playing golf with him at Audubon Country Club in Louisville. This must have been about 1956. He was telling me that Harvard wanted his files and records, and so on. All of a sudden it dawned on me that he was fishing to say, "Don't you want them at Southern Seminary?" I stopped him in the middle of a fairway and said, "Mr. Graham, as president of Southern Seminary, I want to report to you that after a conference with the trustees and faculty of Southern Seminary, I am authorized to request that the Graham archives be deposited at Southern Seminary in the new library we are going to build."

He responded by saying, "After careful deliberation over an extended period of time, I wish to tell you that I am going to accept that invitation." That was done in about five minutes. It did take a lot of doing from there, of course. But this is the way the whole thing was initiated.

That was when the Billy Graham Room was set up?

That's right. But subsequently that whole thing just ran away from us. The Graham archives and Graham ministry snowballed to the point that he needed a building the size of our library to hold his archives. One room wasn't big enough to hold them, and the Minneapolis Graham office didn't like having the archives in a Southern Baptist institution. They are not wholly sympathetic with Baptists—and especially Southern Baptists—for reasons that are known best to them. So we began to have hassles with personnel out of Minneapolis about the archives. We reached the point where we couldn't house the archives. We didn't have room for them, and we didn't have the money to operate an archival system.

Finally, the Graham organization got the offer that related to the Wheaton College campus development. I agreed to that with the condition that microfiche of everything be deposited at the Southern Seminary library. I thought we could handle that. I thought it would be almost as useful as having the original documents, and would serve our educational purposes.

Did they follow through on their $30,000 pledge to help endow the Billy Graham professorship?

Oh yes, the Billy Graham Chair of Evangelism was funded and established. It was the first fund-raising campaign that Southern Seminary used to break the ice in trying to raise money. I figured correctly that nobody was going to tag us out for raising money to establish a chair of evangelism, and especially the Billy Graham Chair of Evangelism, with Billy Graham supporting the establishment of it. So Porter Routh and the Executive Committee discreetly looked in the opposite direction while we went out and raised the money.

So the Graham organization put in $30,000 out of the $250,000 needed? Did they help you raise the additional $220,000?

They helped in a great many ways. And this reminds me of a strange thing that happened during these fund-raising efforts. Grady Nutt came on as director of fund-raising for the seminary, and he threw the old Billy Graham files out because he didn't know what they were. One of the spots on the ceiling in the president's office is where I bounced off of it when I found out he had thrown those files away. They were prospective donor files as well as files of uncollected pledges. While we got enough money to endow the Billy Graham chair, we would have gotten a great deal more if we had had those files.

Was part of the seminary's understanding with Graham that Kenneth Chafin would become the first Billy Graham Professor of Evangelism?

No, there was no understanding with Graham about this. But I went after Chafin as the person I thought would have credibility as a professor of evangelism with the Southern faculty and constituency. Part of my dilemma was to get somebody that our faculty and constituency would accept. Chafin had a positive relationship with the Graham organization. They liked him. Every time they tested him, he passed with flying colors. They put more and more weight on him. His role as Billy Graham Professor of Evangelism at Southern opened the door to his running their schools of evangelism for their crusades, and so on.

Is there any truth to the report that he was removed from that responsibility with the Graham organization because of his support of the moderate position in the Southern Baptist Convention?

Sure, it was Graham's organization trying to get beyond the reach of controversy. Any good evangelist wants to stay away from other people's controversies. He may have a position himself on the issues, but he doesn't want any part of another controversy. This removal of Chafin from that responsibility was done as gently and as cleanly as could be done. They continued to use Chafin in a lot of ways, but they took him out of the slot where he would become controversial.

I understand that Graham has been very instrumental and supportive of you in the work of the Baptist World Alliance?

Very much so. In fact, the Baptist World Alliance, in my judgment, blew it because they were too slow in responding to Dr. Graham's offer to help us raise money for Eastern Europe. He's never withdrawn the offer, but the Alliance was simply not structured to handle fund-raising. But that's another story.

SALARY AND FRINGE BENEFITS STUDY

In 1965 you established a committee of the trustees to study salaries, retirement, disability, and fringe benefits of seminary person-

nel. It was also recommended that Booz, Allen & Hamilton be hired to conduct the study. Do you remember anything about that?

This was to be an updating of the 1957 Booz, Allen & Hamilton report, especially with reference to salaries and compensation. I wanted a pry-pole to lobby for a major increase in compensation. And we needed expert counsel about the best way to fit together the jigsaw puzzle of benefits and salaries and so on. Southern Seminary's compensation structure is a mixed bag of salary and fringe benefits. To talk only about salary doesn't touch the reality at all.

A big chunk of money available for personnel is spent on fringe benefits. The federal tax structure has created this situation for businesses as well as educational institutions. If you give a faculty member one dollar in salary, he only gets 75 cents at best. But if you give a dollar in fringe benefits, the faculty member gets 100 cents.

The seminary made various revisions to its retirement plan in 1964 and 1965. What's your basic philosophy of retirement plans and how they work best?

We were always fine-tuning the retirement plan. I wanted to increase our retirement plan because I thought a mix of inflation would create poverty situations for retired faculty, along with the tendency of faculty members who are underpaid to live to the limit of available funds. We were going to end up with a lot of retired faculty members who would be well below the poverty line and would be hurting when they got to retirement. I did not think you could make a retirement program work unless it was economically feasible for a professor to retire.

I always felt that retirement ought to be a mix of the institution's and the individual's contribution and that the institution ought to match some contribution from each person in the plan. Our plans put those features together. We tried to take several factors into account, such as the young professor starting a family and buying a house. A person in this situation can't do as much in terms of matching his retirement funds as an older person.

We made an effort in our retirement provisions to provide, roughly, 60 percent of the average of an employee's last five years' salary in retirement. That was our goal, but it didn't always come out this way in reality. It sometimes came out better than that. Sometimes it didn't come out that good, depending on length of service, how long a person had worked at Southern Seminary, where else he had been, and the nature of his job.

A foreign missionary could come to the seminary and be in a mess because he had no vested retirement plan with the Foreign Mission Board that he brought with him. So he would lose all that former service. That's the kind of thing that could happen, and we struggled to try to equalize it. We came up with all sorts of gadgets and gimmicks to help. But the main thing was to transfer money to the faculty member, and to transfer it to him at a time when he was going to need it.

How did the trustees react to this?

They believed in retirement programs. They knew that if the seminary didn't have an adequate retirement program, we would have a lot of grief when personnel came to the time of retirement.

And there were two or three instances, I believe, where you received word of some difficulty of widows of former faculty members?

Yes, and the trustees responded. They didn't like to publicize such cases because it tended to promise something that they wouldn't necessarily do for the widow of another former professor.

I understand that a much better health benefit plan was also introduced about this time?

Baptist Hospital in Louisville used to give free care to all seminary faculty, staff, and students, and then hospital insurance came on the scene. After this they provided service based on whatever insurance you carried. Then all sorts of consumer advocate things came on the scene where the hospital couldn't subsidize the seminary out of the charges to the patients paid by Blue Cross. We ended up having to provide health care through insurance programs.

FUNDING FACULTY SALARIES

The trustees also agreed in 1965 that a committee of the trustees would appear before the Executive Committee of the Southern Baptist Convention to urge funding for faculty salaries. Do you want to comment on that?

Normally the trustees expected petitioning of this type to be done by the president on behalf of the institution. But all of our talk in this period about faculty salaries as compared to other salaries within the denomination was not gaining ground. In fact, we were losing ground.

During this period I wrote an article complaining that seminary professors were more poorly paid than foreign missionaries of comparable training and experience.

There was a sense of desperation in the seminary community. We were getting to the place where we were running the school on the sacrifices of the faculty and staff. We had to have more money for salaries, or we ran the risk of diluting the quality of our faculty. This was transmitted to the trustees. They were not willing just to depend on the president to go; they wanted to go themselves and make their own case before the SBC Executive Committee.

Did you suggest this? Was it your idea?

I don't think so. It probably was initiated by the trustees. I welcomed this approach because I knew it would get the attention of the members of the SBC Executive Committee. And anything that gets their attention is more likely to get their action.

How effective was this approach?

It worked rather well; it got their attention. I don't have the numbers, but my memory is that the funds for the formula for theological education were improved.

MANDATORY RETIREMENT AT AGE 65

In October 1965 a number of questions were raised about the mandatory retirement age of 65 for seminary faculty members. What's your opinion of mandatory retirement at age 65?

The mandatory retirement age for the seminary had been 68. By this time the discussion was about retirement moving down, not to 65 but to 60, and Social Security was considering age 62 for full retirement. The assumption was that the retirement age would be moved back to an earlier and earlier age.

The seminary had to deal with the question of retirement age because this impacted what we would do about funding retirement. If we were going to enrich the funding of retirement to be ready for a professor to retire at 65, we had to say he retired normally at 65, not at 68 as heretofore. The seminary was trying to get in step with what was happening in society. It was trying to fund a better retirement program for all of its faculty and staff, and then relate that funding to normal retirement at 65.

ELLIOTT CONTROVERSY

During the time that you served as president, Southern Seminary was not the only seminary to be engaged in controversy. How did the different seminaries relate to one another in the midst of these controversies?

All of the seminary presidents would close ranks to aid any president whose institution was in the midst of controversy. They would not always do what a specific president whose institution was under the gun wanted them to do, but they would always do what they thought would be helpful. They would never do anything the president thought would be harmful.

Did the presidents serve as a sounding board for one another?

Almost always they were a sounding board. They would conduct a ventilating session for him in which he would talk to a sympathetic audience that would gently but firmly tell him he was off base or out of focus at some point. They did that because they cared that much about one another and about theological education. If they thought a president was making a mistake in the way he was handling the controversy, they would tell him so in a very supportive and tender way.

In the early 1960s, a serious controversy known as the Elliot Controversy developed at Midwestern Seminary. This involved a book, The Message of Genesis, *written by Ralph Elliott. Was Southern Seminary involved at all in that controversy?*

First of all, all theological education was involved. Any controversy that reached anything like that level of public knowledge demanded that all the seminary presidents deal with it in some way.

Did you or other seminary presidents make suggestions or recommendations on what should or should not be done in this situation?

You've got me in a very delicate situation. They answer is, Yes, we had some things to say, but we shared them with the president at Midwestern, and then we pulled back. We wouldn't do anything unless he asked for it. I remember at least one dinner for the seminary presidents in Kansas City in the midst of that controversy. We engaged in a lot of conversation about what was happening. I never could make my point. There were forces in the seminary at Kansas City that I didn't understand. I felt that the effort to defend the book was a mistake. I remember trouble in Louisville because somebody wanted me to defend Elliott's book, and I wouldn't defend the book. I responded, "No, I'm not about to defend the book. First of all, I think it was phrased badly."

Unfortunately, the whole affair got positioned as an issue of academic freedom; even the rewriting of the book was interpreted as an attack on academic freedom. There was an effort to permit Elliott to agree to a revision of the book. Some of his colleagues called him "chicken" if he agreed to rewrite the book and modify some of what was involved in controversy. He could have done that without any breach of integrity. What he meant could have been communicated more clearly to the popular mind.

Elliott was a sharp, intelligent professor, but he was also a human being—and a young human being—at that time. His respected colleagues, I think, locked him into an untenable position.

Then he lost his place among Southern Baptists?

He lost his place among Southern Baptists, and some of those colleagues who counseled him also left Southern Baptist life. It was only right that they do that. I was told they had promised Elliott they would do so. In other words, if the principle they wanted him to fight for was worth his job, it was worth theirs; they had no right to remain at Midwestern when he was required to leave. That's the administrator in me talking. I think faculty members are irresponsible if they counsel a colleague to put his career on the line without their being willing to put theirs on the line along with him.

Who are these people you are talking about?

I'm praising Heber Peacock, who left Midwestern. I believe he joined the American Bible Society. Heber did what I think he ought to have done. I take my hat off to him. He gave advice he believed in, and he proved he believed in it by his decision.

Is there any truth to the theory that Elliott wrote that book at the behest of the Old Testament departments of the seminaries as a possible textbook?

He may have written it as a possible textbook. But I can't imagine the Old Testament department of Southwestern asking a professor of any other seminary to do it. He might have done this in connection with the Seminary Extension Department, but that would be the only way. But I don't know any of that for a fact.

What Elliott was trying to communicate was better than the way he put it. He put it in such a way that he would get a backlash from the denomination. Having said that, I want to go on record as affirming this was the most ridiculous controversy you ever saw. Ralph Elliott was basically a very conservative evangelical Christian scholar—a very good professor.

I recommended him to Midwestern. Millard Berquist came to me and wanted to approach Clyde Francisco. I said, "Fine, go after him. But you won't get him. Let me give you the name of one of his younger colleagues who, if I were in your place, I would go after. I don't want to lose him, but his name is Ralph Elliott. He is a conservative, evangelical Christian and a wonderful guy."

Elliott was the least likely candidate for a controversy of anybody I knew. He was a belated victim of the 1958 controversy at Southern. The faculty at Midwestern—and many of them were in the group at Southern—opted to be hard combatants in this controversy. They were going to win the war; they would beat those fundamentalists down in a slugfest. Ralph was too young to realize that he would be the victim of his "friends."

I tried desperately to say to Millard Berquist, president at Midwestern, "Quit defending *The Message of Genesis*. There are defects in the book, and you know there are. If you had written a review of the book, you would have been critical of it. I would have been critical of it. Why do you feel that you have to defend it? Why don't you defend the young professor's right to make a scholarly statement, including being wrong in his first outing, and let it go at that?" I made a special trip to Kansas City to say that to President Berquist.

After Elliott was dismissed, he was in Louisville one day. I said to him, "Ralph, I'm sorry about what happened to you. If you had stayed at Louisville, you would still be a Southern Seminary professor." He said, "I've thought of that many times; I guess I would be." It was not that he was right and lost the war; it was that the war was fought on the wrong terms and the wrong way.

Ralph Elliott didn't deserve what happened to him. Southern Baptists deserved to have Ralph Elliott for life as one of their best Old Testament professors. The caricature of him as a Bible-denying kind of person was totally wrong. What he was saying is exactly what the knowledgeable person who understands the nature of the Hebrew language would have said about the general subject of the message of the Book of Genesis. But today Ralph Elliott could write *The Message of*

Genesis, and he wouldn't make some of the mistakes he made in his first outing.

BAPTIST FAITH AND MESSAGE OF 1963

Looking back from twenty years later, what is your opinion of the Baptist Faith and Message statement of 1963? What reactions did you have as this confession was being formulated?

This statement ran the risk that all confessions run: They generally are formulated in a crisis and therefore they tend to be written against whatever is perceived as the heresy of the time. Consequently, they tend to fall off the other side of a balanced biblical interpretation. So I'm always a little nervous about confessions of faith composed in a crisis. You wonder how balanced the group that composes the next confession of faith will be.

Let me say that the work done in 1963 was done well. I felt this revision of the 1925 Baptist Faith and Message was a good one and that it was well balanced and appropriate. So the concerns in the seminary community at the time of the statement were thoroughly allayed by the document that came forth.

Now the other concern was that the document would not remain a statement of faith but would gradually, like barnacles, accumulate an interpretation that would give it more the force of a creed. And of course, that accumulation has begun. It is a long way from being the source of great anxiety. But we have moved farther toward accepting the 1963 document as a creed than we ever approached accepting the 1925 document as having creedal force.

Why do you think that's the case?

The first contributing factor is the evaporation of homogeneity among Southern Baptists. There was a time when Southern Baptists were basically Anglo-Saxons in the southeastern quarter of the United States, with very similar educational and cultural backgrounds. The spread of the Southern Baptist Convention throughout the United States and the shifting of population within the United States are forces that have developed a situation in which there is suspicion between areas and cultural groups in the country.

The Southwest is thought by some to be excessively fundamentalist, and the eastern seaboard as being excessively liberal. Those are caricatures of an area and, obviously, are inappropriate because there is no homogeneity among Baptists in these areas. There is more conservatism in some quarters than others, but this general statement would include all areas.

Then we have the introduction into the Southern Baptist Convention of some very large segments of Baptists who have not shared the heritage that was Southern Baptist at an earlier stage. They have come in from a background of liberalism that Southern Baptists did not normally deal with, and also from a background of evangelical fundamentalism which was not very strong within Southern Baptist experience at previous periods of our history.

Today, Southern Baptists have this kind of diversity, and the resulting mistrust of one another. Therefore, we have adopted the feeling that it is desirable to use the Baptist Faith and Message to enforce some conformity and homogeneity among all these different points of view.

We're not quite as content as we used to be to raise a standard and let all who will subscribe to that standard be accepted as brothers under the lordship of Christ. We no longer are eager to say, "If they wish to cooperate in the enterprises of Southern Baptists, fine. If they do not want to cooperate, that is their privilege." That was the old standard. Now we want to draw a circumference around Southern Baptists and prescribe the outer edges that define a legitimate Southern Baptist. This pushes us toward creedal definitions.

The Sunday School Board adopted the policy of requiring their employees to sign the Baptist Faith and Message shortly after it was adopted. Is this what you're talking about—the move toward a creedal statement?

This would be one of the evidences of the move in the direction of creedalism, but it was neither a huge thing nor a distressing thing. It was simply the way the grass blows when you toss it into the wind. This indicated that trends were moving in a certain direction.

K. OWEN WHITE

K. Owen White was elected president of the Southern Baptist Convention at its meeting in Kansas City in 1963. He represented a particular point of view in the Convention at that time. He came to

Southern Seminary as the speaker for commencement. Do you remember this event?

I felt rather close to K. O. White, but I did not agree with some of the things he said and did. I had a policy of always asking the Convention president to speak at some formal convocation at Southern Seminary. It seemed to me to be appropriate to ask him to speak at commencement—in recognition of the office rather than as an affirmation of agreement with his ideas.

His election did not seem to bring about any dramatic changes in the denomination. Do you sense that some of those who wanted changes felt they were short-changed in his one-year presidency?

He was the hero of certain elements within the Convention. He spoke vigorously and effectively in behalf of the positions he held and opposed. But at this point the attitude of Southern Baptists was that you did not organize your position; you simply verbalized it. You stated what you believed and called on people to rally to your viewpoints and support them if they were in agreement. This is what K. O. White did. There was a rallying to his position and a rallying on the other side, but no formal action was taken to change things through Convention structure.

That's why I think we could say that White's election did not seem to make any long-term difference in the nature of the Convention. It made a difference only in the sense that positions were clarified and the presence of disagreements was noted.

MULLINS HALL RENOVATION

In the spring of 1965, the trustees spent a great deal of time debating the renovation of Mullins Hall. Tell about this.

Mullins Hall had wonderful brass plumbing that theoretically would last forever. But the original builders in the 1920s had underestimated the water of Louisville, Kentucky, which built up deposits inside the pipes. Over time, half-inch pipes had become quarter-inch pipes in terms of the area for passage. This reduced the water pressure in the four-story dormitory.

There were other factors. The building was beginning to look old in terms of style. Further, the building needed to be air-conditioned. The rooms in Mullins Hall had high ceilings and tall windows. It was not desirable to air-condition all that cubic footage inside a room. The problem was that it was going to cost more to renovate the building than to build a new one of the same size.

Mullins was built like a bomb shelter. In fact, there have been fires in rooms there over the years. It was like building a fire in a stove—the fire was contained inside the room because it couldn't break through those concrete walls. The building had concrete-and-steel floors. It took a workman with a diamond-tip drill bit twenty minutes to cut a hole through the floor for new pipes. It was a major thing to drill a two-inch hole through the floor. There was such a web of steel in the concrete that a workman would probably hit two quarter-inch steel bars trying to drill a hole through six to ten inches of concrete. They didn't spare the cement when they built Mullins Hall! E. Y. Mullins meant for the building to last forever.

The Southern Baptist Convention approved $675,000 for the renovation. Apparently the trustees debated this at some length because this was not nearly enough money to renovate the building.

That amount is probably what was put in the capital needs program for the project. Traditionally, the Southern Baptist Convention funds less than one-half of what is needed for a capital needs project for the older seminaries.

The trustee minutes indicated that you had discussed this matter with Dr. Porter Routh, executive secretary of the Southern Baptist Executive Committee. Apparently he affirmed that you could proceed to raise funds from other sources available to the seminary. What did that mean?

This meant we could raise money for the project from reserves and borrowing, as long as we could pay it back within three years from rentals on the rooms in Mullins. The SBC Executive Committee assumed that the older seminaries were strong enough to find money. Maybe the seminary president didn't know where to look for it, but the SBC Executive Committee was sure he could find it. Fortunately, with the aid of trustees and alumni, he generally did find it, even when he didn't know where to look.

So Dr. Routh was indicating that $675,000 was all the Convention was going to give for this project?

Yes, and that the project was needed and recognized as a legitimate project. He was telling us to go ahead and raise the money from wherever we could find it. There was a suspicion that the older seminaries had pockets full of money that was not visible generally.

Isn't that true for all agencies?

There is a minor sense in which that's true—and it would be very sad if it were not. In other words, there are reserves and there are contingency funds available to most SBC agencies. But it usually creates a crisis if an institution goes that route. And this crisis turns out generally to be more expensive than the denomination recognizes. The reason is that the administrator becomes preoccupied with trying to solve that financial dilemma. This means he neglects some other more important program and personnel issues within the institution.

Did you discuss these issues with Dr. Routh very often?

I would discuss anything of this sort with him for two reasons: One, I thought it appropriate for the SBC executive secretary to be aware of what was going on within the denomination. Two, he was a friend, and he knew things I didn't know. In these discussions I would sometimes be made aware of trends, developments, or issues within the denomination that impinged on the decision I was making. Finally, I hoped I would find him in a happy mood with a soft heart and elicit his cooperation in securing additional funds. But I never found him in one of those moods during those times when I needed help.

I've heard it suggested that the decisions related to funding and Cooperative Program division during his tenure as the executive secretary of the Executive Committee were substantially made by him. Is that true?

It's hard for those of us on the outside to be certain about that. That is the official line and the report. We were aware of the strong influence of Albert McClellan in terms of the analysis of issues. But I was never quite sure whether Dr. Routh made the decision on the basis of data provided by Dr. McClellan.

At the same time as the decision relating to Mullins Hall, the Southern Baptist Seminary Foundation was approved to seek $300,000 to renovate Mullins. At that time how much outside fund-raising could an agency do without violating the Business and Financial Plan?

You could raise funds on your own, but you were supposed to approach the donor one-on-one, unless you were seeking endowment. We did the best we could under these conditions. You would run into criticism from state secretaries and state agencies because you invariably bumped into some of their fund-raising efforts in the process.

INTER-AGENCY COUNCIL

The whole matter of SBC coordination comes into focus here. How big a role did the SBC Inter-Agency Council and its subsidiary organizations play in these kinds of things?

Not very much. I don't remember its being effective beyond the sharing of information about what the agencies were doing. The agencies then were substantially independent entities that tried to work together. They tried to be fraternal in their relationships with one another. They would not deliberately hamper one another or intentionally run into one another. If they knew where the other agencies were and what they were doing, it reduced the possibility of collision.

Did you have any part in developing the Inter-Agency Council?

Not really. The seminaries had to fight to be members in full standing of this council. Some people felt that the agencies that had church-related organizations, such as the Brotherhood, were the key people who should compose the Inter-Agency Council.

I became a kind of maverick at this point because I said, "Go ahead and solve those church programming problems, but the seminaries also have some more issues to discuss. Our problems have to do with how do we relate to the Executive Committee and the Convention. We're seeing a coalescing of new powers within the Executive Committee, and new roles within the Executive Committee, and frequently these are at the expense of one or more traditional agency prerogatives. So why don't we talk about our role, vis-à-vis the Executive Committee and the Convention."

That never got off the ground because Porter Routh and Albert McClellan always attended the Inter-Agency Council meetings. They pressed the point that the Inter-Agency Council was not an agency and had no rights and no responsibilities except to talk to the Executive Committee.

How would you describe more recent years of the Inter-Agency Council compared to some of those earlier years when you met as agency heads?

It was more of a fellowship meeting than anything else. The hard details always got pushed down into one of the suborganizations of the Inter-Agency Council. Those suborganizations tended to be staffed by an Executive Committee staff member. This is where things were hammered out rather than among the agency heads themselves.

Was this a time when the Executive Committee was assuming more power, or the agencies were maintaining their independence?

The agencies had a feeling that the SBC Executive Committee was acquiring power, so they began to band together to protect their vested interests. This was a defensive alliance rather than an attacking alliance. The agencies, even with all their complaints from time to time, are aware that a strong SBC Executive Committee is essential to their welfare. They just wanted to keep the role of the Executive Committee, the role of the agencies, and the role of the Convention in balance.

Did you and James Sullivan of the Baptist Sunday School Board engage in much conversation at this point?

Not a great deal of conversation. It was a subject we would discuss from time to time. Of course, the Sunday School Board had a lot of interest in this subject, and so did the seminaries.

Dr. Sullivan is on record as being strongly opposed to the concept of the Executive Committee becoming the Convention ad interim. *Did the two of you ever discuss that subject?*

Yes. I'm a little more moderate on the subject than he is because there's no other *ad interim* Convention entity. I think the Executive Committee has to be the Convention *ad interim,* but I think it ought to be super-sensitive. Perhaps there ought to be legal constraints around its functioning on behalf of the Convention.

The risk is that the Convention *ad interim* (the Executive Committee) might decide that most of the work of the Convention will be done in the interim. That is the risk, and the point at which I agree with Sullivan. I made a comment about that at the dedication of the present Baptist Building on James Robertson Parkway. I observed that I hoped the Executive Committee would not think of themselves as the senate in session but as the servants of Southern Baptists meeting to further the evangelistic and ministry outreach of Southern Baptists. Porter Routh thought these remarks were not appropriate at the dedication of the building.

INVESTING IN REAL ESTATE—BY TRUSTEES

In 1965 the full trustee board of Southern Seminary advised the financial board "to give further thought to the possibility of more investment in real estate in addition to stocks and bonds." Then three months later the financial board reported that Southern Seminary had property on Broadway in downtown Louisville. Tell us about this.

This happened because some trustees of the seminary from Houston, Texas, were investing in Houston real estate and realizing immense capital gains. They were sometimes critical of the Louisville financial board because it was more conservative than Houston investors would have been. We weren't experiencing capital gains in real estate that Houston was experiencing, and it put the Louisville financial board on the defensive. But the real estate situation in Louisville did not warrant the kind of real estate investments that were occurring in Houston.

Was there reason to believe that the return on investments for the seminary was too low?

Oh no, it was reasonably good. It depended on your understanding of the purpose of your investing—how much risk you were willing to take. If you were willing to take great risks, you could probably improve your return—if you were both wise and fortunate. On the other hand, you could lose your shirt. The point was that the investment climate for real estate was better in Houston. If the seminary had known how to do it, it could have taken its investment dollars and bought a huge tract of Houston real estate and sat on it for twenty-five years and been a lot better off than it is today.

But that's hindsight. There are some other places in the United States, including Florida in the 1920s, that have looked like that from time to time. But then there was a bust that followed the real estate boom in Florida. We've not seen a bust yet in the real estate market comparable to some in the past, but some of these investors for the seminary had seen real estate booms and busts as well as stock market booms and busts. Basically, the philosophy of the seminary was to be prudent investors.

The trustees also took some action on the Broadway property. They indicated they had deferred action on transferring this property from funds functioning as endowment to permanent endowment funds. What did this mean?

The Fifth and Broadway property in Louisville, Kentucky, was the site on which the seminary was built when it moved to Louisville in 1877. Boyce bought that property for $100 a front foot. He was severely criticized for paying such an exorbitant price for the property. I've never worked it out to determine how much he paid for the property. But if it cost $100,000 in 1877, that was a lot of money. The seminary has sold it now for more than $3 million. So even granted inflation and the times, Boyce's investment doesn't look so bad.

That property was left when the seminary moved out to Lexington Road in 1927–28. The seminary used it as an investment plot and first leased it to the Brown Hotel for a garage and then to the Greyhound Bus Company for a bus station. The income on that plot of land was better than the return on the same number of dollars invested in stocks and bonds, so it was a good investment. In fact, the annual return on the Broadway property was about $100,000 net per year.

To get out of that category where we were taking $100,000 per year and lumping it in with rental income from dormitory rooms and other campus property, the Broadway property was designated as funds functioning as endowment. This is a category just short of making it endowment. It means that the corpus, the value of the property, is viewed as endowment with this one reservation—the trustees could alter the use of that corpus. But if it were pure endowment, the trustees would have no control over the proceeds of the property. Legally, the trustees cannot spend the corpus of endowment; they must invest it as endowment for the school.

A trustee meeting in early 1984 dealt with the question of what to do with those funds functioning as endowment now that they were not real estate but cash (after the sale of the property to Morris Brown). So that issue was back on the agenda of the trustees, and they had to ask the question again, "Do we now take this cash and put it in endowment, and thereby lock it up forever, or will we find some intermediate place to use the money?" I went on record as recommending that it stay in funds functioning as endowment.

We put it where the trustees would have to act if the corpus were to become available. Psychologically, they would have to jump a high barrier to take the corpus of funds functioning as endowment and spend it on a building project or something of that sort.

PRESIDENT'S SABBATICAL

In 1966 you gave a report to the trustees as president and indicated that you affirmed the value of a sabbatical you had taken. Was the sabbatical a high point of renewal for you?

Yes. I spent it living in a Union Theological Seminary professor's apartment up against the Riverside Baptist Church in New York City, attending classes primarily at Columbia University and also at Union Seminary. This was the first time I had ever had that much time to back off and read things without some use for what I was reading being scheduled within the next year. Just to do basic study and research without reference to whether it would ever have any practical value was different and refreshing.

I did some study in early church history, an area in which I had almost no training prior to this time. I also did some study in American church history. I did some work in epistemology, consisting of a post-doctoral seminar at Columbia on "how do you know"? My chief helper and friend was a professor of physics at Columbia. We paired up because he was dealing with the area of scientific knowledge and information that presumably is verifiable by experimentation. I was dealing with the abstractions of philosophy and theology. We discovered very quickly that if you pushed the issue far enough, we were both in the same boat—that you still were up against the problem of how a human being identifies reality.

I am trying to illustrate the point that I was engaged in a type of study that presumably would never have any specific value. On the other hand, I did some study in fund-raising, which was very useful to me in my responsibilities as president of Southern Seminary.

OVERSEAS TRAVEL

In April 1966 you secured approval from the trustees to attend a meeting of the BWA in London in 1966, followed by a trip to the Congress on Evangelism in Berlin. Did you handle trips outside the United States differently than your normal travel?

Yes. I always thought it was wise to let the trustees make a decision on overseas trips, simply because I made enough of them that I didn't want them to begin to think that I was coming and going on unauthorized junkets. They actually kept trying to give blanket approval to attend these meetings at my discretion. But then I would come back and ask for approval on the next specific trip. The cost was not all that exorbitant, and the seminary trustees were trusting me to make decisions that required more money than that. But this was money being spent on me. I just wanted to make sure I didn't take advantage of the freedom they gave me.

I traveled a lot in those days. I traveled for the Foreign Mission Board, the Baptist World Alliance, and the United States Air Force. President Eisenhower appointed me a member of the board of visitors of the Air University (1957–59). This was a paper university headquartered in Maxwell Field, Alabama, that was charged with officer training for the Air Force. That did get me an invitation to be the baccalaureate speaker at the first graduation at the Air Academy in Colorado—with President Eisenhower scheduled as the commencement speaker.

There were a few instances in which Mrs. McCall went with you. Did you have discretionary funds for that?

Yes, I nearly always had a discretionary account known as the Jarman Fund. I could pay for her travel out of the Jarman Fund, if the trustees approved.

CHANGE IN TERMS OF TRUSTEES OPPOSED

The trustees voted in April 1966 to express "vigorous opposition to the Southern Baptist Convention Executive Committee limiting trustees to two full terms of four years each." Do you remember the circumstances surrounding that?

This was a proposal within the SBC Executive Committee for recommendation to the Convention. They planned to recommend that the terms of the trustees of all the other agencies be increased from three-year terms to four-year terms, but they wanted to reduce the seminary trustees from five-year to four-year terms. My position was a little more basic. It was that the central documents of the Southern Baptist Convention did not permit the SBC Executive Committee to make this recommendation.

Why?

Because all the Executive Committee could do was to approve or disapprove the charter of the agencies. They had no right to require changes in the charter of an agency. If they started meddling in the agency charters, they were going to open Pandora's box for the future.

So you expressed your feelings to Porter Routh on this?

Vehemently!

And what was the upshot between the two of you?

Eventually he saw it my way. The debate between us was rather vigorous. And I was prepared to fight it on the floor of the Convention and to rally other forces. The Executive Committee is vulnerable to a public fight on a specific issue, particularly if the opponent is willing to detail the areas in which the responsibilities of the Executive Committee have been enlarged. They didn't want that to happen on the floor of the Convention, even though they might think they could win the battle.

There must have been a number of occasions when you and Porter Routh were not on the same side.

We have had several knock-down-drag-out controversies—vehement disagreements. The same is true with Albert McClellan. I love them both like brothers; I trust them with my life; I honor them as great denominational statesmen. But nobody is always right—not even my friends.

BOOZ, ALLEN & HAMILTON—COMPENSATION

In the April 1966 trustee meeting, a lot of attention was devoted to the Booz, Allen & Hamilton faculty compensation study as well as a redefining of the role of the deans. What about this?

You can't take a faculty-operated school and insert an officer between the president and the faculty and do the whole thing at one time. It has to evolve. It has to evolve because the president, the dean, and the faculty must know what the role of the dean is. Then they must agree on the nature of this role.

So the president theoretically could go off and write an ideal job description for a dean and not be able to make it fly. Or, the dean might have the ideal job description, but he's got to make it work with the president and the faculty. So we were constantly tinkering with that idea and trying to refine it, and moving it generally in the direction of making the dean a more important academic officer and giving him more responsibility.

And the goal with the compensation study was just to bring it up to date?

To bring it up to date and to make it manageable so there would be an efficient way to manage it. We had all sorts of evaluation devices that we tested. Perhaps somebody taught us how to do it, and we would try to use it in the seminary. Some of these evaluation devices we tried and threw out. Others we tried and refined. Basically, our position-evaluation process was rooted in an insurance company process that we got from Capital Holding Company in Louisville. They authorized their personnel manager to come out and teach us how to adapt it. That we did, but then we would often go back to consultants to evaluate what we were doing.

Would these plans not work perfectly in the academic institution? Is that what you are saying?

Yes. They don't work perfectly because a seminary doesn't have a bottom line that is measured in dollars. Our problem was not to see how much profit we could make but how much service we could render. That is an abstraction. You will sometimes hear the assertion in academic communities that such abstractions as academic excellence can't be measured. My answer to that is that you had better be able to measure it because you will make decisions based on your impression of what you are doing, whether good or bad, and those impressions may or may not be accurate. Do you just fly by the seat of your pants, or do you have some ways of increasing the odds of an accurate measurement?

The trouble is that somebody makes judgments on the basis of an assessment, which may be a hidden agenda. But if John Doe gets promoted, somebody thinks he's worth promoting. Where did they get their idea about his worth? It's evident to me that everybody, including presidents, ought to be evaluated. For that reason I used to have the seminary staff evaluate me by using professional instruments. They couldn't do anything about my salary and they couldn't get me fired, but they could hurt my feelings by their evaluation. They could also heat up the hot seat for me by their evaluations.

If you respect your colleagues, and they say, "You're good at this, but you're not very good at that," you're likely to believe them. And if you believe them even a little, you will work hard to try to improve your performance in the areas where they are critical.

BLACK STUDENT RECRUITMENT

In July 1966 the trustees urged that the seminary place an increased emphasis on the recruitment of black students. Tell about that.

We employed a retired military chaplain, Col. Robert Herndon, of Social Circle, Georgia, to take on this task. He had worked with blacks as a seminary student when he was a fellow classmate of mine, working in the Fellowship Center in Louisville. He was very committed to ministry with blacks. We employed him for two years, and he spent his full time visiting black college campuses trying to recruit students for us. He managed to double our enrollment of students from about twelve or fifteen to twenty-five or thirty, but he could never get the number any higher than that.

So that effort was not very successful?

No. We waited too long. Since Southern Seminary was an SBC school, black students assumed we were a racist institution that was trying to change its image or something like that. We should have recruited black students aggressively, beginning in the early 1950s. We also would have done better at recruiting blacks if we had set up larger scholarship funds for blacks than we had for whites.

One of the big things that happened was the decline of the number of black ministerial students in general. So many educational institutions were recruiting them that they could get full scholarships to go to places like Harvard, Yale, Princeton, or Columbia. And the result was that if they had any desire for education, there was somebody standing with a check saying, "Come, study with us." And here we were saying, "Our door's open. If you want to come, knock." We were saying to blacks what we said to whites. With the change in the American ethos, that was not adequate.

GRADUATE STUDENT FEE

In 1966 a special fee was instituted for graduate students who went beyond the four-year time limit. Do you remember the circumstances surrounding that decision?

Yes, it was very simple. The seminary presidents agreed that graduate students could not be counted for more than four years, I think it was, in the Seminary Formula. Therefore, if a graduate student continued beyond the fourth year, he was not being funded through the Cooperative Program. The extra graduate fee was designed to cover the seminary's costs which were incurred because of the pace at which he was completing his work.

So this was a decision made at the Presidents Workshop? This was not unique to Southern Seminary?

That's right. The decision was not to count graduate students beyond a certain length of time. But a graduate student could take a leave of absence, if he wished to do so. So if he were not really working full time at the job of being a graduate student, it became advantageous to him to drop out of the program with some kind of leave arrangements. Then he could come back in when he was in a position to spend substantial amounts of time on his graduate program. The presidents of the seminaries reasoned that the normal time for a graduate student to complete his degree was about three years of full-time graduate work.

This would have affected Southern and Southwestern most, I assume. Was this an attempt by the newer seminaries to get a larger piece of the Cooperative Program dollar?

Yes. They objected to counting a graduate student in the Seminary Formula if he was enrolled but was not doing anything substantive about his program. The assumption was that he could finish his oral exams, for instance, and he might stay and loaf two or three years before he got down to serious work on his dissertation. All that time he would be counted as a graduate student, and graduate students received a rather large stipend through the Cooperative Program.

OUTSIDE EMPLOYMENT OF THE FACULTY

Early in 1967 the question of outside employment of the faculty and a policy on absences appear again in the records. What was the problem?

Faculty absences at the seminary was an insoluble problem. The only way you could do anything much with it was to raise the consciousness of the community about the situation. You did that by getting the trustees involved in the problem. If you dealt just with administrative-faculty relations, the faculty would listen politely, then go on doing exactly what they had been doing.

The basic idea was to keep the faculty members teaching. This involved more than their classroom duties. They needed to be available for conducting conferences with students, supervising graduate students, and this type of thing, as over against inordinate amounts of time spent conducting Bible studies, holding revivals, or delivering lectures in places off the campus.

This is one of those ongoing tugs of war between administration and faculty that does not represent any big crisis. It's the kind of thing that just goes on. You keep struggling with the problem. By putting the pressure on, you modify the problem and make it one you can live with as over against letting it escalate until you do have a crisis. You hope to raise the consciousness of the faculty about their responsibility for full-time functioning as a professor at Southern Seminary and their duties to the students.

How does this relate to the issue you raised earlier about the faculty being underpaid? One of the ways they could supplement their income was to do Bible studies, revivals, and supply preaching, or serve as interim pastors?

Now you're giving the faculty's argument. This was always their answer—that they had to take on these outside responsibilities to supplement their income. The answer to this is that we finally had salaries at a level where they could live modestly as full-time professors. I agreed that they were still underpaid. But this is what they had signed on for when they agreed to teach at the seminary.

The professors at Southern were specifically prohibited from teaching elsewhere for profit. What prompted that?

They could get jobs for a stipend at Bellarmine, the University of Louisville, the University of Indiana, or somewhere else. Then they would end up, as some of them actually did, teaching half-time or more at some other institution. In effect, this was pirating the seminary employment of the professor. He could end up giving a lot of his time for a little stipend somewhere else while the seminary was buying his full time twelve months out of the year.

I have no apology for the effort to pressure the faculty into giving full time to the seminary. This was never done in a harsh or mechanical way. There were instances in which somebody was given a bad time for not getting permission in advance from the dean to be away. But usually it was somebody who had a bad track record about that—not the professor who just forgot the policy.

It's very difficult to get a seminary faculty member to view himself as an employee in the traditional sense. I have done consulting in some other institutions, including even a medical school (University of Louisville). And doctors are just like theologians. The doctor on the medical school faculty never sees himself as under the supervision of a president or a dean or a department chairman or anyone else. He's a doctor, and he's doing his thing.

This, in part, is why I could never really solve this problem. I halfway agreed with the faculty member. I really understood what he was saying, and I understood why he felt that way. I halfway agreed that he was an independent entrepreneur, because the really good faculty members are. But on the other hand, they were being paid to be at home teaching students.

The trustee minutes also discussed a procedure for screening outside employment of faculty members. What did this mean? What was considered outside employment?

It had to do with whether you could be pastor of a church or an employee of another institution while being a seminary professor. What about the professor of counseling who puts in forty hours a week in a counseling clinic? Is he going to put in another forty hours a week at the seminary, or will he give little attention to what he does at the seminary?

Frankly, this is a very serious problem because the professor begins to assume that his job as a tenured professor is secure. Therefore, he gives his attention and energy to this second job. The screening procedure referred to a check we would do to make sure one's outside employment was compatible with his work as a professor in the seminary. If it did not enrich his experience in some way, if it did not enhance the life of the seminary, we viewed outside employment of the faculty with skepticism.

How did the screening process work?

It probably meant that the administration would draw up a set of criteria for evaluating outside employment. I don't think anybody ever screened it other than in policy terms.

In other words, a faculty member would keep the dean informed about what he was doing?

Yes. I think of an obvious situation: Perhaps a music faculty member wanted to serve as the minister of music in a church. Would that be helpful or harmful? The answer is that it would probably be helpful to the music faculty member, both economically and as a professor, because he would be conducting the activities he was teaching students to do. On the other hand, suppose he got to be minister of music in a large church and began to come exhausted to his classes without time to prepare his lectures because he was so busy with the multiple choir programs in the church. We had to ask some questions about the amount of time a professor would spend in his outside employment.

WORKING WITH SEMINARY TRUSTEES

In 1967 there is a reference to the attendance records of a couple of trustees. Samuel P. Asper was from Maryland, but he had not attended any board meetings since he was elected in 1962. The other trustee was Abner McCall of Texas who also had never attended a trustee meeting. Both of these were subsequently removed for non-attendance. Was this a routine action toward trustees who didn't take attendance seriously?

The charter of the seminary automatically terminates the membership of a trustee if he fails to attend three consecutive trustee meetings. If these people had unusual excuses, they would sometimes look the other way.

The problem with Abner McCall was that there was a conflict with his role as president of Baylor University. He was a good man, and we would have been delighted to keep him as a trustee. He would have been very useful as a trustee. Frankly, I never did get to know Asper.

I want to make it clear that the attendance of Southern Seminary trustees was high in comparison with that of trustees of other educational institutions. They rarely missed a meeting except when conflicts occurred in their schedules.

The trustees seemed to police their own members, as you have described in this situation.

This is one of those places where the administration of the institution had better tread lightly. You have little to do with the election of trustees. Every time I got involved in a trustee matter, I got my fingers burned. And you certainly had better not be the one who causes a trustee to be dropped. Such an action threatens trustees as a class. The trustees don't like it if the administration is involved in any way in terminating a trustee.

New trustees elected by the Southern Baptist Convention were to be brought to the campus as soon as possible for an orientation. Tell us about these orientation sessions.

Trustees would be elected in May or June of each year, and the seminary's annual trustee meeting was held in late March or April. So you would be a trustee a long time before you did anything. The veteran trustees began to bring new trustees to the campus in October of each year to give them a day of orientation. Then these "freshman trustees" would come to the first trustee meeting ready to function. They would have committee assignments, and they would know their committee and its work.

What things were covered in these orientation sessions?

Basically it started out with breakfast with the president. I would review the controlling documents and the structure of the seminary as a whole. Then they would go through the different aspects of the seminary with the other officers like the vice president for business affairs, the dean of the School of Theology, the deans of the Religious Education School and the Music School, the dean of students, and so on.

These entering trustees would also get a walking tour of the facilities, and they would be briefed about specific projects. If, for instance, you were dealing with the renovation of Seminary Village, if that were coming up, they would be taken out and shown the condition of Seminary Village. Or if you were going to move some program from one place on the campus to another, they would be shown what the problems were in this location and where this program was going to be moved. We would try to orient the new trustees to anything we knew that was on the trustee agenda for the upcoming annual meeting so they would be able to be full participants in making that decision.

How much did this cost? Was it worth the cost?

Oh yes, it was worth it. These orientation sessions required a trip to Louisville from wherever the trustees lived. The total trustee expense at Southern Seminary, as I recall, was about $30,000 a year. Based on the number of trustees we had, this was a reasonable expense. It would have been less if we had had fewer trustees on the board.

Would that have been a good move?

I would never have set up a trustee board as large as Southern

Seminary's board. On the other hand, the way in which Southern Seminary board members were chosen became the pattern for the boards of the major agencies, so apparently it was a good idea.

How did the trustees-at-large system relate to the trustee system at Southern Seminary?

The at-large members were to be chosen from areas not otherwise represented on the board. The number of at-large members was carefully calculated to provide about one trustee for approximately each 100,000 Baptists in areas not otherwise having trustees on the board. But that guideline wasn't followed because politics and ambition got into it. Some of the older states that already had one, two, or even three trustees ended up with one of the at-large members. We had a terrible time trying to keep the at-large members chosen from states or areas not otherwise represented by a trustee.

Southern Seminary wanted a trustee from Michigan for many reasons, although the numbers of Baptists affiliated with Southern Baptists in Michigan was too small a number to provide a Southern trustee as a recurring thing. The Convention elected one man. I think he ended up being from Oklahoma or Alabama or some older state like that the first time he came up for reelection. We don't know what went on in the Committee on Boards that caused that. I would write to the Committee on Boards and explain how we wanted the at-large system to work, but they would read the rules and discover they didn't have to make it work that way.

Did you write to the chairman of the Committee on Boards about such things?

Yes, every year. I don't suppose there was a year in the thirty-one years I was involved in Southern Seminary that I didn't write the chairman of the Committee on Boards at least one letter. I would spell out the problems and the needs. For instance, I might tell the chairman, "We desperately need an educator on our board. If you have an educator from one of these states where a new trustee is to be chosen, we ask that priority be given to the selection of an educator." My strategy was to try to balance the make-up of the board. The needs for specialized skills changed from year to year.

Obviously, this was my perception of the need, and the Committee on Boards could follow my suggestions or not. I was always careful to say that this was a request, and that the seminary would support whatever the Committee on Boards chose to do. I have also been known to write and indicate by name a specific trustee we would like to have. We would describe John Doe as the kind of trustee who could render a great service to the cause of theological education at Southern Seminary.

I didn't buy the idea that trustees are nothing more than the representatives of a group of people from some specific area. I saw the trustees as people who were chosen to render service in the name of theological education for the cause of Christ, but who happened to come from that geographical background.

Did you sometimes encourage the Committee on Boards to place some people of wealth and influence on the trustee board?

Yes, I have been known to spell it out that way by saying something like this: "We need to have people of financial ability and influence in financial circles, and Jim Brown or John Doe from Atlanta, Georgia, or Podunk Hollow, Mississippi, are illustrative of the kind of persons we would like to have." If the Committee on Boards happened to choose the people I named, we were pleased.

Did you ever get someone on the Southern Seminary board as a trustee who presented real problems and difficulties?

I recall a time when a Texas Baptist Convention staff member, Charles Lee Williamson, was elected a trustee: He was correctly labeled as ultraconservative. He took those positions every time it was an appropriate issue. He spoke out, he advocated the ultraconservative theological position every time, but he did it gracefully and effectively. Sometimes he couldn't get a second to his motion. That never seemed to bother him. The board eventually put him on the executive committee of the trustees. This was a powerful committee because it met on an *ad interim* basis to act for the board. The trustees apparently thought Williamson represented a point of view that ought to be heard in the executive committee.

Williamson ended up as chairman of the trustee executive committee. He got the most prolonged applause that any chairman of the executive committee ever got when he relinquished the office, as he was rotating off the board of trustees. The reason was that he was so clearly aware that the theological conviction he held was not always compatible with the majority. He had always been a gentleman, he had always been fair, he had always acted appropriately. The board members were pleased with him; they thought he was a good chairman. This occurred just as Southern Baptists were going into the era of trying to change the agencies by manipulating their boards.

The point of view resonated by most "conservatives" had been most ably represented by the chairman of the executive committee of the Southern Seminary board. It was never a manipulated affair by political action. The man, in the luck of the draw of Southern Baptist life, had been named to the board and had risen to be the chairman of the executive committee of the board.

There has never been much fear of either the extreme conservative or liberal. If you push trustees hard, they will act about like the typical state convention would act on that issue. They see themselves as representative of the Southern Baptist mind-set. That's why I say I don't have any criticism of the trustees that have been put on the Southern Seminary board in the last few years.

I would think it appropriate to object to efforts to manipulate the board. But it would be equally wrong for me to try to control it by getting people on the board who would vote my recommendations or reflect my point of view. I would object to any agency head doing that.

DEGREES IN RELIGION IN BAPTIST UNIVERSITIES

In April 1967 the trustees at Southern Seminary noted the trend of universities to offer degrees in religion. Did this refer to Baylor University's beginning to offer the Ph.D. degree?

It included Baylor, but it was not specifically directed to this school. I objected to this practice on educational and philosophical grounds. My objection was that a doctor's degree in the history of English law is a legitimate degree. That is a different degree from the law school training that leads to a Doctor of Jurisprudence degree. The second degree makes you a lawyer; the first makes you, perhaps, a professor of the history of law, but not a lawyer. The difficulty was that the doctorate was being used sometimes as a short cut—college graduation and a Ph.D., and then you go into the pastorate.

I was complaining that this was not appropriate training, nor was it the training that the layman would think his pastor had to have to function as a pastor. A man practicing law with only a doctorate in the history of English law would be a fraud. I saw the trend as a move that could create future problems. We communicated with the colleges and their presidents and tried to alert them to the potential problems and pitfalls.

KENT SCHOOL OF SOCIAL WORK AND SBTS PROGRAM

Tell us about the seminary's affiliation with Kent School of Social Work at the University of Louisville.

This affiliation provided for Southern Seminary what accreditation was supposed to provide for the Carver School of Missions and Social Work. So we got what Carver School was trying to get, but we got it in a different way. What happened was that Kent liked these Southern Seminary students. They were sharp, able people. Surprisingly, the major scholarships from the University of Louisville for social work began to go to Southern Seminary students who could, if they wished, go on and secure accredited social work degrees.

The dean of Kent School changed just about the time of the merger of the Carver School into Southern Seminary. The new dean was an old friend of mine from Tulane University whom I had known when I was at Baptist Bible Institute, New Orleans. He was sympathetic to this whole enterprise and saw the vision.

But the agreement was negotiated by Walter Delamarter. I didn't have the social work expertise to negotiate it. Walter had the expertise to verbalize the Southern Seminary program in terminology that was compatible with the Kent School program, and then to structure the Southern Seminary program so it meshed effectively with the Kent School program.

KENTUCKIANA METROVERSITY

At the same time we also negotiated an agreement which allowed University of Louisville students to come to Southern Seminary to take courses that were not available at the University of Louisville. We had students from there studying Koine Greek, or Hebrew, or archaeology. History majors would come from the University of Louisville graduate school to study archaeology at Southern Seminary. So there was an interchange of graduate students.

The official name of this interchange of students is Kentuckiana

(Kentucky and Indiana) Metroversity—a consortium of the University of Indiana Southeast, University of Louisville, Southern Seminary, Presbyterian Seminary, Spalding College, and Ursuline College in greater metropolitan Louisville.

This consortium provided an economic advantage to the seminary. Library facilities were shared by all the participating schools. There were programs and courses that we needed to offer at the seminary that we didn't have to offer. Perhaps we didn't have enough students to justify having a professor or even a full class in a particular course. The five or six students who needed the course could go to one of these other schools and take that course.

In what area was this consortium most helpful?

I expect social work was the area in which this cooperative arrangement was most helpful to Southern Seminary, but all sorts of graduate programs were available. And in addition, we had some students who needed additional liberal arts work in certain academic areas that we couldn't offer. Instead of their having to go somewhere else and pay tuition, they could take one course at Bellarmine College and pay the low tuition fees at their home school—Southern Seminary.

TEAM-A

Tell us about the TEAM-A program in which Southern Seminary participated.

TEAM-A is a consortium of theological schools: St. Meinrad's in Indiana (a Roman Catholic school), the two seminaries in Louisville (Presbyterian and Southern Baptist), Asbury Seminary in Wilmore, Kentucky, and Lexington Theological Seminary, a Christian Church seminary in Lexington, Kentucky.

How did this consortium come about?

If you are involved in higher education in a city or an area, you get to know the other school administrators. You begin to dream dreams and talk about problems together. You discuss ways in which you could have saved some money. But there is no mechanism for doing it. You keep on buying the same expensive sets of books for five or six libraries, when as a matter of fact the books are only used three or four times a year by anybody in any one school. One set of the books would have served all the students. But it was an important set, and you had to have it for access by your students.

And you need courses. The TEAM-A situation set up a mid-year course in January in which students from any of these five theological schools could go to any other seminary for a month and take a course.

This arrangement provided opportunity for students to get to know and understand different lifestyles of these various seminary communities. The one rule was that no school ever changed its rules, regulations, or character to accommodate the "outside students." If St. Meinrad students came to Southern Seminary, they had to leave their wine behind because drinking was not permitted on Southern Seminary's campus. On the other hand, St. Meinrad's would do its thing, and if anybody went to that campus from Asbury (which is a very conservative Methodist seminary), they had to conform to the lifestyle at St. Meinrad's.

Under this arrangement, were tuition fees paid to the home institution?

Yes, the genius of the program was that fees were paid to the home institution. So the student who took a course on another campus had no sense of shock, either of being charged more than he or she was accustomed to, or of feeling that his school had been robbing him because he could have gotten training on this other campus at a better price.

So it was a mutually satisfactory arrangement?

Yes, and the exchange of students always stayed in relatively stable proportions. The dynamics of this worked out so that a certain proportion of students would be involved in the exchange. We did have some trouble over the misappropriation of library books, but we had an agreement that the home school was responsible for library books taken from the visited school. So if a Presbyterian misappropriated Southern Seminary books, Presbyterian Seminary reimbursed Southern, and vice versa.

Did that agreement work?

Painfully; but it worked. One student actually ran up a book tab that amounted to several thousand dollars. How he ever got that many books home, nobody will ever know.

LAYMEN'S LEADERSHIP INSTITUTE
In early 1968 there was a change of trustees, and you recom-

mended Howard Butt Jr. of Texas to the trustees. What was your relationship to him?

Howard Butt had been connected with the seminary through the Layman's Leadership Institute, which originated in the late 1950s on the Southern Seminary campus. It was started by a man from Kansas City named Charles Curry. He proposed that the seminary provide weekend courses for laymen in church life and work. Out of that came the proposal for the Layman's Leadership Institute.

I asked Charles Curry what he had in mind for the program of the first meeting. He ran off a list of names, any one of whom would have made a star out of any weekend program anywhere in the country: Bill Hull, the head of New York Life, Billy Graham, Howard Butt, one of the officials of Bank of America in California, and Keith Miller, the Episcopalian author of popular devotional books. Keith really got his start as a speaker at one of these meetings.

My reaction was, "It's an excellent idea, and I will be supportive if you, Charles Curry, will be the chairman." He responded, "Will you get Billy Graham?" I went to Washington and saw Billy Graham at the President's Prayer Breakfast. I approached him about coming. He surprised me by almost falling over himself, saying "I've been dreaming of such a thing; I'll come and bring my whole team."

This was in January 1958. We compiled a list of about six hundred prospective laymen to invite. We wanted three hundred people, so we sent out six hundred invitations to see what would happen. We got more than three hundred acceptances on the first mailing. So it was an idea whose time had come.

Were they housed on the campus?

They spilled over into hotels, but the program was on campus. Men like Maxey Jarman of Nashville and the Russell Brothers of Nashville came. From California to New York they came, and they kept coming. The impact was incredible. This was the first time that active laymen in their churches had jumped denominational lines to get together and talk about personal evangelism and what to do to strengthen their church and its ministry.

These laymen quickly overburdened the seminary facilities. About that time Billy Graham was going to have a campaign in Miami, Florida. He had no organization locally; nobody knew how to put one together in Miami. No denomination was strong enough to do it. There were strong barriers between the denominations. So to help Graham we thought we would experiment one year. We went down to one of the big hotels in Miami and held the Laymen's Leadership Institute meeting there. The attendance jumped to about a thousand, and it never came back to the seminary campus because we couldn't house it in Louisville. The concept has spread and moved all over the world.

Now, the connection with Howard Butt. Howard Butt had an organization called Christian Men, Inc., which is a Butt Foundation-sponsored program. Howard Butt came into the Layman's Leadership Institute as one of the leaders and used his organization to fund it. He subsequently employed staff to service the Layman's Leadership Institute. Now the Layman's Leadership Institute is a program of Christian Men, Inc., but it still functions.

So this was your relationship to Howard Butt. You were not able to convince him to serve as a trustee of Southern Seminary?

No, he served basically with Southwestern Seminary. This was a favorable connection, and he felt that he ought to keep that association.

MORAL SIDE OF THE NEWS

Tell us about your experience as a panelist on the "Moral Side of the News" radio program in Louisville.

Victor Sholis, director of WHAS Radio-Television, asked me to join a group of clergymen on this thirty-minute talk show. This panel was chaired by the editor of the newspaper, with Dorcas Ruthenberg as the producer. The panel consisted of a Jewish rabbi, a Catholic priest, a Unitarian minister, and a Baptist preacher (me). I used to needle the rest of the panel—when we got to be friends—that I represented the "Christians." They had some good retorts to that. Our discussions revolved around moral issues in the community.

One day Monsignor Pitt, the Catholic representative, and I were talking. I said to him, "Father Pitt, you will never know what a nuisance you've been to me." And he said, "How's that?" "Well," I said, "you have upset the Baptists of this community by my sitting by you and, worst of all, agreeing with you sometimes. It's all right when I disagree with you, but when you say intelligent things about the moral issues in the community, and I agree with you, it always upsets my Baptist friends."

Immediately Father Pitt responded, "Duke, you will never know what a nuisance you've been to me. Everybody from the archbishop down in the Catholic Church has been on me about agreeing with you."

Conversations of this type were not common in the early 1950s. "The Moral Side of the News" became the highest-rated locally produced program, in terms of audience, of any program in the city of Louisville. It still continues today. I resigned from it back in the mid-1960s for various reasons. Basically, the personnel had changed, and the personality of the program was not the same. It's still a good program. I miss my old friends and the repartee we enjoyed.

Father Pitt and I used to take on the rabbi and the Unitarian minister every Christmas over the meaning of Christmas. The Unitarian would say that this birth signified the joy that comes to every home with the birth of a new child. Then Father Pitt and I would nod to each other as if to say, "You can get him this year." Then we would light in to say this birth represents the incarnation of the Son of God, born of the virgin Mary. This is the central affirmation of God's love in which, through the incarnation and the crucifixion and resurrection, we have hope of eternal life.

Then the Unitarian and the rabbi would have at us—and that's why the audience loved to listen to it. We didn't pull any punches with one another. But then it began to change, and we were told we had to be careful not to hurt the feelings of the other panelists. It was a little hard for me to pull back into that mode.

CRUSADE FOR CHILDREN

But the main thing the Moral Side of the News panel did was launch the Crusade for Children. This was the idea of Victor Sholis. It reached the point where it raised approximately $2 million annually to assist handicapped children. The resulting medical equipment and organizations were important, but the most important accomplishment was that it let these children out of the closet.

These handicapped children appeared on a twenty-four-hour television marathon at which celebrities performed to raise money. We were first criticized for exploiting them, but it became apparent to the experts as well as the public that the kids loved the attention and looked forward to being on television. Soon the parents of all handicapped children in the region were able to acknowledge their handicapped children in a public way without embarrassment.

The panel of ministers—Rabbi Joseph Rauch, Father Felix N. Pitt, Bob Weston of the First Unitarian Church, and I—with Vic Sholis, manager, and also Wilson Wyatt, lawyer for the newspaper and radio-television station, sat for two hours in the office of Mayor Andrew Broaddus (a Broadway Baptist church member) arguing with the director of social services of the city who wanted to withdraw the fund-raising license of the program.

I remember the Episcopal rector of Elizabethtown, Kentucky, appearing before the panel of ministers asking for about $15,000 to start a program in his church for retarded children. I said to him, "We are not going to give you $15,000 because it will take triple that to serve the kids when word gets out that it is O.K. to have a retarded child in Elizabethtown." He immediately said, "I meant to ask for $50,000." We gave him a $50,000 grant, and the church did a great job.

The crusade finally spilled over into Indiana as well as Kentucky. And the money poured in when the independent volunteer fire departments in the region began to compete with one another to see which one could raise the most money for the crusade.

OTHER LOUISVILLE ORGANIZATIONS

Were you involved with other similar groups in the Louisville community?

Yes, the Conversation Club was a small group of people who selected their membership. It included some very astute, scholarly people, but not all were of this stripe. Also included as members were educators, lawyers, doctors, engineers, and business executives. It was a very exciting group to be a part of.

The Conversation Club met once a month. The host would provide dinner as well as a paper on some literary or critical subject. The issues raised in this paper would be the subject of the conversation for the rest of the evening. All the seminary presidents had been invited to be members of the Conversation Club, going back into the early history of the seminary. E. Y. Mullins had been a member of this group when he was president. Some of the older members remembered him personally. So anything I did or said got compared with Dr. Mullins.

The host of the Conversation Club meeting always provided cigars and cigarettes for the members of the club. I was the host once and had some left over. My boys were surprised to find such articles in our home, and they wanted to try them out. So I finally said, "Pick out whatever you want—a cigarette or a cigar—but there's one rule: you must finish it."

Two of the boys spent the night in the bathtub; the cigars and cigarettes made them all deathly ill. None of the four have smoked anything since then. Perhaps that was one of the permanent values of the Conversation Club.

COMMUNITY CHEST/BOY SCOUTS/MEDICAL CENTER

I would like to say a word about the Community Chest board. I was very proud to be a part of the board of the Community Chest, later called the United Appeal, and also proud to be a part of the Boy Scout Council. I owe the Boy Scouts so much for what they did—not so much for me but for what they did for my four sons—that I always felt willing to work for them. I headed their financial campaign in Louisville one year.

I am still on the Louisville Medical Center board, which is a board that owns the heating and cooling plants, the laundry facilities, and other facilities that service the hospital complex in the middle of Louisville. These hospitals included the Jewish, Norton, Methodist Evangelical, and then the city hospital, which is now in the process of being converted to Humana Hospital University in the center of the city. This board was dominated by representatives of the hospitals, but I was one of the general independent community representatives, presumably on the board to assure that the community interests were always served.

Are there other things you'd like to say about your Louisville involvement?

I could talk about Louisville almost endlessly because it was a great city from my point of view. Oh yes, let's not forget the Rotary Club. Being a Rotarian was a good way for me from my suburban office to get in touch with many of the business and professional leaders of the city. And I always wanted to be a good citizen.

PUBLIC SCHOOL COMMITTEE

You also were on a committee related to the school board.

This was the old Dan Ewing Committee. Dan Ewing was chairman of a general committee to try to solve the problem of the school systems in Louisville and Jefferson County in the face of racial issues. We developed a proposal, partially borrowing bits and pieces from elsewhere, that would have integrated the school system and united the Louisville and Jefferson County school systems.

One of the real tragedies of Louisville, Kentucky, is that the proposal finally worked through both school boards, but action by the Kentucky legislature was required before it took effect. It failed by one vote in the Kentucky senate, and I've never been able to forgive a local politician whose vote kept it from passing. He later became U.S. Congressman Ron Mazzoli—a friend now whom I support. I've always been unhappy because his vote in the Kentucky legislature defeated the integration of a united Jefferson County school system. That was a disaster for Louisville.

The Sixth District Court in Cincinnati later ordered the merger of these two boards and the total integration of the school system by means of busing. But this was ordered without giving Louisville and Jefferson County time to get ready to do either one. (And that reveals my position on courts trying to act as educational authorities.)

The judge who issued this order—Judge James Gordon—is a good Baptist and a long-time personal friend. I admire his courage—he was right in principle and in law—but oh, the chaos this created for the school system! The result was disaster in terms of public opinion and the inability to merge the two staffs from the county and the city systems efficiently. The Jefferson County Educational System is just beginning—and this is many years later—to come out of that disaster.

If the report of the Dan Ewing Committee had been adopted, there would have been complete integration without busing. Merger of the city and county systems would have been brought about peaceably.

PRESIDENT'S COMPENSATION

In January 1968 the trustees recorded that the president's compensation was removed from trustee action. What did that mean?

What actually happened was that the trustees took the president's salary out of the overall compensation program for the seminary. Otherwise, when the president recommended an increase in the salary scale for the base of the full professor, he automatically increased his own salary because his base was 150 percent of the base for the full professor. But what the minutes of the trustees do not note is that this had bothered me so much that I had already stopped taking increases in salary, beginning about 1960.

In fact, I would let them vote increases. I found that if I held the president's salary down, this would keep the total salary scale down. I would accept the voting of a salary increase; I just wouldn't accept the payment of it. So the seminary still owes me, as deferred compensation, most of the increases in salary since 1960.

Did you turn these increases back, or were they placed into a separate fund? How was this handled?

These increases just never were paid; they were treated on the books as deferred compensation. That's why I say they're still on the books—that this money is available to the president of the seminary.

Define "deferred compensation," as you understood it?

The seminary trustees would say, "We will raise your salary by one thousand dollars." I would say, "Thank you; I don't want to accept it; you just keep it. If I need it later, I'll call for it." That's "deferred compensation."

This arrangement does have certain tax advantages?

Yes. I didn't receive the money, so it will not be considered taxable income until I do receive it. I was saying to the trustees, "I'm going to give the seminary some money anyway. Instead of giving you fifty cents on the dollar, I'll give you all of it; you can keep all of this before taxes. As far as I'm concerned, I don't ever intend to take this deferred compensation." But along in the 1970s the seminary trustees put in the record a legal statement that meant that the compensation, which had been deferred and which would be deferred in the future, would meet the government requirements for deferred compensation.

There has to be some point at which this compensation is actually distributed. I have subsequently drawn up a document which says, in effect, that this deferred compensation can only be drawn by Marguerite Mullinnix McCall at her discretion and need, and that if she does not draw it, then it will be added to the Marguerite Mullinnix McCall

Professorship endowment. Her death, of course, means that she cannot withdraw it, and the document remains at the moment unchanged. I could change the document without the concurrence of the trustees. I have made no effort to change it. I won't promise that I will never do so, but I don't intend to.

Are these funds invested?

Yes. At some point in the agreement, the trustees computed the amount and agreed that it would draw interest. That interest is determined by interest received on one of the Seminary Foundation's invested funds. That suits me because it means that a larger gift will be added for this endowment.

This fund was later deposited with the Southern Baptist Foundation. When I resigned as chancellor of the seminary, that triggered the beginning of payments to me. The trustee agreement was that payments would begin when I ceased to be chancellor. The funds will now be put in the McCall Foundation at my death. My sons as the managers of this foundation will decide what to do with the money.

CHAPTER 11
Southern Seminary and SBC Developments

Late 1960s-1970s

In 1968 a strong anti-Vietnam sentiment emerged in this country. This was also the age of student activism. The Southern Seminary trustees had a subcommittee known as the Student Life Committee. Some degree of controversy with the students of the seminary also emerged in 1968. Talk about this.

I don't remember the specific issues, but I remember the era. I described it as the worst time to be the administrator of a school in the history of the United States. It was a very difficult, very discouraging time. The attitude of the students was such that you felt that what you were doing was basically a waste of time. They were so negative with reference to institutions, culture, and even the educational process. Their motto at that time was "burn it down and let's start over and do it right."

They were opposed to everything. They challenged and questioned everything. They felt the church was a mistake that man had made, that denominations were a curse on the face of the earth. Their attutude was irrational, emotionally charged, and vehement; it was a nasty time to deal with students.

Did this attitude pervade the seminary campuses?

Oh yes. We got a milder dose of it, but whatever happens on college campuses the seminaries always get four years later.

One of the issues that emerged was the draft. Some people thought many students were on seminary campuses to void the draft.

284

That's one of those charges that you can't do anything with because it's probably true of some students. But the students who are draft evaders always fade into the woodwork. They were never the activists in terms of Vietnam. They wanted to disappear from view.

The other crowd who were calling attention to themselves were those who affirmed they didn't believe in the existence of God. I never could figure out why they wanted to be on a seminary campus if this was their view. Some church ordained them, or licensed them, or recommended them to a seminary. We got rid of them as fast as we could, but this tended to be a slow process.

ISSUES RELATING TO STUDENTS

Another issue that came up during this time was tuition for non-Southern Baptists. What do you recall about that?

This was a movement within the seminary presidents—to charge higher tuition for students who were not Southern Baptist. It was also a movement within the SBC Executive Committee and certain elements of the Southern Baptist Convention. I opposed this. I thought it was impossible under the Southern Seminary charter to have a two-level tuition system. But this is done now in some of the other seminaries.

You have spoken a number of times about the relationship of Southern Seminary to Baptists north of the Ohio River. Did this enter into your views on this?

This was part of the problem. The argument for charging non-Baptists is also a good argument for charging non-Southern Baptists. After all, non-Southern Baptists don't give to the Cooperative Program either. A non-Southern Baptist student probably is not going to be a Southern Baptist pastor.

I say *probably,* because many of them *do* become Southern Baptist pastors. And, indeed, some non-Baptists end up changing their denomination because of their theological shift while in the seminary. At least one person who is a prime example of that comes to mind. A very able, successful Southern Baptist pastor—Verlin Kruschwitz—was a Methodist when he came to Southern Seminary. He has served as president of the Kentucky Baptist Convention.

I objected to charging higher tuition to these students on the ground that non-Southern Baptist seminaries were also training Southern

Baptist students, so there was a *quid pro quo* in it. I thought it was one of those things that wouldn't raise enough money to make any difference anyway, but it would be an abrasive issue. And the charter of Southern Seminary provides that its training will be available to students of any denomination of Christians.

Your will on this issue did not prevail in the Presidents Workshop, in which I suppose the matter first emerged?

No, it did not. In the President's Workshop, it was finally agreed that each seminary would go its own way. That was partially because the hidden agenda that Southern Baptists had never looked at is the percentage of students who are not Baptists who are enrolled in some of our other seminaries, specifically at Golden Gate. At the time when this issue was discussed by the presidents, about one-third of the students at Golden Gate were not Baptists.

So Southern Baptists were providing training for a large company of non-Baptists there?

Yes. At Southern Seminary I think the percentage of non-Baptist students never got as high as 10 percent, almost any way you counted it—including all the students from TEAM-A, and University of Louisville, and so on. The presidents decided the problems were different in the different seminaries, and therefore each seminary ought to do its own thing.

The trustees also raised some questions regarding the Lord's Supper at the seminary. Do you remember the circumstances surrounding this?

The Student Government of Southern Seminary was determined to have an observance of the Lord's Supper in the chapel. That's one of those things that probably would have been done by Southern Baptists in 1858, but this would be anathema today. In the early days, annual meetings of the Southern Baptist Conventions would observe the Lord's Supper, but that was before the Landmark controversy and its impact on the understanding of the Lord's Supper as the ordinance of a single church.

Was there a sense of combat with the students particularly in this area?

Not with the students but with certain Student Government leaders. In fact, I learned to meet with the new Student Government president and say to him that one of his first responsibilities was to determine what his relationship would be with the administration. If he wished, we could work together and cooperate with each other. If he wished to take an adversarial relationship, that would be perfectly agreeable with me, but he should understand that I would be his adversary if he chose to play it that way.

I learned early that you don't take on hard-nosed young men with one arm tied behind you and pretend that you have to reduce your powers to their power level in order to be fair in a controversy. I would tell them, "I'll win if you want the adversarial relationship. I'll win in ways that won't occur to you until it's over, simply because I know more ways to struggle with you than you know. I've had more experience than you've had, and I have more resources. That's not bragging; that's just a statement of fact."

Any school president who sets out to win against students will win if he will take the time and trouble to do it. So I've had student presidents go both ways. Some Student Government presidents would say, "Let's cooperate." And I would respond, "Fine, we'll cooperate, and if I disagree with you, I'll tell you, and if you disagree with me, you tell me."

I even had one case where a Student Government president came to me and said, "Dr. McCall, I know you'll be opposed to this, so I've not come on that basis, but I've come to get your counsel. If you were in my place, how would you go about trying to do what I want to do?" I replied, "You're right; I am opposed to it, but since you've asked for an honest answer, I'll give it to you." And I gave him the best answer I knew how to give on how he could probably achieve his goal.

Do you remember the student?

Jeff Norris. I've just agreed to preach for him in one of the suburbs of Washington, D.C. He was sharp enough that he could get what the students wanted in that controversial period. He was using me as an asset to get his way. I never objected to that.

HUGH PETERSON RETIRES

Dr. Hugh Peterson, director of admissions, retired about this time. I understand you were concerned about finding a replacement?

He had been an important fixture in the seminary for a long time. I think we offered to extend his service, but he refused. He knew more than we did about his health situation, and he was right. He was having some problems that he was trying to mask in carrying out his duties. I was aware of this, and yet I refused to put it on top of the agenda. He developed Alzheimer's disease. And this was beginning to create memory problems for him. As you know, memory was one of his great strengths.

After Dr. Peterson left, I tried to get him to speak in chapel or do some protocol things like that, just to let new generations of students meet him. He would never participate in an academic procession, once he withdrew from seminary life. For a long time I went to see him at his home. That was fine, but he wanted no part of an official relationship with the seminary. I think he perceived the problem of his ability to function, and it was a very sad thing.

Hugh Peterson was an important person in the life of Southern Seminary. He was integral to many important things that happened, not the man out front, not the fellow with the flag, but he was the person who made things work. After somebody else had adopted the regulation, he would turn it into something that could actually be implemented.

CRISIS IN OUR NATION STATEMENT

Were you involved in the development of the Crisis in Our Nation statement that was adopted at the Southern Baptist Convention in Houston in 1968?

I remember being involved but not the details of the involvement. It was a matter of being one of the agency administrators and participating early on in the formulation of that statement.

I understand that Dr. Arthur Rutledge of the Home Mission Board was the one who spearheaded that statement in the beginning. Is that your recollection?

Yes, although very quickly other people—and I am not now including myself—were very involved and felt that some statement ought to be made, both to Southern Baptists and by Southern Baptists. This statement was unusual in that it originated with agency personnel, who normally see themselves as instruments of the churches in this type of situation. This reflects their feelings about the unusual nature of that critical time.

The Convention that year met just after the assassination of Martin Luther King, and then also Robert Kennedy was killed about the week before. These events must have prompted intense feelings.

Yes. The anger, the bitterness, the hatred of the times were being ventilated in all sorts of circumstances, whether on the school campuses or in the marches. The mood of the nation generally was angry and impatient. These were impossible times. Your own goals and ideals got all fouled up with this angry mood—this irresponsible activity—this absence of caring about what you did in terms of its impact on other people—its rebellion against the past—its rebellion against institutions—its rebellion against any form of authority. All of these things made steering a coherent course or reaching out for desirable goals almost impossible. You would start what looked like a long-term activity, and it would blow up before it got off the ground.

This was true of the seminary campus as well?

Yes, it was true—at least at Southern Seminary—and I think at all institutions because this angry mood permeated our society. The harshest expressions of the times were on state university campuses and college campuses rather than seminary campuses. But the mood and lifestyle of the university is quickly imported into the seminary. While the seminary context modified its expression, it still had its effects.

OBNOXIOUS STUDENTS

Now you look back and say, "Nothing very bad ever happened to Southern Seminary." That's true, but you didn't know it when you were going through the time. (Indeed, a purported survey of student opinion of that era, which appeared to indicate a lack of normal Christian convictions on the part of students, did immense and lasting damage. This, in spite of a report of the views of over 90 percent of the students with reference to their agreement or disagreement with the articles of the Abstract of Principles.)

Can you give some examples of the type of behavior you're describing?

It was the type of thing that would be done to an individual. This person could be anybody from the president's wife to a young professor to a senior professor or a staff member. It was not unusual to have a student chew out a secretary who herself was a student's wife. Because she was a secretary in the seminary, she represented authority to him. More than once I've seen secretaries in tears, so torn apart that you would have to say to them, "Please take the rest of the day off and go home and compose yourself."

Here's a good example of what I'm talking about. Some students tended not to obey the regulations about garbage disposal at Seminary Village. And the result was rats. One night my wife was entertaining guests. Later she found out that our guests had been greeted on the front porch with rats in bottles of fluid that some students had placed there.

We can chuckle at that now. But it was the kind of thing that tended to destroy a happy social occasion. It was a particularly vicious thing because it was aimed at someone who had nothing to do with the problem and could do nothing about it. Certainly the guests at our home could not. Some students came up with inventive ways to be obnoxious.

And that was particularly unique in this era?

Yes. I've never known anything like it at any other time. All school administrators will tell you stories like that, or worse, because we used to share them with one another when we got together. Each one of us could tell a story to outrank one someone else had just told. But I must point out that this type of behavior was not characteristic of all students of that era. It was a very vociferous minority of students. There were students on the other side who were offended and angered by this type of behavior.

PRESIDENT EMPOWERED TO HANDLE EMERGENCIES

There was a statement by the trustees in this era that they agreed to stand by the president in any crisis with the students. Was this at your request?

Yes. Actually it was a little more formal than that. It gave the president almost dictatorial powers if he should declare a state of emergency. His powers to discipline students, and so on, were absolute. But he had to declare a state of emergency to invoke that particular authority.

What did you think could happen?

We had things like students picketing chapel to try to keep fellow students from attending chapel services.

This was when the U.S. chief of chaplains was to speak?

Yes. Students on the other side of that issue have tempers, too, and a riot could start in nothing flat in such an emotionally charged situation. We had the activists, but we also had some strongly opinionated students on the other side. The potential for a clash was always there. This made life miserable for the administrator. He was always trying to buffer the different elements in the student body and keep them from being at one another's throats.

I'm glad to say I never declared a state of emergency at the seminary. But I think having the power kept me from needing to on a few occasions. It was clear to the students that I had such powers. And they knew that it wouldn't take me very long to expel a dozen or so of them.

In a report to the trustees about this time, you indicated you thought there was a new view on "call" to the ministry. What did you mean by this?

I was describing the difference in the attitude of some students. They no longer thought of themselves as called of God in some spiritual sense, but they were called by virtue of the fact that the ministry was what they had rather do than anything else. You were not dealing with people who perceived themselves as uniquely the instruments of God's purpose in the world. Instead, you were dealing with people who saw the ministry as the avenue through which they could reach their goals and implement their agenda.

This was a view of the call that I opposed vehemently. My welcome to new students at Southern Seminary for thirty-one years was this: "If God has called you to the ministry, Southern Seminary can help you become a more effective minister. But if God has not called you to the ministry, we cannot make you a minister at all." I wanted them to realize that if God hadn't called them to the ministry, they didn't belong at Southern Seminary.

In this report to the trustees, you also indicated there was a new activism among students, particularly an anti-Vietnam feeling.

Yes, the anti-Vietnam movement, the pacifist movement—these were on the agenda on campus every day in some form. There was somebody raising an issue, or some faculty member having some peace group like the Berrigans or somebody else on campus. You just couldn't get through the day without Vietnam intruding. I wanted the trustees to give me some authority and direction in how to handle these difficulties during those turbulent times.

JESUS MOVEMENT

Did the Jesus Movement of the 1970s have much effect on the seminary?

Yes, because it affected young people across the country. It was an emotional movement rather than a rational movement. It was at precisely the opposite end of the spectrum from the new fundamentalist emphasis. The Jesus Movement people tended to affirm, "It's experiential, emotional, and it feels good—therefore it's true." This was the source of the new mind-set of the students in the 1970s, and of the surge in enrollment that hit the seminaries in the early years of that decade.

This led to a growth in enrollment that has continued almost without interruption since that time. The first seminary to get the major surge was Southern Seminary. I have always wondered how that happened. I didn't see it coming, I didn't understand it after it got there, and I still don't understand why it hit Southern. I would have guessed it would have hit New Orleans or Southwestern or even Golden Gate first, but the big surge hit Southern before it hit the others. Many people have always thought of Southern as intellectual, rational, sophisticated, and technical.

Yet here was a movement that was not any of those things that broke on the shores of Southern Seminary. Why did the students want to come to this kind of institution? Apparently they didn't perceive it in the same way that the denominational press would have made them perceive it. I guess the answer is that they didn't read the denominational press and didn't know about the controversies.

REVIEW OF STUDENTS' ENROLLMENT STATUS

There also appeared in the minutes in the fall of 1969 a statement about the review of students' continuing enrollment status. What did this involve?

Certain criteria were to be set up as a legal base so a student could be denied readmission to the seminary. If you had students who didn't believe in God and were not preparing for ministry in a church, why should we spend denominational money equipping them? Yet we had no overt charge against them. They hadn't done anything wrong, but they didn't belong in a theological seminary.

The question was whether the seminary was violating its contractual obligations to a student to let him complete his degree unless it had official charges to bring against him. The admissions process could simply say to student John Doe, "You will not be readmitted to the seminary next semester." Then he would have no legal basis to bring charges against the seminary because the catalog and other documents had clearly stated the conditions under which he could continue as a student.

It was what we on the campus called a "clinker removal" system, after the analogy of the old stoker-fired furnace. It was a way to get the clinkers out without having to tear the furnace apart in order to do so. Allen Graves was director of admissions at one time. We had a student who missed the final deadline for readmission, but he demanded readmission. Allen told him, "The deadline has passed, and the emergency deadline has passed as well. You can't be readmitted until next semester."

This student sued Allen Graves, I think, for $125,000, and the seminary for $100,000. In my judgment, the reason was that he was a draft-dodger. I think he was trying to stay out of the Vietnam War. Keeping the case in court preserved his draft-exempt status because he was trying to get back in the seminary. If he had dropped out for a semester, his draft board might have sent him into military service. Incidentally, the case was thrown out of court.

What was your legal strategy in cases like this where the seminary was being sued?

We would employ the best lawyer we could get and tell him to take the case and do with it what his legal training taught him to do. A settlement out of court was always one possible solution. But we never proposed that a matter be settled out of court unless our lawyer negotiating with the opposite lawyers brought that in as a recommendation.

Did you have the same lawyers in such circumstances, or did you have a battery of lawyers?

Different lawyers were used for different situations. Joe Stopher, a member of the board of trustees and head of one of the major law firms in Louisville, was most frequently the lawyer for the seminary during my entire service. Many thousands of dollars of legal advice were given to the seminary by Mr. Stopher during these years.

We sometimes paid some fees that covered costs. In a partnership law firm, if one partner gives the services of the firm, he is making a gift on behalf of other partners. So there were times when we paid fees to cover at least the out-of-pocket costs of the firm on the case. But we never paid Joe Stopher what we would have paid him as an outside attorney.

If you had to characterize your thirty-plus years at the seminary, would this era of the late 1960s be the most difficult?

Oh yes. I would say the late 1960s were more painful than the late 1950s, as far as I was concerned, because the whole reason for what I was doing as president was jeopardized. It was not only controversy, but as the administrator I had a nagging sense of futility about my efforts. Not to be achieving a goal at whatever the price is far worse than to be paying a high price to achieve a good goal. It was by far the worst period at the seminary for me.

STUDENT ATTITUDES TOWARD THE PASTORATE

In 1969 in your report to the seminary trustees, Dean St. Amant reported there was a serious decline in the number of students who planned to enter the pastorate. Tell us about this.

During that era there was distaste among ministerial students for the church, and the pastorate was viewed as an undesirable place of employment. There was a change in attitude toward the call to the ministry. This was one of the things that made it frustrating for someone who was trying to work in a school to prepare people for ministry in the church. It was disconcerting to have a significant percentage of students who were opposed to the church as an institution, and who considered the ministry in the church as the bottom thing on the totem pole of their professional service.

In this report Dr. St. Amant and I were simply trying to keep the trustees aware of the health of the institution. This was a sickness, and we were reporting the bad situations as well as the good things. In fact, that is one of the basic principles on which I operated—that all reports to the trustees must cover the bad as well as the good.

COOKE HALL

In early 1970 V. V. Cooke gave a challenge gift of $200,000 to Southern Seminary. Do you remember the circumstances surrounding that challenge gift?

This must have been the basis for launching an effort to build the music school building that we ultimately named Cooke Hall. That was because the original music school building was a building that V. V. Cooke had bought and given to the seminary. The original "Cooke Hall" subsequently became the president's home at 2800 Lexington Road.

So, taking the name Cooke Hall off the president's home, we kept it as the name of the music school building. V. V. Cooke and the Cooke family have generously supported the School of Church Music through the years. This was interesting because Mr. Cooke was not generally thought of as person who was particularly interested in the arts. But he was very much enamored of music, particularly church music. I think he had played the organ in a little church in western Kentucky. That's why Don Hustad, professor of organ, is the V. V. Cooke Professor of Organ at Southern Seminary. The Cooke family endowed his professorship.

Wasn't Barnard Hall, across Alta Vista from the president's home, used at some point for the music school?

Yes. It was originally the dormitory for women students, and the women students were essentially students in the music school, but the classroom and the school offices were across Alta Vista Road at 2800 Lexington Road, or Cooke Hall.

And then Barnard Hall was subsequently sold?

Yes, it has been sold. The seminary bought considerable additional acreage there because I thought it was a good investment. That proved to be true. We tried to use that property, but zoning regulations and the nature of the residential community abutting it blocked our efforts. The political clout of those neighbors, and even our own sense of what was appropriate, meant there was no possibility in the foreseeable future of using that land for residences of students or faculty or for any kind of academic facility. So it was declared surplus and sold not long before I left the presidency of the seminary.

DENVER CONVENTION CONTROVERSY

Do you remember the 1970 meeting of the Southern Baptist Convention in Denver and the controversy it generated?

Yes, I remember that awful auditorium we were in. It was like a hallway—long and narrow. If you weren't right down front, you felt like you were miles away from the presiding officer. That hindered Dr. Criswell's ability to manage the Convention. He lost control of the situation entirely, and the floor began to run the process, with the person with the loudest voice being in control. It was one of the most bitter and violent annual meetings I have attended.

Would things have been different with a different presiding officer?

They might have been. I think in another setting and another auditorium, Criswell would have been a very successful presiding officer. Showing public disrespect for people in authority was an "in" thing in those days. In an earlier day, if the Convention had overwhelmingly been angry with the president, they would not have let anybody show disrespect to the man who held that office. But suddenly one could show disrespect for the president and still win his point. That was a new development in the annual meeting of Southern Baptists.

Was Denver a poor choice for the meeting, or would this have happened in 1970 anyway?

It would have happened in 1970, but the city and the convention hall were contributing factors. It was a long way from home; you had a lot of people from the far West who were not in the habit of going to conventions. Therefore, they didn't use the patterns of operation that were normative.

I made the SBC Executive Committee unhappy with my criticism of the convention hall. They thought it was unwarranted, but you hear me repeating it. I still think it was a ridiculous choice of a place to hold a meeting of a Convention that is supposed to be a deliberative body. It was an exhibit hall, and it was designed for people to walk down the center aisle and look at the exhibits on both sides.

This was no place for a deliberative body to meet. It was flat, narrow, and long. This put the people too far from the presiding officer; his presence could not be felt from the middle of the auditorium back. The president was a little dot up there at the front of the auditorium, with just his head and shoulders silhouetted above the pulpit. When somebody broke in and had a stronger voice than Criswell—although a stronger voice than his is hard to imagine—his voice dominated the deliberations.

There was a great deal of controversy at this Convention related to the Broadman Commentary. Did that affect the seminaries very much?

Not in a direct way, but it did concern them because the issue of academic freedom was implied in the action. Dr. Davies, author of the

Genesis commentary, had used some inept phrases, in my judgment. What he was trying to say was obviously what the Bible said. By putting it in the British phrasing, he gave the impression that he was not in control of his comments. If I had been writing a review of that particular section of his work, I would have said, "This is inept phrasing and leaves some ambiguity about the relationship of God and Abraham."

WILLIAM HULL AND INERRANCY

A short time later another controversy emerged that did have some effect on Southern Seminary. The Baptist Program *published an article by Dr. William Hull, "Shall We Call the Bible Infallible?" Tell about that.*

That was originally a sermon preached at Crescent Hill Baptist Church. It was not an article written for the *Baptist Program*, or for anything else. I first heard about it from my son, who is a deacon at Crescent Hill Church. He said, "Dr. Hull preached today, and when he started I thought I was violently opposed to what he was saying. But when I listened to all he had to say, I think he preached a very fine sermon." That was a layman's response to the sermon.

Once the sermon was printed, it described the Bible as both a divine and a human book. (Obviously it is both.) The term *infallible*, of course, became a catchword. For Hull to imply that the Bible is not infallible, but that the human dimensions of the Bible introduce the element of human finitude into the book, was a precursor of the more recent controversy over biblical inerrancy.

Did this pose some later problems for Dr. Hull in terms of his selection for other denominational posts?

That may be. I am not being evasive; I just can't comment on that. He is one of the brightest Southern Baptists and one of the best-trained biblical scholars among Baptists in the world today, in my judgment. I think it's a matter of your ability to handle the language that Hull used and to understand what he was really trying to say. He uses language always with precision and in a way that the ordinary person does not. This is a reflection of his high IQ.

If you try to listen to Hull, you discover that his view of the Bible is a high view and that his concept of the inspiration and authority of Scripture is strong. It compares quite favorably with that of his critics in terms of how much control the Bible is given over life and the decisions we make. Whenever any group talks with Hull and really listens to him, he can communicate forcefully with them, and they will almost uniformly rejoice to hear the insight that he brings to Scripture.

How would you interpret these terms that are widely used in the early 1980s—"inerrant" and "infallible"—with reference to the Bible?

I don't want to get into that controversy, but what in the world does one mean by "inerrancy"? What does one mean by "infallibility"? Frequently the people who are trying to destroy somebody on those words don't have the foggiest notion of what they mean when they use them. So you have a thing like my good friend Criswell's defense of the Bible, the inerrant Bible. But he still wants to take a penknife and cut the latter part of the sixteenth chapter of Mark out of the Bible and burn it. I don't believe Bill Hull is quite that vehement with reference to any word of the Bible, much less a big hunk of a chapter.

Has Dr. Criswell really said this?

In sermons, yes; so I'm not making an accusation. I am simply stating that his view of inspiration and the canon of Scripture eliminates the latter part of the sixteenth chapter of Mark. But he's a conservative, and someone else comes along and says we ought to retain that because the issue is not whether John Mark wrote it or didn't write it; the issue is that this is a part of the Scripture given to us by the working of the Holy Spirit.

Of course, the advocates of these positions have already retreated from the inerrancy of the Bible to the inerrancy of the original autographs. This removes the debate from any viable evidence because now they are talking about something we don't have. Of course, I'm on record as having said, "My Bible is true." That is the phrase I keep using. I'm not referring to the original autographs but to "my" Bible—the one I have on my shelf, the one I read in my daily devotions. "My" Bible is true.

It's true, not because of my IQ and my ability to extract from its language eternal truth. It's true because I can be guided by the Holy Spirit in the reading of God's revelation. I insist that if you're going to talk about the inerrancy of Scripture, you have to talk about the reader as well as the writer. It doesn't make any difference about the inerrancy of the writer if the reader extrapolates error out of the writing. So I want the Holy Spirit involved in both the writing and the reading.

The inerrancy dimension is the product of the intervention of God, not of the intelligence of a finite human being, no matter whether he failed to go to the third grade or has six Ph.D.s. Jesus promised that the Holy Spirit would come and guide us into truth.

So this is really not a new controversy or a new issue for you or the denomination?

No, it's a controversy that has gone on in Christendom since the earliest stages of our use of the inspired writings. What we have today is a neo-rationalism that cannot deal with the concept of the Holy Spirit as the source of contemporary guidance. In other words, it is neo-rationalism that is saying, "My mind has to construct a rational basis for the authority of Scripture. The message of the Bible as interpreted by the witness of the Holy Spirit to an individual or even a church is too idiosyncratic for it to have any ultimate authority."

ST. AMANT RESIGNS AS DEAN

There was a change of deans in the late 1960s. What was behind Dr. St. Amant's moving out of the deanship?

Dr. St. Amant is not a predictable person, and he is different from the average human being. He is a character within himself, and he moves to his own drummer. After about ten years, he just decided that was long enough to be dean. So he resigned to continue as professor of church history. That does not make sense, I know, in the lay community, but it is not unusual in the academic community for a professor to say, "I've had enough of administration." The nature of professors generally is not to like organization and its disciplines. They prefer the discipline of scholarship.

Did you and he have any major conflict that would have brought on his resignation?

No, other than my refusal to permit Dr. Wayne Oates to have a local sabbatical. That we did disagree over—and strongly. But that's the only disagreement between us that I know of. And I don't think that our disagreement over Dr. Oates was such as to make him feel that he ought to give up his deanship.

Tell us about the process you followed in selecting a new dean.

We used the formalized dean selection process, and there were disagreements and strong positions among the faculty. The faculty overwhelmingly supported the selection of Bill Hull. I was delighted with that choice. I think Bill Hull is one of the ablest Southern Baptists scholars we have today.

Hull's problem is that he is a tall, imposing figure. And that is an asset unless people are awed by it or feel put-down by it. His use of language is beautiful and precise, and therefore he doesn't talk like I do, or like most people do. The precision of his mind is awe-inspiring in a committee meeting. He will be about three steps down the road dealing with the problem, and the rest of us will be trying to get there. I've found myself more than once having to say to myself while listening to Dr. Hull, "Wait a minute; what in the world are you talking about; that isn't the issue." And then I would realize, "No; it is the issue. I just haven't gotten that far down the rational process." So I have great admiration for him.

After Hull was named dean, there was always a problem between Oates and Hull. In my judgment, Oates thought he would surely be chosen as dean upon St. Amant's retirement. He was being discussed as dean at the point at which St. Amant came back into the picture and accepted the deanship. Actually, there was almost no faculty support for Oates as dean. There was no way the administration at that time could have named him as dean.

Dr. Oates was an empire-builder as a professor. He would want things for pastoral counseling that would serve the interest of that department. He would go in and negotiate with Hull, but Hull was a hard negotiator. Oates wouldn't get everything he wanted, but he would agree to something that would be stated in writing. Hull always used a written document to record their agreement. Oates would go out feeling pretty good. Then he would realize he hadn't gotten everything he meant to get when he went in. So he would start another process to renegotiate the agreement to improve his position or the position of his department.

So Dr. Oates remained in an adversarial role with Hull?

Yes. It was not a vehement thing, but a tug of war was going on between them constantly. Oates was dealing with what is called the Practical Division, including counseling, preaching, etc. Hull was a New Testament professor. The classical disciplines would get Hull's primary emphasis. I think the institution inevitably has to oscillate between emphasis on classical disciplines and the practical. My observation is that it is currently focusing on the practical. But I'll guarantee you that before the 1980s are over, it will be back with an emphasis on the classical disciplines.

ST. AMANT NAMED PRINCIPAL OF RUSCHLIKON

Would you comment on an action taken by the trustees in April 1971 when they refused to withdraw teaching obligations from Dr. St. Amant after his sabbatical when he was named president of Ruschlikon. Do you remember the circumstances?

Yes, I know exactly what this was about. We are dealing again with the issue of faculty sabbaticals and the seminary's policy on sabbaticals. Those policies are clear and inflexible for a good reason—because there are always requests to modify them. Here was a professor, Dr. St. Amant, who had taken a sabbatical but on the sabbatical had been offered a different job and was now proposing to take the other job.

In academic circles the way this situation is handled is that the new institution picks up the sabbatical cost for the sabbaticant. Southern has done that repeatedly in hiring a new professor and paid for the sabbatical that the professor had just taken. But the Foreign Mission Board policy was such that they would not accept any fiscal responsibility for St. Amant's sabbatical, although it had been spent at Ruschlikon teaching for them. That left St. Amant with no external source for picking up these expenses and Southern Seminary telling him he would have to come back and teach for two years or pay back the cost of his sabbatical. The trustees would not modify the sabbatical policy even for St. Amant.

You have previously indicated your opposition to any modification of the seminary's sabbatical policy.

To this good day I'm opposed to modifying those rules because I know what will happen. And once it happens, I also think that within five years the trustees will modify the generous provisions for a sabbatical. So it is my desire to keep this very good sabbatical program intact. That makes me object to any variation of the policy.

How was this situation ultimately resolved?

St. Amant came back and taught at Southern for the period of time required, in order to fulfill the rules of the sabbatical. Then he went immediately to be principal at Ruschlikon. There was no effort to keep him from going to Ruschlikon. I was sorry to lose him, but I had no feeling that it was inappropriate for him to go. We just were not going to modify the policy. There is no way to make an exception for a dean and then not do so for the next faculty member in a similar situation.

SEMINARY VILLAGE

In July 1971 and then again in January and April 1972, the perennial issue over the sale of Seminary Village resurfaced. Apparently there was a firm offer made for the apartment complex at that point.

I know the financial board of the trustees agreed to sell it, but they did not think they could sell it without the approval of the full board of trustees, or the *ad interim* approval of the executive committee of the trustees. When they took the recommendation to the executive committee, they got a sharp debate and refusal to approve the sale.

The trustees who spoke strongly for retaining Seminary Village had lived there when they were students at the seminary, and they thought it was a wonderful place and the seminary ought not to get rid of it. I was in favor of the sale because we could use the money to construct some new student housing units on campus.

We eventually built 100 units of student housing and funded it in another way and kept Seminary Village. But we didn't have the Seminary Village sale money to use as the down payment on the apartments.

Wasn't this during the time when the seminary's enrollment was increasing dramatically?

Beginning in 1974, the enrollment absolutely surged. We had a computer projection on enrollment which, as I recall, showed a 25 percent jump in the entering class. This was a jump of one-quarter in the entering class in a single year, and we had not sponsored any special recruitment program that I knew about. I was sure the report must be incorrect. So I wrote GIGO—Garbage In—Garbage Out—across the report and sent it back to data processing, asking them to refine it.

So they refined it, and it came back the next time showing that the jump in enrollment would be about 35 percent instead of 25 percent. It turned out both computer reports were wrong; the jump in entering students was 46 percent. The actual entering class in September 1974 was 46 percent larger than the entering class in September 1973.

Until this good day, we have never received an adequate explanation of what happened. But I think it was rooted in what had been happening in the Jesus Movement on college campuses. We didn't foresee it because these students didn't come from our traditional sources of students—the Baptist colleges. They came from places like Montana State University. We'd never heard of it, didn't know where it was, and there were only two Baptist ministerial students out there. So there was no concentration that would make them visible—they just showed up that fall for admission to Southern Seminary and also from other similar non-Baptist universities.

How did you deal with this influx of new students?

Every facility we had was suddenly inadequate—classrooms, professors, everything. We had projected too small for the entering class. So we went into a whirling dervish gyration. By magic or ingenuity or invention, you try to come up with new classrooms without building any. And you come up with new faculty members, and you talk some old faculty members into accepting a one-semester overload to buy time so you can find some new people. There's no easy way to do it; you just do it.

So in the fall of 1974 through 1975, this posed some serious problems for Southern Seminary?

Oh yes, it threw the administration into a tailspin. The growth was much too fast. Yet, we don't have any method in Southern Baptist life for manipulating that. You can't stretch it out. We wanted the students, and they were one good batch of students. They were sharp and dedicated, and the church was what they had come to learn to serve. Remember all the things I said in the negative about the late 1960s? Suddenly we had a totally different group of students. They were right down the middle of the track of what we wanted. They were a bunch of conservatives, theologically. They tended to be a little more emotionally committed theologically than intellectually committed, which isn't a bad thing. It's just that this isn't generally characteristic of an academic institution.

FACULTY LETTER TO TRUSTEES DISCONTINUED

Another thing that occurred early in 1972 was the discontinuation of the faculty letter. What was the faculty letter?

This was a tradition that had been going on for many years. The faculty would formally designate a faculty member to read a letter on the floor of the annual trustee meeting. In those early days, this meeting was held at the site of the annual Southern Baptist Convention meeting. That letter would be the communication from the faculty to the board of trustees.

With the change of the venue of the trustee meeting to Louisville, beginning in the early 1950's, the trustees could talk to more than one faculty member, and there was a lot of communication going on between the faculty and trustees. This meant the faculty letter was not needed as much as it was in the earlier days.

In addition, the seminary now had three schools, and we never could get a single letter that represented all these different perspectives. The School of Religious Education wanted to say one thing; the School of Theology something else; and the School of Church Music would say, "The other two schools may be unhappy, but we're happy, and we don't have any of those problems they want to report." So we would get a conflicting report from the faculties of the various schools.

Finally, the faculty letter got to be nothing more than a gripe list. It wasn't really a report on the state of the union; it was a report on the things the faculty wanted changed. More money for the fellows—that would be an issue. Or "we need bigger offices," or "we're working too hard."

But beyond all of these reasons, the accrediting agency objected vehemently to this process. They didn't like the faculty letter and recommended that it be discontinued. They thought this was not the way the faculty ought to communicate with the trustees and that a trustee meeting should not be run in this manner. That was a recurring note in accreditation reports. The seminary had an inspection for reaccreditation about 1971 or 1972. The action that you are reporting is in response to the accreditation recommendation.

The accrediting agency also recommended that in lieu of this letter, the faculty and the trustees should meet together once per year during the trustee meeting. They do it in a banquet situation. They are seated so that faculty members are scattered among the trustees. This means that a faculty member can talk to three or four trustees throughout the dinner hour, and the trustees can do the same thing.

There is generally an adversarial role between the administration and the faculty in academic institutions. What is the best way for the administration and trustees to communicate to the faculty?

The best thing is just to keep the channels of communication open. The way it works at Southern is through the school committees that channel recommendations to the board of trustees. These committees meet with various groups of faculty members on issues that are vital to the welfare of the three schools. In these meetings the faculty and trustees cut loose, talk openly with one another, and say what they think. This is a very formal kind of setting, so whatever is said is on the record.

If the faculty agrees that they want a specific thing done but the trustees don't agree with the recommendation, the school committees will probably go ahead and report the faculty recommendation. With this process, the faculty recommendation is very powerful and it can't be ignored.

VICE PRESIDENT'S ROLE ESTABLISHED

About this time there was a change in the structure of your organization, with Badgett Dillard and Pat Pattillo being elected as vice presidents in 1972. What effect did this reorganization have on the administration of the seminary?

The reorganization of the administration was the final development of a process we had been in for years. We were moving toward setting up the seminary under four separate but related divisions: Business Affairs, Development, Student Affairs, and Academic Affairs. This organization meant the seminary provost was the equivalent of vice president for academic affairs, and the deans of the various schools were under the provost.

This reorganization was an effort to simplify the lines and make the seminary operate more smoothly. For example, it was perfectly clear that anybody in the business operation ultimately went through Badgett Dillard. One of the principles of good administration is that the number of people who report to the chief administrator should be no more than eight. This was an effort for the president to stop trying to deal with twenty-five or thirty different people about innumerable projects.

I'm sure some faculty members continued to want to go directly to the top man with their problems and requests. How did you handle that?

Anybody who wanted to go directly to the president about anything could do so. But the president would listen sympathetically and then ask, "Have you talked to your dean about that? Why don't you go tell him what you've told me. If he recommends it, I'm sure it will get my support."

This approach made the seminary more manageable and more efficient. It also gave the top administration time to think long-term about policies rather than living twenty-four hours a day on hand-to-mouth decisions. Without this type of operation, it's possible for the president and other key administrators to spend all their time and energy just keeping the institution running. This means you don't have time to think long-range and worry about the major issues.

DEALING WITH SEMINARY NEIGHBORS

Why did you list "neighbors" as one of the constituencies a seminary president has to be concerned about?

Believe me, neighbors—the people who adjoin the seminary campus—have power. They can give you fits if you try to put a fence along your property line that they don't want. I know; I did that—put up a fence on the west side of the seminary campus. But I had to do it to stop the fights.

The problem was that the neighbors would come across the line and put their flower gardens and their vegetable gardens over on the seminary property. Then the seminary crew with their gang mowers would come along and mow the outer edge so they wouldn't hurt these gardens. Other neighbors would fuss because the seminary didn't mow up to the property line. If you mowed up to the property line, you would cut down a flower, and that would cause a controversy. So I just got a survey of the property line, put a chain link fence down it (actually one foot inside seminary property), and said "Good fences make good neighbors."

Did you talk with any of these neighbors about this?

Oh, they'll let you converse with them. But it won't work if you try to have group meetings about the problem. They don't come to listen; they come to tell you. I'm a cynic about the ability to take a group like that, once the issue is raised, and persuade them to a reasonable compromise. Maybe I ought to say, "I never could reach a reasonable agreement with them."

To this good day, travel down Godfrey Avenue any day during school hours and notice which side of the street the cars are parked on. They are all over on the seminary side. Why? Because the city officials got so tired of the neighbors fussing about the seminary students parking in front of their houses that they declared their side of the street a fire lane. Then nobody could park over there. Now even the residents have to park on the seminary side

That's nonsense; it's trivial. But it illustrates why the pressure on a school administrator is sometimes irrational and insoluble. He gets blindsided by things that he never dreamed about as potential problems. Sometimes it's the little things that cause more than their share of trouble and frustration.

CONTROVERSY IN 1973–74

In late 1973, did Wayne Oates resign to go to Southeastern Seminary and then actually not go? Did this signal another controversy at the seminary?

As I recall, what happened was that Wayne Oates suddenly announced he had an offer from Southeastern that he was going to accept. I remember talking with him on a Friday about it. Our conversation was very warm and cordial. I regretted exceedingly that he felt he should leave Southern. I thought he had an offer from Southeastern that they could give him because of their smaller faculty. It was a special status as a faculty member, involving secretarial help, research help, reduced teaching load, things of this sort. And he was to have a unique role at Southeastern.

I indicated to him that I had been working to establish a category of distinguished professor at Southern Seminary. This position would not be comparable to the Southeastern offer, but it was of the same general type. I told him that I had hoped he would become one of the first distinguished professors at Southern Seminary as soon as we could get the program implemented.

This was to be a rank beyond a senior professor?

That's right, a rank beyond senior professor, limited to perhaps three or four faculty members at Southern. As it turned out, that was never developed. The title of senior professor was developed, and it's an entirely different concept. What I was talking about to Dr. Oates was later abandoned. After my personal study and discussion with the academic administration, we decided we did not want to go that route. But the point is, I was saying to Wayne, "That's a wonderful opportunity; I'm glad for you. I'm sorry we can't match the offer at this time and keep you at Southern."

We had a cordial meeting, and Wayne was supportive in his attitude on that Friday. That weekend, I was out of the city and came through Memphis on my way home from the Arkansas convention to some other convention. The editor of *The Gadfly* at the seminary caught me in my brother's home in Memphis and wanted to interview me over the phone about Dr. Oates's going to Southeastern.

I gave him a standard reply: "That's Southeastern's story, not mine. I will not announce Dr. Oates's leaving. They must announce his coming. I will comment on his leaving Southern only after they have announced the accomplished fact that he is becoming one of their faculty members."

At that point the editor of the *Gadfly* said, "Let me read a statement that Dr. Oates made to his classes this morning and see if you will comment on that." He read it. Wayne had declared categorically that he was leaving, going to Southeastern. The *Gadfly* editor said, "Now what is your comment?" I said, "I would congratulate him on the excellent position to which he is going. And say that he deserves it, and I regret to see him leave. But we are in a position, fortunately, in the person of Dr. John Boyle (Wayne Oates's associate) to fill the gap. Dr. Boyle will function as the head of the department upon Dr. Oates's departure."

This must have been in November 1973, since state conventions were meeting at the time. I went on to the Florida convention, made no other statement, and was not in Louisville again for several days. My exact statement is available because it was quoted by the *Gadfly* editor. He recorded it on the telephone and published exactly what I said.

You have no quarrel with that?

No, I said exactly what he said I did. I think it was about all I could have said. But I came home to discover that the environment had changed completely between Friday and my return the latter part of the next week. Suddenly Dr. Oates was announcing that he could not get along with either Dean Hull or with President McCall. This was news to me because he had said exactly the opposite during our meeting on the previous Friday.

My guess is that Dr. Oates was not irrevocably committed to going to Southeastern. His resignation, I thought later, was a device to open negotiations with me to secure from the president some things he had not been able to get from the dean. By announcing his replacement, I had, in effect, indicated there would be no effort to talk him out of going or to negotiate with him.

He had given no hint that he was open to negotiation on the matter. When I got home, the verbiage was vehement, it was bitter, it was emotionally charged. Oates had made all sorts of charges about my not supporting him properly. None of these were in his original announcement. Of course, he wound up not going to Southeastern, and that tends to support my assumption that he wasn't all that committed to going in the first place.

Did you and Dr. Olin Binkley at Southeastern talk about this?

Yes, and I agreed there was nothing wrong with their approach to him. In other words, it was a proper offer made by Southeastern to Dr. Oates. The dean at Southeastern, Dr. Raymond Brown, had dealt quite openly and above board. There were no problems with that in my mind. I was surprised that Wayne Oates had accepted the offer.

I was aware that there was some tug of war between the dean at Southern and Dr. Oates. I admired Oates; I thought he was a very useful professor. He was at Southern Seminary before I arrived as president, and I had to fight to keep him. As a matter of fact, he was a target of some of the professors who left Southern in 1958. They did not want him on the faculty and they did not want to see him promoted, because they were opposed to counseling as a subject in the seminary curriculum. So I had been his defender at an earlier stage against some other members of the faculty.

This incident with Dr. Oates seemed to kick off a whole new round of unpleasantries at the seminary. There was name-calling and charges made by several faculty members in the classroom and out. Then the faculty morale went into a nose-dive. A report was made by a committee of the faculty, chaired by Hugo Culpepper, which was critical of the administration.

The situation ran from then on into the spring with numerous meetings between administrators, the Deans Council, and the committee of the faculty, trying to isolate the problems. The administration (president and deans) made numerous proposals to the faculty representatives. Vague charges were made from their corner about administrative style, which seemed to include the deans, president, and staff. They charged that the morale among the faculty was low.

This matter dragged on until May 1974. At that point I told the faculty committee that I had appointed to try to resolve the problem: "We have tried our best to resolve this issue, and we have obviously not established any communication with you that is effective. Therefore, it is time for me to make a statement: There will soon be a regularly scheduled meeting of the trustees. This issue will be brought to the trustees. After that meeting some of you will not be on the faculty of Southern Seminary. I probably will not be president. But at that time we will settle this issue once and for all."

I was simply saying to this group that it was fish-or-cut-bait time. I repeated my statement in the full faculty meeting on Monday. The faculty, some of whom had lived through the 1957–58 controversy, were not inclined to think I was bluffing. They took this as very serious. They went into overdrive to make sure that something was done to resolve the situation.

These older and long-time faculty members asked for a called faculty meeting later in the week and worked out some compromises designed to get us off dead center and move us on to a new era. While I didn't care for the compromises myself, I wasn't really trying to do anything except move the seminary forward. These compromises were eventually accepted by everyone, and we worked the problem out. By next fall everything was sweetness and light.

Did any of the faculty leave over this except Dr. Oates?

No. Oates was the only one. He had left before the controversy intensified.

HOW TO DEAL WITH CONTROVERSY

Looking back over your long denominational career in which you have faced many controversies, what is your philosophy of controversy and how to deal with it?

Let me say first of all that religious controversy is dangerous and real and that people do get hurt in such controversies. Careers get altered, sometimes seriously impaired, by these controversies. More important from my point of view than the impact of controversies on institutional life is what happens inside the spirit of people. I've seen individuals bear ugly scars all of their lives because of what happened in controversy. Controversy is sinful, and I think anyone involved in controversy has cause for repentance, regardless of how it began.

I don't think a person ever gets into a controversy without being partially to blame. But whether a person would admit this at the time of the controversy is another story. Maybe it's just your personality, or the way you part your hair, or the tone of your voice, or your choice of language, or your reputation. All of these things do tend to make you get involved in controversy. But when you get involved, admit that you're in a sinful situation and that you aren't a knight in shining armor with a white banner.

Is that true even when you're right?

Oh, you always think you're right. But if you are going to deal with controversy, one of the things you must do is harbor a suspicion in the far left corner of your mind that you might be wrong. Or that you might be partially wrong. It is very useful to carry this attitude—not to express it. You can't express the feeling that you might be wrong because your opponents will sometimes use that improperly. But you ought to realize that you are a finite creature and that your confidence that you are absolutely right is not soundly based. Your finitude may have caused you to err in understanding.

That's one thing that keeps you a little bit humble in controversy and makes you willing to listen to the other side and to look for a way out of the controversy, including compromises that you think are perhaps not justified. But if the compromise will settle the controversy, maybe a compromise that is partially wrong may be a good price to pay for getting out of the confrontation.

Another thing you need to remember is that you have an official role, so an institution or an organization is involved in how you conduct yourself. That includes winning or losing in the controversy. So don't ever get into a controversy if you aren't going to try to come out winning. Winning sounds a little harsh, but that's what I'm saying. If a controversy is not worth what it takes to win, then it's not worth starting. But remember your responsibility to the larger organization: fellowship.

But having said all of that, survival is also important. You've got to survive the controversy. That doesn't mean you have to keep your job, but it does mean that your psyche must come out relatively healthy, no matter what happens.

I am alarmed when I see people jump into controversy with absolute assurance of victory. I've been in many situations where I was aware that the other side didn't think they could be hurt. But realistically speaking, that stuff on the floor is not ketchup; it's blood—real human blood. People bleed in controversy. And just take for granted that some of that blood will be yours, that you're going to get hurt.

If you think you're not going to get hurt in a controversy, then you're not prepared to go into it. You will overreact when you get hurt, and the overreaction may be withdrawal from the controversy prematurely, or it may mean use of tactics that are not warranted and an attempt to destroy your opponent. So you must assume going into a controversy that you are going to get hurt. This is why those of us who have seen more than our share of controversies don't like them. We will go to great lengths to avoid them.

I think that's true of me; I know it's not particularly my reputation. I had just as soon have a reputation as a person who is willing to get into controversy. It warns people off; it keeps them from starting a fuss in the first place.

You must come out of a controversy with the ability to function as a minister of the gospel, and to be reasonably happy, to be able to get rid of the anger and the guilt that all controversies stimulate in the people involved. I never have been in a controversy that I didn't end up angry and filled with a deep sense of guilt for having gotten into the situation in the first place. This means you must have some techniques for handling the emotional load, the tension, the pressures that result from controversy.

What techniques did you use?

I used to ride a Honda, a trail bike. The angry roar of that engine, a little risk-taking and hill-climbing, and the concentrated effort required to handle the bike would wipe out the other memories. It's childish for a sixty-year-old to do that, but I've done it. I've played follow the leader with a bunch of pre-teens on their little motor bikes in a wooded, secluded area near the president's home.

Another way is to run off to Florida when the pressure gets hot, to change my environment, and so discard the feelings. Another thing I have done is to play golf. You can't play golf and think about anything but golf. This, for me, is a mind-mop that wipes away some of my negative feelings and emotions. But the most important thing is to have a companion, a wife who understands. She knows when I need a little tender, loving care in the form of an extra dessert or something else that says to me in a profound way, "I care for you."

Finally, in the midst of controversy, you need to do some extra praying and devotional Bible study. It is hard to think about God and Calvary and take yourself too seriously or be very angry with others.

Was Mrs. McCall your sounding board in many of these controversies?

Yes, except I tried to limit the level at which I involved her emotionally in these situations. She didn't deserve to have everything dumped on her. So I tried to modify the sounding board. But sometimes I needed that, and she would be the person on whom I would pour all of my emotions.

Did you handle controversies differently at different stages of your life? Do some things work in some controversies that might not work in other situations?

One of the major things I learned was that sitting on my emotions and not communicating my emotions in a controversy tended to mislead the other side. In a lot of stages, I tended to make less effort to bottle up my emotions and to "keep cool," as the phrase would put it, through a controversy. I discovered, in the course of time, that often the only way to counter an emotion is with an emotion.

I know this runs against some theories. Believe me, I understand that when a person is angry you don't get angry with him, because that will escalate the issue. But after you have sought to calm the situation down and taken the edge off his anger, it may be just as well for you to point out to him that there's anger on both sides of the issue. If we're going to solve it, maybe both of us had better control our emotions. That's really what I'm trying to say.

I also discovered that turning the other cheek is a wonderful way to handle controversy. But I'm not sure how many times you do that before it becomes important not to turn the other cheek, but to go on the offensive rather than the defensive. I am aware that this will create theological questions in the mind of anybody who reads this book. But on the other hand, there is a point at which it becomes necessary to harden your own position and communicate very clearly what the consequences of this controversy can be.

Incidentally, I discovered that if people can predict you in a group setting, they find it easier to deal with you. If they don't know how to predict your emotional reaction to things, this sometimes lets them go too far and get into trouble they didn't mean to venture into.

Some people who have observed you in controversial settings have said that you appeared almost to be playing a game at certain points. How do you respond to this?

I understand why someone might think that. I believe there are appropriate and inappropriate responses at particular times in every controversy. What's appropriate in one situation is not appropriate in another, or what was appropriate yesterday may not be appropriate today. Some repertoire, some variety of responses, is necessary in every controversial situation.

I have been known to raise my voice and use a tone as angry as I could muster because someone needed to hear what I was trying to say. When I was speaking calmly, they were not hearing me. They were not understanding the force of what I was saying, so I would give them a signal that communicated in an unmistakable way, "This is important to me."

The most important thing I want to say about controversy is that bearing a grudge or nursing a grievance toward others is absolutely disastrous. It's disastrous in the situation, and it's disastrous personally to the people involved. I think that to a large degree I have avoided doing that. I have tried to discipline myself never to harbor resentment and a spirit of wanting to get even.

Thinking about what I have just discussed, I believe I have been too testy. But even that reflects how this era made me feel and react, so I am still doing it. Tell whoever reads this book to tone down my rhetoric by about ten decibels.

HULL'S RESIGNATION AS PROVOST

Dr. William Hull resigned as provost and dean of the School of Theology at Southern in 1975 to go into the pastorate. Tell about that.

This was a traumatic period for all of us at Southern. This upheaval caused me to question whether it was time for me to leave the seminary. But the decision to stay was rooted in what, for me, was a spiritual struggle with the will of God for my life. Once this was resolved, I had a new commitment to the seminary and to dreams for its future.

I think Dr. Hull had been through the same sort of trauma. He had been through all the controversy and the bitterness that had been ventilated. Suddenly a church—the great First Baptist Church of Shreveport, Louisiana—offered him the opportunity to prove that what he was trying to do in preparing people for the ministry would actually work. If he went into the pastorate and did it himself, that would validate his teachings about a New Testament church. That was a challenge that appealed to him.

The church also offered loving support and emotional response. The absence of such emotional support is one of the difficult things about school administration. Many school administrators complain about it at certain times—the sense of being alone and not a part of a deeply caring community. Now that sense may be a little wide of the facts, but how you feel about it is important.

I regretted to see Bill Hull leave. I thought it was a mistake for him. I thought it was a mistake for Southern Seminary. I thought it was a mistake for Southern Baptists. But I decided long ago that when a person says, "This is the will of God for my life," I will not quarrel with his decision, and I never have.

I've gotten into difficulty on more than one occasion when somebody has said, "I've thought this through, and I believe, under God, I ought to resign from the seminary." I will argue with you about it up until that point. At that point, when you say, "I believe it is the will of God for me to do this," then I suspend judgment and simply say, "It's none of my business; I've got to go on and work with what is left." That was true with Hull.

Bill and Wylodene Hull were close personal friends of mine and Marguerite. His leaving Southern was a personal loss as well as a professional loss, because he was a highly-skilled colleague whom I trusted and admired.

ROY HONEYCUTT AS DEAN

Roy Honeycutt was elected to replace Dr. Hull as dean. How was he elected to this position?

We started out with the regular process of selecting a dean search committee. That's a fairly straightforward process—who is on the committee, and how they are selected. The committee met in my office, and the first effort was to compile a list of the names of all the possible dean prospects from every source, both internal and external to the seminary.

At about the second meeting, the committee, in effect, chose the names of the people the committee would want to consider for the deanship. Then I was given a few days to determine what sequence, if any, I would want to put the names in. Somehow the name of Roy Honeycutt was put at the head of the list to be investigated. I knew him but did not know him well, although I had nothing but high regard for him. I didn't know him as an administrator, or even as a professor, although he had done some teaching at Southern.

Next we assigned different members of the committee different areas to investigate with reference to Honeycutt. Somebody would investigate his work as a pastor in Princeton, Kentucky, somebody else his teaching at Midwestern, somebody else his deanship at Midwestern, and so forth. When the committee reassembled after this phase of the search process, it was absolutely unanimous that Roy Honeycutt was the man. Each person, although he investigated one isolated area, came away from that investigation saying, "He's the person I want to support as dean."

Honeycutt was the only person who ever got serious consideration as the new dean. That is very unusual. The process moved very swiftly, and he was interviewed in Louisville, and he agreed to come. Then his election by the trustees proceeded quickly, and it was done. He came as dean and also as provost.

That was a new position, was it not?

No, Hull had held the position of provost. We were trying to move to a new role where the provost would be the chief academic officer for the seminary, and there would be a dean for each of the schools.

It took a bit of doing and some time before either Honeycutt or the faculty was willing for him to relinquish the deanship. He finally had to admit that he could not carry all the responsibilities. And sitting as one of the deans in one situation and sitting as the supervisor of deans in another produced a certain conflict.

Because of my experience I understood why neither Hull nor Honeycutt wanted to give up the deanship. Actually, there is an emotional involvement in the academic enterprise and with the faculty that is not easy to describe. It is the thing that you think is most important, and that's what you want to be a part of.

How would you describe Dr. Roy Honeycutt?

He is a big man; he's an intelligent man; he is an unflappable man. He never expresses much emotion, either good or bad, pro or con. He moves carefully with an analytical mind that takes the problem apart and then reassembles it in new configurations. And, finally, he makes his decision.

There's a little anecdote about Honeycutt at this point that is significant. One day, J. J. Owens, professor of Old Testament, came into my office laughing from the bottom of his feet to the top of his head. He was just beside himself with humor. He said, "I had to come to tell you about this. We knew we, the faculty, had a dean in Roy Honeycutt, but as president you also have a dean."

It seems that I had declared a vacancy of a senior professorship in a department. But the department had anticipated me and had decided they would look for a junior professor whenever the president got around to declaring a vacancy in the department. (That would mean the new professor would be junior to all of the present members of the department.)

So Honeycutt went to the department in proper protocol to report to them the president had declared a senior vacancy in the department. Whereupon a smart young professor announced, "Dean Honeycutt, we will have to have another department meeting because we have met and decided that we want to look for a junior addition in the department."

Dr. Honeycutt, according to J. J. Owens, responded, "Oh no; it will not be necessary for you to meet again, the president and I have declared a vacancy for a senior professor."

That was the thing that tickled J. J. Owens. It was done without emotion, but with absolute, utter finality. The decision had been made; it was settled; there wasn't any point in anybody reviewing it for any purpose.

This is Roy Honeycutt at another level. I tell this story because it's an insight into the thought patterns of faculty members, including J. J. Owens, who is a very warm, personal friend, as he has been through the years. He was pleased to discover that the dean would function not only on behalf of the faculty but also on behalf of the president. He was telling me, "You can count on Roy Honeycutt; he will represent the president."

Did Dr. Honeycutt have an opportunity to do any teaching in his new role?

Yes, he did teach, because he loves to teach. And that's part of his struggle. He keeps wanting to get back into the classroom. He frets over the fact that he cannot keep up in his Old Testament studies and do all the administration, all the travel, and all the other things he has to do. So he's a man divided in his loyalties, but he has his priorities straight. He knows what his priorities are, and he gets the first things done first.

BOYCE BIBLE SCHOOL

During the 1973 Convention at Portland, there was an attempt to have the Boyce Bible School approved by the Convention as a program of Southern Seminary. What prompted you to give thought to this concept?

Let me respond to that by jumping back all the way to my Baptist Bible Institute days in New Orleans. I was interested then in extension education. My memory is that I took some leadership in setting up the Seminary Extension Department (of the six seminaries). So I was interested in the people not prepared for seminary degree work, going back to 1943.

One of the three proposals of James P. Boyce in launching Southern Seminary was that education would be provided for those who could only take the English program, by which he meant those who would not bring collegiate background to the seminary. That's the root of the Boyce Bible School name.

Didn't Southern Seminary offer a certificate program for people who did not have the academic qualifications for graduate theological work?

Yes, but they had to be older (age 30), and they had to demonstrate the academic competence to perform in a seminary classroom. Not many people were entering the seminary to study for these certificate or diploma programs. Beyond that, I had perceived what was happening in terms of the Seminary Extension Department. This was a fine program and it was successfully executed, but it wasn't reaching a part of our constituency.

That segment was the Great Lakes area. I thought this region was important to the future of Southern Seminary. Southern Seminary has really been on the edge of the Southern Baptist Convention. Now Southern Baptists have expanded into those "pioneer" areas. We at Southern were not training their leadership, and we were going to have on our doorstep an anti-seminary constituency.

The only way I knew to counter that, or to help those churches—and the two were equally important to me—was to try to give proper educational credentials to the pastors of these new pioneer-type churches.

I finally came up with the idea that we ought to have such a school in Southern Seminary. The name "Boyce," by the way, is a bad name because it gets mixed up by sound with the word "boys," and people hear it as BOYS School. But I chose the name for the father of Southern Seminary because it was his principle that was to be embodied in the Boyce Bible School. We planned to educate ministers who had only a "common school" preparation. And I needed his endorsement of the idea to sell it to the Southern faculty, trustees, and alumni.

A SPEECH DELIVERED TO BOYCE BIBLE SCHOOL— AUGUST 27, 1987

"And God said let there be a Boyce Bible School."

I wish I had thought of that title, which was assigned me, because it speaks the truth.

"In the beginning God created the heavens and the earth." Boyce came some time later, but in God's due time.

Paul writes to the Romans, "For whosoever shall call upon the name of the Lord shall be saved. How then shall they call on him in whom they have not believed? And how shall they believe in him of whom they have not heard? and how shall they hear without a preacher? And how shall they preach, except they be sent?" (10:13-15a, KJV). That is a great text for missions, but it is God, not man, who does the choosing and the sending.

This was the perspective of James Petigru Boyce when on July 30, 1856, as he ended his first session as theological professor at Furman University, he delivered his inaugural address entitled "Three Changes in Theological Institutions." In Broadus's *Memoir of James P. Boyce,* he summarized these changes as:

(1) A Baptist theological school ought not merely to receive college graduates, but men with less of general education, even men having only what is called a common English education, offering every man such opportunities of theological study as he is prepared for or desires. (2) Besides covering, for those who are prepared, as wide a range of theological study as could be found elsewhere . . . so that the ablest and most aspiring students might make extraordinary attainments, preparing them for instruction and original authorship, and helping to make our country less dependent on foreign scholarship. (3) There should be prepared an Abstract of Principles . . . which every professor in such an institution must sign when inaugurated . . . (p. 121).

In discussing his first proposal that the new theological school should be open to those who are not college graduates, Boyce said, "Never would I consent to lift my voice upon such a subject as this without a distinct recognition of the sovereignty of God working his will, and calling forth according to that will the many or the few with whose aid he will secure the blessing" (p. 124). The blessing is to meet the need which he described—"Now, when our churches at home are not adequately supplied (with ministers), when dark and destitute places are found in the most favored portions of our own land, when the heathen are at our very doors, and the cry is 'Help! Help!' and there is no help, because there are not laborers enough to meet the wants immediately around us" (p. 123).

From Boyce's vision tossed into the center of the conscience of Southern Baptists by this speech came The Southern Baptist Theological Seminary, chartered in 1858 in South Carolina and begun in 1859 with four professors, 26 students, and 2,200 books. The just-vacated building of the First Baptist Church of Greenville, South Carolina, was divided into two classrooms and a library. Boyce was the chairman of the faculty and later was given the title as the first president. All of the three changes Boyce had proposed were an integral part of the new institution. They continued to be a part of the seminary until the 1970s when the growth in students and faculty and buildings, especially the availability of the Carver Building of the former WMU Training School, opened new doors. The increased technical nature of some seminary classes made them less helpful to students unprepared in that area. Also the organization of the institution into three schools—Theology, Religious Education, and Music—seemed to make it appropriate to add a fourth school specifically designed for those God-called ministers for whom a baccalaureate degree did not appear to be possible.

Because I had a long-standing dedication to the importance of Bible school ministry, I asked Dr. Allen Graves to use his sabbatical at Stanford University in Palo Alto, California, in the fall of 1972 to study new developments in adult education with a view to recommending the best program and structure for achieving Boyce's "first change" in theological education in the current situation of the seminary and the world. When he returned to Louisville early in 1973, we spent many hours discussing and revising his proposals.

It was necessary to get not only seminary faculty approval of the proposal but also to get faculty wisdom in shaping the proposal. The faculty was concerned about the possible dilution of the academic standards of the seminary, the cost of additional faculty members, but most of all, the removal of Boyce-type students from their own classes. After the initial discussion, little opposition remained as attention shifted to the best way to open the school.

The presidents of the six Southern Baptist seminaries were involved in one of their recurring efforts to find the best formula for distributing Cooperative Program funds to the seminaries. A formula expert from Vanderbilt University, Dr. Kaludis, was the consultant. He was trying to apply to the seminaries the complicated procedures in the formulas used in state university systems. Because the levels of teaching as well as the numbers of students and the types of courses would be in such a formula, I advised the consultant in the presence of the other five seminary presidents of our plans for what became Boyce Bible School, although we had not named it at that time.

Southern Seminary trustees received the recommendation for the new enterprise in their annual meeting May 1, 1973. They dealt with it and ended by appointing a special committee headed by the vice chairman of the board, Mr. Joe Jack Hurst, and set a special order for the committee to report on May 2. The recommendation was both complicated and far-reaching. There was sharp debate and motions to amend, but the subcommittee's version survived intact. The main items were as follows:

(1) That 'The Carver School of Missions and Social Work' be utilized as a separate educational institution and that the corporate name . . . be changed to the 'Boyce School of Christian Ministry.'
(2) That the trustees approve the changes in the charter of the Carver School of Missions and Social Work.
(3) That the attached list of persons be elected to membership on the Board of Overseers for the Convention Bible College, which will be a division of the Boyce School of Christian Ministry.
(4) That Allen W. Graves be elected president of the Boyce School of Christian Ministry as the executive head of that school and its several divisions.
(7) That the building and grounds of WMU Hall of the former Carver School be committed for the use of the Boyce School of Christian Ministry and its related programs.

The original motion of Mr. Hurst carried unanimously.

Immediately we released the news to the press and arranged for the SBC Executive Committee to review the matter in their preconvention meeting. Public discussion was strongly favorable.

The private discussion was another matter. Seminary presidents began to lobby the Executive Committee against the proposal. They complained that they had no advance notice and that it would affect the Seminary Formula. It was proposed that I was obviously elitist in my commitment to high academic standards; therefore, I obviously had some other goal than just a Bible school. President Ellis Fuller had at some time talked about making Southern Seminary a full university. It was conjectured that my interest in courses not based on a baccalaureate degree was really to offer college courses in competition with Baptist state colleges and universities. It was remembered that I had turned Baptist Bible Institute into a seminary; no one knew or remembered that I had gone to New Orleans to spend my life in training God-called ministers without reference to academic prerequisites.

The battle was lost in the SBC Executive Committee before it began. No discussion was permitted on the floor. The matter was referred to the Institution Workgroup. Allen Graves, who was our expert and had been chosen to administer the new program, was denied even one minute of explanation before the committee voted against it.

I was shocked and angry—angry at the treatment by the Executive Committee and furious over the lobbying by the seminary presidents without any discussion with me. They responded to me with resentment until something I said finally caused President Harold Graves of Golden Gate to remember my description of the Southern Seminary plans in the formula discussions. Like a Christian gentleman, he not only changed his position but also argued with the other presidents that the procedures of Southern were appropriate in this matter. Over a period of weeks, they gradually withdrew their opposition.

Allen Graves and I came back to Louisville from the Convention in Portland much discouraged. We went back to square one and began all over again so we would not present a previously rejected plan to the Convention in Dallas the next year. I was so upset by the SBC Executive Committee treatment that I refused to route the new plan through the SBC Executive Committee. I insisted on the right of an SBC agency to carry a recommendation directly to the Convention floor.

But time had worked in our favor. The pastors and churches wanted Boyce Bible School established. It was clear that the trustee recommendation was going to be adopted by the Dallas convention. Indeed, the Executive Committee, whose recommendations are the first business of each Convention, beat us to the draw. They recommended to the Convention that a revised program statement for Southern Seminary read: "Maintains three schools and a ministry training center: (1) theology, (2) religious education, (3) church music, and (4) a ministry training center including the Boyce Bible School.* Awards diplomas and certificates to non-college graduates who complete required courses of study."

At the bottom of the page was this footnote: "*Contingent on the approval of the Convention of the ministry training center including the Boyce Bible School (to be presented by the Board of Trustees of Southern Baptist Theological Seminary)," (1974 Convention *Annual,* pp. 58, 59).

The full recommendation of the seminary trustees is found on pages 191–193 of the 1974 *Annual* of the Southern Baptist Convention. The key difference from the previous recommendation a year earlier is: "The center shall be the division of special activities within the Southern Baptist Theological Seminary. It shall be administered by an executive-director who shall report to the seminary president."

The use of the Carver School charter, some autonomy, the title of president, and the Convention Bible College have disappeared. The motion I made on behalf of the trustees was adopted. That enabling action, item 202 of the Convention minutes, reads: "That the Southern Baptist Convention approve the establishment of the Ministry Training Center related to the Southern Baptist Theological Seminary offering programs of adult education for ministry, including the Boyce Bible School."

Because it was an idea whose time had come in the purposes of God, Boyce Bible School was launched in the fall of 1974 with Allen Graves as the first executive director. He had been dean of the School of Religious Education and would be its dean again later. He had been administrative dean of the seminary, a position roughly that of the provost today. But it will always be to Allen Graves's credit that he trans-formed Boyce's dream into the best thinking of the American academic community of this century, and structured it into the fourth school of Southern Baptist Theological Seminary. But he could not have done it without the help and support of the rest of the seminary faculty and staff or without the desire of the hosts of Southern Baptists for Boyce Bible School.

Time would fail to tell of all the faculty members and staff who have worked in Boyce, including the creative and effective leadership of Dean David Byrd, not to mention the members of the Board of Overseers who have volunteered their services.

But the real strength of Boyce Bible School is that it fits a niche in the plans and purposes of God for some of those he has called. May it ever equip them to be worthy ambassadors for the King.

SEMINARY EXTERNAL EDUCATION DEPARTMENT

Tell us about the Seminary Extension program of the six seminaries and how it developed.

Baptist Bible Institute developed a correspondence course, and that put it in competition with Southwestern, which also had a correspondence course. There were conversations back in the early 1940s, when I was in New Orleans, about cooperation among the seminaries in various ways.

I remember we developed a paper on ordination way back then. That was an issue with the seminary. It reflected what we thought was a superficial attitude on the part of many churches toward ordination and its meaning. Then this evolved on down to the days when the Seminary Extension Department had its headquarters in Jackson, Mississippi, with Lee Gallman as the director.

Why was Jackson chosen?

Lee Gallman wanted to put it there, and living costs and office costs were cheap. But it was an inconvenient location; the presidents couldn't keep up with it. The presidents took the initiative in insisting that it be moved to Nashville, where it would join a family of Southern Baptist agencies. Here it would be easy for the seminary presidents to drop in and out. It was moved to Nashville about the time the new SBC building on James Robertson Parkway was completed.

Each of the seminaries pays one-sixth of the cost of operating Seminary Extension, on the theory that they have equal ownership and equal responsibility for its program.

FIRST BAPTIST CHURCH, SARASOTA, FLORIDA

As you began to look toward the closing years of your ministry, did you ever give any thought to doing something else besides being president of Southern Seminary?

Yes, I had always thought I would like to round out my ministry by getting back into the pastorate. We have already discussed the fact that 1974 was a particularly bad time at the seminary. About this time I was invited to First Baptist Church of Sarasota, Florida, to consult with them about calling a pastor. I flew over from Delray and preached for them on Sunday morning. I couldn't stay Sunday night because I had something else to do. So I went over for a Saturday night conference with the pulpit committee. It was a two-hour standard conference with a pulpit committee about processes in calling a pastor.

At the end of the meeting, a lawyer, who is still a dear friend of mine and a trustee of Southern Seminary right now, asked a question. We were in the beautiful boardroom of his law firm. He asked from the opposite end of the table, "Dr. McCall, how can we know whether the man we call as our pastor will love us?"

I have been asked many things in my lifetime, but I had never been asked that question. I don't know the answer. So my answer came out sort of like this: "I really don't know, except that before you call a man, you will know him well. You should know whether, after a business meeting in which you've disagreed with your pastor, you could put your arm around his shoulders and say, 'Pastor, I love you, and I disagreed with you tonight. But I want you to know that I wasn't opposing my pastor. I was doing what you taught me to do—expressing my conscience on the issue."

Then I told the committee, "Could you ever walk up to your pastor and put your arms around him and tell him, 'Pastor, I love you'? If you feel that way about him, he will probably feel that way about you." With that we went on up to the club on the top of the building to have dinner.

I wasn't a prospect in anyone's mind, because I was sixty years old. The next morning I preached in the church. It was a good service. A lot of people were coming down to speak to the preacher after the service. Toward the end of the long line of people, here came the church pulpit committee I had met with the night before. I thought they were coming to tell me good-bye.

There were seven members of the pulpit committee. A woman was the chairperson. One of the men came up, and I reached out to shake hands. He brushed my hand aside and reached over and gave me a bear hug. The next man stepped up and did the same thing. This happened right down the line with every member of the committee until we came to the chair of the committee. She gave me a big hug, and asked, "Do you know what we've just said to you?" I replied, "Yes, but that's not a fair way to say it."

They insisted on taking me out for lunch and telling me that they wanted me to be their pastor. I said, "I won't even talk about that. I've got to leave right away to go back to West Palm Beach. I'll come back some time after thinking about it if there is any reason to talk further. I'll bring my wife."

Well, Marguerite and I did go back down there. I haven't wanted many things very much—but oh, how I wanted to be pastor of that church and those people! I could end my career as a pastor, just like I planned.

Nothing I said discouraged them. Everything I proposed, they agreed to. Whatever I said, they would say it to the nth degree in full support. Think about the privilege of working with a group like that! Seminary presidents don't get much display of affection. And at that time, I could stand a little of that.

In the end, I finally said to them, "I never wanted to be twins as much in my life. I cannot leave Louisville right now; I can't leave the seminary, but I want to come to your church. I can't do both. I cannot get a sense of God's leadership that will turn me loose from the seminary."

I am saying that I don't always do what I want to do, that the sense of God's call in a matter doesn't always line up with my personal preference. That's why I went to New Orleans—I had to go to New Orleans. For me not to have gone to New Orleans would have cost me everything I have always affirmed about being the instrument of God's purpose.

When I turned down First Baptist of Sarasota, I finally admitted that I was not going to realize my dream of making it back into the pastorate. This meant I would retire as president of Southern Seminary.

RETIREMENT PLANNING

What were your thoughts as you moved into the 1970s and began to think about your retirement from the seminary presidency?

When I went to Southern Seminary, the retirement age had been set at age 68. Later I led the seminary to set 65 as the retirement age, with a loose period from 65 to 70 and mandatory retirement at 70. This meant that a seminary employee had to make a decision when he reached 65 about whether he should continue to work past that age.

I became 65 in 1979. Retirement is always at the beginning of the new academic-fiscal year following becoming 65. That means August 1, 1980, would be the point at which the trustees would make the "go, no-go" decision for me on whether I should stay beyond age 65.

Once I decided not to go to the church in Florida, I knew I would stay at Southern Seminary until age 65. My assumption was that I didn't want to be in the middle of a big project at the time of retirement. So that's really all there was to it. Once I decided in 1973–74 to stay on at the seminary, I would have a six-year program that would run out about 1980. And it did, plus a one-year extension.

I'm inclined to think that administrators reach retirement age a little earlier than faculty members do. There was no way for me to take a strong stand for retirement at age 65 for faculty and not hold to this for administrators as well.

You did not announce your retirement, however, until the Convention in New Orleans?

It was not something that needed to be announced. I didn't want to be a lame duck. I figured that the trustees would send out a search committee and find my successor. In fact, what I did was to tell the trustees to go ahead and name their search committee, that I was prepared to leave whenever they had my successor in the wings.

There was a special retirement committee formulated in February 1976.

Yes, and that was to anticipate whatever decisions needed to be made about my retirement. This committee was supposed to investigate everything that related to my retirement, including housing, financial terms, continued relationship to the seminary, and matters like this.

The trustees in April 1976 also agreed that they would provide you in retirement with 50 percent of your salary that you had earned during the last five years of your presidency. Obviously, you had been involved in a retirement plan the seminary had. They indicated that they intended to provide supplemental payments to be sure the 50 percent of your regular salary was paid to you, and that they would provide a house or financing for a house. Did you counsel with the trustees about these matters?

We worked very closely on these issues, although the initiative on any specifics had to come from them. If they raised a question and asked me what I wanted, I told them. I had great concerns at that time because there was reason to believe that Marguerite would outlive me by many years.

You suffered some physical difficulties about that time, did you not?

Yes, I had open-heart surgery in 1978. Marguerite and I were the same age to the day—and actuarial tables say that women will outlive men. So I assumed that would happen; and I was very concerned about it. One of the things the trustees had to do was to find out how much retirement

I had built up. I didn't know. And that is a little more difficult to answer than just to send a note to the Annuity Board. Many different options must be considered. So it got to be a very complicated thing.

Then the trustees decided they would provide housing for us for our lifetime; that put us in the housing market. We had to settle the question, What kind of place do we want to live in? Obviously, we were going to move out of the president's home at 2800 Lexington Road, where we had lived for twenty-plus years. We finally settled on a three-bedroom condominium at 1202 Creighton Hill Road. It belonged to the seminary, but we were assured that Marguerite and I could live there for life. We would pay utilities and other expenses such as that.

The trustees were both very sensitive and very generous in what they did. When I asked for things, they tended almost uniformly to do better than I requested. I'm very grateful for that. There was also the concern on my part that I would be heard as asking for too much, but I did not ask for anything until they brought the subject up.

As we came down to the end when we would discuss compensation, I tried to create certain attitudes on the part of the trustees with reference to my successor. I hoped they would do better by him in several areas. For instance, they provided us with a house but no furnishings and no furnishings allowance. The furniture in the president's home was largely our furniture that we had bought. There were significant exceptions to that in terms of Norton pieces left in the Alta Vista house.

But in general, even the expensive pieces of furniture in the huge public rooms belonged to us. I had purchased the rugs because there was no allowance for furnishings for the president. I insisted that the seminary accept responsibility for furnishing the public rooms. I also asked that help for parties, receptions, and other seminary functions be provided for the president's wife.

The bequest of the Edwin Gheens home to the seminary just as I left made it possible for the seminary to provide for Dr. and Mrs. Honeycutt some beautiful furniture for the public rooms. Even so, Badgett Dillard put a fly in the ointment by insisting that the Gheens furniture must be appraised. Then he recommended that the trustees set a dollar limit on the value of the furniture used in the president's home. That forced the sale at auction of some of the most valuable pieces that had belonged to the Gheens family.

I'm sure Mrs. Gheens turned over in her mausoleum. She intended for all of her furniture to be kept together and used in the president's home.

AD INTERIM ROLE OF SBC EXECUTIVE COMMITTEE

The SBC Executive Committee was formed in the 1920s for efficiency, and you were the first executive secretary who moved it to a business sort of relationship. What is the exact role of the Executive Committee in relation to the Convention?

The key phrase about the function of the Convention's Executive Committee is "ad interim." It functions for the Convention ad interim. It should make only those decisions that have to be made under its ad interim authority. It should not therefore meet on Monday and decide for the Convention, which could have made the decision on Tuesday.

If Southern Seminary had to have Convention action on some matter between sessions of the Convention, I think the Executive Committee ought to handle the matter. Whatever it does, whether the seminary likes it or dislikes it, that's the Convention action. On the other hand, I think the Executive Committee ought to take to the Convention every matter that could not be handled earlier because of time constraints.

I need to go one step further. There is a lot of detailed stuff that simply would clutter the Convention. So it's up to the Executive Committee to package the Convention's decisions in such a way that the messengers who are there one week and haven't thought about the problem can understand the nature of the decision. This means to package the details into a yes-no kind of voting situation.

Let's assume a matter is voted on in a Convention meeting, and the presiding officer of the Convention rules in a particular way. This causes some problems for a particular agency down the way. What can the Executive Committee do about it?

Absolutely nothing. The Executive Committee cannot overturn or change the action of the Convention, even if the Convention was wrong and the officers were wrong. Once the Convention takes a vote, that ends the matter. To talk about the atmosphere of the meeting or everything else is irrelevant. In a recent annual meeting, the Convention did approve the membership of the Committee on Boards on a bad ruling by the president, but the Convention acted, and that settled it. The Executive Committee would have been immoral and illegal to attempt to undo what the Convention had done.

So you are saying that the ad interim status of the Executive Committee is applicable only in a situation where the Convention cannot act, or is not able to act—because the Convention only exists for four days during the year.

That's right. And during those four days the Executive Committee can give guidance to the Convention. Now this is a different function. It can study and recommend to the Convention. That is a very powerful role for the Executive Committee. I am in favor of its doing that and giving recommendations during the Convention. For example, the Executive Committee was not wrong to recommend to the Convention disapproval of the Boyce Bible School or, as it later did, approval.

But in essence they were giving disapproval in not permitting this matter to come up in their agenda item?

That's right. They were trying to stop it, not recommend to the Convention that the Convention disapprove the agency's proposal. This was not a motion to delay for further study.

If a matter of reference is made to the Executive Committee, then it determines whether or not it will act. If it chooses not to act, it simply reports back to the Convention that it has chosen not to act.

Yes, but that is to my mind quite proper. The Convention can refer anything to any agency or any of its sub-units with power to act. It could refer a matter to the Historical Commission, and then the Historical Commission would properly be the body that made the decision because the delegation of authority is a basic principle in any democratic process. And the Convention has the right to delegate. So it can delegate anything to the Executive Committee that it desires. But I don't think the Executive Committee ought to presume that its ad interim authority gives it the right to keep the Convention from dealing with a particular issue.

The agencies report to the Convention through the Executive Committee in a number of instances. They report directly to the Convention, but the funding process means that they are actually reporting to the Executive Committee, does it not?

It's worse than that. You just try to get the Historical Commission to take any major issue to the floor of the Convention without going through the Executive Committee! Now that's the distinction. I have no problem with the agency reporting to the Executive Committee on any matter. I would insist that the Executive Committee has to be the *fiscal agent* of the Convention. But it is not the *policy agent* of the Convention.

So it's quite legitimate for audits to be cleared through the Executive Committee as the fiduciary agent of the Convention?

Yes, because a four-day meeting of 20,000 people can't deal with that function—which is a 365-day-a-year function. And this responsibility is delegated to them by the bylaws and the Business and Financial Plan.

I want to make it clear that the agencies are semi-autonomous bodies that belong to the Convention, not to the Executive Committee. That is why I advocate the election of the directors or trustees of an agency at the time of the report to the Convention by the agency.

Would this not cause some additional problems in the political environment of the present?

In the present environment, but I think we could have avoided some of the present environment if this had taken place because the messengers would have had a feeling of ownership and control of the agencies. Now it would not make life easier for the agency executives. It wouldn't have made my life easier. I can come nearer getting what I want through the Executive Committee than I can on the floor of the Convention. I'm going to have far fewer embarrassing moments before a committee of the Executive Committee than on the floor of the Convention, but I think that's a part of the democratic process that the agency executives ought to have to live with.

AGENCY FUND-RAISING

Why does the Executive Committee of the SBC have so many restrictions on fund-raising by the agencies of the Convention?

These rules against soliciting funds were based on the theory that any money raised by an agency on its own would undermine the Cooperative Program.

But all such rules are dead in the water now. The Executive Committee sank these rules in the late 1970s. Southwestern made the first move to change the attitude, and it was based on the assumption that the Cooperative Program could never completely fund theological education. The Executive Committee decided it had better let the seminaries get in the fund-raising marketplace because this was a big arena, and non-Baptists were raising all the money while Southern Baptists were forbidding their agencies to go after it.

In an Executive Committee meeting about 1978, Southwestern asked for permission to raise $8 million. Permission was granted. Southern promptly countered by asking for permission to raise $10 million, and got permission to do that. This marked the end of active opposition to fund-raising on the part of the agencies by the Executive Committee. Both Southern and Southwestern were successful in these efforts.

Was that a good move? Are we going back to the early days when every agency made its own separate appeal for funds to the Baptist constituency?

No. The economic situation of Southern Baptists and the economic situation in the United States vetoed that old position. Basically the Cooperative Program and its fund-raising concept were rooted in the notion of Southern Baptist church members getting paid in cash on Saturday and taking out a tithe of their dollars and putting them in an offering envelope on Sunday morning. Today, Southern Baptists are no longer primarily blue-collar workers, and even blue-collar workers don't get cash in an envelope; they get a check. And they don't necessarily receive their pay every week; they may get it twice a month. Even if they are hourly workers, they get checks for their wages.

So the whole concept of people living out of the money that is coming in on a weekly basis has shifted. Many Southern Baptists don't live on a salary. They don't know what they made this year until the end of the year when they do their audit on themselves for tax purposes. People don't really know what their income is because it comes in lumps.

Southern Baptists are no longer a people making low wages. A significant portion of them make a lot of money. Many accumulate money, and then they invest it and make a lot more. Even if they did their dead-level best to tithe, they have a lot more money that they could give to church on Sunday morning.

How did you feel personally about Southern's goal of raising $10 million?

This sounded to me like more money than the mint could print. Nobody will ever know how pessimistic I was about the prospect of raising that kind of money in just three years. After a year we had spent a third of a million dollars more than we had taken in, going through three different sets of fund-raising consultants. We fired all the consultants and went to school on what we had learned from them. These consultants were actually very valuable to us, although they failed. They taught us all the ways we couldn't raise that kind of money. And they taught us that there wasn't an expert somewhere who knew how to do it. We just went back to the drawing board and invented our own fund-raising system, based on what we had learned.

What did you learn?

We learned that you have to approach people directly and bring them to the institution. We learned how to present theological education to them. We learned that the educator's understanding of what he is doing is not the public's understanding of what education is all about.

If you want a donor to give you money, you have to talk to him in *his* terms about education, not in your terms. Within a year and a half after we invented our own fund-raising program, we had raised $12 million. We were stunned by our success.

The biggest gift given to Southern Seminary was by one of the persons in Louisville who was helping us raise money. If I had been delegated to ask him for money, I wouldn't have had the nerve to ask for $25,000—and he gave us $1,250,000. He got sold on the seminary in the process of soliciting funds for us. He was a retired army officer. He just walked in and offered to make a gift. And it was the biggest gift that had ever been given at that time to theological education among Southern Baptists. We found there were people like that out there who weren't waiting for us to squeeze the lemon to get something; they were looking for a place to invest their resources in the cause of Christ.

What did you try to show these people when you brought them to the seminary campus?

We tried to show them that theological education would provide better pastors for their children and grandchildren. That is what they would buy into. They didn't care about improving their pastors. They didn't think they could be changed much. But they would invest in a better quality of gospel presentation for their children and grandchildren.

Did you bring them to the seminary during the school year and have them meet the students?

Yes. While they were here, they would talk to students and faculty members. They would sell themselves by investigating the seminary. One of these men who were visiting the campus walked in to my office and asked, "If you had a half million dollars to endow a professorship of preaching, would you be happy, or would you rather I'd give it for something else?"

"Preaching," I replied.

"I'm glad to hear that," he said. "I asked a professor of pastoral counseling (it was Dr. Wayne Oates) what was the most desperate need for an endowed professorship at Southern Seminary, and he said preaching. Because he didn't promote his own department, I believed him. Since you agree with him, I'm going to give you a half million dollars to endow a professorship of preaching."

Nobody asked this man for that; he dug the information out for himself while visiting the campus. It was his idea, and that's why he believed in it. By the way, he and his wife actually later gave $1 million to the seminary.

This is how our approach worked. People were impressed with what was actually already being done on the campus. We tried to get them relaxed enough that they would do their own study and investigation. They didn't buy a pitch from the president or the public relations man; they bought it from the students and the professors.

How did you get people to come to the campus?

We told them honestly, "We're going to try to sell you on Southern Seminary so you'll give." If you didn't tell them that, they would know you were lying. Then we went on to tell them they would not see a pledge card while they were on campus. "If you make a gift while you're on campus," we told them, "you're going to have to stop somebody and get him to take your money; we're not going to ask for it. Now we will ask you later, but we're going to do that whether you come to the campus or not."

So your philosophy was that up-front dealing with these people who were accustomed to being solicited for funds was the best way to do it?

Yes. The main question is, do you have something on the campus that they will buy? If you do, they will sell themselves by watching the students and the faculty. They understood what was going on; you didn't have to tell them. When these potential donors talked with a student, he would talk about his commitment to the cause of Christ and the welfare of people in the name of Christ. These people would buy into the student's dream.

You used the term "investment" in talking about your fund-raising program. Is this how potential donors look at their giving—as an investment?

The term *invest* does describe their attitude, whether they use the word or not. It's their money, and they're going to do something with it. Will they invest it to generate more money for their grandchildren and great-grandchildren? Or would they rather invest in the cause of Christ?

We have discovered that donors want to invest in specific projects that have measurable results. You could say to a potential donor, "We plan to send seminary students on buses into the Great Lakes Area. These students will be visiting, witnessing, and winning people to Christ and starting churches. This is a two-edged project: it will equip better ministers for the future, but it will also provide practical training right now and bring people to the Lord." A donor will invest in a project like that.

He will invest in food for the hungry, maybe, or he may simply say, "This kind of institution, I hope, will continue to exist long after I'm gone. I'll endow it. I will give you a gift of my money so it can live on the income of my endowment, and ask nothing more than that the institution continue to be the kind of school that he or his pastor attended.

We learned to approach potential donors on the basis that their money represented their lives, their dreams, their sacrifices, and their hard work. What were they going to do with it? Put it in the bank? Keep it? Buy real estate? Wait for their grandchildren to spend it? There are many things they could do.

On the other hand, a lot of people with money don't have any family to look after. They are desperately looking for something useful to do with their accumulated wealth. Finding those people is an art. They are not always the people who are on everybody's fund-raising list. In fact,

I've gotten less money from people whom I thought would give big money than from others. These people tend to know all the answers why they can't do what you want them to do. They also know how to handle you. They're experts at turning solicitors off.

I'm not an expert at fund-raising. I've studied fund-raising at Columbia University under the fund-raiser for that great university. But the only way to become an expert fund-raiser is to do it and keep on doing it until you begin to feel at ease in the role.

ACCEPTANCE OF VALIDITY OF CAPITAL FUND-RAISING

Are other SBC agencies besides the seminaries involved in fund-raising efforts?

Yes. Have you noticed that the Foreign Mission Board is doing it, too? Capital funding is being perceived as beyond the capacity of the Cooperative Program. At first the agencies were reluctantly permitted to raise funds on their own. Now they are expected to go out and raise funds for capital projects. It is a subtle but very important shift. Gradually you will see the Cooperative Program funding technique, which began in 1925, being expanded, developed, or destroyed— depending on your point of view.

I think the Cooperative Program is not being destroyed. We are simply seeing new methods of funding coming on the scene. The shift in the socioeconomic status of Southern Baptists prompts this development. That's going to force all the agencies to develop fund-raising staffs.

The new development began with a breakdown of the Cooperative Program idea in the state conventions. Some states began to approve campaigns for special causes. You can't run that very long for the colleges before the seminaries realize that some of their friends might have given money for the new college library that might have been diverted to theological education. There's no villain in this thing; it's the evolution of the entire denominational structure.

Some people said that Southern Seminary went into its "Campaign for Excellence" fund-raising effort because you didn't want Southwestern Seminary to get the jump on you. Is that true?

Sure. Southwestern shocked us all by getting permission for an $8 million campaign. We thought the SBC Executive Committee would stick to its old policies. Southwestern had done its homework before the Executive Committee meeting. To the surprise of all the agencies, that campaign was approved. Fortunately, I had been considering a campaign among individuals in Louisville, Kentucky. So I had a local campaign that could have been done within the SBC Business and Financial Plan on the back burner and a fund-raising consultant in the wings.

Within ten minutes after the Southwestern campaign was approved, Southern Seminary filed its application for approval on a $10 million campaign. Ten million dollars was not "upmanship." It was just to get a round number of about the same amount. Since we hadn't done our homework, we didn't really know exactly how much we needed, and we certainly didn't know how much we could raise.

This $10 million campaign was formulated in less than ten minutes after it was apparent that the Executive Committee had changed its attitude and its policy. By the time they got around to the approval, we had the full consultant's report ready to file and an elaborate campaign. We had identified $32 million worth of needs, of which the $10 million campaign would only raise the first third needed.

FUND-RAISING PROCEDURES

How does an administrator start an effective financial campaign? How do you "put the touch" on people to motivate them to give?

There are some scientific facts that you can learn. One principle is that one single gift will have to equal at least 10 percent of your goal. In other words, you will not raise more money than ten times the largest single gift you receive in the campaign. That's the scientific side. But how does an agency go about constructing a prospect list? Then, how does it develop a "case statement," which basically states why anyone should give this agency any money.

You have to state crisply and clearly why anyone should give you money, and this must be done in terms that appeal to the donor. Then there's the issue of integrity. You tell the truth—which is not always done in fund-raising campaigns.

What about collecting on the promises? Do you hope to collect 50 percent of your pledges?

No, you expect to collect at least 100 percent. In the tax structure in the United States, people will give you only so much money in one year.

So you have to let them spread their gifts out over three to five taxable years. You can't really go for small gifts, by the way. This is why you don't compete with the collection plate dollar. If you do, you're wasting your time and effort.

In the Southern Seminary campaign, our minimum request of donors was $10,000. Now we got small gifts, but we didn't ask anybody to give us money unless we thought they could give us at least $10,000. We wanted $10,000 or more, which is one way of protecting the collection plate dollar; not many people write checks for $10,000 and put them in the collection plate. It doesn't pay for an agency to go after small gifts. The cost of collecting them will be more than they are worth.

You have to go after the big gifts. And Southern Baptists have the donors who can make big gifts. I approached a man who had never given as much as a thousand dollars to his church or to the Community Chest, or any charitable cause. I asked him for a gift for Southern Seminary. He said he had agonized over it and finally agreed that he would give us $3,000.

I said, "That's fine. Let's see, $3,000 a year for five years, that's $15,000." He said, "No, I mean $3,000 total." "Oh," I said, "you wouldn't want to do that. Think about that and pray about that some more—$3,000 a year for five years." He finally agreed to give the larger amount, and you could almost see him grow.

He had grown up in hard circumstances. He wasn't aware that he had succeeded to the point that he could actually give away $15,000. When it really dawned on him that he could give $15,000 to one enterprise, his self-esteem soared. He was made aware of how well he had succeeded by keeping his nose to the grindstone all his life and saving his money.

I won't call his name, but he is a good friend. I'm proud of him. He has been a greater friend to Southern Seminary ever since. He feels good about himself. And he now gives to other causes at a level that he did not think was possible.

Southern Baptists have hundreds of thousands of people like that who are not giving their money in the collection plate, and they wouldn't do so even if they tithed their income. Notice I said "even if" they tithed their income. Much of what they have is in capital gains, and they are moving into a category where they don't get money by the week or even by the month. It comes in big splurges. So a person in this category gives to his church what he thinks he can afford out of his cash flow. Even if that's a tithe, that doesn't touch the hem of the garment of his capacity to give. Southern Baptists are becoming more aware of these resources that are not available to the collection-plate dollar.

There seems to be a movement today away from the Cooperative Program toward individual fund-raising on the part of the agencies. Is this a serious problem for our denomination, or is this just a cycle through which we will pass?

It's a most serious issue. It is the issue that the Convention leadership dares not put on the agenda because it scares the daylights out of every one of them for different reasons. The Cooperative Program, in my judgment, must be redefined within the next ten years—and will be redefined, consciously or accidentally. In fact, it is already being redefined.

Some kind of redefinition is necessary because of the economic situation within the denomination, the churches, and the members of the churches. Their economic situation has changed so much that the basic assumptions of the old Cooperative Program are no longer valid; namely, that people are paid so many dollars at the end of the week and they take a tithe of it and put it in church on Sunday morning. That concept has long been obsolete. Another assumption is that most of our people earn a salary. That is no longer how they get their total income. Even though most of them will be salaried, there are other sources of income beyond the salary.

So several basic assumptions in 1925 for the Cooperative Program have evolved off the scene. New ones have come on; the wealth of our people opens up deferred giving, which the Cooperative Program was never designed to handle. So I'm saying that we have a mish-mash today that has not received thorough study and coherent recommendations. I think the solution is somewhere in terms of a redefined Cooperative Program.

Many agencies have gone out on their own to raise funds. I understand the state executive secretaries have complained about this because they see it as destructive of the Cooperative Program.

I had a part in setting up the old Capital Needs Program funding through the Cooperative Program back at the end of World War II.

This change was actually a redefinition of the purpose of the Cooperative Program. It was an effort at that time to avoid what has subsequently happened. It worked for a while, but then the water in the lake got bigger than that dam would hold.

I think what has happened was inevitable. I think what is not inevitable is our failure to be statesman enough to look at the total picture. I understand the state secretaries. My attitude toward the Cooperative Program tends to be that of the state executive secretaries. They have a vested interest; therefore, what they say must be heard in light of their vested interest. I don't take what the state secretaries say without a grain of salt. But they need to be listened to because they are telling us that they sense the shaking of the foundations of the Cooperative Program. It isn't dead, but it's being redefined, de facto. They would like to go back to an earlier era.

But I must point out that this is impossible. You cannot go back to the old days, because you can't get Southern Baptists to give all of their money through the church budget. There is money that Baptists will give to the Lord's cause that they will not funnel through the present Cooperative Program channels.

Southern Baptists will either find a way to get that money, or it will go to other-than-Baptist causes. And, indeed, I suspect that more money is raised among Southern Baptists by non-Baptists today than the Baptist agencies are raising. That's just an impression I have. Nobody knows the statistics because the state secretaries never count what the state agencies are doing when they complain about what the SBC agencies are doing.

FRIEND-RAISING

I have heard you use the term "friend-raising" as opposed to "fund-raising." What do you mean by this?

I'm talking about cultivating prospective donors. How do you get a list of people who might be good prospects for contributing to the agency? By the way, most agencies throw away valuable information at this point. They are not fund-raising at the moment; therefore, they do not keep information about the people who are interested in their enterprise. And then one day they decide to do fund-raising, and they have to start at square one without a good prospect list.

In the Southern Baptist Convention, the problem is that your prospects are so widely dispersed that it's hard to identify them. Further, you can't just do it randomly because you could spend a fortune and never hit any targets. So you must have a well-targeted prospect list. How to build that prospect list is best described by this statement, "I'm not fund-raising; I'm friend-raising."

There is a very important "friend-raising" dimension to fund-raising. There is a point at which friend-raising turns into frank, point-blank, hard-nosed fund-raising or you never raise it. In other words, friend-raising that never gets around to asking the friend to "sign this pledge card" just won't get it done.

Surely the people to whom one would appeal in these projects are getting many requests for gifts from many sources. How do you make your appeal stand out from all the others?

That's the trick in getting the prospective donors—the people who are interested in and willing to invest in your particular project. For instance, some people invest in endowment and won't put money in bricks and mortar. Others will invest in bricks and mortar but would never give to endowment. There are still others who will invest in live programs that have statistical, measurable results but who won't do either of the other two. You have to know who your prospects are and the causes and appeals that get their attention.

DEFERRED GIVING

What about deferred giving? Is this a delicate thing to discuss with a person?

Not at all. The real problem is, do you know enough about the subject to talk to him intelligently? Sometimes you go talk to some old, crusty, hard-working layman who has made a lot of money, and you think he's not very sophisticated. The truth is that he just paid big money to a professional advisor to give him counsel about taxes and the handling of his estate. If you don't know the tax laws and the percentages and the numbers, you end up sounding stupid to him. Yet you're telling him you can help him with his future.

The problem of deferred giving is to have somebody who knows the highly technical tax laws and the financial procedures available to people. Good advice has to be tailored to each donor's specific situation.

The point is not that it's hard to talk with a person about it; he's looking for somebody who knows the answers. If you are knowledgeable, you not only are going to get a hearing; he will pull you in and sit you down in the easy chair while you tell him. He cares deeply about what's going to happen to this minted investment of his life after he can no longer control it.

But this is a very difficult area to be an expert in, and I certainly am not. An expert is welcome even by people who know a lot because they are always looking for some new insight, some new twist to the procedure, that would improve their situation. Somebody who has been through a couple of seminars does not know what he's talking about if that's all he knows. He's learned a little jargon; he's learned a few gimmicks. But he really doesn't know what he's talking about because deferred giving is a very complicated, sophisticated area best left to the professionals.

Does this area of giving apply only to people with large sums of money?

Is $50,000 a large sum of money? Then anybody who's worth $50,000 is a candidate for deferred giving. This would include everybody who owns a home and most people who have a good retirement program. We haven't begun to even touch this area. The truth is that multi-millionaires are not good prospects for this form of giving because they have already received expensive counsel and advice and they have an estate-planning program in place.

You almost have to cultivate such wealthy persons across a period of time. You don't just go in and say, "Give me money." You live with them. You work with them across the years. They probably are people who once gave you $50.00 gifts—and that meant they believed in you—and then you meet them along the way, and they go further and further.

That's why friend-raising comes before fund-raising, especially on deferred gifts. There are not a lot of deferred gifts that you get by just putting on a campaign for gifts of this type, but there is more money in deferred giving than in any other single source.

ANNUITIES
Some institutions sell annuities and promise high interest rates.

Yes, that's a form of Russian roulette. It may work, and the institution may get a lot of money. Or it may be like some wonderful people out in Jefferson City, Missouri, who gave annuities to Southern Seminary in the 1920s at 8 percent. Southern Seminary was paying them 8 percent on that gift long after all the corpus had disappeared, but contractually the seminary was forced to use current income to pay these annuity obligations.

That didn't turn out so badly in the end. I got off a train one day in Jefferson City and went to see the dear lady to whom we had been paying an annuity. I found her sick in her hotel room. She rented a floor of a hotel. I said to her, "Oh, I didn't know you were sick; I just came to see you and tell you we are interested in you and are praying for you." She said, "Would you look in the top drawer of that chest over there, on the right hand side." There was a check for $70,000 made out to Duke K. McCall.

She said, "When I got sick, I got worried about the fact that the seminary has paid me more money than they got from me. I made that check out to you so you can give it back to the seminary."

I didn't tell her that the check made out to me personally scared the life out of me. Fund-raisers have been known to take gifts for themselves. I promptly wrote, "Pay to the order of Southern Baptist Theological Seminary, Duke K. McCall" across the back of that check and carried it home. It was about a two-hour drop-off between Kansas City and St. Louis on the Missouri Pacific "Eagles" in those ancient days. I had a $70,000 gift to take home that I didn't even go to ask for. And it was from an annuitant who had a conscience.

The changing interest rates can make an institution wish it had never heard of annuities. None of us know what the government may decide about interest rates tomorrow. Southern Baptist agencies are not issuing annuities today, although they did so in the past. One way to guarantee that a person will live a long time is to let him give you an annuity! Annuities are based on an actuarial table that assumes the age of your annuitant at death will be the average of death for the comparable group of people. If you have a group of annuitants who live to 85 and 90 years of age, your agency will go broke.

LOCATION OF THE SEMINARIES
What's your opinion of the location of the six SBC seminaries?

The present seminaries are not all strategically located. In fact, some of them probably ought to be moved, but that is not possible economically and politically. You certainly would never want two seminaries too close together. I would choose a radius of roughly 400 miles for each of the seminaries, but I doubt if you'd ever get one in the Great Lakes area that isn't less than 400 miles from Southern. There will be a seminary in the general Chicago area some day simply because Baptists will grow to the point where it will be needed.

It's a pity Southeastern isn't in the Washington, D.C., area. It's a pity Southern isn't in Atlanta. New Orleans isn't badly located. Golden Gate is absolutely in the wrong spot. In the psychology and sociology of California, in the Baptist growth in California—almost any way you figure it—Golden Gate should have been in the Los Angeles area, not in San Francisco. Midwestern ought to have been farther west, say about Denver, rather than in Kansas City.

Denver was considered as a possible location at one time, wasn't it?

Denver would have been much better for Midwestern, except at the time it was started it would have been premature. Denver wasn't ready for it. Baptists in that area weren't ready for it. Kansas City had the Baptists, but that put it too much under the Southwestern wing. Midwestern has never been able to grow because it has not been able to escape the orbit of Southwestern.

If this is heard as a put-down of these seminaries, notice I deliberately moved Southern to indicate I wasn't just hitting at somebody. I'm just saying that we weren't either good prophets, or wise, or able to escape political factors in the location of seminaries. Southeastern was located for economic reasons. We could buy the Wake Forest campus cheap—and if we didn't buy it the Catholics were going to do so—that was the argument.

Southern was wrongly located originally in Greenville, South Carolina, and then it moved to Louisville—the wrong location again—for economic reasons. If it had to move up on the border, it should have gone to St. Louis, but it didn't. Louisville is not the best location for a Southern Baptist seminary.

The only one of our seminaries I wouldn't move is Southwestern. Of course, it started down at Waco. But Fort Worth was the wrong place historically—it should have been in Dallas, but now Fort Worth and Dallas are becoming a metroplex. It doesn't make any difference whether you are in Fort Worth, Dallas, or Grapevine; you're in the same metropolitan area.

My guess is that one of the compromises of the present controversy might be the acceptance of Mid-America as a Southern Baptist Seminary. But I don't predict that this will happen, not because the old crowd wouldn't finally agree to it, but because I don't think the new crowd will accept it. I think they are better off to have Mid-America as an independent seminary. This way, it can be more individually controlled than if it were within the structure of the Southern Baptist Convention.

Wouldn't that also bring into play the Criswell Bible Institute?

I think you could distinguish between Criswell Bible Institute and Mid-America. Criswell Bible Institute is in no sense a seminary; it is a Bible school. Maybe Southern Baptists could accept it as a Bible school, but it is much too close to Southwestern. There isn't that much difference theologically between it and Southwestern. The conservatism in Criswell Bible Institute also exists within Southwestern. So I tend to reject Criswell not because of its theology but because of its location, and because it is too idiosyncratic as an academic enterprise. It's too much of a one-man show.

TRUSTEE MEETING PREPARATION

How did you prepare for a trustee meeting? Did you swamp the trustees with information?

The technique that gradually evolved was one I didn't use in New Orleans. It was to put in the trustees' hands a carefully-written, carefully-indexed volume that would give them all they wanted to know about every area of the seminary's life. I would say to the trustees, "The financial committee should review chapter 3; the faculty committee should review chapter 2." No one had to read it all, although the information was provided to every trustee. The different chapters of the document were prepared for specific committees.

Did they receive this information before they came to the meeting?

They would receive it in the mail. What they would get when they got to the meeting was a carefully worked out set of recommendations. The idea was to have the recommendations based on the data so they could go from the recommendations to the general report for supporting information. We gradually developed a fairly intricate and sophisticated reporting format.

Each department head among the faculty would make a complete and detailed report of what had happened in his department during the year. He would do this by collecting reports from all of his administrative associates, and then he had to combine and edit and organize this information. We actually used a very precise outline for each division so everything would be covered every year.

The theory back of this approach was that a report doesn't tell you much if it tells you about only one year. But if you can compare this year with last year, you can make a judgment. If you wanted to go back and read what we had said, for instance, about enrollment objectives a year ago and compare it with what we actually reported we did, you could do that because the outline would be the same year after year.

The point of this reporting system (I finally got to where I could say it out loud) was as much internal review and discipline of the staff as it was preparation for the trustees. I considered it to be an important activity if no trustee ever read it. Out of a board of fifty-five trustees at Southern Seminary, if five read the whole thing that would be good. They would not only read it; they would write notes in the margins of the documents and come prepared to raise questions. So that was useful.

If not a single trustee read all the information, at least the internal staff had reviewed their plans and how they had carried them out. I wanted them to report the good things as well as the bad. I pressed hard to say that these reports were not complete unless they carried the bad along with the good.

These reports were organized around the committee structure of the board, which reflected the organization of the institution. For instance, we had a School of Theology and a School of Religious Education; we had a committee on the School of Theology and a committee on the School of Religious Education. The report was broken down the same way.

Did the board of trustees work mostly in subcommittees or in a committee of the whole?

I discovered they would work a lot better in subcommittees and, besides that, they could cover a great deal more ground.

Then you had a limited general board meeting?

The general board meeting would have the whole group come

together and receive the auditor's report and the treasurer's report. These reports covered everybody and had impact on everything that would be dealt with in the meeting. We would go over our fiscal situation. Then we would go to general reports and have a report from the local committee, or the financial board of the trustees. That report would be made at the beginning of the plenary session so everybody would know what had been done during the past year and why.

Then we would break up into subcommittees. Each subcommittee would work through an agenda, along with a seminary staff member who served the committee. The staff member who served the committee and the president and ultimately the chairman of the committee would set the agenda. The final word would come from the chairman of the subcommittee about the order of the agenda and how the various items on the agenda would be dealt with.

But usually that person would follow the recommendations of the seminary staff and president?

Most of the time they would. I would have considered myself out of touch if I couldn't figure out about how they wanted to deal with the matters before them. The sequence was always important. I would put it in order in the way I thought the chairman would want it. I was trying to read his mind. The staff person—the appropriate dean in the case of a school committee—would suggest the items. All of the agenda would be reviewed by the chairman and rearranged to suit his preferences.

What was your role or function while the committees were meeting?

I have gone home and taken a nap a time or two, not often. I would stay on call for each committee that wanted the president. The staff member did not run the committee; he was there to serve the committee. I used to say to the staff member, "While you are working with the committee, follow your best judgment; the only thing I want to say to you is don't introduce anything or propose anything or advocate anything that would surprise me. In other words, if you're going to do it, let's talk about it before the trustee meeting." I wanted them to know that they must not add to the agenda of the committee in the middle of their meeting.

The trustee committee would ad-lib some new ideas. They might make proposals that we of the seminary staff should have thought of but did not. What should the staff member say if that happened? My answer was that the staff should say whatever he or she thought ought to be said without reference to the president.

A good staff member wanted the president's plans to succeed, right?

I would tell the staff members, "If the agenda gets to a sensitive issue and you think I would be upset by the way things are going, propose that the committee invite me to come and share my judgment on the matter." But only rarely did that happen. When it did, I might tell the trustee committee very openly and honestly, "I see the following dangers and risks if you choose to take this action."

CHAPTER 12

Baptist World Alliance President
1980-1985

When did your involvement with the Baptist World Alliance [BWA] begin?

Because of my position as executive secretary of the Executive Committee of the Southern Baptist Convention, I was elected to the BWA Executive Committee at the Congress in Copenhagen in 1947. This part of the BWA is now known as its General Council.

I had been around Southern Baptist life and was not a very reticent type. Mrs. Brown from England objected vehemently to "the young man from North America" presuming to give direction to the BWA. That's the only incident I recall when somebody used my youth as an argument against me. It was my first meeting, I was young, I was a North American, and I expressed an opinion on an issue. All four of these things were against me. That was a typical British reaction, but she and I became friends later.

The issue we were debating had to do with whether there would be nominations from the floor of the BWA for officers, or whether motions could be made from the floor without being processed through the Executive Committee. And there I was arguing, of course, that they should be.

Does that typify the Baptist group out of which you came, as opposed to the hierarchical structure of some other Baptist groups?

Yes, although at that time I wouldn't have understood that. I eventually came to understand that I was dealing both with culture and with familiarity with a certain type of structure. At that point I was a small "d" democrat. Democracy is a way of expressing the priesthood of believers under the lordship of Christ. At least, that's my theological way of talking about it.

I guess your approach conflicted with the British concern for decorum?

Quite so. In those days in the BWA, you observed due process. You named the nominating committee, you heard their report, and you voted for it. But in my opinion, that centralized too much control in the president. Since the outgoing president named the nominating committee, he could appoint people who would look with favor upon his own hand-picked candidate.

What other things do you remember from this 1947 meeting?

I remember that C. Oscar Johnson, pastor of Third Baptist Church, St. Louis, Missouri, was elected president that year. But his term was shortened to three years so the BWA could get back on its regular schedule of electing a new president every five years. He served from 1947 to 1950.

Oscar and I became close friends. While he was BWA president, I traveled with him as his "bag boy" because he had hurt his back in an automobile accident and couldn't handle heavy bags. When he learned that I was glad to help him out like this, he would call and see if I could go if he had an overseas trip scheduled. The SBC Executive Committee would authorize the trip because of the Convention's support of the BWA.

Tell us more about this 1947 meeting of the Baptist World Alliance. I assume it had not met for several years because of World War II?

That's right. It was a small group that met in 1947—probably no more than five thousand people. But this was one of the most emotional meetings I've ever attended, because old friends were getting back together again. The German Baptists were meeting English friends; Americans were meeting Italians. Even if they had been on the same side during the war, they had not seen Baptist friends from other countries throughout the war years. The meeting was a tremendous reunion.

I can still visualize the roll call in the Executive Committee, the twisted heads as friends turned to see the person who had answered "Present." This was the Congress in which Paul Caudill proposed that at least the Americans empty their suitcases to provide clothing for needy Baptists from the war-torn areas to wear home. Many of the Americans went home with their luggage virtually empty because they gave most of their clothes to the needy Baptists at the Congress.

Did you work with Dr. Johnson in any special ways during his term as BWA president from 1947 to 1950?

Yes. The BWA moved its offices to Washington, D.C., during Johnson's presidency. I got involved with him in the fund-raising effort to enable the BWA to make this move. I remember its first Washington office was in a Sunday school classroom of the Calvary Baptist Church. Dr. Lewis was the BWA general secretary during those days.

Why was the decision made to bring the Alliance offices to North America?

Up until World War II, the British had been the major financial supporters of the BWA. They provided office space in the Baptist Church House at 4 Southampton Road in London. But after the war, British Baptists needed this space for their own work. Beyond that, they couldn't provide the secretarial help and other supportive help the BWA needed. The British pound was in shambles, and Baptists didn't want to turn their hard currency into British pounds to run the BWA. The BWA needed North American support as never before. European Baptists just didn't have the money, because they were concentrating on rebuilding after the war.

So the move to Washington, D.C., was Oscar Johnson's idea. He personally raised the $30,000 needed to buy half (with the D.C. Convention) of the 1628 16th Street office building. And I helped him with this fund-raising effort.

BAPTIST WORLD CONGRESS—1950

Talk about the Baptist World Congress in 1950. How were you involved?

I don't remember a great deal about the inner workings of this Congress in London in 1950. I was at London, but I was the busiest person around because they made me chairman of the program committee. I've never been as tired in my life as I was when that meeting was over. I went over to Switzerland, got in a swanky hotel at Lucerne (Bergenstock), went to bed, and slept for a week.

That was the most awful surprise I ever got from a volunteer job. This was because the BWA didn't know what they were asking me to do, and I didn't know what I was accepting. They didn't ask me to serve as program committee chairman until the last minute, and I didn't have time to ask questions.

In spite of all the problems, the program seemed to go okay. Coming out of World War II, everyone was tolerant of planning problems and the resulting *snafu* (*S*ituation *N*ormal *A*ll *F*ouled *U*p), to use the military acronymn. The 1950 meeting was the Jubilee Congress, and it had a large attendance because it was considered a kind of homecoming after World War II.

George Beasley-Murray and I met during this Congress. He was in charge of the music. About half way through the meeting, I said to him, "Friend, these hymns you are singing are wonderful, and we know the words to them, but we don't know the British tunes you are using. That's why we can't get any participation in the congregational singing." George responded, "I thought those were American tunes. We've never used those tunes in England."

We found out that the music committee had arbitrarily picked out its own tunes for the hymns and published them in the program. We were singing all our hymns to tunes that nobody at the Congress had ever heard. I said to George, "Look, I don't care whether we use the American tunes, but let's use either American or British so that somebody here can lead out in the singing."

George is a good musician. But he was British enough that he had been doing exactly what he had been told to do. When I as the chairman of the program committee told him to make a change, he was delighted to do so. From then on we had great congregational singing. And by the way, out of that chance meeting between us came the later invitation to George to teach New Testament at Southern Seminary.

Who was the general secretary of the Baptist World Alliance at that point?

Let me go back and recall the general secretaries I know about even before 1950. In 1920 J. H. Rushbrooke was the Baptist commissioner for Europe, as the first employed staff member of the BWA was called. In 1928 he became the first general secretary. When he became BWA president in 1939, Walter O. Lewis became general secretary. In 1947, at the World Congress in Copenhagen, Lewis agreed to stay one more year until Arnold Ohrn could take over in 1948. Ohrn served until Joseph Nordenhaug was elected general secretary in Rio in 1960.

BAPTIST WORLD CONGRESS—1955

Why was a city like Cleveland, Ohio, chosen for the Baptist World Congress in 1955?

Probably because of a general secretary of Baptists there by the name of Sharpe. American Baptists wanted the Congress in the United States, and Cleveland was a big city and had a lot of people of European backgrounds. This gave it some international flavor. The Baptists under Sharpe were willing to put out the effort and spend money to put on a good Congress.

I understand that some Baptists from Russia attended the 1955 congress?

Yes. I particularly remember Jakob Zidkov, a tall, brilliant Russian. He was an imposing figure, a man who had suffered for his faith. He had been in a concentration camp for his faith, and he was a man of great presence and power.

How many Russian Baptists came?

About five or six, perhaps seven. Their participation had been negotiated rather carefully by the BWA office. We were very pleased that they came. Louie Newton's work in relief probably was a factor in getting them there because Baptists at that time were still having a rough time in the Soviet Union. Their role has evolved over twenty years from being barely tolerated to a sort of despised but tolerated group. And today they are a respected and accepted group, "unfortunately religious," according to the Russian government. Getting permission for them to leave the country was quite a feat in 1955.

NOMINATION OF HERSCHEL HOBBS AS BWA PRESIDENT

I understand that you went to the floor of the BWA to support Herschel Hobbs's nomination as president in 1970.

Yes. Herschel thought he had a right to be elected at that Congress, in my opinion, because he had backed off in 1965 in Miami to let Mr. Tolbert, vice president of Liberia, be elected. I think Herschel's understanding was that if he withdrew when he had the nomination assured, he would automatically be nominated in 1970. He went to the Congress in Tokyo thinking he would be nominated. Unfortunately, some members of his church also thought he would be nominated.

A friend of mine, Venchel Booth, from Cincinnati—a black pastor—was chairman of the nominating committee. Venchel Booth ran the nominating committee the way he would run the nominating committee in his convention, which is not exactly the way you run the nominating committee in the Southern Baptist Convention—a little less democratic.

The committee actually voted *not* to meet in a certain hotel on a certain evening—formally voted *not* to meet then. I called a meeting of the resolutions committee, of which I was chairman in Tokyo, for that hour, since the time slot was open. Venchel announced on the floor of the Congress that the nominating committee would meet at the hotel at the hour the committee had voted not to meet. It was in that meeting that the initial decision was made to nominate Carney Hargroves as BWA president.

There were a number of Southern Baptists on the nominating committee, including me, who could not be at the meeting. Therefore, we felt the meeting was illegal and improper, and we did not accept the validity of the decision made in that meeting. That opened the door, then, for some other things.

The truth is, I did not go to Tokyo as a supporter of Hobbs for president. In deliberations with the official nominating committee, I planned to nominate Leon Chow of Taiwan as president. That was consistent with my effort to break up the passing of the presidency back and forth between Europe and North America.

I had advocated John Soren of Brazil at an earlier date, trying to break that pattern and make the BWA truly international. I was going to do that by trying to get my friend, a great Chinese Christian, elected president. Unfortunately, his government would not let him be elected; he was the chaplain to Chiang Kai-shek, who was still alive at that time. So at Chow's request I did not carry through my plans to nominate him.

I was not anti-Hobbs, but I was against the agreement that had led Hobbs to be so sure of his election in Tokyo. However, I was even more upset by people not keeping their word. My memory is that I got the word that Herschel wanted me to nominate him on the floor for the presidency. I met him in the Liberian reception for Tolbert in Tokyo. We went off in a corner, and I said, "Herschel, I've been told this, but I want to hear you say it yourself. Do you want me to nominate you on the floor for the presidency?" He said, "Yes."

I said, "Then I have another question: Do you want me to nominate you for the presidency knowing that you cannot be elected?" He thought about this for a minute and then said, "Yes."

I told Herschel, "You know you cannot be elected because the ethos around the world is such that there will be resentment of anybody outside of the official establishment organization nominating anybody. This is just not done in most Baptist bodies around the world. Even the Southern Baptists who would vote for you happily if nominated by the committee—some of them will be offended if a Southern Baptist nominates a Southern Baptist against the establishment mechanism."

He told me he understood what I was saying. He could go home, having run and lost, but it would be very embarrassing to go home to First Baptist Church, Oklahoma City, not having been nominated at all.

Although all of this was true, I had a different reason for nominating Herschel Hobbs from the floor. I had seen the editorial that John Hurt of the *Baptist Standard* had written. He ripped the BWA to shreds over the way the nominations were handled and the way the president was chosen, because John knew what had happened in the nominating committee. People like Jim Sullivan, who was on the nominating committee, were furious about this meeting being called at the time and place when the committee had voted not to meet, and about the big decision being made at that meeting.

There is no defense of Venchel Booth on this matter, except that this was how he probably would have done it in the ethos of his own convention. The chairman settles when the committee will meet in his convention; the committee doesn't tell the chairman these things. My position was, if Herschel wants it, and if he has a good reason for it—and I understood his reason—I'm his friend, and I'll nominate him from the floor. If Herschel was nominated and defeated, at least Southern Baptists like John Hurt couldn't go home and say that Herschel Hobbs was not elected president because he was ambushed at the pass.

Harold Stassen was going to nominate his pastor, Carney Hargroves, an American Baptist. Harold Stassen stopped me and said, "Duke, I understand you're going to nominate Herschel Hobbs for president. I told him I was. He exploded with this diatribe: "Terrible! Terrible! With all these Southern Baptists here; it's not fair; it's not right."

"Harold, let's not discuss fair and right," I shot back, "or I might say some things about the nominating committee that would offend you even more than what you've said offends me. I think that what you have done in getting Carney nominated by the committee is improper."

"Well," he said, "if you're going to do that, I'm going to move that the election be in proportion to the membership of the bodies in the Baptist World Alliance, not of those who are present and voting." This would mean that the majority of the large number of Southern Baptists present would vote the size of the Southern Baptist Convention, and so on, but that would mean that a little group of Russians could vote for a million Russians.

I said, "Well, I think that's unwise and unnecessary, but you do what you think is right." He did what he promised, and Hargroves was elected the new president.

Some time afterward, Harold Stassen saw me and said, "Duke, you didn't object to my changing the way the vote was taken. You have a reputation for being a more knowledgeable politician than that. Why did you not disagree?"

I replied, "Analyze the votes, and you will discover that Hobbs lost either way you counted the votes. The fact is, rigging the way you counted the votes took some of the curse off for him because it appears he wasn't elected because of this idiosyncratic vote-count thing."

An analysis of the votes will show that Herschel lost any way the votes were counted because he barely got a majority of the Southern Baptist vote. Nearly half of the Southern Baptists voted for Carney Hargroves. They didn't vote against Hobbs; they voted for the committee's nominee. But the names of Duke McCall and Herschel Hobbs were now mud among the BWA establishment. It was just unheard of at that time to present a nominee from the floor against the official BWA nominee.

SOUTHERN BAPTISTS AND THE BWA

George W. Truett served as president of the Baptist World Alliance in the early 1900s. Then it was a long time before another Southern Baptist was elected to that position.

That's true only if you don't count Oscar Johnson, elected in 1947, and Ted Adams, who served as president from 1950 to 1955. But when I was elected in 1980, it still had been twenty to twenty-five years since a Southern Baptist had served in that position. Before 1980, many Southern Baptists were arguing that it was our turn.

Why was there less interest in the Baptist World Alliance by Southern Baptists after World War II than had been the case in the post-World War I era and in the pre-World War II era?

The biggest thing was that Southern Baptists were not in the ecumenical movement in its structured, organized form, whether we're talking about the National Council of Churches or the World Council of Churches. A British Baptist, Ernest Payne, was one of the presidents of the World Council of Churches. In much of the Baptist world, the World Council of Churches was their life preserver in a sea of Roman Catholicism, Greek Orthodoxy, or secularism.

Having some fellowship with anybody who called themselves Christians is very, very important. And to have some of those important people know you and advocate your cause—there's no way to tell Southern Baptists what that is like for these small Baptist bodies around the world.

But Southern Baptists were ignoring all of these ecumenical considerations—even expressing opposition to them. And you get the "ecumaniacs" within the Baptist fold on the other side of Southern Baptists. They are as nutty as any fruitcake that ever came along, in my judgment. They enjoyed beating up on Southern Baptists as a horrible example of exclusivism. And they did it in the BWA context.

I've had more than one discussion on that subject and have had some nasty personal run-ins with these people who attacked Southern Baptists. They would be as far from accurate as the most extreme Southern Baptists are in attacking the ecumenical organizations. It's possible to exaggerate on both ends of this spectrum.

Then Southern Baptists got so big they didn't need anybody. On the world scene we reached the point where our Foreign Mission Board didn't consult with other mission organizations when it moved into a country—

not even the other Baptist foreign mission boards. The Foreign Mission Board would probably deny this, but I'm talking about how this agency was perceived by other Baptist bodies. They didn't think they were consulted in any definitive sense before Southern Baptists decided to send missionaries into their territories.

Another factor is that some Southern Baptists are a little provincial within the context of the BWA in demanding their rights because of their funding of the BWA. There's nothing that offends people more than for you to fund an organization and then use that as an argument for your right to lead it.

The big boy, no matter how gentle he is, is often perceived as the big bully. I'm not saying that Southern Baptists were the big bully, but a lot of people perceived Southern Baptists as the big bully. Southern Baptists are like an elephant walking among the mice; you don't have to decide to step on a mouse. You're going to step on the tail of a mouse every now and then just because the mouse runs where you were planning to put your foot down. That kind of thing has happened in the role of Southern Baptists in the BWA.

Is it true that many well-known Southern Baptists who might be candidates for the presidency of the BWA would not be acceptable to many BWA people?

There are more potential candidates for the presidency who are acceptable to Southern Baptists than are acceptable to non-Southern Baptists in the BWA. There aren't all that many people among Southern Baptists who are known to the BWA.

Herschel Hobbs was passed over for this position in 1970, and the same thing happened, I understand, to Louie Newton. Have other Southern Baptist personalities felt they were passed over by the BWA?

This happened also to Ellis Fuller. In fact, Louie Newton used Townley Lord to keep Ellis Fuller from being elected. When the moving finger didn't point at Druid Hills, Atlanta, Louie wasn't about to let his old arch-rival in Atlanta move into the slot. Dr. Fuller was pastor of the First Baptist Church of Atlanta at the time.

J. H. RUSHBROOKE AND W. O. LEWIS

How do you remember J. H. Rushbrooke of the Baptist World Alliance? What were your associations with him?

He was terribly British, of course. Physically, he was not a very impressive person. But he was very impressive because of his personality and force of character. I recall him as slow-spoken, but wise. He was a man of his convictions and a man of courage.

How did he relate to Americans?

He was a statesman and a politician. He knew how to handle the American contingent in the Baptist World Alliance, and he did what needed to be done. The BWA often had fraternal representatives at meetings of the Southern Baptist Convention, and frequently he was that representative.

What are your recollections of W. O. Lewis of the BWA?

A Missourian, Lewis was trained at William Jewell and Southern Seminary. He was both a Southern Baptist and a Northern Baptist, in a certain sense. At the 1939 Congress in Atlanta, Rushbrooke was elected president, and Lewis was named general secretary. Rushbrooke died before the 1947 Congress.

What kind of man was W. O. Lewis?

Soft, dumpy in appearance, knowledgeable. He did not have the diplomacy of a Rushbrooke, but he had a bulldog characteristic about him that enabled him to get things done. He was more a plodder, whereas Rushbrooke would sort of take wings and fly. But Lewis did a great deal in terms of study for reconstruction and led the Baptist World Alliance during the critical post-World War II era.

MEMBER OF BWA EXECUTIVE COMMITTEE

When you moved to Southern Seminary, your relationship to the BWA obviously was different than it was during your years with the SBC Executive Committee. How were you able to stay involved and active with the BWA while at the seminary?

As executive secretary of the SBC Executive Committee, I had an automatic spot on the BWA executive committee. But when I moved to Louisville, I had to be nominated and elected to the general council, chosen by Southern Baptists for one of the three or four openings that were not specified by title. This is why I was always surprised whenever I was reelected.

This turned out to be very important for Southern Baptists, by the way. The BWA tended to put a lot of emphasis on seniority among its leaders. So when you rolled over the SBC representatives, Southern Baptists lost a great deal of their leadership in the BWA. These leadership spots kick back then to people like the executive secretary of the SBC Executive Committee, the Foreign Mission Board, and the Home Mission Board.

While I was on the BWA general council, I usually worked as secretary. Among Southern Baptists this is a thankless, awful job; it ties you up so you can't do anything creative except keep the minutes. But in the BWA the secretary serves as a back-up person. He does whatever the chairman doesn't get done. I was there to work for the goals of the BWA, and the secretary's role gave me that opportunity. I was committed to stay in that office as long as I was on the general council.

What kind of BWA commissions did you serve on?

I was on the Baptist Doctrine Commission. I made the motion that set up the commission that dealt with other Christian bodies. This evolved later into the Commission on Doctrine and Interchurch Cooperation. I also served on the commissions on Baptism, Human Rights, and Christian Ethics. I've been on nearly all of these commissions at one time or another because the BWA officials didn't always worry about how many you were on. If you would work at it, and show up for the meetings, they would put you on several committees. The fact that I would show up for all the meetings was enough to get me appointed.

I really was not trying for any office. I preferred to work in the background rather than in the foreground because I considered the chairmanship of committees a recruitment tool to get qualified people to work with the BWA.

RETIREMENT AND ELECTION AS BWA PRESIDENT

So you really never gave much thought to the possibility of being elected president of the BWA?

No. Just the opposite. I thought my nomination of Herschel Hobbs as a candidate against BWA's hand-picked candidate for president in 1970 had wound me up in that department. The BWA General Council met at Southern Seminary, as I recall, in 1974. We used that general council meeting as an effort to promote Southern Baptists' role in the BWA.

But I thought that meeting was my swan song with the BWA. I said my good-byes to the BWA Executive Committee (General Council) at that meeting. I was not trying to be political or anything like that. I thought I had cut my own throat with the BWA with Hobbs's nomination in 1970.

How exactly did your nomination as BWA president come about?

Dr. James Sullivan told me in 1979 that the nominating committee would propose my nomination to the BWA executive committee for the 1980 Congress. At the time I was homebound recovering from open-heart surgery. I thought you only lived so many months after such surgery, but Dr. Lansing promised me five years. I was surprised that the committee did not change its plans.

The thing that impressed me more than anything else about this nomination was that I was told that David Russell, general secretary of British Baptists, had proposed me to the nominating committee. He and I had not seen eye to eye on most things over the years. Our biggest run-in was over my nominating Herschel Hobbs as BWA president in 1970. He was horrified that I had nominated someone to run against the nominee of the committee—of which I was a member.

Did he talk to you personally about this?

Yes. This is the David Russell that I have great respect for. He couldn't feel that way about me and not tell me. He's the kind of literalist who believes that Matthew 18 is to be followed. If you have a complaint against your brother, you tell him. And so he and I have told each other more than once where we thought the other was wrong. We were always getting into little hassles with each other. This is why I was so surprised and delighted that he was the one on the nominating committee who proposed me for the BWA presidency.

Dr. Russell served as general secretary of British Baptists for many years during the time I was at Southern Seminary and the period coming up to my election as BWA president. One of the losses I felt was his retirement as general secretary. I missed him during my tenure as president because I would have leaned heavily on him to represent the viewpoints of those people who differed with me.

Were you retired from Southern Seminary when you began your presidency of the BWA in 1980?

No, I was at the seminary about eight months beyond the time when I was elected BWA president. It should have been only a month, but the trustees asked me to stay to give them more time to seek a new president. I agreed to stay until December 31, 1980. At an executive committee meeting in December, I officially turned over my office with all its perks and powers effective December 31, 1980.

The next day the presidential search committee of the trustees decided to nominate Dr. Roy Honeycutt as president. They asked me to stay until they could call a meeting to elect him on February 2, 1981. I agreed, but I pointed out that I would not be legally president because of my action the day before. I assured them I would sign no legal documents or anything like that. Further, I assured them the faculty and students would pay no less attention to an illegal president than a legal one. The search committee agreed, but the lawyers insisted on a telephone poll of the trustees to make me legal. The first time I was elected president of the seminary, I served for more than thirty years. The next time I was elected, I served for only thirty days. Trustees are getting tougher and smarter!

How did you start your new administration as president of the BWA?

With a mistake! I made the mistake of insisting that with all the change in personnel in the BWA, and with my taking office, we needed an audit. A number of financial decisions, including retirement provisions for Dr. Denny and Dr. Goldie, had been made in the transition rather informally in Washington. Money was spent without specific authorization. I started asking for a detailed treasurer's report that could be approved by the BWA Executive Committee.

My assumption was that if you told the BWA exactly what you did, and they approved it, that locked the door on anybody later saying that this wasn't handled properly. I didn't get any opposition; I just didn't get any response to my request. So I put the needle in and told them that if we were not going to have such a report, then I must ask the Executive Committee to authorize an audit.

The day before the BWA Executive Committee meeting, the treasurer of the BWA resigned, insisting that I questioned his integrity. My letters reiterated that I knew of nothing wrong; I did not suspect anything was wrong. I simply wanted to have a point from which my fiscal responsibilities would start. I had done this when I came to Nashville and Louisville—maybe even New Orleans; and I definitely should have done this when I went to Broadway Baptist Church.

BWA BUILDINGS IN WASHINGTON
Talk about the BWA building in Washington.

The BWA office was first located in one of the churches in Washington. It was very small and inadequate. So Oscar Johnson, new BWA president in 1947, set about to find new facilities. Since I traveled with him, I got into that fund-raising effort for the 1628 Sixteenth Street quarters of the BWA. The BWA half of the building cost $30,000.

With the D.C. Convention paying the other half?

Yes. The BWA and the District of Columbia Convention paid about $60,000 for the large private house we bought in early 1948.

I understand that this original building has been sold and the BWA is moving into new quarters.

Yes, I'm going up for the dedication of the new building at 1633 Curran St., McLean, Virginia, the week of Thanksgiving 1985. I must see whether they fit in the building, now that we finally have a new one. I was frustrated that the old quarters at 1628 Sixteenth Street were inadequate and the building was run down. The third and fourth floors used by the BWA were not desirable.

One of my earliest goals as president of the Baptist World Alliance was to get the organization into a new building. I thought this would be an easy thing to do, and I planned on getting it done during my first year as president. Then I could move on to more important matters.

But I underestimated the Baptist World Alliance and international red tape. So here we are after my five-year term as president, and we are finally moving in to the new building. At least we bought the new building before I left, but we didn't get it paid for—and that was what I thought came first. I wanted to raise the money first and then buy it, but that's the difference between how Americans and Europeans think.

I never was able to get the BWA hierarchy to agree to an architect's prospect of a building that didn't exist. They thought it was unethical to raise money for something that existed only in your dreams. That frustrated me because I had just finished a $10 million campaign for Southern Seminary, and I had the contacts and information needed to raise $2–3 million for an office building. I wanted to raise $5 million in order to endow the office so we could say that all the money given to the BWA budget would go for services. By the time we were ready to raise money, I was no longer president of Southern Seminary and the mailing lists were out of my control.

BWA AND D.C. CONVENTION PARTNERSHIP

When the original building for the BWA was bought in 1947, was the idea to be partners with the D.C. Convention an economy measure?

Yes. Two Baptist bodies needed a new building. Neither one of them could afford it alone, and it looked like a good partnership. I think it was a successful partnership; it was more difficult to dissolve than to set up. By the time it was dissolved, other factors in addition to the space consideration had come to be problems—for example, difference in budgeting ability and maintenance for the building.

The building was a fire-trap, but the BWA couldn't renovate it on its own because it didn't own the entire building. You couldn't do anything to the wiring for just the upper floors of a building. We also had problems with snow removal in the winter. The warm, friendly relations that started out in the Ohrn-Nordenhaug days with Chan Stith in the D.C. Convention had gradually frosted over.

And so the building was finally sold to the D.C. Convention?

Yes, because that was in the original contract—that either agency that wanted out had to give the other the right of first refusal. The price was to be determined by three appraisers, one selected by each agency and the two appraisers selecting the third. So that's what was finally done.

Did you give any thought to the BWA buying out the D.C. Convention?

The BWA couldn't afford to buy them out and then spend a million dollars on the building. We would have needed at least $2 million to pull this off. And raising $2 million to renovate a building is about as difficult a fund-raising chore as you can set your hand to.

BAPTIST LITERATURE DISTRIBUTED IN EUROPE

Were you acquainted with the BWA project that promoted distribution of Baptist literature in Europe?

Yes. David Russell, general secretary of British Baptists, was involved in that because it was done in Europe through the European Baptist

Federation, which is the regional body of the BWA. So the Washington office did not deal with what David Russell had been doing there, but we perceived that as a part of the BWA effort in Europe.

I was the forerunner for David Russell in Bulgaria, for example, in which I tried to crack the door. Then he and Knud Wumpleman (the European Baptist Federation secretary) followed me up in Bulgaria. I was turned down by the Bulgarian officials, but they went in and got permission to distribute literature in that country.

Would you say that David Russell has carried on a long-standing British Baptist tradition of support for Baptists in Eastern Europe?

Yes, I would describe him as the man who wore the mantle of J. H. Rushbrooke.

Talk about another Baptist leader with whom you worked in your early days of BWA work: Ernest Payne.

I knew Ernest Payne quite well. He was general secretary of the British Baptist Union and a co-president of the World Council of Churches—very ecumenical in his approach to things—but a very committed Baptist. He was very knowledgeable, very astute. He was the Baptist statesman for Europe during his leadership of British Baptists.

ROBERT DENNEY AS GENERAL SECRETARY OF BWA

What's your assessment of Bob Denney's leadership as general secretary of the BWA?

Joe Nordenhaug became general secretary November 1, 1960, and then in 1969, upon the death of Joseph Nordenhaug, Denney was asked to assume the post. Bob was elected at the Executive Committee meeting in Baden, Austria, in July 1969. Billy Graham supported Bob Denney's candidacy, and Ted Adams nominated him; that got Bob Denney elected overwhelmingly.

Didn't Bob come from the Sunday School Board?

He was BSU secretary at the Sunday School Board. I nominated Bob for youth secretary of the BWA in 1955, and he became the BWA associate secretary for youth at the beginning of the next year. Then he moved from being youth secretary to becoming the BWA general secretary.

THE BWA AND WORLD RELIEF

How much of the funding for the Baptist World Alliance comes through the SBC Executive Committee and the Southern Baptist Convention?

The Southern Baptist Convention contributes about half of all the funds received by the BWA from the various world bodies of Baptists. But the SBC is about the only major convention that never gives to BWA relief efforts. As Southern Baptists, we have our own Foreign Mission Board relief program, and there is a difference in philosophy between these two Baptist organizations about the distribution of relief.

The Foreign Mission Board works only through its missionaries, and, of course, the BWA has no missionaries. The BWA works through the national Baptist leadership in those places where it does relief work. Personally, I think the Foreign Mission Board relief program is not administered as well as it could be. I think it overloads the missionaries with a task they are not trained to do.

The nationals may mess things up if you depend on them, but the missionaries do, too. And the mess-up is not viciousness or stupidity; it's human nature and inexperience. Nationals can do relief work as well as missionaries. Now, if you keep doing it through missionaries, eventually you will have experienced missionaries doing relief work. But that isn't really the most important thing you have sent missionaries to do. But ultimately, relief aid is a way of expressing our love for people. I am for world relief efforts, however they are carried out.

ADVOCATING RELIGIOUS FREEDOM

The BWA also advocates for religious freedom for its constituency around the world. Is there any aspect of that ministry you can talk about?

This is an important part of the BWA's work, because the governments around the world tend to perceive the president of the Baptist World Alliance in a hierarchical sense. This is just the way they understand organization. This means the BWA general secretary and president can get an audience with government leaders which the nationals of that country often cannot secure. The BWA is able to get a hearing for the interest of the nationals that the nationals themselves cannot develop.

I saw this happen on one occasion in Thailand, a country in which four different groups of Baptists hardly speak to one another under normal circumstances. They're not at war; they just ignore one another, but they are all related to the BWA. First of all, the Baptist leadership in Thailand had to come together. Then all of us went to see the government official in charge of religious affairs. In Thailand this was the minister of education.

It was intriguing to me that they got into a discussion in the Thai language. All of them forgot I was there as the guest of honor. The minister of education, the government official, would be a member of the president's cabinet here in the United States. He got excited about what he was learning about religion in Thailand. He was hearing about some of the tribes that had many Baptists. He was intrigued because of what these Baptist leaders were telling him about his own country.

These Baptist leaders, in turn, were intrigued with what they were hearing about Baptist life from one another. These various tribal groups had been evangelized by missionaries from various Baptist traditions, and they had many linguistic and ethnic differences.

The BWA was serving a useful purpose in making the Baptists aware of one another in that country, and otherwise making the government official aware of the Baptists. The government was hearing the Baptist requests—and they had specific requests. As BWA president, I always received a briefing on those requests before talking to government representatives so I would know how to present the requests.

What kind of requests would they want to make?

They might ask the national government for protection from local authorities. Sometimes it was a request for literature distribution or the right to import literature. Or, it could be a request for the license to establish or build a church. That doesn't make sense to us in the United States, but in many parts of the world you can't have an assembly of any kind without first securing a license for it. And you surely can't build anything without a license.

It could even be a request to get a person out of jail. On one occasion I pled in Rumania for four Baptists who had been jailed by the authorities. A couple of months later, they were released. I don't know what effect my plea had. I do know that two months later these four were out of jail, and seven others promptly went to jail.

The Baptist leaders in Rumania wanted me to come make a plea on behalf of these seven as well. I wouldn't do it in that case. The problem was that the seven had gone to a town on the Black Sea to meet a shipload of Bibles from a Christian who raises money bragging about being "God's smuggler." Unknown to the Rumanian Baptists, he had included anti-Communist literature in the boxes of Bibles. This made the seven Baptists subversives against the government, and they were promptly arrested.

These seven Baptists had moved beyond being Bible smugglers. Now they were anti-Communists and smugglers of anti-Communist literature. It was useless for me as a foreigner from a capitalist country to plead for my Baptist brothers who had been charged with possession and distribution of anti-Communist literature. I knew my plea wouldn't help them.

Now I could plead for a Baptist who had smuggled Bibles, and I usually I did it by making fun of the charge. I would say to the officials, "Surely you don't think it's dangerous for Bibles to be turned loose in your country?" Then I would go on to say, "Surely eight years in prison for trying to share religious literature is a rather hefty sentence, even if what they did was illegal. I don't think it ought to be illegal in the first place, and even if it is, their sentence doesn't fit the crime." The BWA is still doing that sort of pleading for individual Baptists as well as freedom for the churches.

BAPTIST CONCERNS IN OTHER LANDS

Are there other stories you could share about BWA projects in other lands?

In 1964 I asked for the privilege of starting a seminary in Moscow, and in 1985 Russian Baptists finally got the permission. I cannot connect my asking with the permission because I don't know the connection. But the point is that persistence through the years finally paid off. It took twenty years for this request to be granted. As far as I know, I was the first person—on behalf of Jakob Zidkov—to make that request in 1964.

I understand there is a BWA fund in escrow for seminary education in Russia.

This fund comes to about $50,000. Unfortunately, it was frozen so that it hasn't appreciated a great deal; it has simply accumulated interest. This will be enough to get them started, if they are not required to use hard currency. The Russian Baptists have the rest of the money needed for this project. Money is not in short supply in the Baptist All-Union Council.

They have sufficient money coming in, but it can't be taken out of the country?

Right. This is why when any BWA officer goes into the Soviet Union, the last nickel he will spend is before he gets off the plane. In fact, you learn not to express interest in anything if you don't want it, because the Russian Baptists will go buy it for you. If you admire a hat (my actual experience), you will own it. When you admire something, you don't necessarily mean you would pay your money for it or that you would ever wear it, but suddenly you are the proud possessor of a hat because the Russian Baptists will gladly spend their money on you.

Of course, you reciprocate when you have the opportunity. On one occasion, about four or five Russian Baptists came to the United States and visited Southern Seminary. I told them, "Go down to the seminary bookstore and pick out the books you want, whatever you can carry back with you. Just tell the bookstore manager to charge them to my personal account." I called him and told him it was all right. I thought they might spend about one hundred dollars each on books. But was I surprised! They didn't just buy *a* book; each of them bought several! It cost me about one thousand dollars to pay the excess baggage fee for them so they could get the books home!

But I really don't care what it cost. If they got those books into Moscow, God bless. I'm tickled pink because I know those books will be used for a good cause. In the earliest days, I used to take things like Greek grammars to Russia with me because they wanted the grammar for the study of the Greek New Testament. I would take technical theological works because, as a seminary president, I could claim that I needed them for business. I would carry all these Greek grammars and get them through customs and lend them to my friends in the Soviet Union.

The last trip I made to the Soviet Union (1985), Billy Graham promised the Estonians I would bring them one hundred Estonian Bibles. But the problem was that neither the American Bible Society nor the British Bible Society had Estonian Bibles. There's no such thing available commercially. I finally found Estonian Bibles in an Estonian Baptist church in Toronto. Archie Goldie of the BWA staff went up and took my three-suiter, hard-sided suitcase and filled it with Estonian Bibles. The suitcase was so heavy that I could hardly lift it.

I declared these Bibles when I went into the USSR and delivered them to the Estonians by using the BWA president's protocol. At the same time, Roy Honeycutt and Harold Bennett had their Russian Bibles taken away from them. They tried to take in several Bibles just a day or two after I had carried this whole bunch through. The Estonians were beside themselves with excitement.

In trying to help Baptists in these countries, I learned to work the diplomatic angles everywhere I could. David Russell and Knud Wumpleman, by the way, are experts at this. Gerhard Claas is also a wonderful negotiator with government officials on behalf of the Baptist constituency.

Perhaps this is one area that, by its very nature, needs to be kept confidential.

When you fail, you can tell about it. When you succeed, you just shut up and thank God; talk to God about it and nobody else. But there is one marvelous success story that I must tell. I went to see the official in charge of religious affairs in East Berlin. I was instructed by the Baptists to plead that the government not take over their hospital, home for mentally retarded children, and a school.

When I began to make my case, this official said, "Oh yes, I know all about those institutions. The buildings are in bad repair, and the government can provide much better buildings. The staff is also inadequate; we can provide enough people to staff all these enterprises."

I was thinking to myself, "I've failed, because the government is getting ready to take over this ministry." But then he just blew me clear out of the room. He said, "But I know about the way the people are taken care of. The government cannot do this with the love that Baptists demonstrate for the people; therefore, we will not expropriate these Baptist institutions."

I sat there in amazement. He was the main official in East Germany in charge of religious affairs, and he was saying that the love with which these people were ministered to was something the state could not provide. Even though the Baptists didn't have adequate buildings and personnel, he wanted them to continue their ministry.

BULGARIAN PATRIARCH
Did you ever talk with officials of other faiths in any of these countries?

I remember meeting and talking with the patriarch in Bulgaria. He was the highest official of the Orthodox Church in that country. I wasn't allowed to talk to him unless I sat in a chair the same size as his (a stupid but necessary condition).

The patriarch talked about the fact that everybody in Bulgaria was a child of the Bulgarian Orthodox Church. He made it clear that he considered Baptists to be the children of the Orthodox Church. He stated his view that it was terrible that we had weaned ourselves away from our "mother."

When he finished, I said, "I'm grateful that you have chosen the figure of children because that means you care for them, and you love the Baptists, and you look after their interests. But if you mean by this that they are under your jurisdiction because you are the strongest church in Bulgaria, then I would have to say that in my part of the United States, the Orthodox are the children of the Southern Baptists."

This absolutely infuriated the patriarch. But his aide, I later learned, had known Southern Seminary Professor Joe Callaway through the American School of Oriental Research in Jerusalem. This aide took my side. He tried to explain to the patriarch in the Bulgarian language, which I couldn't understand, that he had started this and I had just given him back what he had given me. The aide said, in effect, "In the Baptist world, Dr. McCall is a patriarch, and you don't talk down to him without expecting him to talk down to you."

I learned what the aide had said to the patriarch from the notes made for me by my Bulgarian "secretary" (another status thing). By the way, that story spread among the Baptists all over Bulgaria within twenty-four hours. How they loved that story!

The BWA is able to negotiate on behalf of Baptists in these situations in a way that nobody else can. It's the *perception* of the BWA and its president and general secretary in the minds of the people with whom you are negotiating that gives the BWA clout.

LARGER BUT STILL INADEQUATE BWA STAFF
In the late 1940s when the BWA office was moved to the United States, there was one secretary and one division. Now it has five major departments.

Yes, and nearly every staff member heads at least two programs. Archie Goldie works with both relief and the North American Baptist Fellowship. Either job is more than a full-time job, so obviously the latter gets shorted.

Is there a possibility that the BWA can increase the staff?

They will eventually. I don't know how they will do it because of the financial picture. This increase will have to happen by evolution. The difficulty is that the BWA has run out of money. In fact, we were spending $100,000 more per year than we were taking in for the first three years I was president. That has now been turned around, and for the last couple of years the BWA has actually had a little net after the year's operation.

This problem was brought on by the concept of regional bodies. We brought on board the South American Fellowship, the All-African Baptist Fellowship, specifically brand new ones. And then we strengthened the Asian Baptist Fellowship, and never did anything much with the North American Baptist Fellowship. The Caribbean Baptist Fellowship is up and running. Indeed, the Foreign Mission Board has about taken it over as a way of reaching out to the very diverse Baptist bodies in the Caribbean. The European Fellowship was going great, and is still going great. It's very strong.

Can a lot of this be traced to Wumpleman's skill and ability?

Very much so. It's also because of the ethos in Europe where the Baptists in Europe realize they must work together. So they will cooperate on a foreign mission sending project and do all sorts of things together that their unions are not strong enough to do by themselves.

One of our BWA weaknesses is that we've spent too much time and too many of our resources in Europe. I have argued against the Washington office working Europe so hard. I told them, "Leave it to Wumpleman; he's strong enough and able enough to do it. Let's spend our resources on Africa and South America." European Baptists can teach all of us about leadership.

CULTURAL BARRIERS TO LEADERSHIP IN THE BWA

Some Southern Baptist personalities are not very well received in other countries. What makes a person acceptable to different cultures?

This question speaks eloquently to the challenge of serving in the Baptist World Alliance. A total of 134 national conventions, or unions, make up the BWA. There are many different traditions, cultures, and mind-sets involved in the work of this international alliance of Baptists.

I start by rooting a person's perceptions in the kind of liberal arts education he has. Out of that liberal arts education is the issue of the curiosity of one's mind. Does a person have an appreciation for other cultures and the differences that exist in the world? Some Southern Baptists seem to be able to go into different cultural situations and to do quite well. They know what they believe and they say it quite clearly, but they are also willing to listen. They try to understand the other person's thought patterns.

In my experience, I have found it is much harder to get across the barriers of culture than of color. One of the problems with racial antagonisms is that we tend to think of them in terms of the obvious differences of color. Actually, the problems are often far more difficult because of cultural barriers that neither side has been educated to surmount.

Sometimes the most popular preachers in one culture or country are the worst in terms of getting across the cultural barriers in other countries. They talk to the common denominator of the culture in which they grew up. They speak dogmatically; they speak in terms of concrete ideas rather than abstractions; and therefore they have immense popular appeal. It is a provincial appeal.

But the thing that gives them that charismatic, dogmatic leadership also makes them incapable of transcending their own culture. They are locked in to their own history and their own heritage. So some of the most popular preachers in their own culture are most unpopular outside their own land.

BIBLE STUDY: THE ALL-AGE SUNDAY SCHOOL

Tell about the development of evangelism and Bible study among Baptists in other countries. Is this a contribution that Southern Baptists have made to the BWA?

There's an anecdote here that ought to be put into the record. I was involved in the general program planning for the 1955 Congress of the BWA. Clifton Allen of the Sunday School Board and Gaines Dobbins of

Southern Seminary had urged me to put on the program a period for the discussion of the all-age Sunday school or Bible study for other than little children. I proposed it at the proper point in the program planning, and it was voted down in the committee. So a little later at another spot, I proposed that we insert such a conference and was voted down the second time.

On the world scale, Bible study and Sunday school are for little children, and Bible teaching is supposed to come from the pulpit in the sermon. So in 1955 Baptist representatives from around the world did not want to waste time talking about the Southern Baptist notion that Sunday school, or Bible study, should be made available to all age groups.

For the third time in the program planning meeting, I told the other representatives, "Saturday morning is free time on the program. The people are free to sightsee and shop in London. Let those who want to discuss the all-age Sunday school have some time on that morning to do this." Since this was my third proposal, and everybody would do their own thing at that time anyway, the committee agreed to schedule discussion of this subject as an optional activity.

With that concession, Clifton Allen and Gaines Dobbins set up a program in the Baptist Church House on Southampton Road in London—the headquarters of British Baptists. The crowds of people who came to this conference were so great that they had to run a second section in a nearby church and use the program personnel twice. Every speaker would speak in the Baptist Church House and then go down the street a couple of blocks to a nearby church and repeat his presentation.

That was the beginning of interest beyond North America in the "all-age Sunday school." This is the term used by most other Baptists around the world—not the Southern Baptist terminology, of course. From that point on the thing has developed until today the most active department in the Baptist World Alliance is the department of education and evangelism. In the United States, the word *education* has the ring of higher education. But in the Baptist World Alliance, *education* is an umbrella term that includes all levels of education—seminaries, colleges, Bible study in the local church.

The BWA's department of education and evangelism has three divisions: the collegiate education division, the seminary education division, and the church education division—or, as a Southern Baptist would say, the Sunday school division. This has just exploded all over the world.

Southern Baptists would have difficulty exporting their ideas directly, but through the brokerage of the Baptist World Alliance, Southern Baptist leaders are selling the principles and the purposes of the all-age Sunday school. This is beginning to catch on in indigenous ways. For instance, Bible study may not take place at 9:30 on Sunday morning, or even on Sunday. But there are times in many nations now when Bible classes are provided, with lay teachers as well as clergy teachers leading the study. This is one of the most powerful new tools the Baptist churches around the world are using to reach people for Christ.

How was Dr. Dobbins received among Baptists in the Baptist World Alliance?

In his latter days, he was perceived as an elder statesman and a giant in religious education. His mannerisms did not bother them at all. His ideas were so logical, so succinct, so persuasive that they couldn't argue with him. Dr. Dobbins, and Dr. Clifton Allen for that matter, were able to leave the accidents of Southern Baptist life out of their presentation of the principles of Bible study for all church members. This meant that the principles of Sunday school work could be transported out of North American culture into places like Sri Lanka.

Did both of these men continue to exert leadership in the BWA on this issue?

Yes. We must also pay tribute to others such as Jim Sullivan, the executive secretary of the Sunday School Board. The Sunday School Board put its resources behind this educational effort. They did this through funding of conferences and study sessions, and through the sharing of literature. The Sunday School Board permitted some of its literature to be printed with the outside cover carrying the name and logo of some other Baptist groups. The board was wise enough to understand that the self-image of Baptist conventions and unions meant they could not use Southern Baptist literature too obviously. But they could borrow it if they could "sanctify" it with their own titles.

Many Baptist leaders from other countries have been brought to the United States for training at the Sunday School Board as well as the seminaries. Many of these leaders have returned to lead their conventions or unions in Bible study programs.

Was the travel for this training funded by Southern Baptists?

It was often funded by either the Sunday School Board or the seminaries. The seminaries have provided funds for their faculty members to travel to conferences and schools overseas. The Sunday School Board has done it for its personnel, and then they have hosted people from overseas at their expense.

I understand that Dr. Grady Cothen of the Sunday School Board was also supportive of the educational work of the BWA.

Grady Cothen through the Sunday School Board funded a program to the tune of about a half million dollars to provide libraries for Baptist preachers all over the world. Under Cothen's leadership, along with a Dr. Hadley from Memphis, Tennessee, this project has provided Bible study materials and other books of this sort for churches worldwide.

Another thing that Grady Cothen did was to sponsor a massive conference at Ridgecrest that was attended by Baptist educational leaders from all over the world. This conference focused on educational understanding. It answered questions like these: What is education about? What is religious education? How can we address the needs of the world through religious education?

Cothen's interest in education, both at Oklahoma Baptist University and at New Orleans Seminary, gave him a special background from which he could share a concept of the use of education in the service of Christ in the life of the church.

NEW PERSPECTIVE FOR BWA—1984

In 1984 a system for long-range planning for the BWA was set in place. Tell about this change—and did you have anything to do with it?

As outgoing president, I was trying to change the five-year Congresses from being the summary session for what had been done in the past five years to being the launching pad for the programs for the next five years. We will see in the future whether that was important or not. I thought it was a very important change to lobby for in the BWA.

For the first time in Los Angeles, for instance, the BWA commissions and committees met and organized and launched their programs for the period from 1985 to 1990. Normally, these groups and committees would have been appointed during the Congress, and it would have been a year later before they had their first meeting and got together to decide what they were going to do.

We also had seized the initiative to declare that we would determine the emphases and directions for the five-year quinquennium from 1985 to 1990. The new president, Noel Vose, would make the appointments. As president-nominee he would prepare his slate, and as soon as he was elected he could release the appointments. Then the meetings were held on Friday and Saturday in Los Angeles to begin to carry out the plans that had already been worked out in Berlin in 1984. The theory is that Noel Vose will be the president who will be chairing the planning in 1989, looking to 1990–1995.

BWA CONGRESS IN LOS ANGELES—1985

You concluded your service as president of the BWA at the 1985 Congress in Los Angeles. I understand this Congress had a small attendance. What happened?

Attendance at this Congress was small, as compared with the one at Toronto. There were two factors, in my judgment, that led to this. The popular explanation the BWA prefers to give is that Southern Baptists, American Baptists, National Baptists, and the other Baptist conventions all met at about the same time in the western part of the United States, so that many North American Baptists did not go to Los Angeles. The other factor is that Los Angeles isn't all that attractive to North Americans for a trip. If the BWA Congress had been held in Mexico City, this would have doubled the number of North Americans who attended the 1985 Congress.

Another problem was that the publicity for the 1985 Congress was incredibly low-key. We just never got the word around that we were going to have a Congress. I was opposed to holding the Congress in Los Angeles. I did not think it was a good location, and events proved I was right. We had nineteen Baptist bodies that had never worked together before trying to learn to work together to host a BWA Congress. That was good for them, but not good for the BWA. It made setting up that Congress a tough job.

In terms of the finances, the job was impossible. There was no single convention that invited or assumed responsibility for either the planning for or the funding of the 1985 Congress. This was in stark contrast to the Congress in Toronto, where the Canadian Baptist Federation invited the 1980 Congress, planned it, promoted it, and provided early funding for the meeting.

In another way, the Los Angeles Congress was perhaps the most international we have ever had. It wasn't dominated by any one group—the Americans or the British. It included a balanced mix of Baptists from all over the world.

You used President Jimmy Carter as a featured speaker in the 1985 BWA Congress. How did that work?

Our two featured speakers were Billy Graham and President Carter. The Secret Service called at the last minute to change Carter's schedule. Fortunately, one of the staff volunteers for the Congress was General Earle Cox. He called the right people and suddenly President Carter was back on our schedule.

General Cox had served as commander of the American Legion and ambassador to the United Nations; so he had knowledge and political clout. He was a Georgian who worked in Washington, D.C. He served as my aide in the same way that I had served Oscar Johnson when he was president of the BWA. It's amazing that a general would volunteer to do everything from chauffeuring to pushing the U.S. government around! He remains a great friend and helper.

President Carter's speech would have been better received if he had not used it to advocate the cause of a Russian dissident pastor who had been dismissed by his church in the USSR and who wanted to move to the United States. I think the U.S. State Department played politics with his briefing even as they played politics with Billy Graham's visit to Moscow.

We had some security problems in the arrangements for President Carter, but again General Cox came to the rescue. We also had security problems with Billy Graham because Reinhold Kerstan threw open the doors to a reception to the general public lest we have a small crowd. It was intended to be a select group of financial supporters of the BWA. Graham survived, and no one was aware of the problem except General Cox and me.

Carter is admired by people all over the world and is a genuine Baptist hero because of his action on human rights. "He talks the talk and walks the walk."

BWA YOUTH CONFERENCES

The meetings of the youth conference of the BWA do not seem to capture the attention of youth today as they did earlier in the twentieth century. Why is that?

We're back at the communication problem. The youth conference in Buenos Aires was one of the most exciting, profoundly moving youth meetings that has ever been held. It was of a reasonable size. But there was not enough effort to get the word around that the war was over—to assure parents that they would not be sending their children into a battle zone if they went to Buenos Aires. I'm referring, of course, to the Falkland-Malvinas War.

One of the great things at this meeting was to see the Argentines welcome the British, whom the Argentine people have no use for. The antagonism between Argentina and England on the streets is as vehement as any antagonism between any two countries anywhere in the world. In that conference it was a moving moment when the British were introduced and the Argentines gave them a standing ovation.

It was also an exciting moment when President Alfonsine, the president of Argentina, stood up before that group. A president of that country had never spoken to an evangelical group. He told the group that "religious freedom is the foundation of all freedoms." When he said that, the crowd nearly blew the roof off the auditorium. In the course of his speech he also said, "Jesus Christ is the only mediator between God and man." Imagine him saying that in Argentina—a country controlled by the Catholic Church! I could live a thousand years and never have my spine tingle the way it did when those Argentines and South Americans reacted to that statement.

The BWA office missed getting the word out about this youth conference. Many people were still reluctant to attend because of the recent war. The BWA just didn't have the know-how or the contacts to communicate with the rank and file of the people around the world.

INCREASED THIRD WORLD PARTICIPATION

I think the BWA officials realized that I was trying to be a catalyst and to precipitate a process of decision-making that the community of leaders in the Baptist World Alliance would control. That was helped by the fact that I was trying to bring into active participation many Baptists from Third World countries. My goal was to internationalize even further the decision-making process of the Baptist World Alliance.

Is it possible to include so much of the world in the BWA leadership?

It will work, I believe, because once they move in, getting them out will be a problem. You would have more political problems getting them out than you would have getting them in. Getting them involved in the BWA is an economic problem. But once you get them in and they decide they belong, the Baptist World Alliance will be a much better organization.

Once I was in Kandy, Sri Lanka, talking to a Sri Lankan layman by the name of Richard Gunasekera. I told him, "Richard, you are a layman and you have something to say to the Baptist laymen of the world. We're going to have a lay meeting in Fort Worth in a couple of weeks, sponsored by the men's department of the BWA. I realize you probably can't make that meeting, but I do want to be sure you come to the meeting in Berlin next July."

"Do you want me to come and listen?" he replied. "Or do you want me to come and participate in the decision-making?"

"Oh," I said, "we don't need you to listen; we need you to share your experience and your perspective in outreach as a layman trying to witness for Christ."

He said, "I'll be in Fort Worth in two weeks." And he was—at his own expense. The point of this anecdote is that Richard wasn't coming because he expected the Westerners to speak to him and use him only as a seat-filler in the audience. But if he was going to be active in the decision-making process, he had the money to come; he could do it on his own. He was willing to spend his own hard-earned cash to be involved in a worldwide Baptist effort to get laymen to reach others for Christ.

For a good while North America and Europe will continue to provide the major figures in the Baptist World Alliance. We have to make a special effort to put these other people in the major decision-making roles. If we hear their voices and consider their opinions, they will automatically be included in the decision-making process. This means the BWA will not have to elect somebody from Sri Lanka as president of the BWA just because he's from Sri Lanka. These Baptists from the Third World will make it on their own personal qualifications.

BWA FUNDING

Traditionally, the Baptist World Alliance has been attended by those people who are able to pay their way to these international meetings, or who have some church or institution to pay their way. Will the BWA have the funding necessary to broaden its decision-making process?

No, there will not be enough funds unless the BWA rethinks its funding process. And I don't see any indication that will get on the agenda any time in the foreseeable future. When I say "foreseeable future," I'm talking in decades, not months.

I thought the BWA, with some staff help, could come up with a couple of million dollars to build a new building in about a year. You need a smaller campaign like this in order to get into big fund-raising. I suggested that we conduct a campaign for a building in order to "break the ice," so to speak.

But I never could get the point across to the BWA staff that the way you raise funds is not the way you raise funds in Europe. A campaign has to use some professional activities. It isn't a matter of sitting down and writing letters in longhand to a few prospective donors. But I just couldn't generate any interest among the BWA staff in a more aggressive fund-raising strategy. It finally dawned on me after three years that the problem went beyond the reluctance of people who were new and not yet ready for such efforts. I was pushing against a difference in understanding of what ought to be done, what was legitimate, and how to do it.

For instance, the BWA staff was perfectly willing for me to go raise the money. But when I told them, "We need the organization and the staff to do more," their answer was, "We just don't have the money." But I knew we were not going to get the money unless we got out and got busy at the task. You've got to have some seed money on the front end in order to get going in a fund-raising effort. The money will come in later, but you must spend money to get the effort going. Moving aggressively into fund-raising and generating a higher level of financial support will require a change in the perception of the Baptist World Alliance staff.

The international character of the BWA is nowhere better demonstrated than in its attitude toward fund-raising and financial support. It fails to realize that its own self-interest involves letting the North Americans do something that North Americans do well—raise money.

Isn't this an even more serious problem in light of the fact that the BWA cannot expect substantial increases through the SBC Cooperative Program in future years?

The Lord will have to intervene if they get more support through the Cooperative Program—and that is a reverent statement. The instincts of Claas and Vose and others may turn out to be better than the instincts of us North Americans, or of us Southern Baptists, at this point. But I doubt it. The BWA is near the optimum in Southern Baptist contributions so that they will share only in growth of Southern Baptists and inflation. I don't know of many Southern Baptists who will put a lot more money into the BWA than they have already given.

What about the funding prospects for the new building of the BWA? Have funds been raised to cover this capital expenditure and the additional expenses it will involve?

No. At this point, these funds have not been raised. I'm hoping that when I go to the BWA meeting during Thanksgiving in a couple of weeks, I will hear about plans to raise those funds. I just haven't heard anything about it. I think there is hope in that I finally got Pat Pattillo involved with the development side of the BWA. It finally registered that they were dealing with a highly skilled professional. The question is still open as to whether they will listen to him when the requirements that he might make for fund-raising are spelled out, or whether they will back away, saying, "That's too risky; that's too daring."

Will Pattillo do this as a part of his Baptist commitment?

Yes, Southern Seminary will loan him to the BWA. The seminary has a policy that it will let any of its faculty or staff participate in the BWA almost in any way they are willing to do. This is not a new policy; it's been on the books for decades.

How can the BWA continue to go on with limited funding and a building debt? This seems to pose some rather serious problems for the BWA.

I just can't predict that. I think some things must change. I wanted to change them earlier when I served as BWA president. Perhaps the new president, Noel Vose, will be more adept at achieving these goals than I was.

SBC FOREIGN MISSION BOARD AND THE BWA

How would you describe the relationship of the Foreign Mission Board to the Baptist World Alliance?

One of my surprises upon becoming president of the Baptist World Alliance was that being president apparently erected some barrier between me and the Foreign Mission Board. I thought it would go the other way. I have always been an eager supporter of our Foreign Mission Board and of the mission outreach of Southern Baptists. The only five-year period during which I did not conduct any project for the Foreign Mission Board was the five years I was president of the BWA.

I had the distinct feeling that the Foreign Mission Board was very defensive in terms of relief funds, that they wanted Southern Baptists to perceive that the Foreign Mission Board was the only channel for world relief. We had never raised any question about that, because there's no point in talking about competition between lighthouses. But apparently, the Foreign Mission Board perceives the BWA as a competitor in this arena.

The BWA is in no position to compete with the Foreign Mission Board in terms of personnel, resources, and funds. The BWA is simply another Baptist body with international ties and programs. Keith Parks objected vehemently to the Baptist World Alliance having programs, and he also objected to the Baptist World Alliance being involved in relief efforts throughout the world.

I don't know exactly why he was against the BWA's efforts. Again, we got into the same thing with the organization of the Caribbean Baptist Fellowship. The BWA responded to the Baptists in the Caribbean some years before I became president and agreed to create an organization by that name. But it was after I came in as president of the BWA that it was actually put together and organized. We were planning to do this and name Azariah McKenzie, a leader from Jamaica, as our associate secretary for the Caribbean area.

Just before that was done, the Foreign Mission Board employed McKenzie, and they announced the organization of the Caribbean division of the Foreign Mission Board. This happened to be what the BWA was proposing to do. I called Keith Parks and said, "Look, we don't have any problem with this. We aren't objecting to what you're doing. We just want to get the lines clear because we are perfectly happy to pull out of this project."

As a matter of fact, the Caribbean Fellowship is in a sense an idiosyncratic organization within the BWA. It's small; it's not as large as the others are. It's not homogeneous in any way. It's just not Spanish-speaking. There are points where it doesn't tie in with Central America or South America—it's made up mostly of English- or French-speaking constituents.

As I said to Parks, "Look, we're just asking for information. What do you want? We want to adapt to what you're doing." Parks put the Foreign Mission Board's Caribbean secretary on the line who, at minimum, gave me a "song-and-dance routine."

I know there was Foreign Mission Board objection to forming a South American Baptist Union within the BWA. I don't know at what level. I don't know whether it was an area secretary or missionaries within the mission. I know there was effort to prevent the South Americans from setting up what has come to be known as UBSA— *Union Batista Sud America* (later UBLA—Union of Baptists in Latin America—to include Central America).

When I went to South America for the centennial celebration of the Brazilian Convention, at which time this Union of South America was to be organized, I ran into some Foreign Mission Board-initiated opposition. The Latin Americans never would give me their sources for this information, and I didn't pry for it; I didn't think it mattered. I really didn't want to know because I wasn't going to pay any attention to it. I intended to do the job I had been sent to do for the BWA. What we were hoping to do was to bring all the Baptists in South America together under one continental umbrella. We never have gotten that off the ground, but it will evolve.

I don't understand the exact philosophy of the Foreign Mission Board in its relief program. I know they used the BWA to get relief into Poland during the 1970s. It was organized by Knud Wumpleman in Denmark, and the BWA was able to provide the visas and the governmental approvals to get truckloads of material across the borders. A great deal was made by the Foreign Mission Board about its relief to Poland, which was massive. What the Foreign Mission Board really did was provide money. The manpower and the contacts and the permission came through the European Baptist Federation contacts.

At the visible level, associates at the Foreign Mission Board have been

very active in the Baptist World Alliance and have been very cooperative. So I don't want to create a sense of clash and conflict between the
BWA and the Foreign Mission Board. On the other hand, the absence of
cooperation at the top leadership level of the FMB has been a part of the
problem.

*Do you see any alleviation of that attitude? Do you see it changing
or becoming more serious?*

I'm an optimist. I hope the Foreign Mission Board, after it is com-
fortably involved in its own programs that have been developed, will
reach out to strengthen other world evangelism bodies. Frankly, my
perception, which cannot be proven, is that there is an effort to establish the institutional integrity of the Foreign Mission Board as a world
organization.

Right now the Foreign Mission Board is in a changing environment,
and it is being pulled from many directions by many forces. I know from
experience that it is a massive challenge to Christian statesmanship to
get through those waters. The institution must live through all these
crises in order to keep on functioning. The ideological services that it
might render are subordinated to its staying alive. I'm a realist enough,
having lived with an institution, to know that sometimes idealistic goals
have to be postponed while you swim through the flood.

GOALS AS BWA PRESIDENT

What goals did you set for yourself during your presidency of the BWA?

My first goal was to provide a new headquarters building for the
Baptist World Alliance. This was not the most important need, but I saw
it as necessary in order to permit the development of an adequate staff
and enlarged programs. Another goal was expansion of personnel. But
before we could hire new people, we had to have more office space. We
had people trying to use other staff members' offices when they were
out of the city. The old facilities were totally inadequate.

The new BWA office building is a four-year-old building with approximately ten thousand square feet. We needed more space than this,
because the BWA will probably fill it up the moment they move in. We
really needed something closer to twenty thousand feet in capacity.

My third goal was a reorganization of the BWA staff in terms of job
descriptions and functions as well as the reorganization of the struc-

ture. This was never really fleshed out. We ended up with everybody on the staff being responsible for everything. There were priorities in terms of Archie Goldie, for instance, who had the primary responsibility for relief efforts but who also was charged with other functions. And Denton Lotz had a primary concern for education and evangelism, his first love. But he also served as the youth secretary and a kind of associate general secretary.

The major problem with the office staff was that the secretaries carried on much of the work of the BWA. They were under supervision, but they functioned largely in the absence of their supervisors. They ended up actually trying to implement policies without an overview of the entire operation. So I had great misgivings about the administrative structure of the organization and the traveling nature of the jobs of the men who had responsibility for policy-making decisions. Much of the time there was no one beyond the level of an administrative assistant in the Washington office.

Another goal I had was to enlarge the funding base of the Baptist World Alliance. I had a number of different ways that I thought we could enlarge the funding base of the Alliance. For one, I thought we could generate some endowment funds and some deferred giving funds that would endow certain projects the Alliance does. But as of this date, there is no endowment for the BWA, nor is there any plan to acquire such endowment.

Another goal I had was to generate funds so the general council could help defray the expenses of those who travel to official BWA meetings. The only travel expenses for most members of the general council come from a sort of fund administered by the BWA general secretary. This enables him to get important people to meetings, or to get representation of certain areas of the world to important meetings. I thought it was not worthy of a world organization of Baptists to have people seek their own funding in order to attend a meeting. This practice also restricts attendance to those who are able to fund their travel.

This goal also tied in with another goal—to broaden participation in the decision-making process of the BWA. I realized there were many parts of the world where Baptists had not participated in BWA affairs. I felt the only way we would get full representation was to make it possible for them to attend the meetings. Otherwise, the wealthier nations, specifically North America and certain European countries, would dominate the BWA.

I also wanted to see the BWA flesh out the regional bodies, and we did achieve that goal. The BWA now has regional bodies that cover the world. The exception is Central America, which conceptually we wanted to be a part of Latin America. Central America, for reasons that are not clear to me, chose not to be a part of the Union of Baptists in Latin America and forced the changing of the title to Union of Baptists in South America. (Central America has subsequently joined the South American region.)

BWA SUPPORT PATTERNS

Southern Baptists have often viewed themselves as very generous supporters of the organizational structure of the BWA. How can this support be enlarged?

Of all the Baptist bodies affiliated with the BWA, Southern Baptists give by far the largest amount of money to the Alliance—about one-half of its budget, to be exact. But we need to realize that in terms of available resources, Southern Baptists aren't all that generous with the Baptist World Alliance. The SBC in membership accounts for about one-half of all the Baptists in the world, and we have more than one-half of the resources of Baptists in the world. That doesn't make our support of the BWA something we can brag about.

Some other groups, such as the American Baptists and the Canadian Baptists, give very large gifts to the BWA on a per-capita basis. But they also designate a lot of their gifts for relief. This means their gifts are not available for BWA programs or operating expense. Then Baptist groups in Europe give very generously to the support of the subdivision of the BWA—the European Baptist Federation—and thereby feel they have given to the Alliance. The Washington office gets only ten or fifteen thousand dollars a year from the European Baptist Federation.

Generally, the funding from Baptist groups throughout the world is parsimonious at best. There is no generally accepted yardstick for measuring what a convention or union ought to do for the BWA. As president, I had hoped we could work out some type of support formula. But given the parameters within which the BWA must work, there is no easy solution to this problem.

BWA SUPPORT FROM NORTH AMERICA
What can you tell us about the level of support for the BWA from other North American Baptist groups?

On a per-capita basis some of them do very much better than Southern Baptists in their support of the BWA. But they are relatively small groups, except for National Baptists, and therefore a fairly good per-capita gift is not a very large total gift. So the support is sometimes generous for those smaller bodies but not of great significance in terms of funding a world program.

The National Baptist Convention stopped giving any support to the BWA under the presidency of Joe Jackson in his latter days, or at least for the last five years. I wish to record that this was not an angry thing because he used to send me ten thousand dollars a year every year to use for students at Southern Seminary, while he was refusing to support the Baptist World Alliance. His successor, Dr. Jemison, has recently promised to give fifty thousand dollars to the Baptist World Alliance. So support by these groups is idiosyncratic and difficult to predict. Somebody on the BWA staff ought to be spending a lot of time fundraising with these conventions and unions.

Of course, a great deal of support needs to come from North America—the North American Baptist Conference and the Baptist General Conference. Can you describe their involvement?

These groups are very much involved. They use the BWA to link into larger enterprises than their own body would be able to undertake, and they are very helpful and very cooperative. I spoke on one occasion to a western Canadian group of pastors, which included some Baptist General Conference people. I was intrigued to talk with them and find how very conservative they were. But on the other hand, they seemed to be perfectly relaxed about dealing with the Baptist World Alliance and proud of their relationship. Those two things don't usually go together.

BWA PRESIDENCY IN RETROSPECT
What would you do differently if you were to serve for another five years as president of the BWA?

I don't think I would make many changes in the things I tried to do. By the way, we did have a purpose of strengthening certain programs such as evangelism and education. And that was accomplished during my five years. I would like to have started fifteen years ago setting up some of these committees to evolve new methods and techniques.

Just today the BWA office in Washington called to invite me to a dinner this Saturday night in Washington. That is a big fund-raising dinner, which has some intriguing overtones. To my knowledge, this is the first time something that formal has been structured on fund-raising for the BWA. Maybe something is finally being done about this need.

If I knew how to do it, I would change some things about the role of the president in the Baptist World Alliance. I was often tempted to do this, but I wasn't sure who the next president would be. And to structure the presidency so the BWA becomes dependent on the president's functioning in a certain way would be problematic. Geography, language, personality, traditions—all of these things are factors in the choice of a president.

The new president, Noel Vose, is a seminary president, just as you were, I understand.

Yes, but he's more than that. He's a professor and a president and a fund-raiser for the seminary in Perth, Australia. So he's got about three full-time jobs, plus the Baptist World Alliance, plus half the world to travel if meetings are held in North America.

Will he be able to function in the way you functioned as president?

No, because his time will be more limited than mine was. He will do his travel probably in our winter, which is the Australian summer. This will be his summer vacation period. That will pose some problems for him, but these are problems that he will have to work out.

Thank you for asking what I would do if I had five more years as president, but I'm glad my time has come to an end. Five years is long enough.

CHAPTER 13

Revolution in the SBC

1979-1985

In a speech in Nashville about 1978–79, you addressed the issue of politicizing the Convention's election process. Do you still see this as one of the main issues that confronts Southern Baptists?

Yes, I saw a political campaign whose goal was to change the nature and character of the Southern Baptist Convention and the control of the agencies. It wasn't that people have never done things for political reasons nor was it that board members of agencies were not chosen for their theological bias, right or left. But in the past this was an individual matter that was the product of the thinking of individual members of the Committee on Boards. There was not an organized and concerted effort to put people with specific theological views on the boards of agencies. This is not illegal; I think it's just not in accordance with the spirit of Christian brotherhood or the heritage of Southern Baptists.

What response did you receive to this speech?

I was greeted with a mixture of disbelief. Many people thought I was making a mountain out of a molehill, or that I was an extreme liberal fighting the conservatives, or that I was a conservative fighting the extreme fundamentalists. Later on, people took it more seriously and felt that maybe I had not been crying "wolf" after all.

At first, my good friend Albert McClellan, for instance, thought I was referring to something he had seen happen over and over again among Southern Baptists. Albert later admitted that something new had happened, that this conservative uprising was of a different order and a different quality from previous surges.

POLITICAL TAKEOVER

The Pressler-Patterson group had a long-range plan. There's too much hard evidence—all the way from computer communication systems and maps with different colored pins for the rank of the leader in that geographical area—to assume that this was just a bunch of amateurs. Judge Pressler is a smart professional politician.

The "inerrant Bible" is a political slogan. It is a good one because Baptists divide over what it means. We need to get back to dealing with "how do I obey what I know the Word of God says" rather than fighting over what really turns out to be non-biblical shibboleths on both sides.

My criterion is still, "My Bible is true." If you know some way to make truth truer than true, then go on and use that statement. My Bible is true—and I'm not talking about which version or translation. I think any copy of the Bible under the guidance of the Holy Spirit will guide me to eternal truth. That's enough.

It doesn't bother me if it helps you to feel that a copy of the Bible we don't have was inerrant. That's a symbolic affirmation of faith that's fine with me. But I still want to talk with you about how you are letting the Bible become the rule of faith and practice in your life.

NEW STRATEGY FOR CONTROLLING SBC BOARDS

Is control of the Committee on Boards the central issue in this movement?

The most massive change in Southern Baptist polity has taken place so recently that no one knows where it is going or how long it will last. I refer to the control seized by Adrian Rogers, when he was elected SBC president in 1979. He changed the process for selecting board members.

First, he ignored the obvious intent of the Convention bylaws that require the president to consult with the vice presidents in the naming of the Committee on Committees. (The two vice presidents were not of his political party.) Historically, the three officers have together named the Committee on Committees, which, in turn, names the Committee on Boards. President Rogers ruthlessly shut these two vice presidents out of the process. Later, President Stanley, in his bid for reelection, went through the motions of consultation. All precedents and the bylaws were disregarded so the Convention president could exercise control over the selection of the boards of the agencies.

This, in turn, politicized the election of Convention officers in a new and demonic way. This has changed the polity of the Convention. We have moved from raising a standard—the proclamation of the gospel to the whole creation—to which all people of like mind and spirit might repair, to a control of the perimeters of the Convention as defined by fundamentalist dogma. The question is whether SBC patience will last long enough for this radical change to be altered or modified or whether the unity of the Convention will disintegrate. I hope for the first, but cannot predict which will happen.

Did you ever sit in on the Committee on Boards meetings?

Oh yes. As executive secretary of the SBC Executive Committee, I used to do it fairly regularly, but not of my own volition. The Committee on Boards would go so far in naming the many nominees, and then they would begin to get into a tangle. It's a very legalistic set of regulations, with all sorts of complicated problems. The committee would call the SBC executive secretary to ask about specific issues and regulations, such as whether a certain person had served on a particular agency before—all kinds of questions.

After a little while of this going back and forth, they would call and say, "Look, we're tired of running out here to the telephone to call you. Why don't you come over here and sit in the meeting so we can ask you these questions when we think of them instead of having to send somebody out to call you?"

They were not at that stage asking me, "Who do you recommend?" They tended to get to that stage, but that would be toward the end when they were trying to think of a specific layman from Alabama, and the Alabama representative of the Committee on Boards had left to catch his plane. They couldn't think of somebody who wasn't already on a board from that state. Then they would begin to say, "We've got to leave here in a little while; do you know anybody who could serve?" Eventually you would tell them old Joe Doe down in Montgomery, Alabama, was a very fine layman. With that, he would get named to a board.

The Committee on Boards is made up of good people; they work hard. The problem is they try to do too big a job in too short a time. They are doing better by that, but in doing better, what they've really done is delegate the committee's responsibility to the two state members. The advance work now is done by the state members—the layman and the clergyman on the Committee on Boards, say from Alabama, and they do their work in advance, which is pretty good, except you never get a recommendation from the full Committee on Boards.

THE "CONSERVATIVE" REVOLT

Where and how did this conservative takeover of the SBC begin?

First of all, I don't think it began recently. I think there are personalities that precipitated forces at work within the Southern Baptist Convention. That's simply a background statement to push it back and to indicate that you need to do more than just look at the names of the people and their positions to describe what is currently happening so pervasively within the Southern Baptist Convention.

The next thing I want to say is that I have been perceived for most of my career as at least middle of the road if not right of center toward the conservative side in my own theological position. Not extreme right, but at least right of center, or I would always say "center." The *Religious Herald* of Virginia once described me as "the leader of biblical fundamentalism in the Southern Baptist Convention." I didn't think that was accurate at the time; it was not meant to be a recommendation by the editor.

Another point I want to make is that I have worked happily and congenially across the years with all shades of Southern Baptists in leadership roles in the Convention. Some of these were left of center, some were a little right of center, and some were far right of center.

We had trustees in New Orleans, in Nashville, and at Southern Seminary who were extremely conservative, and they were excellent trustees and close personal friends, people whom I leaned on heavily, and people who became leaders in the work of each agency.

The present situation within the Convention began, in my judgment, after World War II with the enlargement of the Convention beyond its traditional eighteen state borders. That movement began in the San Antonio Convention with the admission of California. The SBC became geographically spread, culturally more diverse, and theologically more diverse. Certain theological positions were greatly strengthened by the influx of new Southern Baptists from pioneer areas. These people were not a part of the American Baptist Convention because they were to the right of that convention theologically.

There was a selectivity in the determination of who wanted to become Southern Baptists in Kansas or Oregon, or wherever, by the very fact that they were not willing to cooperate with one of the other Baptist conventions. People will think of the American Baptist Convention, but there were other alternatives that these people had rejected. Some were more conservative than American Baptists, who were very diverse and not uniformly liberal or conservative throughout the United States.

Many of these people were not strongly established back home, and they were looking for better jobs and newer opportunities. That had some cultural impact on the selectivity process.

Another thing that was happening was the moving from the rural base, the farm, the agricultural base. Earlier Southern Baptists were not all farmers, but even the Southern Baptists in the cities partook of the rural, agricultural culture patterns of the Deep South. The First Baptist Church of Memphis, my home church, sang the same hymns and complained about the BYPU in the same terms as the little open country church at Woodville, Tennessee, where I first became pastor. There was no cultural clash in my experience in moving from the First Baptist Church of the city to an open country church.

Culturally, Southern Baptists had been very homogeneous. Suddenly the nation was moving into an industrial situation where these people tended to be blue-collar workers in the pioneer areas, not farmers. They didn't go to farm; they went to the urban centers to find industrial jobs. This is the place at which the Southern Baptist Convention had begun an evolution in its character. This change would require new understanding, a new willingness to tolerate diversity. All of this stressed the Convention from the beginning, but the Convention was able to handle it until recent years.

Did you feel this change when you took the job as executive secretary of the SBC Executive Committee in 1946?

No, but I felt it later, and it was discussed among the Convention leadership over the expansion of the territory of the Southern Baptist

Convention. This was perceived to be a problem that would have to be resolved in the future.

One of the arguments against the expansion was that we were changing the character of our beloved Convention. There was even some discussion of the problems of the Northern Baptist Convention, as it was then called. We were importing into the Southern Baptist Convention the kinds of problems that had disrupted and divided the Northern Baptist Convention. Some SBC leaders felt we would be confronted with the same situation that Northern Baptists had faced from the 1920s on.

Was there any attempt to make preparation for the future, or did the SBC leaders just recognize it?

It was recognized, and nobody knew what to do with it. I think that ought to be said very flatly. It was discussed, but no one had the wisdom or the understanding to be able to say, "Here is how we ought to prepare for the day that lies ahead." No one in the Northern Baptist Convention had been able to come up with answers, even when the problem overwhelmed them. So it's not surprising that Southern Baptists couldn't come up with answers in anticipation of the problem.

So you would place the beginnings of this controversy back in the 1940s?

Yes, but I think there's one more dimension that ought to be added. In the 1940s there was a change in the population patterns in the Deep South, and there was also growing diversity of culture and economics within the traditional South. Southern Baptists may have had this problem even if we hadn't expanded geographically.

With this change in the South and in the nation in terms of education, the mind-set of large segments of the population, including the church membership, began to change. Education in the public schools changed; emphases in the public schools changed; the efforts to eliminate the sectarian religious influence in the public schools became a factor. And all of this was controversial.

There was a period during which we expected to put at least a junior college within commuting distance of every young person in the United States. We were trying to provide collegiate education for the total youth population of the United States. The political powers-that-be had that in mind. The Democratic Party put that into its platform.

My point is that we were getting a lot more people with a more sophisticated education. This was bound to affect the trends.

I might as well put the seminaries into the picture, too, because the seminaries were reacting to this educational development within the nation. They were becoming more academic in their style, no longer Bible schools. They were moving to become basically graduate schools. So the character of theological education was changing.

The new educational process was providing a new mental process that was moving toward accepting abstractions as reality and as important over against concrete ideas. (An abstract idea like "redemption" over against the concrete image of "washed in the blood," but they both intend to communicate the same thing.)

At that point the old guard was becoming obsolete, and the more conservative theological mind-set was being undermined in Southern Baptist circles. There was a perception of a shift from conservative toward liberal. The reality was a shifting theological perspective or emphasis. Suddenly the L. E. Bartons and the E. P. Alldredges, who exercised immense influence in Southern Baptist life, were becoming themselves obsolescent as far as Southern Baptist leadership was concerned. Their point of view was becoming old hat, and their way of stating the issues and arguing for things was going out of style among Southern Baptists. I suspect I belonged to that new style, which conceived itself as very conservative. In terms of attitude toward the Bible, I held a very conservative theological position.

I think we have a shift in the balance of power within the Convention today rather than a change of the Convention as a whole. The recurring 55 percent versus 45 percent votes for the presidents since the election of Adrian Rogers has been consistent. Apparently it doesn't matter which side does what or how hard they work at changing the vote; they keep coming out with a 55–45 vote.

Some of that is also rooted in the difference in transportation now. The pastor of the small church in the rural section can get into town to the meeting to vote. There was a time when he probably didn't think it was worth the cost or the effort to get in to the Convention. So I'm not sure there has been a sudden change of the percentages as much as the controversy has provided motivation for people to attend the Convention and to vote.

Now I don't know that this is anything more than a personal opinion. It is rooted in my own observation and reflection about the Convention across the years. I've tried to say some of these ideas are not brand new. I've picked them up from forty years ago and have simply brought them up to the present.

Is it fair to say that as early as the late 1940s when you were the SBC executive secretary, there was a sigh of relief when the Convention was over because it had held together one more year? Or is that a little too strong?

A little too strong, but it points in the right direction. You always knew that it could fly apart at any given session. There was always a sign of relief in one sense that no great damage had been done. And then sometimes there was great rejoicing because an Advance Program, or a "Million More in Fifty-Four" campaign or something like that would capture the mind and there would be a great surge forward in Baptist church life.

When did you first see this as a crucial issue?

I saw it all the way back in the Elliott controversy. Then there was the controversy over the Baptist Faith and Message, which issued in the 1963 revision of the earlier document. This is when it became apparent that solutions to the diversity would have to be hammered out.

Then I ran into something new in the Elliott controversy, when I first met Paul Pressler. From that point on, I have been more afraid of him than most Southern Baptists were and I have had more respect for his ability than many of his opponents even today have acquired. They have consistently underestimated him in terms of his ability and determination.

I ran into Pressler in the Elliott controversy days when he was the chairman of a nine-member committee from the Second Baptist Church of Houston to investigate the orthodoxy of the seminaries. I was in Houston in a revival at South Main Baptist Church. Pressler's committee demanded an interview with me. I really didn't relish giving the interview because I didn't think it would help anything.

This committee was investigating all the seminaries. Pressler had gotten his church to say that Elliott was only a symptom of what was wrong with all the seminaries; that they needed to investigate them all. I finally said to Pressler's committee, "I'm here at the invitation of another church, and I'm busy about the work in this revival in South Main Church. I can't see you until Saturday morning, but I'll meet you for breakfast at seven o'clock that day."

The truth is, I didn't think they would show up. But all nine of the committee members showed up at seven o'clock on Saturday morning, at the old Shamrock Hotel in Houston. We sat down, and I didn't get my orange juice down before the key question was posed: "Do you believe the first eleven chapters of Genesis are literally true?"

Instead of answering the question, I turned to the person on my right and asked, "How long has it been since you've read the first eleven chapters of Genesis?" "Oh," he said, "about two years." I went around and asked each of the nine committee members this question. At least eight of them were just plain-vanilla Baptist laymen—the salt of the earth. They really wanted to know the answer to the question, but they came with no hidden agenda. Not one of these nine claimed to have read the first eleven chapters of Genesis within the last year, including Paul Pressler, as I remember.

So I said, "Well, why don't we get ten Gideon Bibles and let's open the Bible and read it. I'll tell you what I believe each word and each verse says, and then you can decide whether I believe it is literally true or not." And so we did that.

I thought we would just test the waters for a little while and go on. But from seven o'clock until eleven o'clock that morning, I sat there and did word-by-word, phrase-by-phrase, verse-by-verse exegesis of the first eleven chapters of Genesis. During these four hours I got up to about chapter 5.

I had taught the introductory course in Old Testament at the seminary level, so this was not new to me. I was not ad-libbing, and I did have some scholarly resources at my fingertips. I recall that one member of the committee said to me at one point—and I'm quoting as nearly as I can exactly what he said: "Dr. McCall, I've always known there was something wrong with my interpretation of the first eleven chapters of Genesis. What you are saying makes this the Word of God to me."

That was the reaction I was getting. They didn't want to quit. About eleven o'clock, I said, "Look, I've got a luncheon engagement. I've got to clean up and dress for my luncheon engagement with the South Main people." I learned later that the committee brought in a report to the Second Baptist Church. The vote was 8 to 1 that the seminaries were in great shape, orthodox, indeed.

But Paul Pressler brought in a minority report to the Second Baptist Church that the seminaries did not believe the Bible and were heretical. Now to explain that, I'll go back. When I tried to leave, Mr. Pressler—he was not Judge Pressler then—said, "But you haven't answered our question yes or no. Do you believe the first eleven chapters of Genesis are literally true?"

I turned that off and said, "Oh, I guess I don't speak very clearly" or something like that, and made fun of myself, and got up and left the room. He followed me out the room. We got to the elevator and he was still asking, "Will you answer the question yes or no? Are the first eleven chapters of Genesis literally true? I tried to brush this off and say, "Mr. Pressler, I've been trying to answer that question since seven o'clock this morning. If you don't understand what I've said, I guess the only way for you to get my answer is to come to Southern Seminary and take the full three-year course."

Were you getting angry?

I was impatient at that point. When I said that to him, he understood the put-down that was implied. I didn't mean it as put-down, but it was exactly what I was thinking. I thought he was pressing the matter beyond good manners. His answer to me was, "I'll have you know I'm a *magna cum laude* graduate of Princeton." The elevator came, and I tried to step on the elevator. He grabbed me by the arm to demand that I answer yes or no to his question.

At that point I was angry, and my temper flared because I didn't like being grabbed and having him physically restrain me from getting on the elevator. My response was, "Mr. Pressler, I don't care if you are a *summa cum laude* graduate of Harvard; you are ignorant." I pushed his hand off my arm and stepped on the elevator.

That last is said with regret. I have regretted that conversation, but I think the conversation is worth repeating in this context because it illustrates attitude and spirit and my inability to communicate with Paul Pressler. I could absolutely win the other eight members of a nine-member committee to the position that I did believe the Bible. I was trying to interpret it in terms of what the Bible itself was saying, rather than to impose some twentieth-century Western rationalistic interpretation.

From that point on, I've had great respect for Paul Pressler's ability. I have also had fear, rooted in my awareness that he is a man with a position that is controversial, that he is a determined individual who is not controlled by the spirit of Christian brotherhood or anything of that sort.

That anecdote is important in interpreting what I would feel in the 1970s when I first saw the liaison between Paige Patterson and the Criswell Bible Institute and Paul Pressler as they began to develop what I thought of as an organized political movement within the Southern Baptist Convention to change the Southern Baptist Convention.

Maybe this is not in the right context, but I want to say I thought that Paul Pressler was one of probably no more than two dozen Southern Baptists who really understood the mechanism of the Southern Baptist Convention. Most Southern Baptists simply let it work but have not examined it as a legal document to find its strengths and weaknesses and how to manipulate it.

Are there any other factors you would single out as contributing to this controversy?

One of the factors is the demise of the BYPU/Training Union as a major force in the life of Southern Baptist churches. The Training Union provided a knowledgeable corps of people in every Baptist church who understood Baptist history and tradition. Tradition is how we feel about church and state, for instance, and how we feel about creeds, and why we fought against this kind of thing.

Another factor is that we are in an era when we are moving back to the past, to the more conservative position. That's expressed in political decision-making. Then we have the confrontational methodology, going back to the demonstrations in the 1960s and the 1970s. Confrontation has become an acceptable way of influencing decision. You raise consciousness by knocking the enemy unconscious. This confrontational methodology has become acceptable in our society and is now routine, even in the Christian community.

AGENCY HEADS ALTER CLOSE RELATION TO SBC MASSES

Another problem is that the agency heads changed their relation to the rank and file of Southern Baptists without meaning to. There was a time when I, for example, tried to speak to each state convention every three years. I spoke to dozens of associational meetings every year. I participated in state convention seminars or conferences on evangelism and other subjects. I would speak to gatherings of pastors and laymen. This allowed many pastors and leading laymen to hear me speak (plus Ridgecrest and Glorieta), and I was able to shake hands and talk with them as individuals.

The result was a great deal of confidence in the agency people by the rank and file of Southern Baptists. But with the growth of the Convention and the agencies, this personal contact was diluted. By the 1960s I was speaking in no more than four or five state conventions a year and almost no associational meetings. The printed page and the public relations officer replaced this face-to-face contact for denominational employees. Thus, the agencies set themselves up for a takeover of the Convention leadership.

Furthermore, when the controversy was a small cloud on the horizon, the agency executives refused to take it seriously. It was just another theological fuss that would soon be forgotten. But when it was obviously very serious, they panicked and did some very foolish things from a political point of view. They almost asked for defeat—and got it!

Credit Pressler-Patterson with being superior politicians, but they get more credit than they deserve for their success. They had a lot of help—including some I gave them without intending to do so.

You first brought this to the public view back in the middle to late 1970s and announced that you saw this takeover as a five-year plan. Tell us more about this.

I dealt with the issue for the first time in a column in *The Tie*—a publication of Southern Seminary—about 1975. The title of my column was, "My Bible Is True." I was trying to say that the Bible is true because it is the revelation of God, and it becomes eternal truth as God's Holy Spirit interprets it to the individual. It becomes transforming truth for people in that way—not because we base our interpretation on an "inerrant Bible" or a specific text or translation of the Bible.

MOVE TO INERRANT ORIGINAL AUTOGRAPHS

I think that article may have had some effect in forcing the movement away from discussion of what was the real "inerrant Bible." It forced the controversy back to "the inerrant original autographs." That is an important change in the nature of the position of the conservatives. Once they take that position, they have moved into the arena of faith and beyond evidence and rational analysis, because nobody has a copy of the original autographs.

I don't think it matters whether the original autographs are inerrant or not if God in his providence didn't give them to us. It's the Bible we have by divine providence that we must deal with. That's why I was saying, "My Bible—the one I have—is true."

My point was that the Bible we have is the Bible we have by divine providence. I will not quarrel with the Bible we have. It is true. Its message is eternally and everlastingly true. Its message is the rule of faith and practice for a Bible-believing Christian. This has been my view since my early training and understanding.

Support of the conservative position on the Bible was obviously present going back several decades. The Convention elected several very conservative presidents—Ramsey Pollard, R. G. Lee, Jaroy Webber, W. A. Criswell. Do you recall others?

K. O. White was also elected in the midst of controversy as an ultra-conservative president. So there was nothing new about that. Both sides in the current controversy have forgotten that we had elected these people. I don't think we've ever had a genuinely liberal elected president of the Southern Baptist Convention.

Why did these early presidents not precipitate the kind of a controversy that we saw in the late 1970s and early 1980s?

That explains why I suddenly became alarmed in the late 1970s and began to talk about the rise of a new Frank Norris-style fundamentalism. I use that particular phrase because I perceived this not as a new theological position within the Southern Baptist Convention, but a new combative, confrontational, political, and manipulative style of conducting debate. That rooted back in my experience that I had with Paul Pressler in Houston.

Frank Norris, who died in 1951, seemed not to get the hearing that some of these later conservatives were able to enlist, although he attended meetings of the Southern Baptist Convention and tried to push his agenda. Why do you think this was true?

Because we had on the other side people like George Truett, who had the confidence of the people. The Norris combative style was rejected as not being legitimate in this era by the Southern Baptist Convention. I knew Norris and was the victim of his ability and skills in more than one combat. I was berated in several issues of *The Fundamentalist,* Norris's publication in Fort Worth. But Norris, by the way, was different from this present group at a very significant point. I had rather quarrel with Norris than some of these present combatants.

While I was executive secretary of the Executive Committee, I met Norris in the Skirvin Hotel at a Southern Baptist Convention session in Oklahoma City, Oklahoma. He tried to embarrass me by announcing in his loud voice, which would penetrate the roar of the conversation in the hotel lobby, "Hello, Duke, old friend. It's good to see you." To which I responded, imitating his volume of voice as best I could, "Hello, Dr. Norris, I've always wanted to meet you. I wanted to tell you that if you ever say anything nice about me in *The Fundamentalist,* I'll sue you for libel."

With that, he broke out in laughter, and we greeted each other as people who were getting along fine. To my knowledge, my name was never mentioned again in *The Fundamentalist* after that encounter. Combativeness and controversy was a game with him, in a sense. If I could respond to him and laugh with him and not be angry or ugly, then I was okay. Not that he agreed with me, but he would focus his guns on somebody else.

But there is no humor, no give and take in the present controversy. Stylistically, it's very different in its leadership. I am told of a conversation in which Adrian Rogers described himself like this: "I am inflexible; I am not given to compromise; I want total surrender of the errant opposition." That is what is different now.

K. O. White was a convinced man and would fight to the death for what he believed was true, but he would not fight to kill anybody. And if somebody could shed light that would change his position, he was willing to listen for truth. He would not just listen to what is said to find a phrase that could be used against the speaker. There's no compromise with the leaders of the current controversy.

Another different element is Paul Pressler's legal ability and lawyer's analysis of the legal documents. This enabled him to find the point of political vulnerability of the Convention. He then organized a skillful effort to exploit that vulnerability by electing a president who would name the Committee on Boards, which then would alter the agencies by the choices of trustees or directors.

And you first saw this coming to the fore in the 1970s?

Yes. There were many indications: the speeches that were being made, the articles that were being written. The leaders of the controversy did not try to hide where they were going. But most Southern Baptists thought this was just another round in that old theological debate that had raged through the years. That's why the establishment crowd got angry and upset with me for being so hard-nosed in my description of what was coming. They thought I was making the thing worse by the rhetoric I was using to describe the nature of the opposition.

Who are some of the people who expressed this to you?

Albert McClellan, Porter Routh, and some of the other seminary presidents. They would discuss it when we met as seminary presidents and tell me I was "seeing ghosts." They thought I was making the controversy bigger than it needed to be. I remember Bob Naylor expressing his opinion that it would blow over. His view was, "Don't give this an importance that it doesn't really have."

Why didn't W. A. Criswell name a Committee on Boards when he was president of the Convention? Did he not know the system?

No, he didn't know the system. I think it's also true that Criswell isn't that political. He would be more likely to depend on speeches, witness, testimony, and eloquent sermons in behalf of his position rather than manipulating the political machinery. So I don't think it would ever have occurred to him to read the constitution and bylaws of the Convention to see how to change things. He would have thought the way to do it was through debate, discussion, prayer, and so on.

Has his position moved to the right during this controversy? Or is he no different than he's always been but is now being more widely quoted and used?

I think Criswell has been pushed to the right, that he's been pushed politically, that he has been pushed within the dynamics and politics of his church, and that he has been pushed by the aging process. I refer to this as the instinct for a "great hurrah" at the end of one's career.

He's been pushed by all of these things until he's become a captive, not of other people, but a captive of the ideas that seem to him to be the best for the future. I think in his best moments that he would not take the extreme position he now takes. But the combatants in a war don't argue that war is good or that everything being done is just and right and good. They argue that the outcome of the war will be on the right side and that the better causes will be supported by winning the war.

I think he really believes that Southern Baptists need to be called back to more direct commitment to using the Bible as the rule of faith and practice. He thinks that if we're going to miss the center of the target, it would be better to miss it on the right side—that the fundamentalist position will do more good than a moderate or liberal position. But I'm reading his mind—and I have no right to do that.

During the SBC meeting in Los Angeles, Criswell told some of the people that he would get rid of Paige Patterson after he got home. He thought Patterson was too combative and too anti-denominational, and so forth. He said this to Herschel Hobbs and maybe Jim Sullivan. They told me about this conversation and said, "Don't worry; Criswell is going to take care of this power structure that roots in the First Baptist Church of Dallas by removing Paige Patterson."

But when he got home, Criswell found that Patterson had the ear of some very wealthy people in the church. The church was in some financial stress, and Criswell couldn't afford to alienate these wealthy members. He had to keep the church from going under in the high-interest-rate period that was in effect in the country at that time. This fiscal situation kept Criswell from keeping his word to his friends in Los Angeles that he would remove Paige Patterson. That's the best anecdote I know to indicate that Criswell was not always totally committed to the techniques and goals of the Pressler-Patterson combine.

Do you feel that the two leaders of this right-wing sentiment are Pressler and Patterson? Patterson, of course, is on the staff of First Baptist Church, Dallas, and is president of the Criswell Bible School.

My evaluation is that they are the brains, the staff of the organization, and it is formidable. They have resources such as computer lists and maps with their lieutenants flagged on the maps, and this kind of thing. My source for this information is a member of First Baptist Church who has told me about what he has seen. This information is about three or four years old, and I don't know that what I am describing is currently true.

You reported that Pressler and Patterson had a five-year plan for gaining control of the Southern Baptist Convention. What was includ-

ed in this plan, and how were they going to implement it?

The five-year time limit was related to some things that Pressler and Patterson had said within their own groups. They thought it would take five years to change the make-up of a board of an agency. It takes a little longer than that, so they miscalculated on this point. They thought that every time a board member came up for election, they could replace him with one of their own hand-picked people. They found that was very difficult to do. They had to let a member of the board of an agency serve two full terms before they could replace him without a controversy.

You will notice there have been controversies whenever they have tried to replace a board member who was eligible to succeed himself or herself. So they miscalculated the time. Legally they could have done it in five years, but politically the dynamics required about eight to ten years.

These people have the organization, the plan, and the ability to stay with their plan. Don't assume that they will quit and go away if you defeat them in one meeting of the Convention. They will stick to their plan and come back on you.

In this controversy we are dealing with something brand new in Southern Baptist life. When the leaders of this controversy say there were political machinations in the Southern Baptist Convention before they came on the scene, they are absolutely right, but previous politics was nothing like their political machinations. No organized group ever before projected a five-year plan, or a long-term plan; they always planned to do it all at the next Convention. Pressler-Patterson planned to take step one and then stay with it. This is what was new.

The change began to occur, I suppose, in 1979 at the Houston Convention when Adrian Rogers was elected?

Yes. Adrian Rogers is the toughest and smartest of the people in their group. He's very astute politically. He has the characteristics and instincts of a political dictator that are not evil in themselves. But the question is, To what are these characteristics and instincts attached? He is an unswerving and uncompromising opponent.

Is his method of administering Bellevue Baptist Church similar to those of the previous two pastors—Dr. Lee and Dr. Pollard?

Absolutely not. He is more the pastor-ruler than either one of them.

The other two were strong pastoral leaders. They were strong pastoral leaders who usually got exactly what they wanted, but they got it in a democratic vote. Adrian Rogers is a man whose psychology is pastor-ruler. This is an old Christian concept of the pastor, bishop, or priest that has come back into vogue in this current controversy within the Southern Baptist Convention. This is true of many of the new and younger pastors who are moving into strong church situations. The atmosphere is that you either accept the pastor's decisions or you move on to join another church.

Jaroy Weber was president of the Convention in the mid-1970s. Then James Sullivan and Jimmy Allen were elected before Adrian Rogers assumed the presidency. Was Weber a part of this takeover group?

I don't think so. I've spent time with Jaroy Weber in vacation settings. I don't believe we could have been together that long without his communicating something about the controversy if he had been a party to it.

Warren Hultgren was very close to Weber, and Hultgren and I have been good friends. We traveled together in various parts of the world in the kind of context in which you get to know what makes people tick. I just don't believe Weber would have been a party to this. He would have been like R. G. Lee, willing to argue for a more conservative theological posture for agencies, seminaries, colleges, and so on. But trying to change the political power structure of the Convention would have been off limits to him, in my judgment.

NEW GROUP IN POWER

So the first time this group really achieved power was in the election of Adrian Rogers as Convention president in 1979?

Yes, and we need to point out that they tried in Norfolk in 1976. Adrian was supposed to have been nominated in Norfolk. He probably would have been elected then if Jimmy Sullivan hadn't agreed to be the candidate. I was not a party to any of that, although I was very much concerned with it. I wasn't involved in choosing Sullivan, but there was an effort of "establishment types" to find a viable candidate to prevent Adrian Rogers from being elected in Norfolk.

Could Rogers have been elected in Norfolk? Did he have the votes?

No, and he knew it. That's why he withdrew from the race at the last minute. Sullivan had the mood of that Convention and the support of that Convention. It swung to Sullivan on the argument that Rogers had not earned his stripes as a Southern Baptist. He isn't really a Southern Baptist; he's more an independent Baptist in his church life and style than he is a Southern Baptist. There were all kinds of arguments and evidence about that—evidence that, incidentally, was politically motivated. Therefore, I'm not saying this was absolutely convincing evidence.

But Rogers would have lost in Norfolk to Jimmy Sullivan. Sullivan was a very popular individual who was beloved and trusted by Southern Baptists. So even as an agency executive, which was a pretty big liability for him, he would have been overwhelmingly elected in Norfolk.

James Sullivan served only one year, and then Jimmy Allen was nominated in 1977. Was there an attempt to get a conservative candidate elected that year?

No, I think not. Allen got in the running very early, he was a popular candidate, and he had good credentials. He was viewed as a very conservative evangelistic pastor who was popular in the Texas convention. So I think that kept the takeover group from running anybody at that time. But when Allen finished his two-year term, from there on there was no good candidate ever proposed against Adrian Rogers in Houston.

Bob Naylor was nominated, but that decision was made within forty-eight hours of the actual election. So there wasn't even time to announce who was going to be nominated to run against Adrian Rogers. Naylor had refused to run up until the very last minute. As I recall, there were efforts to get Baker James Cauthen to run, but he would not agree to be nominated.

There was some claim that the takeover group bused people into Houston to vote for Convention president. How do you respond to that charge?

It's always impossible to prove charges like that—some of which you know are true but can't prove because the Convention didn't have the organization to verify this kind of thing. It was clear that there was an unusually big influx of people for the presidential election in Houston, and that is the proof that I would accept as valid. This is not the way it usually happened up until that time.

Adrian Rogers served as president for only one year. Do you see that as significant?

I think it's possible that Adrian Rogers didn't care that much about being president of the Convention. If it was a conscious political device, it was smart because the opposition was set for him to serve two years. When he dropped out at the last minute at the end of one year, they couldn't generate the support for any alternative.

SBC PRESIDENTIAL RACE—1982

When the Convention met in New Orleans, you ran against James Draper from Texas. Would you relate some of the circumstances around that?

I met from time to time with the people who were opposing the takeover movement. I was not a part of it, but they knew my sympathy was with them. I was asked in April if I would agree to be nominated. I was asked by Ed Perry, who was pastor of the church of which I was a member. I told him, "I don't want to be asked that question. I have done everything the denomination has ever asked me to do, and I don't want to start refusing now. So just don't ask me to run; then I won't have to refuse."

I left the country to go to the Soviet Union and on to Bulgaria and other places. I ended up in the Baptist convention in Italy, which is down on the coast at San Severa where they have a retreat area something like Ridgecrest. I had been there and spoken to the executive committee and the convention. At the point in their convention when they do not allow non-Italians to be present, I asked Brother Bensi, their leader, why I got to be there. His answer was, "You are one of us; we elected you." This was his way of saying they felt they owned the Baptist World Alliance, and therefore I wasn't a North American or anything else. I was a part of them, and therefore I could be there.

After I left the Italian convention, I went back to Rome, and we were visiting with the Ruchtis, SBC missionaries in Rome. The Ruchtis had a big dinner party for us. John Wilkes's wife was a guest at the dinner party. John Wilkes, the European press secretary for Baptists, was supposed to have been down at San Severa covering the Italian convention for the European news and for Baptist Press. Instead, he crashed the dinner party because he had heard I would be at the party.

At the dinner table that night Wilkes said something to me about running for president of the Southern Baptist Convention. I laughed and made fun of it and then he became serious. He said, "No, you're going to be nominated." And I responded, "You've got to be kidding; there's no way I can run for president of the Convention." He didn't have the documents, but he had seen the Baptist Press releases at his home in Zurich, so he began to quote them to me as best he could.

I managed by great effort to retain control and not let my temper explode. I just kept saying to him, "I don't know anything about it." I hadn't talked to anybody in the United States about a nomination for the SBC presidency. After I got home, I called the guilty group together and fussed at them vehemently about deciding to nominate me without getting me to make a commitment.

My reason for not becoming a candidate was very simple: I was president of the BWA, and I did not want this SBC controversy transposed into the BWA. Besides that, I was going as hard as I could go. I felt I was already pushing the limits of my health. I didn't need another job. There was also the issue of my wife's health. She was absolutely, vehemently opposed to my running for the presidency of the Southern Baptist Convention.

I finally agreed to let the group nominate me because one of them said, "We want to nominate you because we need a candidate with name and position recognition and we couldn't get anybody else to run. Besides that, we need somebody to run who is foolish enough to do it when he knows he cannot get elected." I replied, "That's the most persuasive argument you've used because I don't think your candidate can be elected, no matter who he is." The only argument that would get me to agree to run was that I could keep Draper from being elected by a landslide.

Grady Cothen was the person who ended up nominating you, as I recall.

Grady was sympathetic with this group that was pushing my nomination. He was also strongly opposed to the takeover group. He and I were friends from back in his seminary days in New Orleans. They thought he was the best person to nominate me, and I agreed that it would be fine if he was willing to do it.

I remember telling the group, "I don't think it's wise for Grady to nominate me, but that's his decision. Just make it clear that it's not me as a friend asking my friend to do it, so that if he says no, that will not affect our friendship. He must do so in the light of his assessment of all the political implications of his actions." He was president of the Sunday School Board at the time. I thought it would cost him dearly to nominate me.

I knew some of the nasty accusations that would come out because Bill Powell, in his *Southern Baptist Journal,* had been writing about my "drinking problem." That was rooted in a story I told a group of students and state secretaries from the Great Lakes area who were meeting in the lounge of Mullins Hall at Southern Seminary the day I got back from China.

I was in China on a riverboat where the only thing to drink was either strong hot tea containing caffeine or beer. I had a heart condition that prevented me from drinking anything with caffeine. Of the two choices, the less sinful thing for me to do was drink the beer, and I tried to drink the beer. This was used against me by the opposition in the presidential election at the New Orleans Convention.

You really didn't think you'd have a chance at winning in New Orleans?

No. I was convinced there was no way to be elected. I would have had a major problem if I had been elected. In fact, I had told John Sullivan, who was also a nominee for the presidency at that time, "John, the ideal solution to this for me is for you and me to be in a run-off for the presidency, and if so, I will withdraw in your favor."

But it turned out I had to be in the run-off against Draper instead. That was the first run-off election we had experienced in the Convention. At least we made the point that the opposition to the takeover group was significant and had to be dealt with. I think Draper got the message that if he didn't want to divide the Convention, he ought to do something to reconcile those who were in the minority.

How do you assess Jimmy Draper and his SBC presidency?

I think Jimmy Draper is trying very hard to be president of all Southern Baptists. But he was more successful at this in his first term than after he was reelected for a second term.

Draper made the suggestion that there were five basic areas around which Southern Baptists needed to align themselves in order to preserve the unity of the denomination. What's your reaction to those?

I don't think anybody disagrees with his four or five points as such, if they were just ideas to which we would give assent. I think he was calling for unity, and I think he was trying to do a good thing. But I know how easy it is when your attention is focused on a good goal to fail to understand how people can twist, misunderstand, and misinterpret your intentions.

I think he made a mistake, but again I want to give him credit for what he's trying to do. I think he's trying to find ways to call Southern Baptists to walk together.

Things were different when Charles Stanley was elected president. He won on the first ballot, and there was no run-off.

Right, and you will notice there has been no effort to deal with the opposition since Stanley's election. This was total victory from their point of view, and it was up to the opposition to decide how to deal with it.

When Stanley's term came, the issues became considerably more bitter, and the attendance at the meetings of the Convention grew dramatically. What was going on?

Stanley didn't know the first thing about the Southern Baptist Convention, and he still doesn't. He doesn't feel love and loyalty to the fellowship as many of us do. He is an independent operator who has great gifts, and he goes his own way. He has refused to do very much in his second term. He is just holding the title of president and is the channel through which the organization, a la Paige Patterson, will channel decisions and appointments.

I think the situation has changed immensely now, and the lines are very much hardened. The Convention in Dallas demonstrated that the 55/45 percent vote split is going to stay about that way until some fluke comes along.

What was your opinion of the Kansas City Convention, when Stanley was up for election?

Kansas City literally made me sick because of the way that Convention operated. That's when I decided that the war had been lost. I noticed such things as the clear hand signals to the bused-in messengers. They didn't know enough to know how to vote on the issues, but they were voting en masse as somebody turned "thumbs up" or "thumbs down" to show them how to vote. The platforms were patrolled by guards, who kept anybody not acceptable to the establishment from getting on the platform. Then certain resolutions were adopted, including the reversal of historic Southern Baptist statements that had been reiterated for years—the church-state issues particularly.

I was also sickened by the mood of the Convention—the angry, nasty, ugly mood that dominated all of the decision-making. Depending on who the speaker was, he couldn't say anything right if he was from the wrong political background. On the other hand, he couldn't say anything stupid or obnoxious if he was from the right political background.

Grady Cothen ran as one of the candidates.

Yes, and Grady was in exactly the same position I was in. There wasn't any way he was going to win. By the way, I had told him, "If you have reason for running when you can't win, run." But then Stanley appeared to be such a ridiculously weak candidate for the presidency of the Southern Baptist Convention that optimism rose too high. If there was ever any demonstration of the power of the organization to put whomever they chose into office, it was at that Convention. That was why I thought to myself, "My word, there's no way to defeat the organization if it can elect this man."

I'm not underestimating Stanley. In his own environment, doing his own thing, he is a strong man and is probably a very effective Christian witness. But Stanley operating as the president of the Southern Baptist Convention is a fraud and a disgrace. He doesn't know anything; he doesn't care anything; he doesn't plan to do anything except be the empty channel through which the machine carries out its will within the Convention.

THE PEACE COMMITTEE

At the 1985 Convention a committee was established to resolve the controversy. What do you recall about this process?

There was a lot of negotiating about who was going to be on the Peace Committee, and the earliest committee would have been totally unacceptable from my point of view. It would have been a committee to accept the surrender of the opposition, but gradually they did balance the committee out.

Who was involved in those negotiations?

Russell Dilday and Roy Honeycutt, particularly, were the hard-nosed people who would not accept the Peace Committee solution without changes in the personnel of this committee. What I'm probably revealing is my sources of information rather than giving you a complete list of the people who were involved. The original proposal set up the generals from the Paige Patterson side and put some corporals and privates from the other side on the committee.

What kinds of options does the Peace Committee have? What are they negotiating?

What compromises can the establishment side give that would resolve the controversy? In my last conversation with a member of the Peace Committee on that subject, I ended by saying, "I have talked with you in dead seriousness and tried hard to help you find what could be offered as compromise and solution. I don't think the other side—the Paige Patterson side—will accept any compromises that are offered because I don't think they are convinced they have to. They have won the war and they think there is no use in giving away victory at the peace table."

The compromises are such things as to accept one or two seminaries of the Paige Patterson side into the Southern Baptist Convention and give it Cooperative Program support. That would mean Mid-America, at least, and perhaps Criswell Bible Institute. That's one of the compromises. Another is to accept negative designations for the Cooperative Program; meaning that you can give to the Cooperative Program but designate that no money from your church is to go to a certain agency. That is one of the compromises that could be proposed.

None of these seems to me to be a thing that would stop the battle. My perception is that the Paige Patterson group thinks they have demonstrated in Stanley's election and reelection their ability to control the mechanism for naming the boards of the SBC agencies.

Why do they want to have just two seminaries in their camp when they can control all six? Why should they worry about being able to use negative designations to influence the Foreign Mission Board when they can have 99.9 percent of the directors of the Foreign Mission Board control the whole thing? Why worry about the SBC Executive Committee when they can have an overwhelming majority of their people on the Executive Committee and its subcommittees and make all the funding decisions and every other kind of decision?

I think they sense victory is too close at hand for them to compromise anything. I think the Peace Committee is playing into the hands of the group by stopping the debate, the moratorium, and in effect freezing the status quo. So I don't think the Peace Committee is going to be able to do anything. Now I hope I'm a pessimist, but politically I just don't see any reason for Adrian Rogers to compromise. Judging by his statements to certain members of the Peace Committee, he doesn't plan to compromise. I think he will control the vote of that side in the Peace Committee.

There are supposedly three groups represented on the committee—those sympathetic to the Paige Patterson group, the group sympathetic to the establishment, and then the middle ground people who have no agenda—in other words, the right, the left, and the center. Is that true in the selection of the committee, do you think?

We will have to wait and see how they vote to know whether it's true. You can't put John Sullivan in any of these camps, and there are perhaps others on the committee who are in the same category. Therefore, there probably is a swing vote on the committee.

If the takeover group prevails, who will be on their hit list?

The seminary presidents who have been vocal in opposition to them would be totally unacceptable to this group, although it's incredible that anybody would think a Russell Dilday or a Roy Honeycutt was a liberal. However, Roy is on record with some scholarly discussions of some problems within the Old Testament.

I take it from your conversation that you do not see much of a solution coming out of the Peace Committee?

No, I don't think that any logical analysis makes you optimistic. But there is one additional thing that needs to be factored in. You can't predict what God may do, but it will take God's divine intervention of the miraculous dimension to make it work. So I would continue to hope and pray in that direction.

Can the Peace Committee move in the time frame and speed with which it has been urged? Not many viable options for compromise seem to be available.

This is why I hope the Convention in Atlanta will elect a conservative who is acceptable to everybody. Not because that will end the war, but because that will buy time for the Peace Committee process to mature, and for victory to be awarded to people without necessarily having to destroy the structure of the Southern Baptist Convention to prove their power.

Do you think it's significant that it was only as an afterthought that women were added to that committee?

Very significant, and the decision was related to the vote in Kansas City on the role of women, so it was important that they be added.

So as they were negotiating the names of people, this was something that was added at the end, and, of course, naming Winfred Moore and Charles Stanley as ex-officio was also an attempt to sound like a compromise?

Yes. And these are the kinds of things that are very useful to do. That's why time—anything that would slow down the present situation—would be a sign of hope to me. Winfred Moore's election as president at the forthcoming Convention in Atlanta would not make that much difference in the outcome of this whole controversy, but it would buy time that might let other things occur that could make an immense difference.

We can expect an all-out effort of the Pressler-Patterson group to have their people there for the election in Atlanta. I think they have demonstrated that when they do that they can produce at least 55 percent of the ballots.

Where can people go if they are dissatisfied with this trend within the Southern Baptist Convention?

There is no charismatic leader to lead them, so I don't think the Convention will divide. I think we will see the gradual evolution of society-type funding again. Certain causes will get the support of those who are opposed to this trend. You'll find them sending money to those faith missions they think they can agree with. There aren't many of those available now unless you go to the American Baptist Foreign Mission Society. That would perhaps provide an out for some. I'm not trying to say these are very good. There are no good answers, but I think the need will produce the answers.

I've also heard there are many churches, particularly in the Virginia-North Carolina area, that have petitioned for membership in the American Baptist Convention; have you heard that?

Enough to know that the American Baptists are threatened by it; they are smart enough to know that when Southern Baptists expanded geographically we set in motion a change in the nature of their organ-ization and work. If they take in all of these Southern Baptist churches that might prefer to get out of the Southern Baptist Convention, the American Baptist Convention will be changed in the future.

This, then, is not really very viable for either side?

It will be the solution for perhaps a few hundred churches, but that doesn't solve the problem. A redefining of the Cooperative Program method of funding is going to be essential either way, no matter what happens. That's already a demand item on the agenda that has been established for the future. I don't know how long you can postpone dealing with it, and it may never be resolved in one coherent, rational process. It may just evolve into a solution.

If the Cooperative Program ceases to support or limits its support for certain agencies of the Convention, certain churches will turn around and designate funds to those agencies. Some battles are bound to erupt around this issue somewhere down the road.

This would be returning to the pattern that has emerged in the American Baptist convention, where the seminaries are recognized and authorized by the denomination, but they do their own fund-rais-ing.

That's the pattern that would evolve. And the fact that the seminar-ies and the other agencies are already out raising funds means they know who their constituents are and they have some way of guessing at the amount of fiscal support they could generate. But don't hear me saying that I'm proposing something that is likely to happen. It's going to take more provocation than is now on the horizon to force the agen-cies to do this.

Look into your crystal ball and tell us what you foresee for the future.

I can foresee several possible scenarios. One is that the Pressler-Patterson faction wins total control of the Convention, stays together, and carries out the vision of a Judge Pressler or a Paige Patterson and implements it. That, to me, is roughly the same as talking about the world after atomic warfare. I hope that is not to be the future. [Later addition: But it was!—DKM)

A second scenario is that this group has total victory and the better spirits within the group begin to come to the surface and say, "Now it's time for us to act as responsible Christians who will do the right things. We will not excommunicate all who disagree with us; we will try to convert them."

Another scenario is that God will intervene in some miraculous fashion, and the Peace Committee does succeed, and we get a dramatic new sense of direction in the Southern Baptist Convention.

A fourth scenario is for the establishment side to say, "We admit we've lost the political battle. We're disbanding our troops; we're going to go to the next Convention and vote for the best candidate, whoever he is, but somebody else must find him; we're not going to push any candidate. And then they would settle in, just as the Japanese did after World War II, to rebuild a future in peace time by moving away from the war scene as quickly as possible.

The fourth scenario is the most optimistic one I have because it's the only one that is in the control of the establishment side. That's the only thing they can do—declare that the Pressler-Patterson group has won the victory and then settle in quietly to win the peace. But the peace is not to be won by political maneuvering; it would have to be won by force of character and spiritual power. [Later addition: The Moderates did not withdraw from the SBC but kept the battle going by organizing their own group. I helped them.—DKM]

It does not seem that the Pressler-Patterson group has been as successful at capturing state conventions as they have been in capturing the Southern Baptist Convention. What does this mean?

This verifies what some of us have been trying to say for a long time: We are dealing with a political organization, and that political organization focuses on the Southern Baptist Convention. It is successful in that arena. But without that same political structure and process, it doesn't work—the ideological warfare doesn't guarantee victory. So we have a strange situation in which the parts—the state conventions—function one way, and the whole—the Southern Baptist Convention—functions a different way. That's the reason I would be optimistic about winning the peace.

Since the Pressler-Patterson group cannot control the state conventions, it's possible they would not always be successful in their choice of Committee on Boards members. The state convention people could say these people do not represent their viewpoints.

It's hard to keep the battle mentality going when nobody is fighting against you. And their people are bound to be as tired of the battle as the folks on the other side are. I'm not talking about leadership now; I'm talking about the rank and file. The rank-and-file Southern Baptists would love to say, "A plague on both your houses; why don't you all go off somewhere and let us get on about the Lord's business." That would be the sort of 90 percent vote of Southern Baptists if they could figure some way to have that option. But as long as the superpowers keep battling, the common folks don't have that option.

And they become embroiled in a battle they don't want?

That's right. They don't want the battle, but they have to choose sides. And since the perception is that it's those who believe the Bible *most* against those who believe the Bible *least,* most Southern Baptists will side with those who "believe the Bible most." Southern Baptists will never do anything that would raise a question about their commitment to the Bible as the authoritative, inspired revelation of God.

My personal position is one of anguish that we're in the controversy. One of my recurrent prayers is that God will manifest his presence and power in whatever way he chooses to do. I am not sure that God would answer my prayer the way I would want it answered, but I think that is the hope that I have for the Southern Baptist Convention.

The Southern Baptist Convention is important to the degree that it is an instrument of what God is doing in the world. I think it's important—but I don't think it is absolutely necessary—for God to have us as his instruments. What I fear is that Southern Baptists may be taking the path that other religious bodies have taken. They ended up splintering and disintegrating, not in a sudden division, but in a gradual fraying until the power to be useful was gone.

COUNTERPROPOSAL TO FUNDAMENTALIST TAKEOVER

This is a copy of my first public move to counter the SBC "takeover." I was a director of *Baptists Today* at the time.

June 23, 1988
Mr. Jack Harwell, Editor
SBC Today
Atlanta, Georgia

Dear Jack,

In the light of years of working with and promoting the SBC Cooperative Program, I want to put in print the best way to give moderates a means of acting without doing permanent damage to the Southern Baptist Convention. But also, a way to change or at least influence the course of the SBC agencies appears important.

Moderates have, in my judgment, proven that they cannot in the foreseeable future win an election in the SBC. The other side has announced and exemplified their intention to mold the SBC and its agencies in their image. That is simply unacceptable for any old style Southern Baptist—even those of us who have lived and worked for decades with fundamentalists. The *Religious Herald* once called me "the leader of biblical fundamentalism in the Southern Baptist Convention." So much for associating with fundamentalists! What we now have is not theological fundamentalism but Fighting Frank Norris Fundamentalism.

What a pity to see the successor of Frank Norris in First Church Dallas—ugly spirit, bad taste and all! But without Norris's sense of humor. I weep. It must be our old age. That is my excuse. We have, indeed, returned to the bad old days. So we return to the desert, and Moses must lead us out one more time. Maybe a younger Joshua is available.

Enclosed is a copy of what I would say to him. It distills my experience of fifty years since I graduated from the seminary. My fear is that without intimate knowledge of the road we have traveled, we will repeat yesterday's stupidities—mine and Criswell's and Routh's and Newton's and Barton's and Alldredge's. Worse, we may abandon permanently our heritage and the resources it has created. So let us not divide and go with the Annuity Board, but let us step off to the side a little way and walk as close to all the SBC agencies as we can. Maybe what we cannot do with ballots; we can do with our gifts. It is worth a try, and I think that road is open-ended way down the future.

So I write to you as a leader who has been true to your convictions, and earned the right to speak up. If what I propose has any merit, combine it with all you know and lead us out of this wilderness; learn from the ten-to-two report of the spies—83.3 percent majority vote to stay in the wilderness.

I want to provide only constructive help. No reply desired.

Cordially yours,

Duke K. McCall

A CALL FOR ACTION BY "MODERATES"

Here is a copy of a June 1990 proposal I made to the leaders of the moderates:

DREAM IT AGAIN!
Duke K. McCall
Past Executive Secretary, SBC Executive Committee

Baptists united under the banner of the Great Commission to reach a lost world for Christ—that was the dream in Augusta, Georgia, in 1845 that brought Southern Baptists together. Together we have done far more for Christ our Lord than our churches could have done alone.

The world is still lost. God still wants a chorus; not just solos from his people. Jesus prayed His Father "that they all may be one . . . that the world may believe that You sent Me" (John 17:20–23).

Atlanta, Georgia, August 23–25, 1990, is not too far from Augusta in 1845 for us to DREAM THE SOUTHERN BAPTIST DREAM AGAIN—not a new convention but new ways for our diversity to flow together as the Holy Spirit leads.

No church needs to leave the Southern Baptist Convention! I know all the complaints. I belong to the 40 percent minority too. But I still want to work with Southern Baptists and minister through my state Baptist convention.

So I have dreamed of a way for "Moderate" Southern Baptists to keep on working together—supporting the missionaries and professors we all appointed—and following as God guides us. The instrument is the BAPTIST COOPERATIVE MISSIONS PROGRAM, Inc. in Atlanta that will use our Cooperative gifts forwarded from each state Baptist convention the way we vote in our churches.

Our Cooperative Program gifts beyond the Baptist state convention will go through Atlanta instead of Nashville, but the SBC agencies like the Foreign Mission Board and other causes such as the Joint Committee on Public Affairs will be supported by cooperating "Moderates." Whether our vote is important or not, we can use our Christian influence—wrapped in our stewardship.

I do not belong to Baptists Committed or the Southern Baptist Alliance, but I urge all "Moderates" to join Daniel Vestal in the "open" meeting he has called in Atlanta. Register to be there in person or in prayer. My proposal is one option. You may have a better one.

Let us "Moderates" stay together in our Christian witness, in the Southern Baptist Convention if conscience permits—and the majority allows. We ask only for space, not to fight against, but to bear witness to our convictions. Now it is time to dream that uniting dream again—in partial fulfillment of Jesus' prayer.

A copy of my proposal to the Atlanta conference follows. Edit, revise, replace it with what you think God would have us do. Alas, I will be in China at the time the Atlanta meeting is called—so my fellow Christians will have to form the dream.

A COOPERATIVE PROGRAM FOR "MODERATES"
THE PROBLEM

There are many issues: biblical inspiration, separation of church and state, abortion, role of women in ministry, priesthood of believers, authority of the pastor, purging of moderates from all positions of leadership, firing or forced resignations from seminaries and Baptist Press, etc. Issues are weighted differently by individual "moderates" with some dissent at specific points. Every issue is important, but no single issue will unite all of the Moderates *across the SBC territory* to the point of action. (See Note #1)

After twelve years of effort, the Fundamentalists have a solid 53–58 percent majority of the votes and Moderates have 42–47 percent. That gives Fundamentalists 100 percent *control* and Moderates have none—and almost no influence. This has continued long enough for the Frank Norris-type Fundamentalists to get working control of the boards of all the SBC agencies and organizations. They will have control of the agency staffs within the next five years.

Having lost a billion dollars worth of assets, and having no programs administered by compatible people, what will moderate churches support? They are currently mounting their horses and riding off in all directions! A uniting procedure is required.

PRINCIPLE

The basic principle to use is *the right of every donor to direct his/her stewardship.* All true Baptists can act on this principle. The

Christian spirit requires action in concert with fellow Christians to seek to express the mind of Christ. The Great Commission belongs to all of us.

WHAT TO DO

Continue to use the Cooperative Program to support state convention causes and some SBC agencies. But cut a channel around the Fundamentalist-controlled SBC Executive Committee in Nashville, Tennessee. (See Note #2)

Incorporate the Baptist Cooperative Missions Program, Inc. in Georgia, the original site of the Southern Baptist Convention, 1845. (See Note #3) Arrange for the trust department of a major bank in Atlanta to receive Cooperative Program funds *from* any state convention (after the state portion is taken out) and disburse them to the agencies or organizations according to agreed percentages. (I will have such a Georgia corporation ready for use, if wanted.)

A church needs to take only one action different from the past. Ask the state convention office to send the portion of the gifts of the church that would have gone to Nashville, Tennessee, instead to Baptist Cooperative Program, Atlanta, Georgia. (See Note #4)

Funds received by the bank in Atlanta would be sent at least monthly to the SBC agencies or other causes as instructed by the contributing churches, whose vote would reflect the amount contributed by each church.

To give each church its proper share in directing the use of the funds, each one-hundred dollar donation through Baptist Cooperative Missions Program, Inc. would represent one vote. Ballots would be distributed to the churches with the correct number of votes (shares) encoded; so a vote with that ballot would equal the voting power of that church. Voting in a meeting would be similar to a stockholders meeting. As in the SBC now, a machine would read and count the ballots.

A church in its business meeting (lay participation) could determine how to vote its shares in the Baptist Cooperative Missions Program, Inc., or it could send uninstructed delegates to the meeting, or it could vote by mail or by proxy. One person or two dozen people could represent and cast the ballot for the church—the church would control. (This prevents stacking the ballot or busing in children to vote or non-contributors holding leading positions as has been common recently in the SBC.)

During the remainder of 1990 all Cooperative Program funds received would be distributed on the percentage in use right now. (See page 31, 1989 *Southern Baptist Convention Annual.*) A meeting of representatives of cooperating churches would be held to determine distribution of 1991 undesignated receipts. (See note #5)

Lottie Moon Offering funds would be transmitted to the Foreign Mission Board as designated. Initially, it would be best for other designations to be made through state convention offices that have experienced personnel to handle them.

However, because the Baptist Joint Committee on Public Affairs and the Baptist World Alliance are not included in the percentage budget, funds could be designated to them, and they would receive a part of the 2.34 percent allocated by the SBC to the Convention Operating Budget—to reflect the dollar amounts promised in the 1989–90 SBC allocation. Thus this 2.34 percent would be distributed as follows:

Baptist Joint Committee on Public Affairs	.3 percent
Baptist World Alliance	.3 percent
Baptist Cooperative Missions Program, Inc.	
Expense and Reserves	1.74 percent
Total	**2.34 percent**

THIS PROPOSAL

This mechanism for working together is under review and subject to revision by some of the best minds among Baptists. No individual will be its author. No individual owns it or the corporate structure that is available. The directors of Baptist Cooperative Missions Program, Inc. will turn that corporate shell over to the chosen representatives of the churches immediately without strings. It is offered publicly as a gift to any group of moderates who will use it, or it will be dismantled if a better mechanism is found.

May God guide us all in spirit and action to the end that His kingdom may come, His will be done on earth as it is in heaven!

NOTES AND OPINIONS

Note #1: The Fighting Fundamentalists forced the news media to use the terminology "Conservatives" for themselves and call the rest of us "Moderates." I have used the term "Moderate" for convenience only. We are mostly theological Conservatives, but we proudly include some intelligent Fundamentalists. We all believe that the Bible is the God-given rule of faith and practice. A new inclusive designation for all "Moderates" is needed.

Note #2: Churches making their Cooperative Program gifts as here proposed would continue to meet the current requirements for membership in the Southern Baptist Convention. Because these are subject to change, a church may wish to send at least $250.00 to some SBC agency—perhaps send the Lottie Moon Offering directly to the Foreign Mission Board or the SBC Executive Committee in Nashville, Tennessee. Thus when the Southern Baptist Convention returns to normal operations (meaning without political party organizations and creedal requirements), the closing of all breaches would be relatively simple.

Note #3: The use of a version of "Cooperative Program" is essential to enable many churches to act. Churches, associations, state conventions, and the SBC have developed it as a way of working together for world evangelism and ministry, especially in foreign missions. No wise pastor should ask his church to stop giving to missions, but it should not be hard to get people to vote to send their money to the version of the Cooperative Program that their church has a voice in directing. Their desires being completely ignored by the SBC elected leadership, all that is left for influence on our Baptist agencies is stewardship. A new instrument for uniting almost half of us is needed.

Note #4: It is important to support the state conventions that thus far have fought off the Fighting Fundamentalists. It is important that state convention structures be safe-guarded. Indeed, redirecting the national Cooperative Program should provide an argument for state conventions to reject one-party control. State personnel and agencies are the next target of the Fighting Fundamentalists. Let us not be moderate in our support of stable state conventions.

If any state convention office finds problems in sending funds to the new national Baptist Cooperative Program, a church could send all cooperative program funds to the Atlanta bank trust department *first* for return of the state portion from there. This probably will not be necessary.

Note #5: This proposal postpones important changes until a mechanism for the donors to make them is in place. That avoids debate now about what, if any, changes should be made in the objects funded. It is hard not to advocate now the elimination of certain objects and the inclusion of others. But that is left to the vote of the participating churches. At this time not all members of many Moderate churches are aware of the drastic redirection of the SBC. That will come with the elimination of Moderate candidates for the mission fields and a few seminary dismissals, and the end of freedom of the press for Baptist Press.

Time is needed for churches to redirect the national and world portion of their Cooperative Program and qualify to vote on the future shape of their united efforts. Then they will be free to make choices in the light of current situations.

It does seem wise and right not to abandon too quickly agencies staffed by dedicated missionaries and professors and others who for at least the near future will require support from "Moderates." The 100 percent change in control of the agencies will not immediately alter the character of every agency. Perhaps continued support from Moderates can slow the process, but annual review by the churches will be possible. Future decisions are open!

The Baptist Joint Committee on Public Affairs and the Baptist World Alliance should be included adequately in the percentage budget in 1991. There may be other good organizations to include.

One of the earliest needs of a new enterprise is reserves for start-up funds for new efforts and emergencies.

CHARTER OF THE COOPERATIVE BAPTIST MISSIONS PROGRAM

Below is the proposed charter for the Baptist Cooperative Missions Program, Inc. that was sent to former Georgia Governor Carl Sanders as the basis of a Georgia charter for the corporation that received more than

$4 million in the first year of its operation. Thus a channel was cut for moderates to support the SBC agencies in which they had confidence.

REVISED COPY

The Baptist Cooperative Missions Program

A Georgia Corporation

In affirmation of the Christian unity and freedom of those who believe in Jesus Christ as Savior and Lord, the Baptist Cooperative Missions Program, Inc. is chartered:

For the purpose of eliciting, combining and directing the energies of Baptist churches and individuals for the propagation of the gospel throughout the world through Christian missions, Christian education, Christian social services and benevolent enterprises, as they deem proper and advisable.

It shall provide means for Baptists to support any Southern Baptist Convention agencies and/or other appropriate organizations. It shall function to the best of its ability in friendly cooperation and support of Baptist associations, conventions (state and national), the Baptist World Alliance, and other Christian enterprises.

A basic principle of the organization is that churches and individual donors have a right to give direction to their Christian stewardship. Such direction shall be in approximate proportion to the size of their gifts.

Representatives of supporting churches may give instructions to the directors of the corporation. The directors shall adopt such bylaws as are needed to direct its actions. They shall seek divine guidance in the conduct of its affairs and be guided by the teachings of the Bible and the leadership of the Holy Spirit.

WHAT WE DID

Governor Sanders declined to do this legal work *pro bono* because it would involve his partners in a Baptist fuss. I then asked him to accept me as a client who would pay for the work. He did and I did.

The effort to find directors for this new corporation hit a wall. I turned to all the bright young pastors who had produced fiery speeches and articles about the SBC situation. They uniformly proposed a layman in their churches as a director. I assumed a layman smart enough to be useful would be smart enough to see the risks and problems in the venture; so I did not contact them. Originally I turned to my two lawyer sons as directors to get the corporation off the ground.

Dr. Jimmy Allen and the Texas "Baptists Committed" organization became the source for a list of strong directors. To this list I added Dr. Grady Cothen, who agreed to serve as chairman if I would do most of the work as vice chairman.

We shared equally in the effort. For example: I paid the lawyers and he paid for the post office box to give us an address. The opposition shot at him as president of the new SBC alternative, and I held his hand over the telephone.

We never thought of ourselves as anything but loyal Southern Baptists using our Baptist freedom.

Dr. Daniel Vestal, in a letter dated July 18, 1990, stated our position: "Many of us do not want to leave the denomination, but neither do we want to continue to fund the institutions in ways that violate our conscience and the principles that inform our conscience."

BOARD OF BAPTIST COOPERATIVE MISSIONS PROGRAM

The officers and board members who launched the Baptist Cooperative Missions Program were:

Grady Cothen, chairman, living in Coral Springs, Florida, at that time

Duke McCall, vice chairman, Highlands, North Carolina

Mrs. Frances Prince, secretary, then commissioner, Tennessee Department of Education, Nashville, Tennessee

Mrs. Hettie Johnson, treasurer, Decatur, Georgia

John Baugh, Sysco Corporation, Houston, Texas

Raymond Boswell, Boswell Insurance, Shreveport, Louisiana

Lavonn Brown, pastor, Norman, Oklahoma

Harold Cole, former executive secretary, South Carolina Baptist Convention

Mrs. Carolyn Weatherford Crumpler, former executive secretary, Woman's Missionary Union, Cincinnati, Ohio

Drew Gunnells, pastor, Mobile, Alabama

Mrs. Ophelia Humphrey, Amarillo, Texas

Randall Lolley, pastor, Greensboro, North Carolina
Mrs. Esther McCall, Kansas City, Missouri
John McCall, attorney, Louisville, Kentucky
Bill Poe, Charlotte, North Carolina
Gene Triggs, Yazoo City, Mississippi
Dan Vestal, pastor, Atlanta, Georgia
Brooks Wicker, Jacksonville, Florida
Each of these was selected because of his or her leadership in Southern Baptist life.

Duke McCall Jr. dropped off the organizing board in favor of his brother John McCall, who had served as a member of the SBC Executive Committee. Duke McCall Jr. lives in Greenville, South Carolina, near my summer home. He was, therefore, in a position to be my legal counsel in the very beginning of plans for a new corporation because I was spending my summers in Highlands, North Carolina, only eighty miles away.

HETTIE JOHNSON, OFFICE MANAGER

Grady Cothen and I discovered Hettie Johnson through her pastor in Decatur, Georgia. She had been the director of business and personnel of the SBC Home Mission Board for twelve years. She knew Baptist life. She knew most SBC leaders. She had great administrative skills. She was a volunteer.

When named the office manager and treasurer of Baptist Cooperative Missions, she could not even get reimbursed for small out-of-pocket expense. All we gave her to begin with was P.O. Box 450329, Atlanta, Georgia 30345-0329.

She had to find an office. She found one with *SBC Today,* later named *Baptists Today,* near her home in Decatur, Georgia. It was not much, but the rent was free in the beginning. She had to purchase office equipment and open a bank account at First National Bank. A designated gift for $500 enabled her to do all that. The gift came from Dr. and Mrs. Orville W. Taylor of Clearwater Beach, Florida.

FINANCIAL SUPPORT FOR BCMP

Without any organized effort or solicitation, $250,000 was sent through the Atlanta office in the last three months of 1990. By March 1991, I predicted $4 million would flow through this new mission program during that year. I felt that was an optimistic projection, but it proved to be accurate.

Unless otherwise designated by the donor, receipts of the Baptist Cooperative Missions Program were divided and sent to the agencies as follows:

Foreign Mission Board	50.00 %
Home Mission Board	19.54 %
Annuity Board	.78 %
Golden Gate Seminary	2.07 %
Midwestern Seminary	1.76 %
New Orleans Seminary	3.47 %
Southern Seminary	4.33 %
Southeastern Seminary	2.99 %
Southwestern Seminary	5.85 %
Southern Baptist Foundation	.19 %
Baptist Brotherhood	.72 %
Education Commission	.36 %
Historical Commission	.37 %
Radio/TV Commission	4.00 %
Stewardship Commission	.36 %
Joint Committee on Public Affairs	.67 %
Baptist World Alliance	.67 %
Baptist Cooperative Missions Program	1.65 %
TOTAL	100.00%

Only the last two items were added to the SBC Executive Committee distributions for the year. These replaced the allocation to the SBC Executive Committee itself.

TRANSFER OF BCMP TO THE BAPTIST FELLOWSHIP

From the beginning in 1990, it was made clear that the Baptist Cooperative Missions Program would not stand alone. It would fit in and serve any general Baptist organization created by Moderates. Indeed, its corporate structure was offered, subject to amendment by the new body, as a corporate structure ready for use.

At the first meeting of the Baptist Fellowship board, the BCMP directors offered to resign after electing the finance committee of the Fellowship as their successors.

Clarification of the legal niceties was required to assure the Fellowship that only by some such procedure could the BCMP transfer its tax-exempt status and resources to another body. Thus the brief life of the Baptist Cooperative Missions Board was merged into the Cooperative Baptist Fellowship, giving to it support and funding and programs. The programs and objects to be supported were quickly redefined as was intended.

The Baptist Fellowship would have come into being without the Baptist Cooperative Missions Program. In the beginning no one could have predicted the future shape of the movement of a million Southern Baptists away from the conservative takeover of the Convention. Even the eagerness of the conservative leadership not only to disfranchise their critics but also to separate them from the Convention in all ways was unpredictable.

A million Baptists would have been left to wander in the wilderness and squander their stewardship without some structure. The Baptist Cooperative Missions Program rushed to provide such structure. The Baptist Fellowship is a more comprehensive umbrella under which Baptists can gather and work together to serve the kingdom of God.

All of us must end by saying, "Nevertheless, not my will but Thy will be done!" That necessarily includes Jesus' prayer for the unity of his disciples found in John 17:20–21: "I pray also for those who will believe in me through their message, that all of them may be one . . . that the world may believe that You have sent me."

CHAPTER 14

Friends Along the Way

Tell about some of the friends you made and the people you dealt with during your denominational career. Were you involved at all with Dr. J. B. Lawrence of the Home Mission Board?

J. B. LAWRENCE

I was very much involved with him—both with him and against him—in certain circumstances across the years. He was dedicated to the welfare of the Home Mission Board and its work. He believed in this agency with all of his heart and could not understand why everybody else didn't see its importance. If we didn't win America, he reasoned, we couldn't send missionaries to the rest of the world.

So his perception was that the Home Mission Board was the most important thing that Southern Baptists were supporting. He was so committed to his enterprise that he couldn't see that in order to have missionaries we had to have strong churches, and the Sunday School Board's programs were important for all the mission outreach.

Dr. Lawrence came to the Home Mission Board following the Carnes defalcation. Was he perhaps so concerned about getting the agency out of debt that he really never saw the opportunity of outreach? Some people think debt reduction was so much a part of his psyche that he couldn't get past that.

That's a good way to say it. He arrived at the Home Mission Board in a crisis. He was somewhat defensive on behalf of his agency, feeling that it was under assault and suspicion. His perception of the problems with the Carnes defalcation really did that to him. By the time I knew him, the debts had been paid, but his defensiveness on behalf of his agency remained.

COURTS REDFORD

How would you describe Courts Redford of the Home Mission Board?

Courts Redford was a schoolman, a sort of educational administrator type. He came at the whole home mission enterprise, it seemed to me, from an institutional approach. He didn't come up with anything that was new and exciting. I saw him as an effective business-as-usual administrator. Even with the addition of new territories, the Home Mission Board stayed with its tried-and-proven formula. However, race relations was an exception. In a critical time, Redford was a genuine denominational statesman. I must not overlook his catalyst role in race relations for Southern Baptists.

FOREIGN MISSION BOARD LEADERS

Describe the Foreign Mission Board leaders whom you knew in the 1950s era, before Dr. Rankin became executive secretary?

Charles E. Maddry was an impressive fellow and an able leader, but I never thought of him as a great world statesman. I thought of him as the leader of this agency with its headquarters in Richmond. But it was different with Theron Rankin. I thought of him as a missionary statesman, a man with a world vision that didn't start outside the borders of the United States—it started right where he was and then reached around the world.

Dr. Rankin came back to the United States in 1944 as one of those missionaries repatriated and then, not long after, went to be the executive secretary of the Foreign Mission Board. So my years at the Executive Committee spanned very closely the years he served at the board.

What sort of a man was he?

He was a teacher—a professor almost—rather than an evangelist. But he was eloquent, and he could be a fiery speaker. He was always the teacher, teaching you about your responsibilities in the world.

What was your impression of Baker James Cauthen of the Foreign Mission Board?

Baker James Cauthen was a charismatic missionary. He could wave the flag of missions so effectively that he would rally people who weren't particularly in favor of missions. He was an eloquent speaker, and his fervor communicated. As a great motivator, he kept Southern Baptists focused on the mission enterprise.

During Dr. Cauthen's administration, the foreign mission enterprise was growing dramatically. He was always a missionary at heart, and he saw the task from the perspective of a missionary on the field. The administrative office in Richmond served as a support service for the missionaries. Many major decisions were pushed out to the personnel on the field. He thought they were the best authority for problem-solving.

My impression was that Dr. Cauthen had no love for sitting behind a desk in Richmond. He did that because it had to be done to support the foreign missions effort.

T. L. HOLCOMB

Tell about T. L. Holcomb of the Sunday School Board.

He was the epitome of the denominational executive of the times—the pastor who was drafted into an administrative role and told to get on-the-job training for the task he faced. That's the kind of people we chose in those days for our specialized denominational jobs. He was a good leader, but he was not a highly knowledgeable educator in terms of religious education. He learned administration as he went along, and he expanded his abilities every step of the way. He was a small, feisty fellow—quick to respond to anything.

I've heard that he was always ready to fight, and sometimes seemed to do so when it was not necessary.

Yes, I think we all felt that. And we all fought with him some of the time. Sometimes when we didn't mean to, we found we were in a fight. But that was more characteristic of that era. I wouldn't put Dr. Holcomb down with that statement. He would stand up for his convictions, but many people were willing to criticize him for what he did or didn't do. He was very conservative theologically.

Dr. Holcomb would have been quite at home with the elements that are now wanting to change the direction of the Southern Baptist Convention. He would not have joined such a movement, but he would have been absolutely sympathetic with what they are trying to do.

JAMES SULLIVAN

Another person whom you knew quite well was James Sullivan at the Sunday School Board.

Sullivan was the pastor par excellence when he came in, surprisingly gifted in administrative ability. You couldn't have known that he would be as effective as he turned out to be. He was very adept in talking the language of the common people. It's a pity he was not a denominational executive during recent years, because he could verbalize the denominational point of view in language that anybody could understand. He was great with figures of speech that could carry an emotional message to rank-and-file Southern Baptists.

At the same time, he was a man of absolute integrity and honor in his dealings. Whatever he told you, you could count on it. I think he had a fairly difficult time with the personnel situation and the expansion of the Sunday School Board. There was a huge expansion of the Sunday School Board operation during his administration. Constant reorganization was needed to implement these new programs. But I thought he handled it very well. He was always a wise speaker whenever he spoke on denominational issues.

When did you first meet him?

I've known Jim Sullivan since he was pastor in Ripley, Tennessee, and I was pastoring Woodville Baptist Church out in the country from Ripley. We also served in the same area when he was pastor at Beaver Dam, Kentucky, and I was pastor at Centertown, Kentucky, three miles away. So I knew him during seminary days.

He was one of the older students to whom I looked up with admiration and respect. He was from Sullivan's Hollow, Mississippi. My father had some association with Sullivan's Hollow. I would have known him; he wouldn't have known me. My memory is that he was a graduate student when I entered the seminary, along with Herschel Hobbs, W. A. Criswell, and that crowd.

JOHN R. SAMPEY

Tell us about Dr. John R. Sampey, president of Southern Seminary.

He was gruff and sometimes rough, but he was always controlled by his convictions. Jesus was indeed his Lord. He believed the Bible is the

Word of God. He wanted every student to know the contents of the Bible. That was the thrust of his Old Testament survey course taken by every student in my student era.

Of course, Robert E. Lee was his hero. I heard Dr. Sampey ask a student, "Could Jesus lie?" "No," said with emphasis, was the correct answer. Then Dr. Sampey asked, "Could Robert E. Lee lie?" The student hesitated. Sampey supplied the answer, "Of course not. He was a Christian gentleman!" Dr. Sampey intended for that to characterize his views. Neither a Christian nor a gentleman should ever lie.

ELLIS FULLER

Tell us about your relationship with Dr. Ellis Fuller, your predecessor as president at Southern.

Dr. Fuller and I were good friends. It broke his heart that he could not do what he thought the president of Southern Seminary should be able to do. Yet he did some things that are important. For instance, the music school, the chapel building, the acquisition of land on Alta Vista. He made some good decisions with reference to a better administrative structure. When he was dealing with staff, he could make it work, and the staff would love him for it. But he moved into a taboo land when he told the faculty that he was to be the chief executive officer of the seminary.

THE J. M. DAWSONS

Did you know J. M. Dawson well?

Yes. He was very active on the SBC Executive Committee in my early days there, and Mrs. Dawson was a powerhouse among the women. My wife was a friend of Mrs. Dawson, and we traveled together one time—probably in connection with the BWA Congress in 1947 in Copenhagan.

"Thoughtful pastor" is the way I would describe Dawson. He thought things through carefully. I am not thinking of a profound scholar but a very thoughtful man, personable, careful, accurate in his work. He was an excellent choice for the role he filled, because he could think through some of the shibboleths on separation of church and state that Southern Baptists tend to live by. He could think them through and verbalize thoughtful, intelligent positions. This would give him more power with the powers-that-be among the government officials in

Washington. On the other hand, he could retain the support generally of Southern Baptists.

HERSCHEL HOBBS

Tell us about your association with Herschel Hobbs.

He was a fellow student at Southern Seminary, and we have remained friends through the years. I recommended him to Dauphin Way Baptist Church in Mobile when he went there from Alexandria, Louisiana. Then I recommended him again when he went to Oklahoma City from Dauphin Way. I am not trying to claim credit for getting him the job; I'm just trying to say I believe in him that much.

I remember Herschel as always the biblical theologian. He approaches things from a biblical perspective rather than from a sociological or philosophical point of view. There is usually a rational, theological framework for what he does. He has a quick wit, and he is very courageous. He has the confidence of a person of great conviction who has had great success. I have great admiration for Herschel Hobbs. We haven't been together all that much, but he's done everything he could to be helpful to me, and I've done everything I could to be helpful to him.

During my time at Southern Seminary, he served on the board of trustees. He was a good trustee, and he handled some of the theological problems as a trustee with great skill. Many theological problems arise inevitably at a seminary, because theology is the seminary's baby. It was very helpful to have him on the board to help us deal with some of these problems.

You are thinking primarily of problems with professors and their teaching?

Yes, or the president, for that matter. I haven't had a lot of challenge on my theology until the rise of the current Frank Norris type of fundamentalism. Herschel has been on the SBC Executive Committee, and his membership there has been good for the whole Convention, including Southern Seminary. He has been a strong supporter of theological education over the years.

I am not saying that he was a supporter of me as such. But he always understood what I was trying to do. If he thought I was making sense, he would be an advocate of what I was asking. He would also take the other side when he didn't agree with me. When he thought I was wrong, he would tell me and try to persuade me that I was wrong. If he couldn't persuade me, he would vote what he thought was right.

W. A. CRISWELL

What kind of person is W. A. Criswell?

Criswell is a remarkable person, but he also tries to justify the means by the ends. He justifies what he says and does in terms of the achievement of his goals.

He is very aware of his audience and responsive to it. When he hits a note to which his audience responds, he raises the rhetoric at least one octave and repeats it. That's what gets him into trouble; it's also what makes the crowd come to hear him. Even he doesn't know what he is going to say some of the time until he has heard himself say it.

Yet, he is a very careful student. He knows what he is talking about. He knows it better than his hearers will sense because he will use the material that will get the desired results. There is a goal-orientedness about Criswell that betrays him sometimes, in my opinion.

He and I traveled around the world together in 1950. Both of us were in Nigeria for the centennial celebration of the Nigerian Baptist Convention. At the time, Criswell was a trustee on the Foreign Mission Board and a leading pastor. On the way home from this engagement, we ended up traveling together and speaking at different churches and Baptist agencies for about three months. Part of our assignment was to try to secure visas for Baptist missionaries to enter various countries.

During this time Criswell and I got to know each other rather well. He could tell stories about me, but I could also tell yarns about him for an hour. Some of them would make him out a hero and some of them would portray him as an "Ugly American." But so would his stories about me.

When we wrote our book, *Passport to the World*, which was really Criswell's idea, it consisted of articles I was writing for the *Nashville Banner*. Then these were put together, and I took them and added Criswell's diary. *Passport to the World* was put together that way.

Maxey Jarman, president and owner of General Shoe Company (Genesco), made a trip around the world the next year. He told me, "Duke, I read *Passport to the World* to get ready for my trip, but none of the things that happened to you and Criswell happened to me." I said,

"Maxey, are you telling me you don't believe those things happened to me, or did you find evidence that those things really happen in those countries?" "Oh," he said, "you did not write about your wildest experiences that the missionaries are still laughing about."

There was something about Criswell and McCall together that would precipitate problems. Our agreement was that I would get us to a destination and Criswell would find us a place to stay. We alternated bringing greetings and preaching in every service. By agreement with each other and prayer commitment, the one who was preaching would always give an invitation regardless of the situation. At least one person responded at every invitation in every country.

Criswell was a wonderful traveling companion. He was used to taking charge of things. And he was a lot of fun! We enjoyed Bible reading, talking, and praying together.

Criswell has the reputation of moving toward the right in our Convention now. Was that true of him in those days?

No. He was not anything but a very conservative Southern Baptist. Criswell is basically, in his views, a small "f" fundamentalist. He knows the critical material, but he has arranged it in the fundamentalist pattern. That's who he is, and that's what he believes. The angry, fighting, Frank Norris Fundamentalism development—that's new for him. I am surprised at that, and I regret it.

I think somebody sold him a bill of goods. Or maybe with age he has fallen for the common temptation to stamp his contribution in the history books. Perhaps he thinks this is the way to make all Southern Baptists share his convictions. Up to now he has been content to witness to his convictions and to do it persuasively and powerfully. He is not, in my judgment, a good politician. I think he is used by politicians rather than being a politician.

Criswell is a powerful pulpiteer. He is at his best doing expository sermons and at his worst, in my judgment, when doing a convention-type speech where he tends to slip over into a little demagoguery. Some of the rest of us do that, too. That is not meant to be too negative. It's meant to be descriptive of the difference between a sermon in a church and what he will do in a state convention or evangelistic conference program.

*You were with the other seminary presidents in Dallas just about the
time Dr. Criswell raised some questions about liberalism in Southern
Baptist seminaries. Can you tell us what happened?*

My off-the-cuff memory is that this happened probably about 1979 or
1980. It was in the early stages of the current discussion about inerrancy.

It was an accident that the seminary presidents were meeting in the
Dallas-Fort Worth airport. I have forgotten what the purpose of that
meeting was. It was not about the Convention controversy; it probably
had to do with something in terms of formula for theological education
that would apply to the Cooperative Program.

While we were there for this meeting, the Dallas newspaper carried a
story about Dr. Criswell's broadside attack on liberalism in the seminaries. This was a statement that he had made in different forms on
more than one occasion, but this was hometown stuff. He was talking
to a hometown reporter.

It was pure coincidence that the seminary presidents were there and
read the story. Since we were in town, it was appropriate for him to give
us the evidence. We had a great deal of difficulty getting an appointment
with Criswell. Russell Dilday pushed the matter and got kind of stubborn about it, saying, "We'll meet you any time day or night. Let's do it
while we are here in town. You've said something about the institutions
we serve. We think it's a matter of integrity whether you are willing to
tell us what you told the reporter."

A meeting was finally set up in Criswell's office about nine or ten
o'clock at night. All six of the seminary presidents were there. The current chairman of the seminary presidents group asked Criswell about
his quotes. Were the quotes accurate? Did he really say that? If so,
would he elaborate? I've already referred to the fact that Criswell has
courage. He was one against six, and those odds aren't good psychologically or any other way. He stood his ground that there was some form
of liberalism in the seminaries.

Each president said to Criswell, "I'm president of such and such seminary. My relationship to you is thus and so. Now be specific; talk back
to me." This was done for three schools. Let it be said that Criswell
wouldn't back down.

He kept his charge focused at each of the seminaries until he got to
Golden Gate. Dr. William Pinson, after hearing Criswell's criticism,

came back with a disturbed and emotional response. The presidents are human beings, too, which people often forget. Pinson told about how, as a young fellow, he had stayed in the YMCA, which was across the street from the church in Dallas. Criswell had visited Pinson and had been meaningful to him in Pinson's spiritual experience. This was a very emotional thing in which Pinson expressed his indebtedness and love for Criswell. His statement was made in the context of, "I can't believe you are doing what you are now doing." That changed the mood of the encounter. It became very personally confronting.

The presidents were trying to say, "Isolate your charges and identify the offenders."

Did he name names?

He did not name names of professors, but he talked about some incident, some publication, or some article about the school or a lecturer on a certain campus. When it came my turn, I simply said to Criswell, "We've been friends for a long time. But I have ought against you, brother. You do not believe the Bible. You are making charges, but you are not following Jesus' instructions in Matthew on how to deal with the brother you think is in error. You have made blanket charges against my friends and colleagues, and that includes all six seminaries. I don't know whether you are attacking Southern Seminary or not. We are in the target area, so we are being charged. You haven't named a seminary, and you haven't named a specific professor. But worse than that, you haven't talked to the professor to find out whether your understanding of his views is accurate. You are making some charges, and let me make one. My charge is that you do not believe the Bible has authority over your conduct. Your conduct is contrary to the biblical instruction in Matthew 18."

Criswell didn't back down—and I admire that in him. I would think a lot less of him if he had collapsed under the attack. This report about that meeting is going to be inconclusive, because the meeting was inconclusive. It broke up, not in anger, but as a group of friends disagreeing. We disagreed with each other, but at least we had followed Matthew 18 in that there had been a face-to-face confrontation. I think the story may be more important for describing something about the people than the particular event. There is a feeling that when you get into these controversies you always end up as enemies.

Was this just one in a series of charges from Criswell about liberal-

ism in the seminaries?

My feeling was that Criswell was verbalizing the basically fundamentalist position, which has always been his view. It was true before he came to Southern Seminary. It was true when he got his doctor's degree from Southern Seminary. This was his doctrinal position. He was now prepared to verbalize this view in a controversial setting and to stand his ground with those who disagreed with him. This was what was new, as I perceived it. The conclusion the presidents reached was that Criswell had entered the fray as an antagonist of theological education as it has been carried on in the Southern Baptist Convention.

He has become, either intentionally or accidentally, the stackpole of an organized movement within the Southern Baptist Convention. He has people very close to him who are fueling his views. They are making him feel that he must give leadership to this fundamentalist movement, lest the whole Christian enterprise go down the drain from godless liberalism or anti-biblical liberalism or "secular humanism."

Why would Criswell be seeking a power base at this point when he had been president of the SBC in 1968 and 1969?

I don't think that's what was involved with Criswell. I think for him it was the "one last hurrah" syndrome. Life is drawing to a close; your career is coming to an end, and you've had all these wonderful opportunities. Suddenly you want to do something grandly heroic as a finale to your life's contribution.

I've seen this happen more than once where people suddenly change toward the close of their career. They hope to go out with one great flash of lightning and do something that will mark their contribution for posterity. Or it may be more piously oriented—here at the end of my life, I'm going to do for God what God always needed doing. My view is that if we try to spend our lives doing the will of God, then there is no way we can suddenly do something better than this at the close of our careers.

Criswell did have a degree of influence and power in the latter 1960s, since he was elected president of the Convention. Was he not aware of the political machinery that would have allowed him to capture the will of the Convention?

Obviously not. He didn't use his appointive powers as president to do anything different from what every other president had done—and that was to place strong representatives of the total Southern Baptist Convention in places of leadership. He didn't try to "stack the Supreme Court." That syndrome was not in his presidency

I have seen this happen more than once. Men have been elected president of the Southern Baptist Convention without understanding the machinery of the Convention. The organization of the SBC is not what they're interested in. They're interested in moral and spiritual leadership. And, I might add, Criswell proved to be a very good president between Convention sessions.

Another Convention president like that was R. G. Lee. He never bothered with the mechanism of the office. The office meant a platform and a hearing for his convictions and his views. And I think that was basically true of Criswell.

R. G. LEE

How would you describe R. G. Lee?

I was not a member of his church, Bellevue Baptist in Memphis. But during my seminary days I volunteered to work in the youth program at Bellevue one summer for the opportunity to be close to him and to see how he operated the church.

What did you learn from that experience?

I learned that there was only one R. G. Lee in the world and that you'd better not try to imitate him. I tried during seminary days to imitate his preaching style—with disastrous results. There was such a charismatic quality about him that he carried his church along with him.

Whatever Lee recommended or wanted always got done. He did not depend on preaching to get the job done. He depended on the Sunday School and the Training Union organizations as the way to involve church members in the outreach and Bible study and membership-training programs of the church. This intrigued me at the time—how good he was at organization.

He was good at delegation. He knew how to tell somebody what he wanted and then leave that person alone to get it done. He did expect it to be done the way he told you to do it. His description of the process you were to use was not just suggestive; it consisted of precise instructions.

I found him a very pleasant guy to be around, and I enjoyed our relationship. When I was at Baptist Bible Institute in New Orleans, I brought him in as a lecturer. He was proud of his association with BBI and New Orleans Seminary. I tried to get him to raise $100,000 for BBI, and he claimed he was proud to be thought of as being capable of doing that, but he never did it.

Dr. Lee and I received the same "General Excellence" medal as graduates of Furman University, and that also gave us a special camaraderie. He was elected Convention president while I was at the Executive Committee, and I traveled with him quite often during the three years of his presidency.

I could almost have delivered some of the speeches that he made over and over, since it was his style to repeat. He worked hard on a speech, and then he used it whenever he needed it. I sometimes use that technique myself. I learned it from him—to work hard on a speech or sermon and polish it, and then not be too worried that somebody might hear it twice.

How would you assess Lee's effectiveness as president of the Southern Baptist Convention?

I think R. G. Lee did one of the most important jobs for Southern Baptists that has been done by any president. I'm thinking of the Alldredge amendment at the Oklahoma City Convention. President Lee saved the Convention's unity when the Foreign Mission Board was attacked because it appeared to have trustees who were related to the Federal Council of Churches. It took great courage for him to act as he did.

Lee actually sided with a position that he was not sympathetic with, but he did so because he thought a higher cause was being served. He was being president of all of the Convention, not the partisans who represented a particular point of view. He served the larger interest.

Tell us about the Alldredge amendment.

The Alldredge amendment was aimed at Ted Adams, pastor of First Baptist Church of Richmond, Virginia, whose brother was involved in the National Council of Churches. I've forgotten exactly how Ted Adams was supposed to be involved in the National Council of Churches, except that he participated in the local Richmond Council of Churches.

The Alldredge amendment was designed to say that no person related to the National Council of Churches could have any leadership role in the Southern Baptist Convention. This would have taken Ted Adams and the members of his church off the board of the Foreign Mission Board.

THERON RANKIN

My anecdote about the Alldredge Amendment involves Theron Rankin, then the executive secretary of the Foreign Mission Board. It was a very divisive proposal by Dr. Alldredge. It looked like it would pass, especially in Oklahoma. There would be no sympathy in the western section of the country for the eastern understanding of relations with other Christian bodies. I think it is clear that there was a difference in attitude between the East and the West, and the Convention was meeting in the western part of the nation.

Dr. Alldredge was the statistical secretary for the Sunday School Board. As executive secretary of the Executive Committee with an office in the same building as Alldredge, I had discovered—and could prove—that he was writing for the Frank Norris *Fundamentalist*. This publication printed attacks on the Sunday School Board and other Southern Baptist Convention agencies. Alldredge was writing these articles under a pseudonym. This is why the Sunday School Board's inner workings could get reported with a fundamentalist bias.

I had experienced some sharp run-ins with Alldredge along the way (over my attending the organizational meeting of the World Council of Churches in Amsterdam). I came into possession of these incriminating documents that he had written quite by accident. They were carbon copies of articles that appeared in the *Fundamentalist,* and I had secured copies of them before they appeared in print. I had these documents with me at the Convention in Oklahoma City.

Theron Rankin was absolutely up in arms. His whole board structure was going to be torn up if this amendment passed. It would have affected more than Ted Adams; some other Virginia members of the Foreign Mission Board, including the lay chairman, were related to their local councils of churches. These might not have any connection with the National Council. But you would never prove that to the people, particularly in the far West, who were antagonistic to all councils of churches, The structure of these councils would have been too complicated to explain on the floor of the Convention.

Theron Rankin came to me. I had a desk as the executive secretary does on the platform of the Convention. He said, "Duke, I've heard that you have some documents that prove that Alldredge is working hand in glove with Frank Norris in attacks on the Southern Baptist Convention." I don't know where he got that information, except by the same kind of grapevine that runs all through Southern Baptist life.

"Yes, I do," I told him.

He said, "Can you get them quickly?" He assumed they were in my hotel room. "If you will let me have them, I am going to use them."

"If you use them," I replied, "you will destroy Alldredge's leadership, but you will also destroy your own. The Southern Baptist Convention will not let you use that kind of tar without its being spattered all over the user, so you will wreck your own usefulness."

"For the sake of the Foreign Mission Board, I would use them," he replied. "Can you get them?"

"Yes, they are in this locked drawer right here in my desk," I told him. "I thought I might have to use them." I unlocked the drawer and gave the papers to him.

He took the documents and walked up and asked for recognition by the president of the Southern Baptist Convention. This was during the debate on the Alldredge amendment on the Convention floor. But R. G. Lee didn't want Rankin to speak. Perhaps it was his instinct, or insightful leadership on his part.

"Wait just a moment, Dr. Rankin," Lee said. "I have a statement I want to make." Then Lee spoke on behalf of the unity of the Southern Baptist Convention and the integrity of the foreign mission enterprise. Lee's support was very influential, and the vote went against the Alldredge motion. I can see Theron Rankin right now as he breathed a sigh of relief and walked away from the podium.

My feeling is that Lee protected Rankin and the Foreign Mission Board in that heated situation. I think Lee knew exactly what he was doing. He didn't know what Rankin was going to say. But he didn't want the Foreign Mission Board executive director to have to get into the confrontation. Whenever that happens to any denominational executive, it impairs his effectiveness and leadership. The public thinks denominational executives ought to be Sir Gallahad, high above the controversy and the political activities that go on in a controversy.

I think Lee's goal was to elicit, combine, and direct the energies of the Baptist denomination of Christians for the more effective propagation of the gospel to the lost. He saw what was happening as division and loss of strength, and therefore he swung his full weight as president into the breach.

No Convention president wants the Convention to divide during his presidency. I could cite some recent presidents. Just read their statements and see how they always become advocates of unity rather than division, once they were elected president. This is an interesting psychological effect that the presidency has on people. (Updated note from McCall: But this attitude was actually reversed in the 1980s. For example, SBC President Patterson called for division in 1999.—DKM)

RAMSEY POLLARD

Ramsey Pollard succeeded R. G. Lee at Bellevue and was also elected SBC president. How well did you know him?

He was a very close friend of my mother and father, and he and I were friends. Pollard went to Bellevue from Broadway Church in Knoxville, Tennessee. He and Dr. Lee were similar in their theological persuasions, but stylistically he was a very different kind of person. It's amazing that he was so successful as Dr. Lee's successor. Lee would have been a hard man to succeed, and Ramsey's success reflects to his credit.

During your time at Southern Seminary, the presidents of the Convention frequently spoke at graduation ceremonies or some other important occasion. But I understand that Pollard never did speak at Southern. Why?

About the time I should have invited Ramsey Pollard, he came out with some attack on the seminaries. It was a situation where I would have created problems for myself with faculty and alumni and with some other people by inviting him to speak on campus. So I just never got around to issuing the invitation. It was just not the right time.

LOUIE D. NEWTON

Louie Newton, pastor of Druid Hills Church in Atlanta for many years, was a long-time member of the SBC Executive Committee in the days before the rotation pattern came in. Describe Louie Newton from your experience in dealing with him.

I never think of Louie by himself. I always think of him in a group of friends—John Buchanan, Jim Wilkerson, and so on—who were always coalesced around Louie Newton. He was the center of a coterie of friends, all of whom were bright, strongly committed to Southern Baptist life, and deeply involved in the organizational life of Baptists.

I understand that if you could convince these three people to support a cause, you could carry the rest of the Executive Committee.

Yes. And they would decide to agree or disagree on an issue over a Rook game that might last until two o'clock in the morning before the meeting of the Executive Committee. In the old days, they met in the Sam Davis Hotel in Nashville, or they would ride the train together and play Rook.

If there was some issue in the Convention, Louie Newton might ride the train over to Birmingham to talk to John Buchanan. Or John might ride the train to Atlanta to spend the day with Louie. Their friendship was very strong and very trusting. They were so open with each other that they could take opposite sides on an issue. That never affected their friendship.

But the odds were that they would end up on the same side because they generally thought alike and they would hammer out their differences before the meeting. And they might even do a little working out of strategy for the presentation—who would make the motion, who would second it, who would speak to it, what points each would make, etc. They were very powerful people.

This "group side" of Louie Newton needs to be pointed out, because he is generally perceived of as such a powerful person that he tends to loom over the crowd. I think of him, for instance, after we had the microphones throughout the audience in the Southern Baptist Convention sessions. He wanted to object to something. Louie had access to the platform, and he could have spoken from the platform mike. Instead, he rose up in the balcony and called out with that nasal twang, "Mr. President." The president recognized him and said, "Dr. Newton, go to a microphone." "I don't need a microphone," he responded. "I just want to say a word."

And then for five minutes he spoke without a microphone, absolutely fascinating and captivating the crowd. The ten thousand people in that auditorium heard him clearly because he could really project his voice. With his homespun humor and his country anecdotes, he would put the issue in down-home terms that everybody could understand. Generally, the people would be on his side because of his effective use of those illustrations.

He was a difficult man to handle if you happened to be on the other side. But he was a great friend. His preaching style was anecdotal, even in the cultured and sophisticated atmosphere of Druid Hills Baptist Church. He was always down to earth, and he talked about the things that the congregation wanted to hear.

Louie was a great committee man. He would come early and stay late for committee meetings. He would also do his homework before the meeting. He would sit quietly until everybody else had established their positions, so he would know how to handle the group.

He had a remarkable debating technique. If he was violently opposed to a proposal somebody had made, he would get up and say, "I am in agreement with Brother So-and-So's proposal, but I think we ought to divide the motion. Then he would get the maker of the motion to agree to divide it. The first motion would be that we're in favor of God, country, motherhood, and apple pie—idealism. Louie would make an eloquent speech in favor of that motion. And the group would vote almost unanimously for that motion, which was half of what the original maker of the motion had presented. The other half would be the part that implemented what the original motion was intended to accomplish, the half that Louie opposed. At this point Louie would have some doubt about whether we ought to do it this way. Then he would get a unanimous vote not to implement the idea that he presumably was supporting.

The poor fellow who had made the motion would be sitting there stunned, not knowing what had happened to him. Once out of sheer sportsmanship I used that same tactic against Louie. It worked as well against him as it worked for him against other people. It caught Louie by surprise. But it didn't take long for him to realize what had happened, and he laughed at himself. He thought it was great sport.

Louie was a happy-spirited fellow. Nobody could stay angry at him very long, even if that person had taken an awful whipping at his hands. He would make it a point to make friends again. He didn't want you to get on the opposite side from him for long. But there were people in the Convention who were anti-Louie Newton people. If Louie was for it, they were against it. J. D. Grey was one of those who were against Louie Newton.

JOHN BUCHANAN
Tell something about John Buchanan, pastor at Southside Baptist Church in Birmingham.

John "Buck" was a big man physically. He had a big, booming voice, with all of the self-confidence that this size, coupled with high intelligence, would give to a man. I've already pointed out that he was a close friend and confidante of Louie Newton. John was more open in some ways toward other Christian bodies than Louie Newton.

In fact, John "Buck" almost ruined himself politically in the denomination by advocating membership in the World Council of Churches. George Truett was chairman of the committee, and John Buchanan was a member of the committee. John brought in a minority report in favor of joining the World Council of Churches.

Buchanan was an open-handed, open-hearted sort of fellow who had a sharp mind. He was not as eloquent or as persuasive in debate as Louie Newton, but there was a kind of ponderous power to his logic and to the way he presented his proposals.

John "Buck" was in some ways my father in the ministry. I tend to say that about more than one person, but he certainly was one of them. He was a very powerful influence in my early days. He took me under his wing and brought me into the Louie Newton/John Buchanan/Jim Wilkerson group. I would get invited to play Rook with them at night while they were debating Southern Baptist affairs.

How did an executive secretary of the Executive Committee who lived in Nashville survive in meetings where these fellows came from out of town and set up camp?

I joined them when I was in New Orleans, so I could be one of them, and I could go home and get some sleep. After I became executive secretary of the Executive Committee, I stayed away from the Rook games. That was more than my constitution could handle. They created enough pressure on you just to deal with the denominational issues. I didn't need the added pressure of trying to win at Rook while discussing these matters.

GEORGE RAGLAND

You've mentioned an SBC world relief effort right after you went to the Executive Committee in which a man named George Ragland was involved. Tell us about him.

George Ragland of the Executive Committee eventually got into the Newton/Buchanan/Wilkerson group, which is the most incredible thing. From the First Baptist Church of Lexington, Kentucky, Ragland was put on the Executive Committee in a political effort to get a sharp, knowledgeable, ultraconservative Baptist to straighten out the liberals on the Executive Committee.

After he got on the Executive Committee, he decided Newton and his boys really did believe the Bible and loved the Lord and were trying to do right. So instead of fighting with them, as he was supposed to do, he joined them. That doesn't mean he always agreed with them. He learned that you didn't have to agree in order to be a part of this friendly group. That was the most incredible combination I ever saw.

This is one of the marks of the past that I wish we could resurrect in the present. George Ragland thought Louie Newton and John Buchanan were a little more liberal than they ought to have been. But on the other hand, he respected their knowledge of the Bible and their commitment to the Bible as the rule of faith and practice.

I've heard them have some horrendous arguments about what the Bible taught on certain subjects. They would argue about any subject, and they would really have at each other. George Ragland would pull out his Greek New Testament and beat Newton and Buchanan with it. They ended up walking together about 85 percent of the time. Then about 15 percent of the time, George Ragland would be on the opposite side.

In one big debate on the floor of the Executive Committee, George Ragland and I took on Louie Newton and Jim Wilkerson. The debate was over the establishment of a Southern Baptist Relief Center in New Orleans at the end of World War II. Ragland and I wanted the center established for the distribution of relief by Baptists to other Baptists. Louie Newton and Jim Wilkerson wanted Southern Baptists to send their money through Church World Service.

As a matter of fact, we ended up doing both, and Southern Baptists gave eight times as much through Church World Service as did the Methodists, who were in second place in using that channel. In addition, Southern Baptists sent millions of dollars of relief through the Baptist program in New Orleans.

George and I wanted a Baptist agency that would forward materials to Baptist churches in Europe for distribution. Church World Service tended to put these relief goods in the hands of the state churches for distribution. The New Orleans Baptist Relief Center meant the Baptists in Europe after World War II could be the distributors of relief in their communities.

We wanted Baptists not only to receive our SBC relief gifts, but also to become the distribution channels in Europe. We thought this would strengthen the weak Baptist bodies if they became the channels of relief distribution. The Church World Service channel confirmed the strength of the state church and made the Baptists the people who came with their hands out.

George Ragland said in our presentation to the Executive Committee, "I think that Louie and Jim are quoting the Bible as saying, 'Do good unto all men,' but Duke and I are quoting the whole verse, 'Do good unto all men, especially to those of the household of faith.'" That little twist in Scripture quotation won the debate.

Normally I would not have been thought of as an ally of George Ragland against Louie Newton. I would have been sitting over on the other side of that equation, but in this case the issues determined the combination.

J. D. GREY

Tell about J. D. Grey.

J. D. and I were friends from my BBI days. I had more friends in his church than in any other church in New Orleans, and I spoke more often in the First Baptist Church than in any other church in New Orleans. But I was not a member of his church. I didn't think that J. D. and I ought to be harnessed up too tightly because of our stylistic differences.

It worked out because we became good friends. I am indebted to J. D. Grey. I owe him for many things, and I never got any chance to start to repay many of these.

He was the sort of cigar-smoking type of preacher who, if you rebuked him, would say, "I'd rather smoke here than hereafter," and go right on doing it. He had a slam-bang quality about him. He was the sort who was never risqué but sounded like he was about to get there in his stories. Even in the pulpit he would pull some things that you would never think a Baptist preacher could get away with—but he did.

The men of New Orleans thought he was great. He got a reputation for being "Saint J. D." But with all of his slam-bang, man's-man, secular kind of veneer, there was a lot more to J. D. Everybody detected a deep spiritual commitment in him.

You never could predict him; he would say anything that occurred to him, and yet somehow he communicated a deep piety. People felt that he had a basic integrity about him. They believed that if J. D. Grey said he could do something, he would do it. He had the distinction of being a very powerful Protestant clergyman in New Orleans, a Roman Catholic city.

When J. D. came on the SBC Executive Committee, Louie Newton had been the powerhouse for many years. J. D. Grey told me, "I'm going to bump Louie Newton out of that control of the Executive Committee." Essentially, J. D. Grey succeeded in pulling it off.

The rotation pattern that was adopted in the Executive Committee in part replaced Louie Newton, didn't it?

That was J. D. Grey's doing. They finally rotated Louie Newton off the Executive Committee. Most of us, including Louie Newton, opposed this move to a rotation system. We did so on the basis that this was using a meat ax to do what a scalpel ought to do. We thought that the people who didn't really function ought to be removed, but the rotation system got the good ones off as well as the bad ones.

Was J. D. Grey involved at all with BBI when you served as president there?

He was an opinionated guy who had ideas about everything, but he would share his ideas with me, and we would talk about them. We never really clashed. I'm saying that with a little surprise. I think it was because each of us left the other some maneuvering room.

Was he in favor of renaming BBI as New Orleans Seminary?

He was the man who seconded the motion to do this at the Southern Baptist Convention. Dr. Anderson of the BBI faculty was given the job of reading the recommendation that I had written. Then acting president Wash Watts (by that time I had moved to the Executive Committee in Nashville) would make the motion at the Miami Convention. J. D. Grey's job was to second the motion with authority, because Watts's voice was a little thin and wouldn't carry power and conviction.

J. D. seconded that motion, and he did it in such thunderous tones that there was a stunned silence for a few seconds. During that silence President Pat Neff said, "The motion is moved and seconded; all in favor say 'Aye'; those opposed by like sign. It is so ordered." Neff didn't even take a breath during that declaration. It was done! And it was supposed to have been a controversial issue that would generate debate.

J. D. Grey had the self-confidence and the astuteness to be able just to say, "Second the motion," and say it with such enthusiasm that it would carry the crowd along, and then quit and let the president put the motion before the assembly.

When J. D. Grey was elected president of the Convention, I take it he didn't always fit the classical presidential mold?

No, because he had a rough-and-ready style, although he was a Kentuckian by birth. He projected what would have been thought of as a "west Texas" style.

M. E. DODD

Give us your impressions of M. E. Dodd.

Dodd and I became friends when I was at Baptist Bible Institute because he was a kind of godfather to BBI and a source of financial support for the school. I can laugh at some of his foibles. But I need to tell you that I was greatly impressed by him.

Mandeville, I believe, is the encampment of Louisiana Baptists. There was a pastors conference there once. I can't remember what happened—a strike or something. No one could be hired to wait tables. Dodd came to me and said, "Let's serve the tables." So he and I became the waiters for the country preachers who had gathered there at Mandeville. I watched him work with those less-educated preachers in difficult rural situations.

I came away with an appreciation for Dodd and his concern for that group of preachers. I liked Dodd; and he and I hit it off well when I was in Louisiana. We hadn't done it before then. I had crossed him years before at Ridgecrest. I was serving as a bellhop there, and he was the "big preacher" come to town. He made me take his luggage to three different rooms in different buildings before he accepted a room. I made him tip me for my trouble, which was against the rules for Ridgecrest staff members.

But I learned to love him and respect him in Louisiana. Fiscally, Dodd had a very relaxed approach to finances. He tended to think that a few hundred dollars spent on this or that couldn't hurt much, especially if it contributed to his convenience. Dodd got a bad reputation in leadership circles for his easy way with SBC expense accounts. He wanted what he wanted, and he would put it on his expense account.

KYLE YATES

You studied with Kyle Yates at Southern Seminary. Talk about him.

Kyle Yates was my old professor and pastor of Walnut Street Baptist Church in Louisville and Houston Second Baptist Church. He was a very gracious man. He never saw you without telling you how wonderful you were and what three churches he had recommended you to lately.

This approach didn't impress me. I got to the place where I couldn't be effusive in gratitude and appreciation of people. To this day I'm not likely ever to tell a person I recommended him or her for a job. I'll do it, and if you find out about it, that's all right. I can't tell you about it because nothing may come of it. I guess I'm talking about the human foibles of great men.

Was he really the pulpiteer rather than the scholar?

Kyle Yates was a very intelligent man, and he had done his homework. He had read the books; he knew what was being said. But he was calculating about the results of what he said and did. He tended to want to manipulate the outcome. Therefore, he wouldn't teach something that would create a controversy or upset somebody.

That's why he always let me teach the Book of Daniel for him when I was his fellow at Southern Seminary. I noticed that the time to teach Daniel always came when he was out of town. I don't think he ever taught the Book of Daniel while I was a graduate student because this book was a hot potato.

There was nothing you could say in those days about the Book of Daniel that wouldn't create a controversy. If you linked it to the hard-line premillenialist view, you offended people on the outside of that. If you didn't, you were going to get chewed up. If you didn't have the right chart, you didn't fit Daniel into the right track the critics had learned. So there was no way to teach the Book of Daniel to any group of Southern Baptists, and certainly not to a group of ministerial students, without evoking violent emotional opposition to what you said, or did not say. Kyle Yates did not like that kind of emotional confrontation, so he avoided it. I think this weakened him as a professor.

If you follow that line of thinking, you end up preaching only what is palatable to people; you also develop a style that is appealing to them. Kyle Yates did have an appealing preaching style; people enjoyed listening to him.

I have heard him teach the Psalms both in the seminary and at Ridgecrest. He could teach the Psalms in a very attractive way, but sometimes he might ascribe the authorship of a particular psalm to the person who fitted the sermon he was writing. That choice would be one of the live options but not necessarily the one the more technical scholars would have advocated.

I went into his office on many occasions to discuss a very sophisticated, technical, critical problem in Old Testament studies. I didn't think he knew anything about it. I had never heard him mention it. But when I started talking to him, he would take it up right away. He knew what I was talking about, and he could add information that I didn't know about. He knew the critical issues, but he wouldn't discuss them even in a graduate seminar. This disturbed me because I thought he ought to volunteer this information to all the students.

I believe the Bible is the Word of God, and I do not believe any *truth* about the Bible will weaken anything except superficial assumptions about the divine revelation.

Dr. Yates left the seminary in the middle of the year rather than at the end of the term. Why?

Because a church called him at that particular time. This was Walnut Street Baptist Church, the largest church in Kentucky, a great evangelistic church of Findley Gibson. A church of that stature didn't sit around and wait for a seminary professor to finish a semester. I think the pressure was on him either to say yes or no, come on or stay—and do it now.

That was an interesting move for an Old Testament professor—to go to an evangelistic church like Walnut Street.

But Dr. Yates was that kind of preacher. He was an attractive, popular pulpiteer. Walnut Street was a populist type of church, so his preaching was compatible with the people. He did a good job as pastor at Walnut Street. While he was not an organizer or a detail man, he made friends easily. If you were a beggar on the corner, you were the finest beggar he had ever seen, and you were a blessing to everybody who came by that corner. So the beggars thought he was great, too.

GEORGE NORTON JR.

What was your relationship with George Norton Jr. of Louisville?

He and his father, who was also treasurer of the Southern Baptist Convention, were leading trustees of Southern Seminary. Their relation to the seminary dated from 1877, when the school moved to Louisville.

George Jr. owned WAVE radio and WAVE television, which has just been sold for $110 million to Cosmos Broadcasting. He was also a major stockholder in Citizens Fidelity Bank; and as somebody said, they bought a little real estate that became useful in some place called "the Chicago Loop." They bought some arid land where they couldn't get water. When they drilled they always hit black stuff called "oil." So George Norton had a lot of "bad luck" in his business affairs.

The death of George Norton Jr. in an automobile accident in Jamaica was one of the great tragedies in my administration as president of Southern Seminary. We lost something we never could replace. He was the one man who could call the president of Chase National Bank in New York and go straight through to talk to him. He had access to business interests across the nation like nobody else we've ever known at Southern Seminary.

George Norton and his wife had been members of Broadway Baptist Church when I was pastor there. We had ties of personal friendship, and still have ties of friendship with his wife. She has gone back to the Episcopal Church, St. Francis in the Fields, which she helped found on the eastern edge of Louisville.

The friendship there is very warm and genuine, but the seminary now has no official connections with the family because George Norton's son was killed in an automobile accident just a couple of months after his father's death. There are no male heirs, and the daughter is married to an Episcopal rector. Suddenly all of that family connection disappeared from Baptist ranks. This family was not just a Southern Seminary family. This was a Southern Baptist family of great prominence, great wealth, and astute business judgment.

CHAPTER 15

Conclusion

How do you feel about the Southern Baptist Convention now—in retirement—living in Florida in the winter and the North Carolina mountains in the summer?

An anecdote, a story from the past, is my best answer. I flew from the Kansas City Southern Baptist Convention meetings to an insurance company (Presbyterian Minister's Fund) board meeting in Philadelphia. The Kansas City SBC meetings literally made me sick at my stomach. I was deeply depressed. I got to Philadelphia the night before the board meeting about dinnertime. My wife and I went into the Hershey Hotel, which is across Broad Street from the Arts Auditorium.

I couldn't watch television. I couldn't read. I couldn't sit still. I couldn't prepare to chair the board meeting the next day. I finally said, "Marguerite, I'm going across the street to see what's going on at the theatre tonight, and to check to see if we can get tickets." I did, and "Camelot" was on.

We went to "Camelot." I've never identified with anybody like I identified with King Arthur that night, with his dreams of a roundtable and right makes might, and all the idealism. Then there is the human frailty that breaks in—with greed and lust for power. The play ends with King Arthur getting ready to go to battle against his friend, who had stolen his wife, Guinevere. She is now in a convent. His home is shattered. The roundtable is destroyed, and peace is gone. He has lost it all.

Tomorrow is battle. And the little boy Tom comes up to volunteer for the army because he wants to be a knight of the roundtable. King Arthur asks Tom, "What do you know about the roundtable?" and Tom replies, "I've heard the stories."

With that King Arthur knights the little boy but refuses to let him go into battle. Instead, he sends him out to tell the stories of the roundtable. He recognizes that the dreams and ideals of the roundtable are not dead as long as the little boy is telling the stories.

I came out of "Camelot" that night thinking, "Well, I've been in despair because so many things I worked for and dreamed of among Southern Baptists are gone. They are history; the war has been lost. But the ideals are still there, and the dreams are still there, and we still have new generations of young people." Of course, I applied this to seminary students: They will go out and rebuild the roundtable.

This new table may be oval instead of round; these new seminary graduates may do a lot of things differently, but the dreams of unity and love and compassion for a lost world will live on. What God is doing through the Southern Baptist Convention will not be lost, and the Convention will live in a new form. It will go through new crises and new eras, but it will come out as God wills. Now that ought to be my closing statement, because that's exactly where I am. God is still in his heaven, and all is not right with the world today, but in God's purposes it will be right. This oral history interview is my way of telling the stories of the Southern Baptist roundtable in the twentieth century.

RETIRED

Are there other things as we come to a conclusion that you would like to share?

I'm at the point of a major transition right now in this month of November 1985 because, having moved back to Florida for the winter, I've really closed up my office at the seminary for the first time. The seminary continues to provide me as chancellor with office space and all the secretarial help I need.

My long-time secretary, Clara McCartt, has retired again as of November 1, 1985. What's an office without a secretary to keep it straightened out and functioning? So I'm at a transition point in my own working life. But invitations do continue to come in, and I enjoy staying active. I've said repeatedly that the things that Baptists have paid me to do, I ought to have paid them for the privilege of doing. It's been a great life. I've enjoyed it.

I'm really settling back. I'm moving out of active participation in organized denominational life. Someone called me recently and said, "What do you think about so and so." And I replied, "You must understand that if you don't go to the meetings, your sources of information are cut off." In the past I attended five or six state conventions every fall, attended associational meetings all over the Southern Baptist Convention, and then attended Baptist meetings, more recently, all over the world.

If you do that, you meet the people and you hear what is going on, and you are told the interpretation of events by this person and that person. So you really end up hearing both sides in the discussion without having to dig for it. I have been able in the past to talk about what was happening among Baptists as if I were very smart and very wise. I had wonderful sources of information and unique sources of opinion.

There are some doors closing at this point because I have neither the official position nor the occasion to attend all these meetings. I haven't the energy and strength, frankly, to try to keep on attending them.

I had a letter today from Noel Vose, the president of the BWA. He asked if I was coming to the meeting in Washington and ended by saying, "I wouldn't blame you if you went out to the airport and waved at ten planes leaving for Washington while you stayed at home." He was making fun of a statement that I had made to the Baptist World Congress that I was going to retire and go to the airport and watch ten planes take off without me.

Although I really have had all the flying I care to do, I'll keep traveling and participating. But the nature of my involvement will be considerably different from this month on. I will be in retirement in a real sense, but I hope it's going to be an active retirement.

ADDENDUM: RETIREMENT PLANNING

I anticipated retirement as early as 1959 by asking myself how I would finance it. I did not want to cut back to the lifestyle provided by my contributions to the Annuity Board.

I was in Athens, Greece, in three consecutive summers during the 1950s, twice with the U.S. Air Force. I left once with two 20,000 drachmae bills that I could not convert to dollars. When I went back the next summer, these two bills were worth only 20 drachmae. The government had just dropped the last three digits on their money. That made me aware of inflation even more than Maxey Jarman teaching me in the 1940s that average inflation is about 4 percent a year. Thus, I thought, a long retirement could begin well, yet run out of money.

I made a study of the kind of investment I might be able to handle that would be lucrative. My conclusion was that a mobile home park would be wonderful. I did not know how to start one.

During a 1958 revival at the West Bradenton, Florida, Baptist Church, I went to dinner with Lynn Gilmore, chairman of the deacons. He dreamed out loud of developing a mobile home park. I pulled out the $100 dollar bill I carried for emergencies and offered it to him, saying, "Let's be partners and do it."

To make a long story short, with seven other partners enlisted by Lynn using my one hundred dollars, we developed a 780-unit mobile home park named "Golf Lakes Mobile Estates."

I hoped my share would provide me with $1,000 per month in retirement. Instead, the park sold in 1989 for $14 million. I will omit the trials and tribulations along the way, but Lynn Gilmore was the managing partner. He was and is a genius. His primary characteristic is integrity drawn from the Christian faith of his Baptist-preacher father. He grew up in the backwoods of Florida with limited educational opportunities. He never got to algebra in school, but he could solve an algebraic problem with his own logic.

He and I never disagreed except when he refused to buy the adjoining golf course. He said that we could not make money on it, but I claimed inflation would make us money. Double-digit inflation in the early 1980s (the Carter presidency of the U.S.) was the secret to the sale price of Golf Lakes.

However, in retirement I have never missed the profit on that golf course. I never expected to have one retirement home in the mountains of North Carolina and another on the coast of Florida. I moved from Louisville because the changes at Southern Seminary created faculty and staff trauma that I could not stand or help.

My beloved wife Marguerite died just over a year after we retired from Southern Seminary. Winona McCandless and I were married in 1984.

We both used JJB Hilliard/Lyons Investment, Inc. in Louisville. Gayle Dorsey was our account executive. We were very lucky people because she did very well with our investments.

Winona's father, Mr. Harper Gatton of Madisonville, Kentucky, was a leading Baptist layman in Kentucky, superintendent of schools, the CEO of the Kentucky Chamber of Commerce, and something of a political power, president of Kiwanis International, and a Sunday school teacher all the while.

Winona came out of that kind of Baptist background very similar to my own. Her mother had died when she was a very small child, and an aunt had reared her younger sister, born just before her mother's death. She had stayed in the home of her father and been reared by him and another aunt, who lived with them for a while.

She married Paul McCandless, whom she met when they were students at the Baptist College of Kentucky—Georgetown College. He went off to World War II, then came back to go back to work for the telephone company. They traveled and lived all over the South—Miami, Jacksonville, and Atlanta. He had come back to Louisville to be head of South Central Bell Telephone of Kentucky and, I add, to head up fundraising efforts in the state for Southern Seminary. So he and I were friends when he had a heart attack and died three years before Marguerite died.

Winona and I were members of the same church—Broadway Baptist Church in Louisville—and so we have felt that God led us both to a happy, new resolution of our situation. She is a trustee of Georgetown College and in her own way is quite active as a Baptist lay woman. I've talked about Marguerite in earlier discussions, so I'm just putting in this addendum on Winona.

Winona and I set up the McCall Foundation to share our good fortune with Christian causes. She made the first $250,000 gift to Georgetown College. Her parents and her sister as well as she graduated there. Her father and her first husband were both trustees at Georgetown.

I intended to endow the Marguerite McCall Professorship at Southern, but the reaction to a gift to the Baptist Theological Seminary at Richmond, Virginia, and five-point Calvinism and attacks on E. Y. Mullins have put a fly in the ointment.

Conclusion

As I write this, both Winona and I are in our eighties with some of the health problems that attach to old age. We feel that we may yet become really old, but life is too good to worry about it. Three golf games a week coupled with visits to the gym are routine for both of us.

Our children, grandchildren, and great grandchildren are the source of lots of joy and pride. We are both still members of Broadway Baptist Church in Louisville, Kentucky. However, we joined and worship usually in either First Baptist Church, Highlands, North Carolina, or North Stuart Baptist Church in Florida. Membership in three Baptist churches should be enough for any Christian!

Our efforts to help found Central Baptist Church in Jupiter, Florida, were successful, but an eloquent Southern alumnus and friend, Dr. Douglas Waterson, is our pastor in Stuart, Florida.

We are semi-retired in that Winona no longer serves as chairperson for the women's member/guest day or as an officer of the Women's Golf Association. I no longer give blocks of time to property owners associations or as condo president. Praying at the opening and closing of golf banquets in Florida is my only ongoing religious responsibility. At age 85, I enjoy the view from the pew.

God is good!

Index

About Duke McCall

Duke Kimbrough McCall was born in Meridian, Mississippi, in 1914 and reared in Memphis, Tennessee. He attended public schools in Memphis and graduated from Furman University (B.A., 1935) as valedictorian and from The Southern Baptist Theological Seminary (Th.M., 1938; Ph.D., 1942). He holds six honorary degrees: Baylor University (LL.D.); Georgetown College and Shurtleff College (Litt.D.); and Furman University, Stetson University, and the University of Richmond (D.D.).

He served as pastor, Broadway Baptist Church, Louisville, Kentucky, 1940-43; president, Baptist Bible Institute (later New Orleans Baptist Theological Seminary), 1943-46; executive secretary, Executive Committee, Southern Baptist Convention, 1946-51; treasurer, Southern Baptist Convention, 1946-51; founding executive, Southern Baptist Foundation, 1947; president (1951-82) and first chancellor (1982-90), The Southern Baptist Theological Seminary; and president, Baptist World Alliance (1980-85).

McCall's other offices included Board of Visitors, United States Air Force, Air University (appointed by President Dwight Eisenhower); vice president and chairman of Commission on Accrediting, American Association of Theological Schools; National Council of Boy Scouts of America; Chairman of the Board, Covenant Life Insurance Company; Board of Directors, Louisville (KY) Chamber of Commerce; Board of Directors, United Way, Louisville, KY; Founding Member, Louisville (KY) Crusade for Children; Board of Directors, Louisville (KY) Medical Center, Inc.; Board of Directors, Louisville (KY) Fund for the Arts; and President, Southporte Condominium Association, Jupiter, Florida.

McCall's books include *God's Hurry*, *Passport to the World* (coauthored with W. A. Criswell), *Broadman Comments*, *What Is the Church?* (editor), and *A Story of Stewardship*. He has written hundreds of articles for Baptist and non-Baptist publications.

McCall married Marguerite Mullinnix of Greenville, South Carolina, in 1936. They had four sons: Duke Kimbrough Jr., Douglas Henry, John Richard, and Michael William. Mrs. McCall died in 1983. McCall married Winona Gatton McCandless in 1984. The McCalls live in Jupiter, Florida, in the late fall, winter, and early spring, and in Highlands, North Carolina, in the late spring, summer, and early fall.
